T0331260

PARTICIPATION FOR SUSTAINABILITY IN TRADE

Global Environmental Governance Series

Series Editors: John J. Kirton and Konrad von Moltke

Global Environmental Governance addresses the new generation of twenty-first century environmental problems and the challenges they pose for management and governance at the local, national, and global levels. Centred on the relationships among environmental change, economic forces, and political governance, the series explores the role of international institutions and instruments, national and sub-federal governments, private sector firms, scientists, and civil society, and provides a comprehensive body of progressive analyses on one of the world's most contentious international issues.

Also in the series

The Politics of Irrigation Reform
Edited by Peter P. Mollinga and Alex Bolding
ISBN 978-0-7546-3515-4

A World Environment Organization
Edited by Frank Biermann and Steffen Bauer
ISBN 978-0-7546-3765-3

Sustainability, Civil Society and International Governance
Edited by John J. Kirton and Peter I. Hajnal
ISBN 978-0-7546-3884-1

Bilateral Ecopolitics
Edited by Philippe Le Prestre and Peter Stoett
ISBN 978-0-7546-4177-3

Governing Global Desertification
Edited by Pierre Marc Johnson, Karel Mayrand and Marc Paquin
ISBN 978-0-7546-4359-3

See page 279 for more titles

Participation for Sustainability in Trade

Edited by

SOPHIE THOYER
Supagro-Lameta, France
and
BENOÎT MARTIMORT-ASSO
*IDDRI, Sustainable Development and International Relations Institute,
France*

LONDON AND NEW YORK

First published 2007 by Ashgate Publishing

Reissued 2018 by Routledge
2 Park Square, Milton Park, Abingdon, Oxon, OX14 4RN
605 Third Avenue, New York, NY 10017

First issued in paperback 2021

Routledge is an imprint of the Taylor & Francis Group, an informa business

Publisher's Note
The publisher has gone to great lengths to ensure the quality of this reprint but points out that some imperfections in the original copies may be apparent.

Disclaimer
The publisher has made every effort to trace copyright holders and welcomes correspondence from those they have been unable to contact.

ISBN 13: 978-0-815-39102-9 (hbk)
ISBN 13: 978-1-351-15188-7 (ebk)
ISBN 13: 978-1-138-35709-9 (pbk)

DOI: 10.4324/9781351151887

Contents

List of Boxes and Tables

Boxes

Tables

List of Contributors

Stephen Bass is Senior Fellow at the International Institute for Environment and Development (IIED). He is a forester and environmental scientist with 25 years experience, principally in Southern Africa, Southern Asia and the Caribbean, and in international processes. He is currently researching the links between poverty reduction and environmental management, and has published several books on sustainable development and forest management (e.g. http://www.iied.org/pubs/). He has been on advisory boards for groups as diverse as UNEP, WWF, Shell, Chatham House, and Oxford University, as well as editorial boards. Until recently, Stephen was Chief Environment Adviser at the UK Government's Department for International Development. He was awarded the Queen's Award for Forestry in 2001 for services to international initiatives.

Isabelle Biagiotti works as an Editor for the French quarterly review *Le Courrier de la Planète* since 1996. She holds a PhD in political science, on good governance for the US and German Assistance in Sub-Saharan Africa (EHESS 1996, Fullbright Visiting Scholar, Brown University, 1995). She has since conducted and published several research works on different aspects of global governance: governance of development assistance, governance of international negotiations (mainly illustrated by the Biosafety Protocol), and the role of civil society in international governance. Interested by actors' strategies in international governance processes, she is currently working on the dynamics leading to the definition of a common political culture in the World Social Forum.

Tom Dedeurwaerdere is Research Director at the Centre for the Philosophy of Law and professor at the Faculty of Philosophy, Université catholique de Louvain. He is a graduate in polytechnical sciences and philosophy, with a PhD in philosophy. He is in charge of the direction of the biodiversity research of the European REFGOV network (6th framework program) and the Belgian Inter-university network IAPV/29 on democratic governance. Recent publications include 'From Bioprospection to Reflexive Governance' in *Ecological Economics* and a special issue on the Microbiological Commons in *The International Social Science Journal* (Fall 2006).

Olivier Godard, PhD in economics, is researcher at CNRS in France and professor at Ecole polytechnique-Paris, Chair in Sustainable Development. Doing research on environment and development policies since 1973, he joined the Ecole polytechnique in 1998, where he developed work on decision-making under scientific controversy, the precautionary principle, emissions trading (acid rain and climate change) and sustainable development. He has regularly been a consultant for the OECD Environment Directory about the use of economic instruments. In 2002, he co-authored a book on 'new hazards': *Traité des nouveaux risques. Précaution, Crise, Assurance*, published by Gallimard, Series 'Folio-Actuel'.

Benjamin Görlach is a Senior Fellow and environmental economist with Ecologic. He focuses on the economic valuation of environmental goods and the use of economics for policy support. He was involved in several projects that have assessed costs and benefits of environmental policies, including groundwater protection, soil protection or the EU Water Framework Directive. In addition, he works on impact assessment methodologies, on the relation between environmental policies, growth and competitiveness and environmental policy integration.

Jessica F. Green is a PhD candidate at the Woodrow Wilson School at Princeton University, and a visiting researcher at United Nations University-Institute of Advanced Studies (UNU-IAS). Before coming to Princeton, she worked as a Researcher at UNU-IAS, where she directed a project examining participation of developing countries and civil society actors in international governance for sustainable development. She is co-editor of *Reforming International Environmental Governance: From Institutional Limits to Innovative Solutions*, UNU Press, 2005, and *The Politics of Participation in Sustainable Development Governance*, UNU Press, 2006. Green served as a Lead Author in the recently concluded Millennium Ecosystem Assessment, and has worked at the UN Framework Convention on Climate Change and the World Resources Institute. She holds a Master's degree in Public Policy.

Stéphane Guéneau works with the French Institute of Sustainable Development and International Relations (Iddri) since 2003. He is in charge of the Forest and Standards programme of this Institute. His main work is in the area of global governance of sustainable forest management. He coordinated the French white paper on tropical forests, a multi-stakeholder initiative. Before 2003, Stephane Gueneau has worked for 14 years with the French NGO Solagral where he was responsible of the trade-environment issues. He has also worked as an expert for Unctad and the European Commission. During year 1999–2000, he was an invited researcher at CPDA (Programa de Pós-graduação em Desenvolvimento, Agricultura e Sociedade) of the federal rural University of Rio de Janeiro (Brazil) where he worked on the impact of the liberalization of the paper fibre industry on sustainability.

Peter M. Haas is professor of political science at the University of Massachusetts Amherst. His recent work focuses on multilevel networked governance and the role of science in international environmental regimes. His most recent book is *Global Environmental Governance*, co-authored with Gus Speth.

Chloé Keraghel is a sociology PhD student at the French School of Social Science Studies (EHESS). Her research work focuses on the dynamics of the World Social Forum, more specifically on interactions between social movements in India and anti-globalization NGOs. She is the coordinator of a special issue of the *Revue Internationale des Sciences Sociales* on 'Explorations in Open Space: The World Social Forum and Culture of Politics'. She also works with the Education department of Unesco for the management of projects on education to HIV dangers and on the synergies between formal and informal education.

Markus Knigge works with WWF's European Policy Office in Brussels. His focus is on the European Common Fisheries Policy, Fishery Partnership Agreements with third countries and the fisheries subsidies negotiations in the WTO. Before joining the WWF, Markus was Senior Fellow with Ecologic, Institute for International and European Environmental Policy, Research Fellow at the American Institute for Contemporary German Studies and McCloy Fellow in Environmental Affairs. Markus Knigge studied international relations and international economics at the School of Advanced International Studies, Johns Hopkins University and Urban and Regional Planning at the Technical University Berlin and the Instituto Universitario di Architettura.

Nicole Kranz is a Fellow with Ecologic, Institute for International and European Environmental Policy. In this position, she is involved in projects in the environmental policy arena related to water governance and public participation in policy-making. In previous appointments she was a researcher at Lawrence Berkeley National Laboratory, worked as sustainability consultant for BMW Group Designworks-USA and held a fellowship at the American Institute for Contemporary German Studies at Johns Hopkins University in Washington DC. She is currently a PhD student at Berlin Free University concentrating on the formulation of environmental policy in areas of limited statehood. Nicole holds a Master degree in Environmental Management from the University of California and a degree in Environmental Science from Braunschweig Technical University.

Sélim Louafi is since 2001, Research fellow at the Sustainable Development and International Relations Institute (Iddri) in charge of the biodiversity programme since 2001. He holds a PhD in agricultural economices (political economy of wheat price policy in Tunisia). Formerly, he was Research assistant at the Centre of Philosophy of Law at The Université Catholique de Louvain-la-Neuve (2000–2001). He has worked on the different theories of governance applied to biodiversity negotiations. His current research projects are in the fields of traditional ecological knowledge and access to genetic resources. He has coordinated a collective book on the French experiences of protection of traditional ecological knowledge (Quae editions, Paris, 2005).

Benoît Martimort-Asso was assistant coordinator of the European Sustra network on sustainable trade between 2003 and 2005. He is presently in charge of the International Environmental Governance programme at Iddri (Sustainable Development and International Relations Institute – Paris) and coordinates Iddri's activity dissemination programme. From 1996 to 2002, he worked in Canada on projects related to the treatment and the diffusion of environmental information for French-speaking countries at the Global Ecopolitic Observatory (UQAM, Canada). He worked as consultant for various ministries in France and in Canada, NGOs, research centres and private companies. Benoît Martimort-Asso has an initial training as an engineer (University of Perpignan, France) and obtained a postgraduate diploma in Environment and Prevention (University of Montreal, Canada), a master degree in Environmental Science (UQAM, Canada). He has completed the academic part of political science PHD programme at UQAM.

Carlos R.S. Milani holds a PhD in development socio-economics (EHESS, Paris, 1997) and is a permanent professor at the Organizational Studies Department in the Federal University of Bahia (UFBA, Brazil). He worked at Unesco's Social and Human Sciences Sector between 1995 and 2002, and also taught 'Development Policies and Politics' at *Sciences-Po* between 1997 and 2002. He has been an invited professor at University of Montreal (2004), Sciences-Po (2005), and University of Colima in Mexico (2006). His recent publications include articles and books on transnational social movements, international relations and environment, as well as the critical analysis of discourses and practices of international cooperation agencies in the fields of democratic governance and local participation. He is currently the coordinator of the LABMUNDO (World Political Analysis Lab), within UFBA.

Patrizia Nanz is Junior Professor of International Relations and Political Theory at the Graduate School of Social Sciences at the University of Bremen. She is also Executive Leader of the research project 'Participation and Legitimation in International Organizations' at the Research Centre 'Transformations of the State' at the University of Bremen. She has completed her PhD at the European University Institute in 2001 with her dissertation 'Europolis. Constitutional Patriotism beyond the Nation State'. Thereafter, she has been Senior Fellow at the Max Planck Institute 'Common Goods: Law, Politics and Economics' (Bonn) and Marie Curie Fellow at the Centre for the Study of Democracy, Westminster University (London). Her current research and publications focus on democratic theory and transnational governance (in various areas including immigration and asylum policy in the European Union and risk regulation in the WTO), and, in particular, on new forms of civil society participation in international politics.

Jona Razzaque is a barrister and a senior lecturer in law at the University of the West of England (UWE) in the United Kingdom. Before joining the UWE, she worked as a staff lawyer at the Foundation for International

Environmental Law and Development (FIELD) on cross-themed environmental projects involving trade, biodiversity and climate change. She holds a PhD on international environmental law and recently published a book on 'Public Interest Environmental Litigation in India, Pakistan and Bangladesh'. She is a member of the Commission on Environmental Law, IUCN. Her research interests include public participation and access to environmental justice and she published numerous articles on these issues.

Marcus Schaper is a doctoral candidate in the Department of Government and Politics at the University of Maryland. His research deals with transatlantic policy issues from a comparative institutionalist perspective with an emphasis on regulatory and environmental topics. Prior to pursuing his doctorate, he was a project manager at the Aspen Institute Berlin where he was in charge of developing and conducting projects which sought to defuse potential transatlantic disagreements. He also held fellowships at SWP (the German Institute for International and Security Affairs) and the American Institute for Contemporary German Studies (Johns Hopkins University), and worked at the World Bank Institute. Marcus Schaper holds graduate degrees from the University of Maryland (MA, government and politics) and Universität Potsdam (Diploma, political science.

Jens Steffek, a political scientist, is Assistant Professor in the Research Centre 'Transformations of the State' at the University of Bremen. He holds an MA degree from the University of Munich (1998) and a PhD from the European University Institute (2002). His research and publications focus on the role of moral and legal norms in international governance. His most recent book is *Embedded Liberalism and Its Critics: Justifying Global Governance in the American Century*, published by Palgrave Macmillan. Together with Patrizia Nanz he is currently studying new forms of civil society participation in politics beyond the nation-state.

Sophie Thoyer is the coordinator of the European Sustra network on sustainable trade. She is a senior lecturer in agricultural and resource economics at Ensam (University of Montpellier). She holds a PhD in economics from the University of London (1996), she was lecturer for four years at the University of London (Imperial College at Wye) and was an invited academic at University of Western Australia in 2003. Her research work focuses on the political economy of economic reforms and on environmental negotiations both at local and international levels. Sophie Thoyer has coordinated several research projects for various ministries in France, on the issue of trade and biodiversity, on European biosafety regulation and on negotiated water management rules. She also worked as an expert for the FAO, the European Commission and ODA.

List of Abbreviations

AB	Appellate Body
ABONG	Associação Brasileira de Organizações Não Governamentais
ACP	African, Caribbean and Pacific (countries)
AFLEG	Africa Forest Law Enforcement and Governance
AIDS	Acquired Immune Deficiency Syndrome
BASD	Business Action for Sustainable Development
BCH	Biosafety Clearing House
BSWG	Open-ended ad hoc working group on bio-safety
CAC	Codex Alimentarius Commission
CBD	Convention on Biological Diversity
CCD	Convention to Combat Desertification
CCEURO	Co-ordinating Committee for Europe (FAO/WHO)
CCGTs	Combined-cycle gas-fired turbines
CDC	Conservation for Development Centre
CEESP	Commission on Environmental, Economic, and Social Policy
CEM	Commission on Ecosystem Management
CEPLA	Commission on Education and Communication, the Commission on Environmental Law
CFC	Chlorofluorocarbon
CIFOR	Center for International Forestry Research
CIMI	Conselho Indigenista Missionário
CITES	Convention on International Trade in Endangered Species of Wild Fauna and Flora
CNPPA	World Commission on Protected Areas
CNRS	Centre national de la recherche scientifique
COIAB	Coordination of the Indigenous Organisations of the Brazilian Amazon
Comifac	Conference of Ministers in charge of Forests in Central Africa
COP	Conference of the Parties
COP/MOP	Meeting of the Parties to this Protocol
CPF	Collaborative Partnership on Forests
CSA	Canadian Standards Association
CSD	Commission on Sustainable Development
CSOs	Civil society organizations

CSR	Corporate Social Responsibility
CUT	Central Workers' Union Confederation
DG	Directorate General (EU)
DSU	Dispute Settlement Understanding
ECA	Export credit agencies
ECGD	Export Credits Guarantee Department
ECOSOC	Economic and Social Council
EDC	Export Development Canada
EFIC	Export Finance and Insurance Corporation
EIA	Environmental Impact Assessments
ELC	Environmental Law Centre
EPI	Environmental Policy Integration
EPR	European pressurized reactor
ERG	Export Risk Guarantee Agency
EU	European Union
Euler Hermes	Euler-Hermes Kreditversicherungs-AG
Ex-Im	Bank Export-Import Bank of the United States
FAO	Food and Agriculture Organization
FDB	Foods Derived from Biotechnology (Task Force on)
FLEGT	Forest Law Enforcement, Governance and Trade
FSC	Forest Stewardship Council
GATT	General Agreement on Tariffs and Trade
GDP	Gross Domestic Product
GEF	Global Environment Facility
GFTN	Global Forest and Trade Network
GHG	Greenhouse gas emissions
GIC	Global Industry Coalition
GIEK	(Norwegian) Garanti-Instuttet for Eksportkreditt
GMOs	Genetically modified organisms
GNP	Gross National Product
GONGO	Government – organized NGO
GPG	Global public goods
GRI	Global Reporting Initiative
GTA	Amazon Working Group
GTZ	Gesellschaft für Technische Zusammenarbeit
GWP	Gross World Product
GWPI	Global Warming Potential Index
IAF	International Arrangement on Forests
IATP	Institute for Agriculture and Trade Policy

ICCP	Intergovernmental Committee for the Cartagena Protocol on Biosafety
ICRAF	International Center for Research in Agroforestry
ICSU	International Council for Science
IDPM	Institute for Development Policy and Management
IFF	Intergovernmental Forum on Forests
IFIA	Association Inter Africaine des Industries Forestières
IGOs	intergovernmental organisations
ILO	International Labour Organization
IMF	International Monetary Fund
IO	international organization
IPCC	Intergovernmental Panel on Climate Change
IPF	Intergovernmental Panel on Forests
ITTA	International Tropical Timber Agreement
ITTO	International Tropical Timber Organization
IUCN	World Conservation Union
IUFRO	International Union of Forest Research Organizations
JBIC	Japan Bank for International Cooperation
LMOs	Living modified organisms resulting from modern biotechnology
MIA	Multilateral Investment Agreement
MEA	Multilateral environmental agreements
NAFTA	North Atlantic Free Trade Agreement
NBFs	National Biosafety Frameworks
NGLS	Non-Governmental Liaison Service
NGOs	Non-governmental organizations
NSMD	Non-state market-driven governance
ODA	Official Development Assistance
OECD	Organisation for Economic Co-operation and Development
P&C	Principles and fifty-six associated Criteria
PAFC	Pan-African Forest Certification Scheme
PEFC	Pan-European Forest Certification Scheme
PP	Precautionary principle
PPP	Public-private partnerships
PPT	Permanent Peoples' Tribunal
SD	Sustainable development
S–E	System-Environment (Complex)

SFI	Sustainable Forestry Initiative
SIA	Sustainability Impact Assessments
SPP	Social Policies Programme
SPS	Sanitary and Phytosanitary Measures
SSC	Species Survival Commission
TBT	Technical Barriers to Trade (Agreement on)
TOES	The Other Economy Summit
TRIPs	Trade Related Intellectual Property Rights
UN	United Nations
UNCTAD	United Nations Conference on Trade and Development
UNDP	United Nations Development Programme
UNEP	United Nations Environment Programme
UNEP/GEF	United Nations Environment Programme/Global Environment Facility
UNESCO	United Nations Educational, Scientific and Cultural Organization
UNFCCC	United Nations Framework Convention on Climate Change
UNFF	United Nations Forum on Forests
WBCSD	World Business Council for Sustainable Development
WCS	World Conservation Strategy
WEF	World Economic Forum
WHO	World Health Organization
WRI	World Resources Institute
WSF	World Social Forum
WTO	World Trade Organization
WWF	World Wildlife Fund

About Sustra

Sustra[1] is a research network of European social scientists, who have worked together for three years in relation with policy-makers and stakeholders, in order to analyse the interactions, complementaries and tradeoffs between trade rules and social and environmental protection objectives. The objectives of Sustra were to provide analytical keys to interpret the needs of the civil society, the underlying motives of collective preferences and the gradual building up of international collective action in the area of sustainability in trade. The network organized five international workshops on the following themes: (i) global public goods and global governance; (ii) the institutional architecture of the global system of environmental governance; (iii) the methodologies for assessing the process of trade liberalisation from a sustainability perspective; (iv) vested interests and resistance to trade and sustainable development reforms; (v) civil society participation in the European policy-making process.

The whole analytical approach of the Sustra network was based on the general recognition that sustainable development is not a stabilized concept: different categories of stakeholders, nations, decision-makers and international organizations have different – and sometimes diverging – expectations about what sustainable development should achieve. Developing a theoretical framework and identifying benchmarks against which progress towards sustainable development could be measured is therefore not a technical decision only. It is typically an area for which deliberative processes could help improving the legitimacy of policy making. Therefore Sustra has chosen to leave aside the technicalities of sustainability impact assessments of trade policies. It has focused instead on the theoretical justifications of deliberative processes for defining sustainability priorities; it has then made a critical survey on principles and guidelines for participatory procedures and it has drawn a number of general recommendations for the architecture of the global system of governance. Sustra has also analysed the role that the European Union could play in promoting sustainability in trade.

Sustra Partners:

- Ecole Nationale Supérieure Agronomique de Montpellier, France (Coordinator)
- Centre d'Etudes et de Recherches internationales – CERI, France

---

[1] Financed by the European Union's 5th Framework Programme under the Key Action 'Improving the socio-economic knowledge base'. For more information: <www.agro-montpellier.fr/sustra/>.

- Ecole Polytechnique, France
- Foundation for International Environmental Law and Development - FIELD, United Kingdom
- Ecologic, Germany
- Institut du Développement Durable et des Relations Internationales - Iddri, France
- Institut Français des Relations Internationales - IFRI, France
- Solagral, France
- Université Catholique de Louvain, Belgium
- Universidad Politecnica de Valencia, Spain
- University of Sussex, United Kingdom
- Vrije Universiteit Amsterdam, Netherlands

This book is dedicated to Konrad von Moltke

Konrad von Moltke was strongly involved in the SUSTRA European network.

Konrad passed away on 19 May 2005. He was an important figure in European and global environmental politics. Cosmopolitan, researcher, humanist, environmentalist, lobbyist, polyglot, inspiring guide for many of us, Konrad was a visionary person, with innovative arguments and an incredible facility to create and sustain networks.

Before dying, Konrad tried to finish the projects he was involved in. This book was one of them, although he did not have the time to write up the two chapters he had planned. These chapters were provisionally entitled 'Investment after Cancún' and 'Improving the Procedures in the WTO to Take Account of Sustainable Development: Lessons from Multilateral Environmental Agreements'. Konrad wanted to develop the idea that the WTO's efficiency is insufficient, and that Multilateral Environmental Agreements, due to their diversity and institutional richness, can be a source of inspiration to elaborate more efficient international regimes.

Despite his absence, Konrad continues to inspire research and practice. All members of the Sustra network have fond memories of his enthusiasm and of his challenging interventions in debates.

Foreword

Promoting Knowledge Based International Governance for Sustainable Development

Peter M. Haas

Introduction

Globalization comprises the dominant context for contemporary international relations. The challenge for decision-makers is how to navigate the interstices of an increasingly complex global agenda. Sustainable development has become the new mantra for a coherent multilateral approach to addressing globalization. Sustainable development entails a widespread and comprehensive approach to dealing with such interlinked issues as environmental protection, economic development, democratization, the pursuit of human justice and peace. Such an emergent paradigm or global vision appears to underlie the United Nations Millennium Development Goals.

Promoting sustainable development on this scale entails global governance that reflects guidance from an interdisciplinary knowledge base and that is capable of generating accurate assessments of the world, and which relies for its legitimacy on a deliberative process that engages states and multiple non-state actors, including civil society, expert networks, the private sector, and possibly local communities as well (Held and Koenig-Archibugi 2005; Reinecke and Deng 2000; Ruggie 2004).

Adequate global governance is unlikely to appear solely from national leadership, or 'hegemony'. The USA is reluctant to address a broad agenda of issues, and lacks the legitimacy to command sustained voluntary support from the allies and the rest of the world (Ikenberry 2004; Reus-Smit 2004; Tucker and Hendrickson 2004). Europe is reluctant, and probably incapable of unilaterally providing global governance. Thus governance has to rest on formal and informal institutions. This means an increased role for international organizations, transnational scientific groups, civil society organizations and the private sector, for articulating consensual views about governance.

Knowledge-based Governance and Usable Knowledge

Global environmental threats embody many of the defining characteristics of globalization: ecosystems are complex so that management decisions must address multiple interacting subsystems, decision-makers are often uncertain about the choices available to them; and accurate policy advice and guidance is at a premium. States and individual policymakers cannot clearly anticipate or address environmental threats without better mechanisms for environmental policy advice. The nature of and magnitude of environmental threats and the associated policy responses are often unclear to decision-makers, who require expert advice about the technical details of such challenges, including the connections to other issue areas, such as balancing economic development and environmental protection. Governance principles for managing complexity are controversial and contested. NGOs and some European governments urge application of the precautionary principle in such cases, whereas others urge a use of scientifically informed policies.

A major informal institution for governance is usable knowledge. While there is broad deference to science in policy-making circles, widespread research has demonstrated that decision-makers only selectively defer to science. Recently social scientists have focused on 'usable knowledge' as a better-defined subset of 'scientific knowledge' that is most likely to be converted to effective governance. Constructivist approaches to policy analysis suggest that to be usable, science must be developed authoritatively, and then delivered by responsible carriers to politicians. 'Authoritative' and 'responsible' in this regard refer to procedures that are viewed as socially legitimate by mass publics who will ultimately be effected by decisions resting on these expert judgements. In most instances this means that the procedure by which usable knowledge is developed will be by transparent international panels of experts who enjoy reputations for professional and impartial expertise. Of course all experts have their own preferences and norms, but if they are widely seen to be willing to subordinate their personal beliefs to their socialized professional training – i.e. the scientific method and consensus approaches to truth – then their arguments are more likely to reflect broader technical consensus as well as being accepted as being politically acceptable by various policy consumers (Haas and Haas 2002).

Epistemic communities are the actors involved in formulating and disseminating usable knowledge. The more autonomous and independent science is from policy, the greater its potential influence. Consensus in isolation builds value and integrity, and then its consequences should be discussed publicly. Measures of autonomy and integrity include the selection and funding of scientists by international organizations rather than by governments, their recruitment by merit on important panels and reliance on individuals whose reputation and authority rest on their role as active researchers rather than policy advocates or science administrators. Accuracy can be achieved via peer review, interdisciplinary research teams and independence from sponsoring sources.

Substantively, usable knowledge is accurate information that is politically tractable for politicians and policy-makers. Such knowledge frequently exceeds the mastery of any individual disciplinary approach. Recent studies of global environmental assessments (Haas 2004; Siebenhuner 2002, 2003) apply the criteria of credibility, legitimacy and saliency.[1] Credibility means that the key knowledge producers and their consumers believe their product is true. Legitimacy means that the claims are believed to be legitimate, that is, developed through a process that minimizes the potential for bias and is more equitable in terms of participation by those who are dependent upon the information. Current research from comparative politics, international relations, policy studies, and democratic theory suggests that science remains influential if its expertise and claims are developed behind a politically insulated wall. Lastly, saliency means that such information is provided in a timely manner and contains information that is useful for public policy making: that is, in practice, that it arrives in conjuncture with the policy process and provides advice that can be converted into laws or decisions by decision-makers. In practice, credibility and legitimacy are mutually reinforcing, as a procedural approach to developing consensual knowledge is likely to generate both accurate and acceptable knowledge. Yet saliency and credibility may be at odds, as the lengthy time often necessary for developing credible knowledge may interfere with the short-term needs for applying the knowledge to making policy. Existing knowledge that precedes the policy process is more likely to be usable than is knowledge that is being developed concurrently with the policy process, because it will be less likely to be seen as politically tainted by its proximity to immediate policy decisions.

From Usable Knowledge to Networked Reflexive Governance

This process of developing and circulating usable knowledge provides a provisional and rudimentary road map for a new model of reflexive governance, based on processes of social consensus. Participants create shared tangible understandings about how the world works and how national interests are affected. A new collective pattern of voluntary governance can emerge based on new appreciations of self-interest. Such an approach to governance is part of a broader system of governance without government that involves reasoned discourse and usable knowledge by many actors in international society (Haas and Haas 2002; Rosenau and Czempiel 1992).[2] Reflexive governance replaces the

---

[1] For a review of usable knowledge and science policy, see Haas 2004.

[2] This concept has been advanced most fully in the context of the EU through a notion of multi-level governance. See Hooghe and Marks (2001), Martimort-Asso and Tubiana (2005), Schimmelfennig and Wagner (2004) and Schimmelfennig and Sedelmeier (2004). Similar ideas about environmental governance can be found in the literature on sustainability science, for instance Clark and Munn (1987) and Kates et al. (2001).

traditional dichotomous concepts of global governance organized hierarchically or anarchically with a network model of complex decentralized global governance. The political dynamics are those of social learning.

Reflexive governance requires the participation of multiple actors. Private firms, NGOs, civil society and scientists all contribute elements of usable knowledge for decision-makers. The broader process of reflexive governance parallels that of the process by which usable knowledge is formulated. Groups of relevant experts are brought together to formulate a view of the world. After reaching provisional group consensus, their views are refined and presented to decision-makers in a structured discursive setting. The ideas are then applied as policy experiments. Social scientists *cum* policy analysts then appraise the effectiveness of such policies, and engage in similar discussions with policymakers as those that occurred initially with epistemic communities. In turn, following focused discussions among epistemic communities, relevant experts, policymakers and social scientists, broader policy doctrines are formulated and ultimately institutionalized as they are converted to international regimes, national policies and administrative procedures. Eventually, policy evolution and innovations through reflexive governance give rise to incentives for the emergence of new markets. Such a process provides a way to triangulate between the normative poles of globalization, regulation and democratic sovereignty. This slowly leads to robust institutionalized orders of governance through processes of social learning, which come to embody regulatory approaches that may not reflect the initial interests of the major parties, as actors learn about the nature of the issues they seek to govern and about their own interest through the structured interactions with others (Frankel 2005).

In the environmental realm, incremental social learning about the behaviour of global ecosystems; their influence on national environmental and broader social conditions; and the need for meaningful collective action led states to endorse increasingly more comprehensive environmental treaties, stronger national environmental regulations and ultimately to send sufficient market signals to firms to increase attention to environmentally friendly technology, leading to the creation of a new environmental technology market that did not previously exist, and may contribute to more effective environmental protection for the future. Reflexive environmental governance proceeded through a number of institutional channels. International conferences, from the United Nation Conference on the Human Environment (UNCHE, Stockholm 1972) through United Nation Conference on Environment and Development (UNCED, Rio 1992) to the World Summit on Sustainable Development (Johannesburg 2002), expanded the number of actors engaged in environmental governance and helped consolidate beliefs around a broad vision of sustainable development. This new vision had procedural and substantive components calling for more comprehensive environmental policies linked to other issue areas (including trade), as well as invoking broader participation in a discursive process of sustainability. International organizations helped to develop and popularize doctrines of ecological management, as well as enhancing the political profile of individuals (epistemic community members) involved in developing such usable knowledge. States also helped create a more comprehensive and sweeping body of international law for international environmental governance (Bernstein 2001; Caldwell 1996; Haas 1996, 1997, 2001, 2002, 2004; Hoffman 2001).

Gradually, the social goals of environmental protection have become expanded, through the application of usable knowledge over a 30-year period, to include a broader international agenda that focuses on the linkages between security, international economic relations and environmental protection, most recently expressed in the acclamation of the Millennium Declaration and subsequent creation of the Millennium Development Goals. The aspirations and presumptive means of collective action been reframed toward broader governance. New principles of sustainability have been forged in which individual issues can be nested, based on a socially learned set of causal connections.

Conclusion

This volume, and the broader SUSTRA network, marks a step in a new direction in sustainable development and reflexive governance. It seeks to advance multi-level governance through a conscious effort at pragmatic construction: bringing together the relevant expert and policy communities in an ongoing setting that promotes interchange and learning. Through the various stages, the interplay between trade and sustainable development becomes better understood, and provides a stronger foundation for more effective policy to promote sustainability in trade.

References

Bernstein, Steven. 2001. *The Compromise of Liberal Environmentalism*. New York: Columbia University Press.

Caldwell, Lynton K. 1996. *International Environmental Policy* Durham, NC: Duke University Press.

Clark, W.C. and R.E. Munn, eds. 1987. *Sustainable Development of the Biosphere*. Cambridge: Cambridge University Press.

Costanza, Robert, ed. 1991. *Ecological Economics*. New York: Columbia University Press.

Frankel, Jeffrey A. 2005. 'The Environment and Economic Globalization'. In Michael M. Weinstein, ed. *Globalization What's New*. New York: Columbia University Press.

Haas, Peter M. and Ernst B. Haas. 2002. 'Pragmatic Constructivism and the Study of International Institutions'. *Millennium* 31.3: 573–602.

Haas, Peter M. 2004. 'When Does Power Listen to Truth? A Constructivist Approach to the Policy Process'. *Journal of European Public Policy* 11.4: 569–592.

————. 1996. 'Is "Sustainable Development" Politically Sustainable?' *Brown Journal of World Affairs* III.2: 239–48.

————. 1997. 'Environmental Issues and Evolving International Environmental Governance'. In Jin-Young Chung, ed. *Global Governance*. Seoul, Korea: The Sejong Institute.

————. 2001. 'Environment: Pollution'. In P.J. Simmons and Chantal de Jonge Oudraat, eds. *Managing a Globalized World*. Washington, DC: Carnegie Foundation.

————. 2002. 'UN Conferences and Constructivist Governance of the Environment'. *Global Governance* 8.1: 73–91.

————. 2004. 'Addressing the Global Governance Deficit'. *Global Environmental Politics* 4.4: 1–15.

Held, David and Mathias Koenig-Archibugi, eds. 2005. *Global Governance and Public Accountability*. Malden, MA: Blackwell Publishing.

Hoffman, Andrew J. 2001. *From Heresy to Dogma*. Stanford, CA: Stanford University Press.

Hooghe, L. and G. Marks. 2001. *Multi-level Governance and European Integration*. Boulder, CO: Rowman and Littlefield.

Ikenberry, G. John. 2004. 'Illusions of Empire: Defining the New American Order'. *Foreign Affairs* March/April.

Kates, Robert et al. 2001. 'Sustainability Science'. *Science* 292: 641–2.

Martimort-Asso, Benoît and Laurence Tubiana 2005. 'International Environmental Governance: The Next Steps'. *Les Syntheses de l'Iddri* No. 7. Paris: Institut du développement durable et des relations rnternationales.

Reinecke, Wolfgang H. and Francis M. Deng. 2000. *Critical Choices*. Toronto: IDRC.

Reus-Smit, Christian 2004. *American Power and World Order*. Cambridge: Polity Press.

Rosenau, James N. and Ernst-Otto Czempiel, eds. 1992. *Governance Without Government* Cambridge: Cambridge University Press.

Ruggie, John Gerard. 2004. 'Reconstituting the Global Public Domain'. *European Journal of International Relations* 10.4: 499–531.

Schimmelfennig, Frank and Ulrich Sedelmeier. 2004. 'Governance by Conditionality'. *Journal of European Public Policy* 11.4: 661–79.

Schimmelfennig, Frank and Wolfgang Wagner. 2004. 'External Governance in the European Union'. *Journal of European Public Policy* 11.4: 657–60.

Siebenhuner, B. 2002. 'How do Scientific Assessments Learn?' *Environmental Science and Policy* 5.5: 411–27.

————. 2003. 'The Changing Role of Nation States in International Environmental Assessments'. *Global Environmental Change* 13: 113–23.

Tucker, Robert W. and David C. Hendrickson. 2004. 'The Sources of American Legitimacy'. *Foreign Affairs* November/December.

Chapter 1

Introduction: Participation for Sustainability in Trade

Sophie Thoyer and Benoît Martimort-Asso

The final Declaration of the Hong Kong World Trade Organization (WTO) ministerial conference in December 2005 is presented as a success. Yes, Ministers agreed on a common declaration that 'put the Round back on track' in the words of Director-General Pascal Lamy, and this can be named a 'success' compared to the failures of the ministerial conferences in Cancun in 2003 and in Seattle in 1999. Delegates were under pressure to find an acceptable way-out for a round which seemed doomed to fail. Their proposals were motivated more by this objective than by genuine efforts towards substantial liberalisation outcomes. The contents of the Declaration confirmed this fear. They are so feeble that their impact is really mitigated. Although WTO members were not ready to fully negotiate the content of the Doha Round in Honk Kong, they clearly demonstrated that the need for a multilateral framework for international trade is shared.

The success, in a very specific context, of the Doha ministerial conference in 2001, when the Development Round was launched, has to be found in fact more outside than inside the WTO dynamics. After the September 11 attacks, nation states needed a symbolic success of international cooperation, especially in Arab countries. Moreover, following the collapse of the Seattle meeting, another failure in Doha could have had a major impact on the trade multilateral regime in a time of abundance of regional and bilateral trade negotiations. The failures of the Seattle and Cancun WTO ministerial conferences and the modest success in Hong Kong in 2005 have confirmed the mounting difficulties in reaching international agreements on trade.

The tensions and disagreements are intense, both on the objectives pursued by liberalizing trade and on the pace at which the process should take place. In the analysis of the dynamics of trade negotiations following the creation of WTO in 1995, three factors are particularly worthy of note.

First, there has been a growing interdependence between trade and social and environmental concerns. Though sustainability questions were already being addressed in the agenda of international negotiations, they emerged during the WTO Seattle meeting in 1999 as a major trade-related issue. Two questions were to become focal points of the trade debate: social and environmental norms, and the management of global risk. These issues have raised some major obstacles to the pursuit of the WTO negotiation process. On the one hand, they are suspected to introduce new biases in trade competition and are therefore challenged vigorously by nations fearing that their market shares might be unfairly reduced by hidden protectionism. On the other hand, were they to be managed within the WTO system, there would be a risk that sustainability development objectives would be reduced to trade liberalization objectives. By highlighting the need to clarify the links between trade rules and multilateral environmental agreements, the WTO debate on environmental norms and on the precautionary principle has brought the exceedingly complex issue of the architecture of the global system of international rules to the fore. The preamble to the 1995 Marrakech Agreement establishing the World Trade Organiz ation recognizes that 'relations in the field of trade and economic endeavour' should allow for 'the optimal use of the world's resources in accordance with the objective of sustainable development, seeking both to protect and preserve the environment and to enhance the means for doing so in a manner consistent with their respective needs and concerns at different levels of economic development' and the 2001 Doha Declaration reaffirms, in paragraph 6, the commitments of Members to act 'for the protection of the environment and the promotion of sustainable development'. Yet, the WTO is not an international institution created to promote sustainable development. The relationship between the WTO and multilateral environmental agreements (MEAs) on the one hand, and institutions in charge of social matters such as the International Labour Organization (ILO) and the World Health Organization (WHO) on the other, is not organized in a clear and constructive way. Indeed, the relationship is more often seen as one with impending conflicts, rather than as an area of cooperation and mutual reinforcement.

Second, developing countries have radically changed their negotiation stance: from a fairly passive role, particularly evident in the General Agreement on Tariffs and Trade (GATT), they have adopted a much more proactive bargaining attitude. Although the United Nations Conference on Trade and Development (UNCTAD) has already demonstrated that consistent positions rooted in robust coalitions could help to gain momentum in trade negotiations, it is certainly within the fora of MEAs that developing countries have learnt to position themselves and to claim their due share of bargaining power. Their capacity to edict their preferences and priorities was reinforced by the increasing collaboration between the official delegations of developing countries and NGO activists, although such cooperation was sometimes embedded in ethical conflicts and mutual suspicion. The 'Sectoral Initiative in Favour of Cotton', which was presented on 10 June 2003 to the Trade Negotiations Committee by Burkina Faso is a good illustration: when four Sub-Saharan African countries (Benin, Burkina Faso, Chad and Mali), backed up by powerful development NGOs such as Oxfam International[1] and the

---

[1]   The Cotton Initiative is mostly based on the 2002 Oxfam study, *Cultivating Poverty. The Impact of US Cotton Subsidies on Africa*, <www.oxfam.org/eng/pdfs/pp020925_cotton. pdf>.

Institute for Agriculture and Trade Policy (IATP), required, in the name of fair development, that developed countries phase out their subsidies to their cotton sector and pay compensation to traditional cotton exporters, it created upheavals at the WTO and developed countries could not afford to ignore it. Moreover, developed countries have understood that they are not protected from litigation pursued by increasingly determined developing countries. The victory of Brazil in the recent dispute settlement panel (March 2005) on the cotton issue, which ruled that US cotton subsidies violate international trade laws, has reinforced the feeling that the bargaining power in trade talks is changing hands. From a practical (and probably quite cynical point of view), the increased presence of rapidly developing countries – led by China, India, Brazil and South Africa in G20 – in the WTO negotiation process, has certainly contributed to accentuating the difficulties in reaching a trade agreement. The implicit principle of reciprocal trade concessions, which was the driving force of the trade negotiations until 2001, cannot be put into play in the same way with the entry in the bargaining game of these new partners: they want more access to developed countries' markets (in particular agricultural markets) but they are not offering any interesting trade prospect in exchange for developed countries – which therefore wish to extend trade discussions to new areas (services, intellectual property, environment etc.). Meanwhile, leading negotiating parties such as the European Union and the United States have had to learn that bilateral 'green room' negotiations are no longer acceptable. The increased role that developing countries – who represent three-quarters of WTO members – wish to play has created some procedural 'gaps' pertaining to the forms that cooperative coalitions might take and the means by which transparency, democracy and trust might be acquired.

Third, there has been a surge in demands by civil society to participate in a negotiation process that remains very much limited to member states. The demand for greater participation is clearly associated with a deep wave of protest against further trade liberalization and globalization. Although disorganized at its early stages, civil society has proved its capacity to coordinate efficiently and its potential to influence the decision-making process. Civil society groups have been particularly dynamic and vindictive on a wide range of issues linked to sustainable development, and have contributed to demonstrating that trade rules could not be designed in isolation of other burning global issues such as poverty, debt, North–South relations, environmental protection, labour rights, human rights and democracy. On these issues, their contributions, either in the form of street demonstrations, or in the (more cooperative) form of position papers and side conferences, have served to enrich the agenda of international negotiation and to enlarge the issues publicly debated.

The Objectives of the Sustra Network

The Sustra[2] network was launched, following the Doha meeting, in 2001. The overarching objective was to create a network of European social scientists and NGOs, analysing together how trade regulation could be designed or improved to be more supportive of sustainable development objectives. Sustra's aim has been to contribute to the development of a theoretical framework for analysing the interactions, links and trade-offs between trade rules and social and environmental protection objectives. Another, and equally important, objective of Sustra's work has been to interpret the needs of civil society and to seek a better understanding of collective preferences at the international level. Sustra has been working as an independent research group, but it has also had exchanges with the European Commission, more specifically with the Cabinet of Trade Commissioner Pascal Lamy, who had emphasized, shortly after the Seattle debacle, the urgent need to 'ensure that the rules of the game support not only economic growth but also equitable economic development in the emerging economies, the sustainable use of natural resources and the protection of the planet'.

The work of the Sustra network has focused on the definitions of sustainable development and on the fact that it is not a stable concept. Although the term 'sustainable development' was used as early as 1972 at the United Nations Conference on the Human Environment in Stockholm, it was not until 1987, in a UN report entitled *Our Common Future,* that the term was fully defined as development that meets the 'needs of the present without compromising the ability of future generations to meet their own needs'. The World Bank has also defined sustainability in terms of opportunities for future generations, based on three pillars; economic, social and ecological objectives, which have to be pursued simultaneously over the long term. More precisely, economists have tried to provide a benchmark against which sustainability could be measured, in terms of capital preservation (human-made capital, natural capital, human capital). In 1992, at the Rio Earth Summit, prescriptions for achieving sustainable development were agreed upon in 'Agenda 21', which recognized that the 'integration of environment and development concerns and greater attention to them will lead to the fulfilment of basic needs, improved living standards for all, better protected and managed ecosystems and a safer, more prosperous future'. Since 1992, it is interesting to note that almost all international agreements refer – directly or indirectly – to the sustainable development objective.

However, despite international negotiations and policy prescriptions, there is no consensus on what the principle pillars of sustainable development should be.

---

[2]   Sustra is a 'thematic network' financed by the Directorate General Research of the European Commission under the 5th European Union Framework Programme, under Key Action 'Improving the socio-economic knowledge base': it stands for SUStainable development and TRAde. More information can be found at <www.agro-montpellier. fr/sustra>.

Different categories of stakeholders, governments, international organizations, businesses and NGOs define it within their own interpretative framework and following their own priorities and preferences. It is therefore difficult to develop a theoretical framework that can assess and measure progress towards sustainable development objectives. In fact, claims for more equity, transparency and civil society participation in the decision-making process are also indirect demands for new forms of social and political relations in which stakeholders can present their understanding of what sustainable development should achieve, and under what conditions it should be implemented. It is an area in which traditional top-down approaches to the public decision lack legitimacy, and for which deliberative processes could help to improve the quality and acceptability of policy making.

The emphasis on more deliberative and participatory approaches to governance has been actually one of the most important changes in international rule making in the last twenty years.

The Increasing Interest of Civil Society for International Issues

Already in the first years of the 1980s, demonstrations in several third world countries had led to accusations against the International Monetary Fund (IMF), and to a lesser extent the G7, for their role and responsibility in creating poverty. At the London meeting in 1984, activists at The Other Economy Summit (TOES) challenged shareholders of the International Monetary Fund (IMF). However, with the end of the Cold War and the imposition of policies based on the 'Washington Consensus', the structure of international relations has changed. The G7 (now G9), the IMF, World Bank and the WTO have become prominent actors of what is called 'liberal globalization'. The different anti-globalization movements were to finally converge in their criticism of the liberal doctrine, in particular the more conservative and authoritarian version, to organize coordinated action for a different model of globalization, less liberal and more sensitive to sustainable development issues. The demands of these groups, though quite diverse, shared a common leitmotif; that of more direct citizen participation in the international rule-making process. In particular, the functioning of international institutions in charge of trade and finance was accused of being opaque, inequitable, non accountable and as such, illegitimate.

The outcry against these institutions led to counter summits being organized during the official ones. The informal civil society meetings (NGOs and trade unions) turned into independent civil society fora, the World Social Forum (WSF) being the most substantial illustration. The participation of individuals is at the heart of the World Social Forum's success. Indeed, the WSF is a self-described democratic alternative space for dialogue and debate with the aim of proposing alternatives to the current system.

Participatory Approaches in Development and Environmental Issues at the National Level

These claims for more participation in global governance have not emerged spontaneously from a suddenly convergent popular demand for participating in the international decision-making process. They are in fact rooted in the older movement of decentralization and participatory development approaches.

Responding to criticisms and assertions as to the failure of centralized top-down approaches of development projects, the 1970s and early 1980s have witnessed a new emphasis placed on bottom-up 'people-centred' development. The increasing recourse by local and national governments, as well as by NGOs and (later) international development agencies, to various forms of participatory approaches were rooted in the expectations that community-based initiatives would help to design more proactive, more innovative and better-adapted responses to the development issue. The justification was also that by taking into account different knowledge, values and preferences, the participatory processes would improve the legitimacy of local policy responses and would create a greater sense of shared responsibility and a greater commitment to implementation. Priority was therefore given to capacity building, participatory action research and people's empowerment at the local level. At the national and regional levels, emphasis was placed on the subsidiarity principle, in order to bring decision centres closer to the communities concerned.

Beginning in the early 1990s, consultation and participation have also become the keywords of successful environmental decision-making. It was then emphasized that environmental issues are complex, and characterized by multiple conflicting interests, within and between communities, because the environment relates to various aspects of life (leisure, production, consumption, technology), for which people may have very different and often competing preferences. Moreover, the problem of diffuse responsibilities and lack of personal, social and even political responsibility (because of the large distances covered and long time-span of many environmental impacts), lead to free-riding options, and therefore to an absence of action, aggravating environmental problems. Environmental policies, it was deemed, were therefore extremely difficult to design and implement. Participative and deliberative processes were expected to lead to better policy decisions, built progressively and collectively through a shared diagnosis of the issues at stake and the co-construction of common long-term objectives. In developing countries, this has taken the form community-based environmental management. In developed countries, emphasis has been placed on participatory rule-making for local environmental rules and also on various deliberative fora at the national level, such as the famous citizen conferences on controversial subjects (biotechnologies, climate change) or commissions for public debate. It has also influenced the legislation: for example, the Negotiated Rule-Making Act was enacted in 1991 in the USA to give priority to negotiated solutions to environmental conflicts. The Aarhus Convention was signed by the

European Union in 1998 and made compulsory the provision of information to the public, access to justice and greater public participation for matters related to environment.

These new forms of collective decision have given rise to a number of theoretical and policy debates. On the philosophical and political side first, they raise questions about the nature of democracy itself, by highlighting the respective advantages and limitations of representative and deliberative democracy. It also raises questions concerning the 'right' level of decision and subsidiarity, and the coordination between different levels of governance. On the more practical side, the success of deliberation depends also very much on the design of participation: who is entitled to participate, with what rights or duties, how to prevent the lack of accountability or representativeness of certain participating groups, what are the decision rules, what role should public authorities play and so on. Although social science research has recently invested in those questions, there is still a large gap in knowledge that leaves decision-makers and coordinators of deliberative processes with too few recommendations and little guidance. The consequence is that it casts suspicion on such processes, throwing discredit on decisions. It is interesting to highlight that the same enthusiasm, and also the same reticence, exists concerning participatory decision-making at the international level.

Participation for Global Governance

At the international level, the issue of legitimate and democratic decision-making is even more crucial since nation states are sovereign and cannot be forced to abide by the law of an international treaty. The issue of global governance has, of course, received considerable attention, more so since citizens and decision-makers are aware that a number of global issues (mainly environmental) can only be solved by international cooperation.

Theoretically, two visions have been traditionally opposed. In the libertarian approach, decisions are made by inter-state bureaucratic bargaining on the basis of voluntary participation of sovereign nations. Global federalism, on the opposite side of the spectrum, defends governance based on a democratically elected global government. Whereas the first approach implicitly assumes that global governance is a non-issue, the second approach implies that there is no solution to global governance since there is no possibility, at the present time, of nation states relinquishing their right to sovereignty. However, claims rooted in the successes of participatory processes at the local level, and voiced by grassroots movements and NGOs in various international meetings, have made it clear to governments and international institutions that a third option could be developed and defended for global governance, the option of deliberative democracy.

The first international fora acknowledging the idea that participatory approaches were essential were those on sustainability issues: in 1992, the United Nations Conference on Environment and Development adopted Agenda 21, which clearly stated that sustainable development must involve the participation of all stakeholders. In 1996, the US President's Council on Sustainable Development recommended that collaborative processes be fostered to achieve sustainable development. The European Commission's General Consultative Forum on Environment and Sustainable Development published similar conclusions a year later, in 1997. It is a fact that international organizations dealing with the environment have adopted from the outset a more open attitude to effective participation by stakeholders. For example, the Convention on Biological Diversity has created a number of open-ended working groups and conferences, in which NGOs, grassroots movements, indigenous groups and private lobbies have been invited to voice their opinions and claims. The UN has also chosen to increase its consultation process by accrediting a large number of NGOs in its Economic and Social Council. On the other hand, so-called 'member-driven' organizations, such as the WTO, have been much more reluctant to move in this direction, although efforts have been made to favour equitable participation of member states as well as more rapid and transparent information for associations and the general public, both through press conferences, websites and so on.

Many of the questions already raised in the case of negotiated decision-making at the local level are also left unanswered in the case of international decision-making and create even more acute debates on the forms of participation, the legitimacy of participating organizations, the impossibility of identifying an international civil society and the like. Most analysis is in fact provided and publicized by NGOs and is a blueprint for more information, greater transparency and improved accountability of international institutions. Their guidelines include recommendations for an improved dialogue and good consultation practices between international administrations, governments and civil society organizations. However, little is said on the risks of badly conducted or badly designed consultation processes such as high-jacking the debates or circumventing the solutions. This has provided arguments for the opponents of deliberative approaches, who claim that such decisions are illegitimate or impractical.

Objectives of the Book

To address these challenging issues, Sustra has organised three expert workshops on trade and governance in a sustainable development perspective. The forms of participation in international negotiations were taken on as a cross-sectional issue to all the workshops. In the first workshop, which addressed the issue of global public goods, it was emphasized that one of the characteristics of global public goods was that the policy-making process through which they had to be identified and prioritised had to be inclusive and participatory. The second workshop, which took up the institutional architecture of trade and sustainable development, devoted much discussion to the role of non-state actors in global governance. The third workshop focused on sustainability impact assessments and developed innovative proposals on the 'reflexivity' of the trade evaluation process, through a process of consultation and dialogue between decision-makers and stakeholders.

The issues of participatory and deliberative processes raise political, social and ethical questions, cutting across several disciplines: researchers in sociology, political science, law and economics need to establish a common language in order to be able to debate together and to identify the common areas of research that could benefit from 'cross-fertilizing' contributions.

This book provides theoretical background, as well as case studies relating participatory processes to sustainability and trade. It analyses participation and deliberation at various levels and for different types of formal and informal stakeholders (states, non-state actors, international institutions). It focuses on the four main phases of the international negotiation process, where participation appears to be critical: agenda-setting, decision, implementation and evaluation.

Organization of the Book

Part 1, entitled 'Theoretical Analysis of Participatory Processes' provides an introductory evaluative framework to the issue of participation in international decision-making (chapter 1). In a debate too often driven by normative views, it provides different competing theories analysing participatory and deliberative processes within the context of sustainable development and global public goods.

In chapter 2, 'Is Sustainable Development an Alternative Principle of Justification?', Olivier Godard emphasizes that there is no pre-established hierarchy between man and nature. Since most environmental issues are embedded in controversial universes, sustainability cannot be defined in a unique and unambiguous way. Olivier Godard illustrates why the sustainability concept refers to various coexisting justification orders, on which there are rival claims in competition with each other when priority actions must be identified. He then examines the conditions and the procedures that could ensure that sustainability policies pass the legitimacy test.

In chapter 3, 'Global Public Goods and Governance of Sustainable Development', Sophie Thoyer reviews the concept of global public goods (GPG). She illustrates their links with sustainable development objectives and argues in favour of a participatory approach to identify them, based on Samuelson's principle (which requires identification of the willingness to pay of societies) and on the fiscal equivalence principle (which requires identification of the right level of subsidiarity). She then analyses different types of global public goods according to their supply technology: the 'additive' public good, the 'weakest link', the 'best shot' and the 'essential player'. For each of them, she describes the difficulties of international collective action and suggests institutional responses to ensure adequate supply.

In chapter 4, 'Deliberation and Democracy in Global Governance: the Role of Civil Society', Patrizia Nanz and Jens Steffek argue that the democratization of global governance depends upon the creation of a genuine transnational public sphere in which the civil society would play a key role. Such process would entail exposing global rule-making to public scrutiny, bringing citizen's concerns onto the agenda and empowering the most disadvantaged groups.

Chapter 5, 'Assessing Civil Society Participation: An Evaluative Framework' concludes part 1. Jessica Green demonstrates that civil society often remains disenfranchised from international policy making. This chapter provides a conceptual framework for understanding how to evaluate the successes or failures of civil society participation in sustainable development governance – both from the perspective of civil society groups, and through assessing institutional rules.

The starting point of part 2, 'Participation in International Agenda-setting and Decision-making' is that globalization is not only a competition for market shares and for economic growth opportunities. It has also evolved into a social and political competition for imposing values and preferences. This competition starts at the level of agenda-setting, when stakeholders try to persuade the international community to take on board the global issues they wish to see tackled at the international level. This is not only an interstate competition, revealing hegemonic behaviour. It is also a phase of the negotiation process in which all categories of actors are mobilized to influence both the underlying values and the way the debate is going to be formulated and structured. International organizations have increasingly acknowledged the need to include the civil society in the international decision-making process. They have sought to improve transparency, participation and accountability by reforming their structures, creating consultation and expert groups and by formalizing the links with accredited groups. However, are these reforms sufficient to ensure that a genuine deliberative process takes place and that the risks to see it high-jacked by a few pressure groups for their own purposes are minimized?

In chapter 6, 'The International Agenda for Sustainable Development: International Contestatory Movements', Carlos Milani and Chloé Keraghel show, through the analysis of anti-gobalization movements in World Social Forums, how civil society networks have translated the notion of sustainable development into practical actions and how they have naturally linked it to the participation issue. They also highlight the limits of a radical democratic approach.

In chapter 7, 'Epistemic Community and International Governance of Biological Diversity: a Reinterpretation of the Role of IUCN', Selim Louafi illustrates how the International union for the conservation of nature (IUCN) has been instrumental in formalizing the issue of biodiversity, and in influencing the debates during the negotiations of the Convention on Biological Diversity. He argues that the IUCN did contribute to the emergence of an epistemic community on these issues, even though it lost its leadership after 1992, and never completely regained it.

In chapter 8, 'Emerging Corporate Actors in Environment and Trade Governance: New Vision and Challenge for Norm-setting Processes', Isabelle Biagiotti explores the changes brought about by the emergence of corporate actors as full actors of the global governance process. She assesses their actions and influence within the sphere of trade and environmental norms setting. She analyses how corporations have displayed a new attitude based on social and environmental responsibility, and she describes the new institutional mechanisms created to activate the contribution of private actors. In conclusion, she suggests new avenues to investigate further the strategies used by corporations in order to gain influence in international negotiations on global environmental and trade governance. She also assesses the risk of a privatization of governance processes.

In chapter 9, 'Transparency and Participation of Civil Society in International Institutions Related to Biotechnology', Jona Razzaque examines empirically (within Codex, WTO and the Biosafety Protocol) three dimensions of the participation of civil society on international issues related to biotechnology: the regulatory structure for accommodating inputs from the civil society; the effective influence of civil society in the decision outcome; and internal and external transparency, which improves public trust.

In chapter 10, 'Global Forest Governance: Effectiveness, Fairness and Legitimacy of Market-driven Approaches', Stephen Bass and Stéphane Guéneau show how private actors can be a driving force in replacing ineffective public governance with effective private governance. They assess the advantages and difficulties of this type of solution, based on a detailed analysis of the Forest Stewardship Council.

In part 3, 'Participation in Implementation and Evaluation', authors focus on the value of participatory procedures at the implementation and evaluation phases of global governance. This is a much less debated issue in the theoretical literature, although non-state actors are becoming increasingly vocal about the necessity to reform such procedures in order to improve both efficiency and accountability.

In chapter 11, 'The Role of Scientific Expertise in Assessing Sustainability under Uncertainty and Controversy – Lessons from the Case of Climate Change', Olivier Godard illustrates the role of integrated impact assessment approach in the context of sustainable development. He unveils what happens to scientific results when they are used in a context of expertise, that is, a context framed by the needs of collective decision-making and action. After reviewing different models of expertise, the paper describes the work of the Intergovernmental Panel on Climate Change (IPCC). It highlights how the IPCC experts were placed under the double constraint of scientific scrutiny and stakeholders' approval. It led the IPCC to recommend to switch from a cost-benefit analysis approach to a sequential decision approach. The various roles that experts had to play, implicitly or explicitly, in controversial contexts, are thoroughly described. The chapter concludes with an example drawn from the French policy for energy futures, illustrating possible voluntary misuses of expert evaluation results, feeding frequent mistrust between scientists and politicians. As a conclusion, doubts are cast on the high expectations placed on integrated modelling to resolve controversial issues.

In chapter 12, 'The Contribution of Network Governance to Sustainability Impact Assessment', Tom Dedeurwaerdere reviews the shortcomings of traditional forms of governance, both of command and control types, and of a deliberative nature. He then proposes new forms of participation and cooperation in Sustainability Impact Assessments (SIAs). This method is inspired by the analysis of network governance developed by Clark, and by the organizational learning of epistemic communities developed by E. and P. Haas, both seeking to improve upon the more traditional participatory assessment approaches.

In chapter 13, 'Public Participation in the EU's Sustainability Impact Assessments of Trade Agreements', Markus Knigge and Nicole Kranz argue that the use of SIAs to integrate sustainability concerns into trade policy poses new challenges in terms of research, causal chain analysis, timing and legitimacy. Of major concern is the question of how to better take account of civil society opinions into these processes. This chapter gives a short review of the benefits and costs of public participation in impact assessments. It then identifies and analyses the major challenges and obstacles to participation by looking in detail at the composition of stakeholders, the structure of participation in the different stages of SIAs and the links between SIAs and trade agreements. Special emphasis is given on the SIA process within the European Union.

In chapter 14, 'Transparency, Information Disclosure and Participation in Export Credit Agency Cover Decisions', Benjamin Görlach, Markus Knigge and Marcus Schaper explain the fundamental role of transparency and public participation in the activities of export credit agencies (ECAs), with particular reference to their cover decisions. They discuss whether and how increased transparency could have an impact on those decisions. This chapter also sets out the international negotiation process leading up to common, binding standards for ECAs at the OECD level, pointing out the difficulties in reaching a common position.

To conclude, part 4 provides, in chapter 15, 'The Effectiveness of Participatory Procedures: Actors' Viewpoints', a round table with various actors directly involved in the practice of participatory procedures. The round table is based on interviews with Bernard Collomb (Lafarge and WBCSD), Juan Mayr (former Minister of Environment – Colombia), Daniel Esty (Yale School of Forestry and Environmental Studies), Jorge Eduardo Durao (ABONG – Brazilian Association of NGOs) and Daniel Hartrige (retired Director, Trade in Services Division of the WTO). Although their perceptions of the role of stakeholders differ, all panellists agree on the importance of participation but insist on the fact that participation is not an end in itself. They insist that participation at the global level must be associated with participation at the national level.

Most discussions developed in this book show that improving sustainability in trade could be condensed under two headings: legitimacy and effectiveness with resilience. Authors argue that there are many more sources of legitimacy in practice than institutions and elected representatives are generally willing to acknowledge. Constant criticism of international institutions, specially those in charge of trade and finance, put into question the traditional legitimacy of interstate negotiations in the international system and claim for more effective participation of directly concerned stakeholders. It has become a challenge to encompass all interests when negotiating collective norms, together with promoting democracy and equity: the right balance between representative and deliberative democracy at the international level has not been found yet, but this book shows that it has to be fine-tuned, according to the different phases of the negotiation process, from agenda-setting to evaluation. Without getting into the debate of the various understandings of effectiveness, this book points out also the question of the adaptability of institutions to the global issues at stake: how should the international agenda, norms and law be re-designed to take into account changing national and international collective preferences? How to link different issues together rather than adopting a 'tunnel vision' approach?

Proposals to strengthen the sustainable development regime range from providing more financial resources and political power to the existing institutions, to a reorganisation of MEAs, to a complete new global environmental governance system, embodying possibly a World Environmental Organisation or an International Environmental Court. However, we show that a drastic reform of existing institutions in order to improve their leverage could be extremely costly and that stakeholders are in fact reluctant to follow such path. Authors point out that there is space for an evolutionary process which would make better use of existing institutions and participatory tools. To be effective, the process should encourage the reform of national institutions in order to foster a genuine national debate on cross-cutting global issues; ensure that public opinions are adequately relayed at the international level by guaranteeing participation of non state actors; improve the accountability of international agencies by nominating GPG committees to whom they have to justify their policy and budgetary choices; reform the guidelines of sustainability impact assessments to include the preferences of stakeholders in a more reflexive way; encourage public-private partnerships when they serve the common good.

In such prospect, the experience of the European Union – in its successes as well as in its failures – is invaluable. The European Union is a true institutional laboratory in which the notions of subsidiarity, political superstructures and horizontal management of cross-cutting issues have been progressively refined. Furthermore, it is increasingly aware of the necessity to re-regulate its domestic markets in order to better integrate sustainable development requirements and it has dedicated much thought and efforts towards this goal. Europe could seize here an opportunity to exert stronger leadership on the international scene.

The issue of the participation and sustainability at the global level was also analysed from the North American perspective in recent book publish in the same series.[3] We hope that this book will provide the reader with an enlarged vision of how participatory and deliberative approaches can contribute to improve the relationship between sustainability objectives and globalization impetus, by helping to build universal values to be preserved across time and space.

---

[3]   John J. Kirton and Peter I. Hajnal, eds. 2006. *Sustainable Civil Society and International Governance*. Aldershot: Ashgate.

PART 1
Theoretical Analysis of Participatory Processes

Chapter 2

Is Sustainable Development an Alternative Principle of Justification?

Olivier Godard

Introduction

Sustainable development (SD) has been adopted as a new benchmark by UN organizations, governments, NGOs and principal economic actors. It is used at different level of political governance, from local scenes to the global one. For instance, it has become a constitutional goal of French public policies when the Charter of Environment passed the last step of adoption by the French Congress in 2005 – the two chambers together. Asked to make choices compatible with sustainability, bureaucracies and managers try to translate this broad concept into manageable indicators and criteria, with the general assumption that if people ask for sustainability, this 'thing' should and could be measured approximately the same way as a physical characteristic (length, weight ...) or an economic one (income, GNP ...).[1] It could then be standardized as an object of administration. The implicit view is that, in order to achieve such a result, it would just be a question of methodological investment in building sustainability indicators (Kuik and Verbruggen 1991; Ministère de l'écologie et du développement durable 2004) and sustainability impact assessments of given projects or policies (Commission of the European Communities 2002; Kirkpatrick and Lee 2002).

Such an approach takes it for granted that sustainability can be measured in a unique and unambiguous way, once data are provided. Furthermore, there is the implicit or claimed view that SD has been – and can be – turned into a new

---

[1] For instance, the International Institute for Sustainable Development based in Winnipeg (Canada) states as a strategic intellectual position: 'Societies measure what they care about. Measurement helps decision-makers and the public define social goals, link them to clear objectives and targets, and assess progress toward meeting those targets. It provides an empirical and numerical basis for evaluating performance, for calculating the impact of our activities on the environment and society, and for connecting past and present activities to attain future goals. Measuring sustainable development – just as we currently measure economic production – makes it possible for social and environmental goals to become part of mainstream political and economic discourse', <www.iisd.org/measure/>.

legitimate principle of assessment and justification of actions on its own. In 2006 the concept was not that new – it was introduced in the early 1980s by the World Conservation Union (IUCN) and popularized by the Brundtland UN Report on Environment and Development in 1987. A huge literature has burgeoned since then. Thus it is still necessary to take the time to think about these two assumptions: both of which have to be duly examined and challenged.

Elsewhere (Godard 1998), I have argued that sustainability was still not qualified and equipped to be seen as a legitimate principle of justification of its own. Limitations were shown to originate in difficulties with both normative requirements to be met by justification principles in modern Western societies (Boltanski and Thévenot 2006; Godard 1990), and in practical shortcomings. Both are linked. Unsustainable states and dynamics seem empirically easier to grasp than to characterize SD. How could we develop systematic measurement tools and indicators before we know enough about the very nature of concepts and values at stake? At the very least, measures and indicators should be targeted to be intrinsically robust and not committed to one ideology or another. For instance, for some NGOs and scientists, the nearer an ecosystem and natural resources are to a state not influenced by human activities, the greater the guarantee for ecological sustainability.[2] The popularized 'Ecological Footprint' (see Box 2.1) (Wackernagel and Rees 1995) is a synthesis index that can be said to be framed by this controversial idea of a strong opposition between human activity and ecological sustainability, as if less of the former would automatically imply more of the latter. Many people who find the Ecological Footprint attractive at first sight may nevertheless not agree with the values and conceptions hidden in its building; that is, a philosophy in which the environment is suffering competition with man, and the best that man can do is to reduce his impact and avoid interfering with natural processes as far as possible. This example shows that by fixing our attention on some specific manageable and simple indicators, we may be embarking on validating implicit goals that have not been tested according to agreed social values and justification principles acknowledged in our democratic societies.[3]

---

[2]   When presenting the AMOEBA approach adopted by the Dutch government for water management, Ben ten Brink (1991: 78) explains: 'A system which has not at all, or only slightly, been influenced by human activities may provide clues to define parameters and processes essential for sustainability. Such a system contains the conditions for the evolution and survival of organisms, including man, living in and around it for millennia. The assumption is made that an ecosystem which is hardly or not at all manipulated, offers the best guarantee for preservation of these fundamental values: the REFERENCE system. The closer one comes to the point of reference, the larger the guarantee for ecological sustainability, and vice versa ... The search for a concrete ecological objective can therefore be reduced to the question: "what is the maximum acceptable distance to the point of reference?"'

[3]   For instance, it is clear that deep ecology and eco-centric values do not constitute a generally accepted basis for policies of sustainable development. This comes back to the historical emergence of sustainable development on the international agenda: an important

Box 2.1: The Ecological Footprint

After defining sustainability as avoiding 'ecological overshoot', Wackernagel and Rees (1995) suggest to measure it by determining how much biological capacity is available and then comparing this supply with human demand. The 'ecological footprint' methodology is intended to provide a natural capital account in order to determine at various scales, from the global down to the household, how much of nature's services are appropriated by considered entities (a country, a city, a firm, a consumer) to support their activities. The amount of bio-productive capacity that humanity has available worldwide is given by the size of the planet's areas that are biologically productive. To determine the per capita supply of ecological capacity, the biologically productive land and sea that exist in a given year are divided by that year's population. For the year 2000, this resulted in an average of 2.1 hectares per person. But people should not use the whole mean area to which they could be entitled if some place for living is to be preserved for other species.

Human demand for biological capacity is calculated by adding up the various areas from all over the world that are occupied to produce the resources being consumed and to absorb the waste generated. This total represents a population's ecological footprint. Non-renewable resources are reflected in the accounts only to the extent that their use damages the biosphere, for instance through mining, processing and consumption. They are presently accounted for the embodied energy associated with their use. To make footprints internationally comparable, they are expressed in standard hectares. One standard hectare is one hectare of bio-productive space with world average capacity to produce biomass. Impact of use of fossil fuels is estimated from the area needed to absorb emitted carbon into biomass and ground. Under calculations based on 1996 data, the average American required approximately 12 hectares to provide for his consumption (over five times more than is available per person worldwide); the average German lived on a footprint of 6.3 hectares, which is three times the mean sustainable footprint per inhabitant (Wackernagel 2001).

To go further, we have first to face the ambiguous theoretical status of SD within the field of social and normative values. Taking for granted the fact that the main conceptual challenge of SD is to find ways to go on with development without putting the natural environment at peril, one problem lies in understanding what the environment really involves as a concept embracing Man–Nature relationships. Environmental events cannot escape interpretations,

bifurcation happened when IUCN abandoned in 1980 strictly preservationist goals in favor of a conservation strategy embedded in a strategy of sustainable development that raise the level of satisfaction of basic needs of human populations.

and interpretations depend on legitimate interpretation frameworks. A common set of axioms supports existing legitimate justification principles in Western societies (Boltanski and Thévenot 2006). How do environmental issues fit this axiomatic constraint? A second problem is linked to the plurality of justification principles and legitimacy orders across the world and within each Western society: hence it is not easy to identify the relevant principles to use in a given situation, and self-defeating to expect that one single principle can solve environment and development controversies.

This chapter is intended to contribute to the setting of an appropriate theoretical background, grasping the very nature of environmental issues and its implications for the debate on ways and means to bring SD to reality. Section 1 is devoted to an explanation of the concept of a system-environment (S-E) relationship. Section 2 introduces controversial universes in which environmental issues have to be thought and tackled. Section 3 questions SD as an alternative principle of justification. As a conclusion, it is stressed that SD cannot be measured as a physical characteristic, because it can only acquire meaning and have practical translations through the interpretation and elaboration brought by several coexisting social frameworks (justification orders and principles). However, these social frameworks have various degrees of relevance according to specific situations. Like other social values (freedom, justice), SD is a stake-carrier for enhancing democratic debates and reappraisal of meanings. Indicators and measures are useful, and contribute positively to the extent they are robust with a variety of social values or where there is a broad consensus on embedded social values that may be pursued with their help. They are misleading if they do not correspond to basic social values, or embody hidden choices that oppose agreed principles.

The System-Environment Relationship: an Entangled Hierarchy

Uncertainty and controversy have been the common background of environmental policies during the past thirty years. They should have reserved a central place in our thinking on sustainability and the integration of environmental issues by public policies and economic activity.

Issues of Qualification

Environmental issues raise difficult questions about the ways and means to integrate human beings and non-human beings into one unified representation. Behind all-pervasive sources of uncertainty lies a deeper hesitation as regards the appropriate qualification and status we should give to 'environmental beings'. The standard utilitarian economic concept and the political model of the 'common good' are framing the world they institute from an initial partition between 'subjects' – human beings – and 'objects' – all other beings. At the same time, standard systems approaches and eco-energetics give the same ontological status to all beings, human and non-human; both categories being viewed as vehicles of energy and material flows. As regards environmental issues, each of these patterns, being incomplete, is condemned to open up to others, although the prospect of getting both categories combined in one integrated model is problematic! The problem to solve is not reducible to the usual one of linking different boxes or compartments that have the same physical nature. We must envisage the building of specific interfaces and other forms of integration that acknowledge a rupture between the semantics used in both sides.

We should therefore consider a type of integration based on a circulation between polar viewpoints, i.e. between two types of integrated approaches. This is the view we gain from an exploration of the very logical structure of the environment-system relationship in the context of self-organizing systems.

The Environment-System Complex

Uncertainty is not just a contingent and temporary feature of some environmental problems, as it is for many new emerging concerns in society. There is a logical link between a state of critical uncertainty and the very nature of what 'environment' means in self-organizing systems theory[4] (Godard 1984, 1995, 1997b). Within this framework, it has been shown that the complex formed by a system and its environment is an 'entangled hierarchy' between two orders of emergent sense, or matrix of meaning (see the definition in Box 2.2). In one order, the overall meaning emerges from the system. In the context of this paper, human society is logically the first, being the definitional reference of the other pole, its 'environment'. The environment is the subset of the world that is meaningful for this reference system, either as resources and conditions of existence and development, or as sources of relevant perturbations and threats. An element of the world that is not relevant for the system under consideration does not belong to the environment of the latter.

Meanwhile, there is an opposite order in which the meaning emerging from the environment is posited as logically anterior to the meaning from the system, because the very existence of the environment appears to be a condition of the existence of the system. For this second order, the system is just a subset of the

---

[4]   Mainly since the Second World War, systems theory has had to grasp a challenge: to elaborate concepts and models that allow explanation and simulation of the process of self-organization of natural entities and systems (not man-made). Among them, the development of living organisms was at the heart of a new thinking that departed from engineer-type viewpoints and metaphors of external 'programmes'. The names of Ludwig von Bertalanffy, Heinz Von Foerster, Francisco Varela, Henri Atlan, Ilya Prigogine and Douglas Hofstadter are linked to the development of this new understanding of systems able to organize themselves.

Box 2.2: The System-Environment Complex as an Entangled Hierarchy

1   Given a self-organizing system S, interacting with its environment E
2   Given a hierarchy of sense H on $\{S, E\}$: $S > E$, which means that S is
    logically anterior to E, and that identity of E proceeds from S,
3   Given the opposite hierarchy $\mathcal{H}$: $E > S$,
4   The $(S\text{-}E)$ complex is said to have a structure of 'entangled hierarchy'
    since:

(a) it is paradoxically coupling ($\cup$) two opposite hierarchies of sense, H and
    $\mathcal{H}$
$$(S\text{-}E) : H \cup \mathcal{H}\ (1)$$
This particular coupling is such that:

(b) each hierarchy comprehends the other one ($\supset$) as a component of itself
$$(S\text{-}E) : (\mathcal{H} \supset H) \cup (H \supset \mathcal{H})\ (2)$$

(c) dynamically, each hierarchy implies, at one moment and just for a moment,
    to switch ($\Rightarrow$) to its opposite (reverse hierarchy), in a movement of eternal
    circulation analogous to the one generated by a Möbius ring.
$$(S\text{-}E) : (\ H \Rightarrow \mathcal{H} \Rightarrow H \Rightarrow \mathcal{H} \Rightarrow \ldots)\ (3)$$

In the case of the Man–Nature complex, the entangled hierarchy $\{S, E \rightarrow H,$
$\mathcal{H}\}$ is ultimately cognitively dominated by H: $S > E$, since the question cannot
but be raised by men, but practically dominated by $\mathcal{H}$ as far as the existence
of Nature is a logical precondition of the existence of mankind.

From Godard (1995, 1997b).

---

environment, one that takes part in its global functioning and dynamics and can influence or disturb the global environment.

Each order of meaning generates its own key benchmarks and factors of integration and reproduction, which is reflected in the different semantics used by scientists for their description and understanding.

Developing a comprehensive concept of the environment requires the association of the two orders as basic components of one unique complex functioning: they are entangled. The first one, qualified as self-referent, considers the behaviour and interest of the system regarding its environment from its inside; the environment is viewed from the system's viewpoint as a whole set of resources and opportunities, and at the same time as constraints, obstacles and sources of perturbations and threats. The system defines by itself the borderline between itself and the environment. This borderline is directly related to the issue of self-reproduction, since it separates the part of reality that is organized to ensure its self-reproduction – the system as a reproductive, recursive network – from the rest of the world, the reproduction of which is not incorporated in the relationship patterns that support the self-organizing, self-reproducing system. In this sense, it is intrinsic for a self-organizing system to externalize its environment, meaning both that there is an active process of not including elements of the environment as regular components of the system, and there is an active process of ignoring the conditions of environmental reproduction, however important the environment may be for the survival and development of the system. The environment can be defined in this regard from the system's viewpoint as an important but externalized component.

An illustration of the self-referent order projected by the system is to be found in the main concepts economics currently used for organizing the representation of the natural environment of human societies. They do not express components of the environment taken for themselves, but a human look at these components.[5]

The second order, qualified as hetero-referent, is about the structure and running of natural systems viewed from the inside, and reveals what the environment makes of the action of the system on its own organization and functioning, and what feedback goes to the system. In fact, both orders are linked in such a way that each one includes the other as a part of its own functioning and accomplishment. For an observer, to explain one order in action involves, at one moment and only for a moment, switching to the other one.

Take a standard pollution case and its economic interpretation as an 'external effect'. Such an effect involves a change in the physical environment and emerges between two economic agents when this interaction is not regulated by voluntary trades on the market. In order to elucidate its full meaning for the economic system and human society (altering utility functions), human beings have first to try and elucidate the full sense of the involved biological and physical phenomena from the viewpoint of the environment[6] and only then link the picture to human welfare considerations. In order to achieve this step in practice, they have to switch from self-referent semantics – utility functions, subjective preferences, social values – to environment-centred ones – systemic resilience, population dynamics, energy flows and multiple equilibriums.

In a symmetric way, humans cannot directly know the very meaning of the environment for itself. It is made manifest to them first through natural events, fluctuations and catastrophes, and second, through the knowledge activity

---

[5] Consider the concept of natural resources: there is no place to speak of natural resources if the targeted components are not referred to a human usage or to some value defined by men. If, alternatively, we consider the use of some resources by biological units (predator–prey relationship), there is no basis to qualify them as 'natural', that is in the context of an opposition with human attributes (culture, technology ...). It is the same for 'quality of life', 'habitat', 'landscape' and so on.

[6] Here we find a sort of reminiscence of the extraordinary formula of Aldo Leopold (1987): 'To think like a mountain'.

of humans, be it intuitive and empirical or scientific, both being linked to interpretative frameworks available within society. What humans can capture of the 'meaning of the environment for itself' is still a construction emanating from the human system: there is no pure hetero-reference in the same way as there is no pure self-reference. Scientific research is a contingent human activity, dependent on human concerns and decisions (goals and priorities in financing Research and Development, fighting for influence resources allocation, symbolic power between disciplines and so on) and human faculties; science does not provide a direct access to reality. The sense attributed to the environment unavoidably results from a conjectural and potentially controversial social construction embedded in cultural grids and socio-economic and political games. The implication is that no position can be viewed as the absolutely appropriate one. The ultimate meaning of the environment for itself is a question mark for humans.

According to the 'entangled hierarchy' concept at the core of the *S-E* complex, the basic condition of the professional life of scientists interested in the environmental field would be to circulate in their minds between the two orders of meaning, both of them being considered as partial but still being necessary viewpoints on the production of sense involved in the Man–Environment relationship. The main question is not to choose between, for instance, neoclassical economics and ecological economics or bio-economic studies, since each of them is occupying a specific polar position. Neither is it to look for some unified theory based on a homogeneous, all-inclusive semantics such as efforts to integrate all natural elements in economic evaluation, but to achieve a meaningful circulation of viewpoints. This requirement provides a theoretical foundation for trans-disciplinary approaches to environmental issues.

An Additional Source of Complexity: the Plurality of Principles of Justification

An additional source of complexity and uncertainty arises from the system under consideration, i.e. modern and postmodern contemporary societies: present Western democratic societies are framed by a plurality of coexisting principles of justification, supplying a pluralistic framework through which a conscious collective management of interactions with Nature can be thought and practically organized: they are called 'market', 'industrial', 'civic', 'domestic-traditional', 'opinion and fame', 'inspiration-based' principles (Boltanski and Thévenot 2006; Godard 1990, 1998) (see Box 2.3). Each one defines a specific way to apprehend human subjects and things that shape a specific world; each one is organized around a specific normative concept, and depends on specific tests of value and procedures to solve conflicts. Environmental issues are not built the same way within each of these orders (Godard 1990), and social conflicts raised by environmental issues often oppose different views regarding the right principle to use as a reference; it is all the more true that the solutions should differ according to situations considered and that each principle is only partially successful to address the issues of environmental management and SD (Lafaye and Thévenot 1993).

Box 2.3: Principles and Orders of Justification

1   The *inspiration-based* concern for environmental matters takes up ideas of a Nature having a transcendent value and being incommensurable; personal commitments, individual sensitivity and desire for authentic natural environments are at stake. Here, a quasi-religious relationship to Nature supports environmental protection. Practical expressions of this order (in protests, when proposing solutions and so on) are marked by a tendency towards radical alternatives, utopia and rejection of compromises. Basically argumentation refers existing, concrete situations to a 'transcendent elsewhere', such as true wild, virgin nature, a natural paradise or divine creation, with which communication is made through the channels of intimate desires and inspiration. This order may feed a benevolent attitude towards the general cause of the environment and is a possible source of social acknowledgement of 'existence values', although the fix on uniqueness and invaluable natural beings is an impediment for systematic comparisons. The general form of tests in this order is to be found in embodiment and personal commitment; it gives a high standing to prophetic characters and mystic speech.

2   The *domestic-traditional* order includes the will for conservation in a general project of transmission of heritage, the focus on traditions in environmental practices and a concern for a right ranking of people and things in a stable hierarchy related to the intergenerational link. The value of heritage is attributed to culturally marked objects able to both embody the identity of a cross-generational group and to crystallize polyvalent resources for allowing holders to face nasty surprises in life. As such, cut off from their cultural and social meaning, nature and wilderness have the lowest ranking. Domestic animals (horse, dogs) have a higher standing than any wild species, which, in some cases, are treated as harmful species doomed to destruction (foxes, snakes, mosquitoes).

3   The third order is organized around a concern for *opinion and fame*. It embodies the idea that the value of beings depends on their fame; an action is all the more valuable as it draws the attention of the largest number of people. Public perception and opinion is what really matters. Gaining celebrity and having existence in the media is the very source of value. Indices of notoriety (have you ever seen the Eiffel Tower? Did you climb up?) are the true tests to use for choosing priorities.

4   The *civic order* shapes a political society based on a concern both for a basic equality of citizens who should have an equal access to the environment and natural resources, and the superiority of general interest and will over private ones, and of public bodies in charge of the common good over private entities: law is taken as the expression of general will of citizens, hence a focus on effectiveness of law enforcement; other concerns are

related to the importance of collective action, a higher standing given to public management against private one and attention attached to a fair democratic representation of all communities. Within this order, access to greatness implies an abstraction of individual singularities and specificities for the best profit of the common good of society.

5 The *market order* is framed by the desire for commodities; as a collective device, the market points out what the valuable goods are that people are invited to desire. It requires people and objects to be detached from roots, land or community in order to be totally available for trade and market valuation. Achieving an affluent society stimulated by the satisfaction of individual desires is the value of this order. Private property rights are the means to integrate environmental assets into the market game. Nature is valuable if it can be made profitable through trade one way (extractive uses for commodity markets) or another (tourism) ...

6 The sixth and last type of order, *the industrial order,* extends to the whole society and the environment the type of order developed by big *industry* during the nineteenth and twentieth centuries. It is focused on a productive use of resources and land in order to satisfy objective needs. Excellent technical performance in production and management is sought, and is expected to be reached, by giving a key role to engineers and scientific experts. A strict hierarchy of social status and roles and a clear division between conception and execution are two features of this order. This is also the reign of objectivity and figures; decision-making is to be based solely on sound science and objective data; the future is apprehended through rational plans and investment. Regarding Nature, this order basically urges that natural systems and resources be put to a productive use: there is no greater scandal than resources lying in an unproductive state ...

Source: Boltanski and Thevenot 2006; Godard 1990.

Competing views about which principle should take precedence is a type of competition without clear generally accepted tests for arbitration: there is no mechanism – a marketplace, a negotiation procedure, a democratic vote or the like – to compare their respective performance, because there is no universal meta-criterion against which to judge their achievements. Each justification principle is a way to define the essence of society and the essence of the world, and tends to colonize any part of social life. But this tendency to expansion is slowed down or neutralized by the same tendency of others and the fact that, according to individual situations, different justification principles do not demonstrate the same intuitive level of relevance – some are assessed as more relevant, although various principles are used as a reference by the various stakeholders. For example, there are strong limits on the way to submit production and trade to the sole logic of the civic order (one man, one vote). In each society, history has produced a broad allocation of spheres of economic and social activities to the different justification orders, whereas concrete organizations can be interpreted as institutionalized compromises between some of those principles. Social frontiers are not located at exactly the same place from one country to another,[7] which reinforces difficulties of coordinated action and cooperation at the international level.

In this respect, environmental issues are a source of social controversy, because they generally cross existing frontiers between social spheres: they concern consumption as well as production; they do have an economic dimension, but also a civic one resulting from the public good and transgenerational characteristics; they depend on public institutions, but also on business and NGOs; they touch business strategies of multinational firms, but also personal choices and ethics regarding lifestyles; local issues find meaning through global interpretation (biodiversity, climate change) and so on. Thus, environmental issues are a permanent source of embarrassment and conflict regarding justification. The key difficulty is related to the ways and means to reach agreement between stakeholders supporting opposite views on the shape of issues and priority of concerns.

Living in 'Controversial Universes'

With roots in the structure of the *S-E* complex and in the plurality of orders of justification, environmental issues are touched by critical uncertainty and long-lasting scientific controversies. The latter are not restricted to scientific communities, but spread through society, fuelling social controversies. Both sources combine to generate 'controversial universes' (see Box 2.4), in which scientific theories and 'visions of the world' become social stakes around which strategic games are developing among economic and social actors (Godard 1997a).

Such contexts contrast themselves with '*stabilized universes*', which have been explored at length by environmental economics in the framework of the theory of public goods and external effects: making pre-determined individual preferences the ultimate source of assessment; building on clear causal relationship between actions and environmental damage; assuming reversible damage. Within '*controversial universes*', the standard temporal precedence of knowledge on action ('learn then act') has to be partly reversed ('act then learn') because what is at stake is the prevention of a presumably irreversible damage: action has to be determined on the basis of a partial and controversial knowledge.[8] Hence, cognitive issues and stakes of collective action are intertwined, giving rise to new forms of strategic competition among social and economic actors. Here, competition is about the framing of issues in order to control the shape of policies. Alternative scientific theories and environmental uncertainty tend to be

---

[7]   One example is the various ways to organize the same services to the public, such as power distribution or railways.

[8]   Here we enter the domain of the precautionary principle to which we come back later.

Box 2.4: Controversial Universes

1   Individual representations of issues are not based on direct perceptions, but mediated by a preliminary scientific, administrative and social construction; so the ultimate reference of judgements cannot be genuine individual preferences taken as already shaped.

2   All people of legitimate concern are not 'here and there' in order to express their preferences and judgements; a specific issue is raised about the appropriate procedures to represent the interests and rights of absent third parties (other people in foreign countries, future generations). Various spokesmen claim to be the legitimate representatives of absent parties.

3   Because of potential irreversibility, there is a strong perception, at least among some social actors, that there is a need for immediate and firm action, without waiting for the momentum of certitude; then design of action cannot be based on certified knowledge.

4   A long-lasting controversial state of scientific knowledge on critical parts of phenomena relevant for policy making do not allow decisions to be deduced of a scientific characterization; in this case, new forms of competition between visions of the world arise; issues are reframed, and action is eventually taken on the basis of available and socially acceptable technological options; scientific controversies are then indirectly arbitrated by policy and technological choices; in a reversed movement, the formulation of problems depends on the availability of solutions, but is deemed to be eventually revised with progress of scientific knowledge, although strong inertia can supersede.

---

instrumentalized by social and economic actors according to their interests and goals – stopping the development of a technology, ensuring a market and so on. To some extent, the level of uncertainty acknowledged in public debates becomes an endogenous variable of social games: it reflects the will of various stakeholders to find an agreement, in which case the importance of scientific uncertainty is reduced, or alternatively to pursue a strategy of conflict and disagreement, in which case uncertainty is magnified.

When the environment is at stake, the very process of controversy echoes the incompleteness of each order of meaning in the complex S-E, their confrontation and, at the same time, their inescapable link.

Conventions and Social Coordination when Objects are Uncertain

Controversial universes exacerbate the role of social conventions in the process of coordination: conventions do stabilize contexts for action in order to avoid paralysis, even when the threats that trigger decisions are still uncertain, and not precisely defined and assessed. For instance, we may want to protect the global climate, but we do not know to what extent this climate is being scarred by human actions, and what will be the magnitude and location of damage. Should we wait for perfect knowledge? If not, how should we organize action? The weaker our knowledge of the world, the more the collective coordination of action is dependent on somewhat arbitrary conventions in which the basic autonomy of human society expresses itself. The logic of conventions is embedded into the perception of practical possibilities – a question regarding an uncertain and controversial environmental problem is translated into a question of technological capabilities, economic feasibility and social acceptability – into secondary interests (for instance gaining a diplomatic success, capturing new competitive advantages and so on) and into key features of justification orders. For instance, policy decisions *decide* that such a trend or such an ecological problem is mainly attributable to such-and-such human activity or natural factor, or that technology at the level of production processes will be sufficient to solve problems, avoiding making a commitment to additional and painful structural changes. Critical uncertainty and controversies pertaining to the environment allow social processes to decide about the framing of issues and action beyond inescapable scientific facts and data. This is the reason why I suggest considering environmental threats as a trigger for a process of social self-organization, the result of which can be far enough from the initial shaping given by scientific alarms.[9]

The Precautionary Principle as a Way Out?

Under scientific uncertainty on the very existence of some hazards or about the causal relations involved in some environmental phenomena, threats of serious and irreversible damages to the environment and public health pushed the precautionary principle (PP) to the forefront in various domains: marine fisheries, climate change, waste management, air pollution, food safety, public health and even working conditions (Godard 2006b). This principle has been intended to overcome the rhetoric argument used by some stakeholders according to whom preventive policies should only be implemented under scientific certainty. The PP gives legitimacy to the idea that it is necessary to take an early account of

---

[9]   In the German forest decay crisis in the 1980s, a feeling of emergency arose regarding a process of degradation that was perceived as very fast: damage seemed to progress by a rate of 10–20 per cent of forest areas a year. The policy response has not triggered those actions having the most immediate impact on suspected sources (for instance with strong measures regulating road traffic and speed on highways), but instead, bet on technological changes that have been phased in at a much slower pace (such as installing scrubbers on coal-fired power plants and switching to lead-free petrol for cars). These initiatives might not have a fully developed impact on the decay process before fifteen or twenty years, in which time all forests would have died, in the worst case scenario. In technical terms, those measures were not appropriate solutions to the perceived problem. They have nevertheless been efficient from a political viewpoint, because social protest has been calmed down (Godard 1997a).

threats and early preventive actions within risk management. Typically the most authoritative definitions of the PP state that the lack of full scientific certainty should not lead to postpone efficient preventive measures addressing potential risks of damage (O'Riordan and Cameron 1994; Godard 1997a).

In spite of broad acknowledgement in environmental law[10] and pervasive references in the literature, the PP is suffering from as many controversies as there are cases in which it was invoked to overcome paralysis due to uncertainty. Sustained conceptual confusion is still lasting, although considerable efforts were made in Europe to specify the meaning and the practical requirements of this principle (Godard et al. 2002; Godard 2006c). The EU politically validated doctrine insists upon scientific assessment, proportionality, considering costs and benefits of all sorts, coherence, non-discriminatory treatment, provisional measures leading to periodic revision of measures taken initially; it has no direct incidence on criminal or civil liability. All this is at odds with the viewpoints often developed in the USA. For instance, since the Wingspread conference (Raffensperger and Tickner 1999), the PP is often understood in the United States, by both supporters and opponents, as a system requiring the reversal of the burden of proof and implying a new foundation for civil and criminal liability. In the same vein, many scholars are still confusing the PP with a Principle of Abstention that requires a proof of no-risk. It is for instance the case of Cass Sunstein (2005) in his book, the *Laws of Fear*: assimilating the PP to a reversed burden of proof, he rightly concludes that this concept leads to no direction at all, since there are risks on the way of each option. Leading a similar discussion, Godard (2006) shows the self-contradiction of a catastrophist approach to risk management, but also points out that the proportionate EU concept of the PP escapes self-contradiction and validates itself as an expression of Reason. Sunstein and others are in fact missing their target when they think they are dismissing the PP.

Other contributions in the academic circles, such as the one by Steve Gardiner (2006) who follows the way opened by John Rawls in his Theory of Justice, postulate a direct link between the PP and the maximin criterion.[11] As a matter of fact, the key reference of the PP to proportionality of measures (Godard 2003, 2006; Godard et al. 2002) does not stick to the maximin rationale, which is in fact inappropriate to scientifically uncertain situation: in context of uncertain hazards, framed by partial and piecemeal knowledge, the worst-case scenario cannot be identified with certainty because all possible states of the world are not identified ex ante. Then the so-called 'worst case scenario' is a conventionally bounded scenario to which it is not wise to give an excessive weight in decision-

---

[10]   Since its inclusion in the Maastricht Treaty in 1992, the PP is a key law principle on which EU environmental policy has to be based. More recently it is also part of the Charter of Environment that has been added to the French Constitution in March 2005.

[11]   When using the maximin criterion for making decisions, each act is appraised by looking only at the worst outcome this act can achieve and the best act is the one having the best score among worst outcomes.

making. Were decision-makers willing to wanting to consider equally all possible prospects, whatever realistic they could be, they would reach a state of levelling-out of all alternatives, each of them being credited of the potential to lead to a disaster under a specific set of hypotheses and circumstances.[12] It means that the maximin approach is useless in really scientifically uncertain contexts.

As a principle, the PP should not be confused with a decision criterion determining a complete order on a set of alternatives such as maximin or maximizing expected utility. The PP is not computable and calls for a case-by-case judgement taking account of various concerns and values. Once an agreement on an early consideration of a new potential threat is achieved, very important questions remain about what to do. In this regard, the PP only gives some landmarks and procedural directions. Although the PP has been a major breakthrough for environmental risk management, it cannot by itself put an end to social controversies about the right actions to take in controversial contexts. By asking to address long term issues without deferring their consideration to a far distant future, the PP bring policy resources to sustainable development but does not allow to avoid conflicts and debates when interpreting requirements of SD.

Such is the context brought by environmental issues. It provides fundamental reasons that explain why SD discourse and analysis can only be of a hermeneutic type, built on conjectures and conventions, in order to face objective data riddled with uncertainty and indecisiveness. This inescapable context should be addressed by any approach aiming to give an operational translation to SD.

Of Sustainability and Justification

Needs of Public Justification

The search for agreement on collective actions and rules that would regulate individual conduct and solve conflicts over the use of the environment is subject to a general requirement of public justification. Debates, tests and judgements involved are framed by justification orders and principles that we have already introduced. It is at the end of such justification work based on specific tests that actions undertaken or new norms and classifications adopted will be seen as legitimate. Examples of ordinary tests for ordinary situations can be found in court cases, motor races and economic calculations of the profitability of an investment. Even though they correspond to different situations, they are all tests intended to determine the appropriate action or relative value of various competing options or claims.

---

[12]   Think of the usual trade-off put forward in the field of energy policy: climate change due to intensive use of fossil sources on one side and nuclear hazards due to massive development of nuclear power plants on the other side. With imagination, a major disaster for Humanity may be associated to both options. It just means that worst case scenarios attached to each technology are useless to come to a policy choice.

The requirement of tests is twofold: to find a suitable response to the specific circumstances of the situation requiring a judgement and to link the situation to a more general representation of an ideal order, supposed to sustain a common good shared by all members of society. The justification orders identified in Section 1 are deemed to be legitimate in Western societies because they are compatible with a common set of general axioms,[13] as detailed in Box 2.5.

Box 2.5: The Axiomatic Base for Western Legitimate Orders of Justification

A1   The Principle of Common Humanity
1   A basic distinction is established between human beings, who are members of the 'City' and non-human beings
2   Only human beings, as members of the 'City', are entities having rights[14]
3   To be a member of the 'City' implies mutual recognition and basic symmetric relationship

A2   The Principle of Dissimilarity
There are several possible social positions for members

A3   The Principle of Common Dignity
Each member has an equal formal potential of access to the various social positions

A4   The Principle of Greatness Ordering
Differences in social positions are turned into an ordering of greatness

A5   The Principle of Sacrifice (or Investment Formula)
Access to Greatness (upper social positions) has a cost, implies a sacrifice

A6   The Principle of Superior Common Good
Having a high rank provides a common good for all members, and not only a personal satisfaction (happiness, power, reputation ...)

Source: following the 'Polity' model, Boltanski and Thévenot (2006).

---

[13]   The reader should note that these axioms do not pretend to characterize the real state of Western societies, but the ideal reference of what would be considered fair, just and legitimate by people when they search to find an agreement on a collective issue or are in a position of evaluation of contributions to social achievements, not private ones. For instance, it may turn out that accumulation of fortunes within the hands of some happy few is considered legitimate, only if action of rich people generates a common good (wealth, development, safety and so on) benefiting everyone else in a sufficient manner.

[14]   This is a critical point, one that gives rise to a lot of debates and controversy within circles interested in environmental protection, since it separates anthropocentric and eco-centric systems of values. See Ferry (1995) for a critical appraisal of the idea that non-human beings could have rights.

Understanding the concept of justification in this way, it is quite clear that the idea of SD is presented and used today by many groups, organizations and institutions as a new standard for criticizing or promoting actions taken in the many areas of technological and economic development, international relations, trade and environment, demographic growth, town and country planning, natural resource use and exploitation and protection of the biophysical environment, to name but a few of the fields. To what extent does SD give rise to a new and alternative justification principle?

Sustainability, Mostly a Resource for Criticism

Far from being firmly established for its positive content, the SD rhetoric is first and foremost used to back up arguments criticizing current situations, practices and projects. Such statements are not just objective or neutral scientific observations, but rather socially interested objections and criticisms. The history of the emergence of the concept of SD is littered with denunciations and alarms.

Generally speaking, turning the idea of sustainability into an effective standard of justification depends on a group of operations:

1   gathering data to achieve a shared understanding of interaction patterns between human activities and the environment;
2   using tests to evaluate threats and environmental assets that would be touched, with open questions on sustainability or unsustainability thresholds;
3   making a decision on practical sustainability objectives;
4   finding an agreement on rights of various groups of people and defining rules for allocating obligations and limited access rights in relation to the chosen sustainability norms;
5   defining transitional mechanisms;
6   designing incentives and penalties to ensure compliance with the new regime of rights and obligations.

If SD is to become an acknowledged principle of justification, all of these stages should be organized precisely and achieved successfully, particularly regarding the invention of appropriate tests to resolve disagreements and arbitrate contradictory claims. The ordinary logic of denunciation and social criticism relies on a set of statements mixing positive and normative elements presented as self-evident, in order to produce an effect of revelation about the 'real nature' of a situation. For instance, Ecological Footprint indexes are used to convince Western people that their consumption patterns are unsustainable since, the argument goes, five or six planets would be needed to support the same level of consumption for all inhabitants of planet Earth (Wackernagel and Rees 1995). Clearly, such statements combine a specific way to produce 'facts' and a normative orientation formulated in the name of SD. Are they convincing?

Regarding the practical equipment of SD, we are far from a well-established justification principle. It is expected from justification tests that they can put an end to conflicts and disagreements, and notably avoid endless rhetorical exercises that would take place if tests were to be seen as purely argumentative procedures without any involvement of the physical world.[15] Justification tests mobilize a set of precisely qualified objects and conditions that all members of society can firmly rely on to decide among rival claims.[16] We cannot presently find such features with SD.

The context of scientific controversies and incomplete understanding, sketched out in Section 2, actually reflects the inability of present states of ecological objects (CO_2 emissions, the spread of chemical compounds in the sea, deforestation and so on) to establish guaranteed equivalence with future environmental states. What we know of the present state of the environment does not allow us to predict its future state accurately.[17] The social pacification expected from the world of things committed to tests awakes a cruel disappointment here. The same shortcoming is found in the link between local and global phenomena. Complexity is the name given to the lack of information and knowledge needed by the human observer to access the global sense on the basis of knowledge of local mechanisms and realities (Atlan 1979): we know some parts of the puzzle, but not enough to fully understand the global functioning and the direction that the whole system will take. Such gaps open the way to various strategies of stakeholders backing contradictory interpretations.

These are the practical consequence of the 'entangled hierarchy' structure that underlies the *S-E* complex. But SD also has to face more fundamental problems, linked to the axioms characterizing a legitimate justification order.

Theoretical Issues with Sustainable Development as a Justification Principle

It is not uncommon to hear comments on the vagueness and inconsistencies of the concept of sustainability, even if rhetorical mentions of SD in business or political discourses are still more frequent. Some mainstream economists have long expressed doubts on the relevance, scientific value or rationality of SD as a

---

[15]   Real-world things, beings and states, at least through their representation (scientific measures and data), play a key role in social coordination for at least two reasons: human interests and lives cannot be separated from their material and technical basis, a component of which is their dependence on the bio-physical environment; objectivity of facts imposes their presence to everybody, and can only be denied by being in bad faith or through hard work of de-construction.

[16]   Think of a race to determine who really runs faster.

[17]   The much, and rightly, contested book by Lomborg (2001) is a typical demonstration of the error provoked by the confusion between gathering data on past and existing states of the environment and making statements on future states and issues: in a rather dishonest way, Lomborg tries to dress his personal views and priorities for the future as if they were a direct expression of the present real state of the world!

criterion for public management and economic planning.[18] Most analysts writing about SD evoke the large number of conflicting definitions and approaches at some point in their papers. This is certainly no reason to reject the concept and the problem as a whole, but such statements hint at the fact that the SD concept is still in a creation phase. Beyond, there are some theoretical difficulties in the way of making SD an alternative justification principle.

Two divergent perspectives, generally called anthropocentric and bio-centric, coexist in the literature on sustainability. Our previous analysis on the *S-E* complex confirmed the entanglement of a self-referent anthropocentric viewpoint and a hetero-referent bio-centric one. Yet the last word necessarily belongs to the self-referent anthropocentric one, since only humans raise the question of SD. This implies that a simple-minded anthropocentric approach will be at odds with SD, although there is hesitation on the appropriate way to progress.[19] The bio-centric view has been contemplated and developed by various scholars, but it rapidly leads to a dead end (Larrère 1997). Other experts show reluctance to limit the normative background to the strict application of a functionalist or narrowly economic anthropocentric concept, but do not want to choose sides in the bio-centric/anthropocentric controversy (for example, Kuik and Verbruggen 1991).

Regarding axioms of justification orders, the bio-centric view clearly comes up against a major problem, in that it violates the axiom of 'common humanity' (Axiom A1 in Box 2.5), which defines the legitimate reference community as a community of humans who mutually acknowledge each other as fellow men. Paul Ricoeur (1993: 15) stressed this difficulty when he stated his belief that the notions of rights and duty cannot be extended beyond the human sphere. Each time an approach considers ecological sustainability or survival of non-humans as superior goals or goals in their own right, and not as a means to guarantee a future for Mankind or to provide welfare, it is rendered invalid from the point of view of the 'common humanity' axiom.

The anthropocentric view does not come across this particular problem, but does suffer from two other important difficulties. To be suited to the stakes of sustainability, a principle of justification would have to provide a coherent representation of the future. This is a general point of tension, since the 'Polity' model frames a synchronic order on the people and social states. This is the case because it focuses on the conditions for reaching an agreement between the people who form society 'here and now'. This is why axiom A1, which establishes

---

[18]   On the contrary, see Asheim (2001) for a formal plea in favour of SD against standard optimal growth models.

[19]   For instance, the classical economic concept of optimal internalisation of external effects is quite inappropriate for shaping SD actions. As David Pearce (1976) showed, the conventional way to define the optimal pollution is part of the process by which the environment is progressively destroyed. The conceptual innovation introduced in economics by the SD concept is to consider natural components as capital assets, the reproduction of which has to be routinely integrated in the economic process (Godard 2006a).

a basic difference between other beings and the humans faced with the problem of finding a mutual agreement, also posits a fundamental equivalence and symmetry between all the members of the human community considered. This does not fit well into historical time, which introduces asymmetry between generations – one that is redoubled by the procreation relationship – and introduces a radical gap between remote generations. Both features have to be highlighted:

1   Remote generations do not belong to the same community of living people and the same physical world, and cannot communicate with each other in order to agree on a common good or an inter-temporal strategy of exploitation of natural resources; the successive generations are incapable of having the 'same power of access' to the different physical and social states (axiom A3), whereas the set of accessible states changes considerably over time (the 'irreversibility effect').
2   The former generations procreate the later generations and give them, at the same time, their unique identity and the world in which they are going to live their life. Former generations have the power to allow later generations come into existence or not.

These basic features that go with the development of Mankind since its beginnings do not fit the requirement of symmetry postulated by the 'Polity' model. They have considerable effects on the way to consider trans-generational equity, which cannot definitely be defined within the same framework as with the concepts and values put forward for intra-generational equity. For instance, some have claimed that the present generations cannot harm future ones under any circumstances. How is it possible? To each behavioural regime, however little it may modify the decisions of the present generations, there are corresponding future generations that will be different in both quality and quantity: those yet to be born will not be the same people; they will therefore not be in a position to criticize their parents for the state of the world the latter would have left them, because they would not have come into the world had their parents behaved differently.

Different attempts have been made to overcome this 'problem of identity'. One of them is to adopt a utilitarian framework (Beckerman and Pasek 1993, 2001; Birnbacher 1994); it gives a strong pre-eminence to a criterion of maximizing global welfare, and relatively[20] poor consideration to the specific achievements of identified individual people. But this utilitarian approach faces with both the issue of predicting long-run growth trajectories and future states of the world, which does not fit the radical uncertainty that prevails in practice, and the unresolved

---

[20]   I say 'relatively poor', not 'zero attention', because a utilitarian will take account of the growing marginal utility of an individual whom society tends to sacrifice for the sake of the general good of the whole society.

issue of discounting.[21] One alternative is to acknowledge minimum basic rights for all humans, in order to make ensuring human dignity possible for all individuals in all generations to come. The latter solution leads only to a partial ordering. It may be the same for SD, since there are presumably very different development combinations that can be said to be sustainable.

Another solution has been proposed on the institutional field: giving future generations an explicit and institutionalized representation today within the community formed by the present generation. The aim is to overcome the structural incapacity of ordinary democratic regimes to give weight to long-run human interests (Jonas 1984). The argument is as follows. As environmental changes are the remote 'links' from present generations to future generations, symmetry would be re-established by placing the representation of the latter in the present time. Certainly this solution would involve changes in the political modes of democracy; for example, with a council of future generations that would be given the right to censure existing parliaments, like constitutional courts. It would have the theoretical advantage of re-installing an initial community made up exclusively of co-present members, although with different roles.

Yet it remains to be seen how weights can be given fairly to future and present generations respectively, and how the representation mechanism can be compatible with the common dignity axiom (A3). As a social state, the function of representative should also be accessible in principle to all present members of society. Institutional innovation should not lead to the creation of two classes within the community: those only entitled to speak for themselves and those authorized to speak for the absent third parties. Above all, the envisaged solution raises the issue of authentication of the capacity of a number of individuals or bodies to represent future generations, as the usual validation procedures (elections by those to be represented and so on) are not available in this case. What tests could be used to judge self-proclaimed and contradictory claims to represent future generations?

Another direction to explore is provided by logics of transmission of heritage that are not linked primarily to equity concepts. For instance, the *domestic-traditional* justification order views the obligation of intergenerational transmission within a patrimonial group as a necessity to ensure the practical and cultural survival of the group, not primarily in order to be fair for future generations. This has a direct impact on the type of assets to transmit. They combine: valuable assets for future survival and adaptation of the group; assets inherited from past generations and having received a symbolic founding value; and assets that are considered by present generations as the most significant among their own contribution to human culture or to defining their own identity; in the latter case, the ethics of transmission is related to a search of a post-mortem extension. To rejoin SD, this concept of transmission has to raise the level of

---

[21] See the special issue 'Reflections on Discounting' of the *International Journal of Sustainable Development* (Hampicke and Ott 2003).

collective interest that it takes in charge in order to reach a level of generality beyond the limits of families or local groups or communities, but this may be conflicting with its group-identity foundation. At the same time, it should avoid considering members of the patrimonial group as nothing more than useful means to ensure group survival, as is the case in some traditional non-Western societies.

It is basically the value of responses to asymmetry between non-overlapping generations that tests the suitability of approaches of justification to be mobilized when sustainability may be at risk. All those considering the successive generations as a human community similar to that of a society of co-present people, such as extensions of Rawls' veil of ignorance to the trans-generational relationship, are inappropriate, because they ignore the fundamental asymmetry introduced by historical time and the procreation relationship. Such asymmetry does not have to be denied by artificial means, but overtaken by restoring some form of symmetry, such as indirect reciprocity.[22] This requirement holds true in spite of the fact that, since the condemnation of eugenics, attempts are being made to tone down the implications of this relationship as much as possible. Such a get-out is found, for example, by considering demographics as belonging to statistical laws on which forecast approaches can be based, rather than calling on principles putting a responsibility on the head of each generation for its procreative behaviour.

In view of all these problems, the question has to be raised as to whether SD is a new generic justification order, or whether it should rather be looked as an application of existing orders to a specific field of action and concern. The former case would require a change in the basic common set of axioms that frames justification orders in Western societies. It would amount to a fundamental revolution, but the profile of the alternative axioms is still not clearly defined at the theoretical level, to say nothing of concrete political aspects. If SD is an application of existing justification orders, the discourse and tests of sustainability have to be built from inside these orders. This is the position of authors such as Boulanger (2004), for whom SD amounts to a full and joint acknowledgement of requirements of classical intra- and intergenerational equity, which means an extension of the single civic justification order. In fact, to refer to justification orders already in place implies an acknowledgement of their plurality. Unlike Boulanger's position, I contend that not one of the existing orders can by itself provide the overall framework needed for thinking about SD. To have some chance of approaching the requirements of SD, we need to consider all that can be brought by the various active justification orders in democratic societies.

---

[22] Indirect reciprocity takes the form of an obligation to transmit to children, the source of which lies in the fact that parents have inherited assets from previous generations. It does not generate a backward transfer to the generations from which parents have benefited themselves, but a forward one to future generations; so the central generation is in a position of both receiver and giver; symmetry is restored. See the critical discussion of this solution by Gosseries (2001).

Conclusion

Unless our modern society is ready to turn the axiomatics supporting its justification orders upside down, theoretical limits as well as practical difficulties to finding appropriate and workable tests imply that SD should not be considered an alternative justification principle. Its status would then be that of an intermediate norm that has to be built and understood from inside the various classical justification orders that presently coexist in our modernity. In other words, SD would not be the ultimate foundation of assessment and judgement of development patterns and trajectories, but would have to be confronted with the specific tests of justification belonging to existing orders. Which one will provide the right test in a given situation is a question of mapping orders and contexts: different principles are felt relevant to different parts of economic and social life of our pluralist societies.

If we accept this broad direction, it follows that achieving sustainability cannot have a uniquely determined content, and that going to sustainability implies no unique way. SD has to be understood as an enterprise giving a chance to several interpretations and normative frameworks, each one being shaped by a specific justification order.[23] It would also open the way to various strategies to combine them in different ways. Even if, under specific circumstances, it may happen that these various constructs do converge in concluding that given courses of action or specific evolutions are definitely not sustainable, the core of sustainability cannot be seen as conceptually homogeneous: it is made of various rival claims put forward to give an appropriate translation of sustainability requirements.

This view of the normative status of SD certainly has consequences for the practical approaches and strategies that can be rightly developed. The relevance of any programme aiming at measuring sustainability with the help of a unique system of indicators should be questioned, as should the trust some actors seem to give to positivist sustainability impact assessments. Meanwhile, once pluralism is acknowledged to be co-substantive to the issue of sustainability as it is for modern liberal societies, there is still room for assessment exercises and the use of indicators. Any justification order is equipped with specific tests to resolve disputes and settle agreements. The interesting question raised by SD is how to develop relevant and useful tests and models in a pluralist society in which several constructs claimed by various stakeholders compete with each other.

Inasmuch the full development of the SD problematique can only be global and concern Humanity as such, but there is no such thing like world government, the issue of pluralism of concepts and translations of SD requirements takes a particular flavour in the context of international relations. This is a matter of

---

[23]   Underlying the pluralistic content of SD in relation to plural justification orders does not mean that any statement about SD is acceptable and should be accepted in the name of pluralism. Each justification order offers specific tests to assess claims. SD is not a way to escape the logic of public justification.

fact: other political and cultural communities do not wholly share the Western axiomatics of justification. Beyond formal United Nations statements on human rights, the question is open as to whether it is possible to find some truly universal benchmarks to apprehend the requirements of SD and prioritize action.[24] This is all the more true that present international governance is mainly framed by military threats and strategies, and trade issues, not by environmental ones. Would it be possible for a world in which rules of trade are more important that regimes aiming at preserving the global environment to be sustainable?

References

Agarwal, Anil and Sunita Narain. 1992. *Towards a Green World: Should Global Environmental Management be Build on Legal Conventions or Human Rights?* New Delhi: Centre for Science and Environment.

Asheim, Geir B. 2001. 'Justifying Sustainability'. *Journal of Environmental Economics and Management* 41: 252–68.

Atlan, Henri. 1979. *Entre le cristal et la fumée: essai sur l'organisation du vivant.* Paris: Seuil.

Beckerman, Wilfred and Joanna Pasek. 1993. *Environmental Policy: The Economics-Philosophy Relationship.* Annual Conference of the Society for the Advancement of Socio-Economics. New York, March.

———. 2001. *Justice, Posterity and the Environment.* Oxford: Oxford University Press.

Birnbacher, Dieter. 1994. *La responsabilité envers les générations futures.* Paris: PUF. Coll. Philosophie morale.

Boltanski, Luc and Laurent Thévenot. 2006. *On Justification: Economies of Worth.* Princeton University Press. Series 'Studies in Cultural Sociology'.

Boulanger, Paul-Marie. 2004. *Les indicateurs de développement durable. Un défi scientifique, un enjeu démocratique.* Les Séminaires de l'IDDRI 12. Paris: Institut du Développement Durable et des Relations Internationales, Juillet. http://www.iddri.org/iddri/telecharge/mardis/s12_boulanger.pdf

Brink, Ben ten. 1991. 'The AMOEBA Approach as a Useful Tool for Establishing Sustainable Development?' In Onno Kuik and Harmen Verbruggen. *In Search of Indicators of Sustainable Development.* Dordrecht: Kluwer. 71–87.

Commission of European Communities. 2002. *Communication on Impact Assessment.* Brussels, COM (2002) 276 final, 5 June.

---

[24] John Rawls (1999) tried to address the same type of issue, i.e. finding a minimum basis for an equitable international society made of collective bodies including both states and peoples, without assuming that all countries share the basic rules of equity that a democratic society based on justice would adopt according to his own theory of justice (1971). Is it possible to avoid relativism in the sphere of human values? See Dallmayr (2002) for a discussion of human rights in the context of 'Asian values' and Parikh and Parikh (2002) for an analysis of the position of India regarding the idea of taking action to mitigate climate change.

Dallmayr, Fred. 2002. '"Asian Values" and Global Human Rights'. *Philosophy East and West* 52.2. April: 173–89.

Ferry, Luc. 1995. *The New Ecological Order*. Chicago: University of Chicago Press.

Gardiner, Stephen M. 2006. 'A Core Precautionary Principle'. *Journal of Political Philosophy* 14.1. March: 33–60.

Godard, Olivier. 1984. 'Autonomie socio-économique et externalisation de l'environnement: la théorie néo-classique mise en perspective'. *Économie appliquée* 37:2: 315–45.

———. 1990. 'Environnement, modes de coordination et systèmes de légitimité: analyse de la catégorie de patrimoine naturel'. *Revue économique* 41.2: 215–41.

———. 1995. 'L'environnement, du champ de recherche au concept – Une hiérarchie enchevêtrée dans la formation du sens'. *Revue Internationale de Systémique* 9.4: 405–28.

———. 1997a. 'Social Decision-making under Scientific Controversy, Expertise and the Precautionary Principle'. In Christian Joerges, Karl Heinz Ladeur and Ellen Vos, eds. *Integrating Scientific Expertise into Regulatory Decision-making – National Experiences and European Innovations*. Baden-Baden: Nomos Verlagsgesellschaft: 39–73.

———. 1997b. 'L'environnement, du concept au champ de recherche et à la modélisation'. In François Blasco, ed. *Tendances nouvelles en modélisation pour l'environnement*. Paris: Elsevier: 407–15.

———. 1998. 'Sustainable Development and the Process of Justifying Choices in a Controversial Universe'. In Sylvie Faucheux, Martin O'Connor and Jan van der Straaten, eds. *Sustainable Development: Concepts, Rationalities and Strategies*. Dordrecht/London: Kluwer: 299–317.

———. 2003. 'Le principe de précaution comme norme de l'action publique, ou la proportionnalité en question'. *Revue économique* 54.6: 1245–76.

———. 2006a. 'La pensée économique face à l'environnement'. In Alain Leroux and Pierre Livet, eds. *Leçons de Philosophie économique – Tome II : Économie normative et philosophie morale*. Paris: Economica: 241–77.

———, ed. 2006b. *La question de la précaution en milieu professionnel*. Paris: EDP-Sciences and INRS, Coll.: Avis d'experts.

———. 2006c. 'The Precautionary Principle and Catastrophism on Tenterhooks: Lessons from a Constitutional Reform in France'. In Elizabeth Fisher, Judith Jones and René Von Schomberg, eds. *Implementing the Precautionary Principle: Perspectives and Prospects*. Cheltenham/Northampton, MA: Edward Elgar: ch. 4, 63–87.

Godard, Olivier, Claude Henry, Patrick Lagadec and Erwann Michel-Kerjan. 2002. *Traité des nouveaux risques. Précaution, crise, assurance*. Paris: Gallimard. Coll. Folio-Actuel.

Gosseries, Axel. 2001. 'What Do We Owe the Next Generation(s)?' *Loyola of Los Angeles Law Review*. 35.1: 293–354.

Hampicke, Ulrich and Konrad Ott, eds. 2003. Special issue 'Reflections on Discounting'. *International Journal of Sustainable Development* 6.1.

Jonas, Hans. 1984. *The Imperative of Responsibility. In Search of an Ethics for the Technological Age*. Chicago: University of Chicago Press.

Kirkpatrick, Colin and Norman Lee. 2002. *Further Development of the Methodology for a Sustainability Impact Assessment of Proposed WTO Negotiations*. Manchester: Institute for Development Policy and Management, University of Manchester, 5 April.

Kuik, Onno and Harmen Verbruggen, eds. 1991. *In Search of Indicators of Sustainable Development*. Dordrecht/London: Kluwer.

Lafaye, Claudette and Laurent Thévenot. 1993. 'Une justification écologique ? Conflits dans l'aménagement de la nature'. *Revue Française de Sociologie* 34.4: 495–524.

Larrère, Catherine. 1997. *Les philosophies de l'environnement*. Paris: PUF. Coll. Philosophies.

Leopold, Aldo. 1987. *A Sand County Almanac and Sketches Here and There*. New York: Oxford University Press (first published 1948).

Lomborg, Bjorn. 2001. *The Skeptical Environmentalist. Measuring the Real State of the World*. Cambridge: Cambridge University Press.

Ministère de l'Ecologie et du Développement Durable. 2004. *Indicateurs nationaux du développement durable: lesquels retenir?* Paris: La Documentation française.

O'Riordan, Timothy and James Cameron, eds. 1994. *Interpreting the Precautionary Principle*. London: Earthscan.

Parikh, Jyoti K. and Kirit Parikh. 2002. *Climate Change: India's Perceptions, Positions, Policies and Possibilities*. Paris: OECD and Dehli: Indira Gandhi Institute of Development Research.

Pearce, David W. 1976. 'The Limits of Cost-benefit Analysis as a Guide to Environmental Policy'. *Kyklos* 29.1: 97–112.

Raffensperger, Carolyn and Joel Tickner. 1999. *Protecting Public Health and the Environment. Implementing the Precautionary Principle*. Washington DC: Island Press.

Rawls, John. 1971. *A Theory of Justice*. Cambridge, MA: Harvard University Press.

———. 1999. *The Law of Peoples*. Cambridge, MA: Harvard University Press.

Ricoeur, Paul. 1993. 'L'éthique, le politique, l'écologie. Entretien'. *Ecologie Politique. Sciences, Culture, Société* 7: 5–17.

Sunstein, Cass R. 2005. *Laws of Fear: Beyond the Precautionary Principle* (The Seeley Lectures). Cambridge: Cambridge University Press.

Wackernagel, Mathis. 2001. *Advancing Sustainable Resource Management. Using Ecological Footprint Analysis for Problem Formulation, Policy Development and Communication*. Prepared for DG Environment, European Commission, 27 February.

Wackernagel, Mathis and William Rees. 1995. *Our Ecological Footprint – Reducing Human Impact on the Earth*. Gabriola Island, BC: New Society Publishers.

World Commission on Environment and Development. 1987. *Our Common Future*. Oxford: Oxford Paperbacks.

Chapter 3

Global Public Goods and Governance of Sustainable Development

Sophie Thoyer

Introduction

Unknown ten years ago, the concept of global public goods (GPG) has become a central theme of discussion not only amongst researchers but also in institutions and negotiation arena, governing development, international trade and the management of global risks. Between 1990 and 2002, numerous scientific papers on the subject were published (e.g. Barrett 1990; Kindleberger, 1986; Sandler, 1998), and several international institutions began to make substantial contributions to the debate. After the 1999 publication of *Global Public Goods: International Co-operation in the Twenty-first Century* (Kaul et al. 1999), the United Nations Development Programme (UNDP)'s Office of Development Studies published a second book devoted more specifically to the supply of global public goods, *Providing Global Public Goods: Managing Globalisation* (Kaul et al. 2003), which drew considerable response both from the academic world and from policy-makers.

In 2001, the World Bank published a report evaluating financing mechanisms believed to contribute directly to the conservation of global public goods (World Bank 2001). Subsequently, many international development agencies began to include the concept into their aid programmes (Severino 2001; Tubiana and Severino 2002). Finally, France and Sweden launched a 'task force' devoted to global public goods in 2002. This task force has initiated several international meetings to promote the idea that international cooperation should be better coordinated in the national interest in order to achieve higher living standards around the world, benefiting recipient and donor countries alike (Secretariat of the International Task Force 2005).

The GPG concept has been instrumental in highlighting the growing interdependence among countries, and in pinpointing a number of major shortcomings and unresolved issues in the efforts to undertake joint action for preserving global assets or producing global services. It has therefore contributed to invigorating the debate over international cooperation and coordination.

The objective of this chapter is to examine to what extent the notion of global public goods can provide new insights into the issue of the governance of sustainable development, following three main directions:

1   The non-rivalry and non-excludability characteristics of global public goods are linked to the notion of sustainable development. By clarifying those links, there is scope to bring the international discussions on development aid and trade rules to be held on a more equitable playing field, by changing the perceptions of what the global common good is and by introducing different expectations on the outcomes of international cooperation.

2   The theory on the collective provision of global public goods emphasizes the need to tie supply decisions to the willingness to pay of populations concerned. It indirectly reintroduces the question of the acceptable trade-offs between managing heterogeneity in preferences and preventing free-riding behaviours. It therefore points at the issue of the right level of governance, highlighting the interests of a decentralized provision of public goods and giving new theoretical grounds to participatory decision-making processes.

3   Looking at international issues through the global public good lense brings new insights into the discussions about the institutions for global governance. In particular, there is a growing literature in economics focusing on the way in which national contributions to the provision of public goods aggregate into global public goods. It is useful to make recommendations on optimal financing schemes at the international level and on better-designed institutional solutions to the issue of international cooperation.

Despite its success in international organizations and discourses, the fact that the analytical content of the definition of global public goods remains weak cannot be overlooked (Constantin 2002). Detractors argue that expansion of the concept of global public goods results in a mishmash of economic efficiency concepts and socio-political considerations concerning equity and social justice, thus losing its analytical rigour and becoming a mere ideological slogan. However, this chapter argues that the global public good notion can lay the foundations for a strengthened legitimacy of sustainable development policies by renewing the theoretical basis on which sustainability principles are defended. In the rest of the chapter, we will therefore examine the three issues – global public goods and sustainability; global public goods and participation; global public goods and global governance – in more detail.

Global Public Goods and Sustainability

Economists have traditionally defined public goods as those goods whose inherent characteristics in terms of non-exclusion and non-rivalry make their production by the private sector improbable. State intervention to supply and preserve such goods is therefore justified.

The notion of non-exclusion is frequently defined as the fact that it is impossible or technically very costly to forbid access to a good or service to those who wish to benefit from it. This is typically the case of roads or street-lights. It is therefore difficult to establish and enforce property rights and to make users pay for the good. Non-rivalry is associated with the fact that consumption of the public good by an agent does not prevent the consumption of the same good by others. The good is not altered by the consumption process. A radio programme can thus be heard by an infinite number of listeners. In certain cases, the effect referred to as 'congestion of use' can affect the property of non-rivalry. This is the case of traffic jams on a road or crowds of people on a beach.

When surveying the range of public goods, we can distinguish two types: man-produced public goods and natural assets and resources. There are costs associated with their production in the former case, and costs associated with their preservation in the latter case.[1] Whereas markets are a powerful instrument for relating supply to demand of private goods, they fail to provide and preserve public goods adequately because they face the well-known free-rider problem: typically, a provider cannot keep non-contributors from consuming the good's benefits. Therefore no profits can be made and markets are unlikely to develop. Moreover, even if a group chose to make up for the market's failure by pooling resources to collectively provide the public good, no member would have any strong incentive to reveal his true willingness to contribute to the financing of the good. Although economists have designed complex preference-revelation mechanisms to induce recipients to adopt truth-telling as their dominant strategy, such theoretical solutions are often difficult to implement in practice (Cornes and Sandler 1996). The issue is therefore threefold: (1) how to promote collective action for the provision of public goods; (2) how to choose which public goods should be produced and in what quantity since there are no price signals to reveal the hierarchy of preferences; and (3) which burden-sharing mechanisms should be established to finance the costs?

The Global Dimension of Public Goods

Considerations of global public goods build upon such questions. Thus global public goods came to be understood as those goods – or bads – with non-rivalrous and non-exclusive features, not only with regard to individuals but also between different populations and countries. Some of them are truly global and affect the whole planet, whereas others can have a more regional impact across several constituencies in the same area of the world.

---

[1]   Such costs can be foregone benefits of choosing not to use the resource up to the privately optimal point.

The first global public goods were identified – without being named as such – in the context of global environmental risks and transborder externalities. In the early 1970s, several studies confirmed the hypothesis that air pollutants could travel several thousands of kilometres before deposition and damage occurred. In particular, scientists established the links between acid rains that badly affected Scandinavian forests and lakes, and the rate of sulphur emissions in neighbouring countries. It provided grounds for the idea that cooperation at the international level was necessary to control and reduce such environmental impacts. In 1979, the Convention on Long Range Transboundary Air Pollution was signed to reduce those emissions: it was the first legally binding instrument to deal with air pollution problems at a regional scale. It was followed by the signing of the Montreal Protocol in 1987, which sets limits on the use of ozone depleting gases. The quality of the atmosphere and the ozone layer were thus defended as global natural resources and pure global public goods. Since the Montreal Protocol, the substantial media coverage of the global warming debate and the notorious difficulties to set the Kyoto Protocol in motion have contributed to publicizing this notion. Less well-known, the negotiations to protect oceans as common heritage of mankind culminated with the adoption of the 1982 United Nations Convention on the Law of the Sea. It provided the basis of a universal legal framework for the rational management of marine resources and their conservation for future generations.

It was emphasized that the production or preservation of global natural resources requires the joint, coordinated action of several countries. However, since countries that do not participate in the provision or the conservation of such goods cannot be prevented from using or consuming them, the temptation either to free-ride, or defect after having signed an agreement, is strong. In the absence of a legitimate supranational government, the resolution of environmental issues requires that a voluntary agreement should be signed between independent sovereign states 'in the context of anarchy' (Axelrod and Keohane 1985). The risks of under-provision are great. In the domain of economics, it gave rise to a whole stream of game theory literature dedicated to the issue of international environmental cooperation (for a review, see Batabyal 2000; Neumayer 2001): cooperative game theory focuses on the process of coalition formation and stability, whereas non-cooperative game theory analyses the scope for reaching self-enforceable and renegotiation-proof agreements through bargaining, reputation effects, credible threats and the exploitation of information asymmetries between negotiating parties (Barrett 1990; Carraro and Siniscalco 1993; Chandler and Tulkens 1997).

With the acceleration of the globalization process, social and economic interdependencies between countries have deepened. Globalization has made the threats of international negative externalities and the opportunities of positive externalities more acute. Clearly, the integration of financial markets increases the risks of an international financial crisis jeopardizing the prospects of economic growth at a global scale. Facilitated travel and trade expansion have multiplied the risks of a rapid spread of pests or contagious diseases: the massive mobilization of the international community following the Severe Acute Respiratory Syndrome (SARS) outbreak confirms the global challenge posed by such threats. It is thus argued that – beyond the preservation of global natural resources – the eradication of contagious diseases, the stabilization of global financial markets, or the promotion of world peace and security also display non-rivalry and non-exclusion properties that make them good candidates for a 'global public good' definition (UNDP 1999). The initial focus on environmental issues was rapidly enlarged to include global social and economic stakes, therefore imposing the provision and management of global public goods – to manage such externalities – on the priority list of the international policy-making agenda.

This is not a recent phenomenon: following the Second World War, the international community had acknowledged that international rules had to be collectively designed and enforced to facilitate exchanges and economic stability. There are technical and safety rules: the International Civil Aviation Organization enacts regulation to promote air safety; the International Telecommunication Union seeks to harmonize standards and to improve the standardization of equipment. There are also economic rules, such as the Bretton Woods rules, which were designed to stabilize the international monetary system, or even the World Trade Organization (WTO) trade rules, which are expected to promote trade and prosperity. Although such international rules imply some loss of autonomy in national decisions, most of them allow enormous gains in terms of spared transaction costs. They provide non-rival and non-excludable benefits: the international community has known how to produce global public goods well before naming them. The issue today is to extend this type of cooperation beyond the limits of common safety rules or trade standards and to include solutions to the sustainable development challenge.

Discussions on global public goods have shifted to the poverty issue, therefore inducing both a more philosophical debate on the status of public development aid and very pragmatic negotiations on the forms and tools of international cooperation. The international taskforce on global public goods has identified six challenges – peace and security, disease control, global commons, financial stability, knowledge sharing and open trade – which all contribute to the world's physical and economic security, and are therefore important drivers of poverty eradication. The underlying rationale is that more equitable and sustainable prosperity in the South will benefit everyone in terms of stability, reduction of conflicts, opportunities for trade etc ... and not only the poorest. Efforts towards the provision of global public goods should not be conceived as mere assistance to developing countries, but as a joint coordinated action to improve the welfare of all present and future generations. By linking economic issues to social and environmental issues, the notion of global public goods re-emphasizes the three pillars of sustainability and can impose itself as a fruitful theoretical basis for tackling sustainable development objectives (and, in particular, the Millennium Development Goals) from a global perspective.

Inclusiveness

A number of authors have proposed departing from the strict definition of global public goods. They suggest broadening the concept based on the social construction of exclusion and rivalry properties. From their perspective, the 'public' nature of the good is a socio-political decision rather than an inherent quality of the good. It is a fact that the properties of exclusion or non-exclusion are not innate properties despite what is often described in the literature. For example, it can evolve with technical progress: the transmission of television images can now be encoded, thereby reserving viewing rights for channel subscribers. Similarly, societies can design regulatory rules to set-up exclusion devices, such as intellectual property rights that force users of innovations to pay royalties to those who have produced this new knowledge.

If exclusion devices can be set up, then there is also scope to design inclusion. For a number of advocates of GPGs, decision-makers should aim at building the conditions for non-exclusion and non-rivalry – not only between countries but also between all citizens of the world. The UNDP's definition of the GPG's triangle of publicness states that a governing principle of GPG provision should be that three publicness dimensions be respected and balanced: *publicness* in consumption (in that everyone must have access to the good), *publicness* in decision-making (in that the political process through which the good is selected and financed, must include consultation and dialogue with all stakeholders in an open process) and *publicness* in the distribution of net benefits (in that everyone is entitled to benefit from the good).

Such a conception obviously entails a radical change in the nature of international cooperation: the objective is no longer to set up 'exclusion' devices in order to establish a market value for a given GPG, but to make 'inclusive' a good that is not necessarily so, in the name of the 'global general interest'. In such cases, it is collectively decided that a given good or service be made available to all without restriction for the common good. The inclusiveness of the good is therefore socially built. From this enlarged perspective of a GPG definition, a number of recommendations can be drawn in terms of access rules, participation, and GPG 'value'.

Global Public Goods and Participation

Since global public goods cannot be supplied without international coordination and cooperation, it is necessary to be able to identify the collective priorities of joint efforts – in terms of financing and changes in technological orientation. In the absence of a democratically elected global government, should we entrust existing inter-governmental agencies with this responsibility? What should be the appropriate decision-making process for choosing collectively the public goods that should be produced, the quantities and the financing mechanisms?

From a neoclassical economics perspective, the provision of local or national public goods is theoretically guided by two principles: the 'Samuelson condition' (Samuelson 1954) – a public good is optimally provided when the marginal cost of supply is equal to the marginal willingness to pay by society – and the 'fiscal equivalence principle' (Olson 1969) – the decision for collective expenditure should be taken preferably by those who are directly affected by the decision. These two principles are interesting to help defining the scope and mechanisms of global governance.

Subsidiarity and Globalness

The issue raised by the Samuelson condition concerns the willingness to pay by society. At the national level, we have already seen that it can be very tricky to identify this willingness, since all benefactors have an incentive, either to understate their benefits (when they expect their participation in costs to be calculated on the basis of their share of benefits) or to overstate them (when they expect the quantity of public good to be produced according to declared benefits). At the global level, the issue is made even more difficult: although GPGs affect all countries, the benefits derived from their production or preservation are not necessarily evenly distributed. Each country, each group of stakeholders might give a different ranking to GPG priorities. Moreover, the production of two global public goods might be in conflict with each other. For example, how should the international community reconcile the food security concerns expressed by one population – which could be answered through the generalization of genetically modified crops – with the priority for the conservation of biodiversity expressed by another – which could preclude GMO crops? Even a single GPG can entail several forms of values, which do not accrue to all stakeholders equally. Let us take the biodiversity example: it offers public-use values, such as ecological services or environmental amenities, valued by nature-loving citizens. It also has public non-use values such as heritage value, of greater interest for a member of a traditional forest community than for an urban dweller; and existence value, which again might be different when assessed from the point of view of a high-income citizen or a low-income citizen.

There is a need to aggregate those different preferences into a single, stable, collective-preference function. Social choice theory provides some keys to get around the issue of non-transitive collective choices.[2] However, apart from the General Assembly of the United Nation – which has little power in terms of prescription – there is no formal process of collective decision and no equivalent

---

[2]   When using a majority rule for collective decision, we can end up with circular votes such as: choice A is preferred by the majority to choice B, choice B is preferred by the majority to choice C, but choice C is also is preferred by the majority to choice A. This paradox was initially described by Condorcet and was later formalized by Arrow in his Impossibility Theorem (Arrow 1951).

of a 'global government' that could legitimately exert authority to ensure that a decision is taken and respected. Policy-makers are aware of this issue, especially since the massive demonstrations expressing distrust of the globalization process and denouncing the lack of democracy in international decisions.

One solution –which would be a remote equivalent of the Coase bargaining solution – would be to let communities (countries or supranational groups of countries such as the European Union) choose their priorities but compensate other countries for the negative externalities that such choices might entail for them. In the context of trade, Pascal Lamy, as head of Directorate General Trade of the EU, suggested the use of a special WTO safeguard clause to 'ensure that trade integration will not pose a threat to legitimate collective preferences' (Lamy 2004). Such a clause would have been subject to two conditions, namely a requirement to demonstrate that there is a coherent underlying social demand to justify the measure; and the demonstration that the measure complies with the basic principles of the trading system. The clause would also have been accompanied by a compensation mechanism, which would have served to partially compensate the affected exporters, thereby placing the responsibility on communities to bear the external cost of measures that reflect their societal choices.

Of course, this proposal was seductive: it tried to strike a balance between subsidiarity and globalness. However, it suffered from major shortcomings: in particular, it left partially unanswered the question of the amount of compensation. Since people value public goods differently, it is very difficult to reach an agreement on compensatory transfers between the 'victim' and the 'incumbent'. For example, if the EU insists on subsidizing its agricultural producers in the name of environmental protection and landscape preservation, it could maintain such a policy provided it compensated exporters for losses in market shares. This can be done provided only market losses are taken into account. But what about indirect losses associated with the reduction of food security in exporting countries? Moreover although the applicability of such a solution is conceivable for trade choices, it is much less the case for activities entailing irreversible effects; what would be the compensation that the USA would have to pay for its contribution to global warming?

The hierarchy of global issues and the priority they are given in terms of negotiation efforts and financing depend thus on the mobilization of different groups (various interest groups, civil society organizations, experts and researchers and policy-makers) defending them in the international arena. International competition is no longer uniquely an economic competition: it is also a social, intellectual and political competition for imposing norms, values and preferences in the process of international agenda setting. However, such competition is all the more pernicious because it is uneasy to observe and analyse. Interstate hegemonic pressure, diplomatic threats and corruption, can also be come into play at this level.

The question is therefore the following: how do we make sure that this competition is accepted by all and that decisions taken on those arenas have legitimacy?

Civil Society Participation

Civil society groups claim that the answer lies in more participatory decision-making process. They argue rightly that global public goods are rarely the sole responsibility of state authorities and that in fact their production and preservation depend on the cooperation of many actors and require both public and private spending. They therefore demand that international institutions be adapted to be made more democratic, more transparent and more open to non-state participation. This is echoed by the extended definition of publicness given by the UNDP, insisting on the importance of an open and participatory decision. Arguments for more participatory procedures are also in line with the recommendations found in Agenda 21 for sustainable development. The question of course is whether such changes would be sufficient to ensure the expression of the diversity of stakeholders and preferences.

It relates also to the principles underpinning good global governance. They encompass the traditional policy-design issues of openness (more communication with the general public), accountability (more responsibility of decision-makers), participation (more inclusive approaches to consultation and participation of stakeholders) and international conflict resolution.

However, the claims so far are that international negotiations are plagued by lack of transparency, absence of genuine participatory processes and unbalanced bargaining power. Some developing countries backed up by civil society groups denounce this new form of imperialism, which consists in imposing one's vision of the world and preferences upon the rest of the international community in the name of the collective well-being. However, some international institutions have succeeded in fostering interesting participatory experiences: the Conferences of the Parties of the Convention on Biological Diversity have included a vast array of interest representation, from biotechnology transnationals to indigenous and local communities. These open-ended meetings have certainly contributed to enlarge considerably the scope of the Convention and to include issues that were initially overlooked or downplayed, such as the protection of traditional knowledge.

Type II initiatives promoted at the Johannesburg World Summit on Sustainable Development have opened the way for a new form of action, combining NGOs, local communities, public partners and private enterprises. They demonstrate an innovative potential for the development of economic projects participating in the production of global public goods. They reveal the possibility of new forms of cooperation, which are less directly dependent on the intervention of states. The success of such endeavours therefore leads to a reconsideration of the conditions of production of global public goods, which can combine public and private efforts more efficiently. Another example of such a supply is associated with the tradable rights instrument. When the international community decides to create user rights on the GPG, which are then allocated to countries, and possibly traded (for example, transferable fishing quotas or emission permits), they are in fact delegating the production/preservation of the GPG to private agents, through their elected governments. This allows better subsidiarity in the choices that each government can make to encourage its private sector. Moreover, the greater reliance on market mechanisms is expected to improve efficiency and to enhance the respect for local preferences concerning the GPG provision. However, such a solution is only available when the global public good is the joint product of a private activity. What can be done for GPGs that cannot be produced as a by-product of economic activity or for which it is impossible to create user rights?

Moreover, it does not solve the issue of the choice concerning the amount of GPGs that should be produced. The harsh negotiations on CO_2 emission quotas which have preceded the signature of the Kyoto Protocol in 1997, and the ensuing difficulty to obtain ratification, remind us that markets are an interesting tool to boost efficiency but do not solve the issue of initial allocation of rights. We are back to the initial question: how to create the conditions necessary for the emergence of a consensus concerning the ranking of global public goods?

Global Public Goods and Global Governance

This brings the issue of the best institutional fit for providing global public goods to the fore. Four areas of practical recommendations are summarized in the overview of the 1999 UNDP book: (i) refurbishing the analytical toolkit; (ii) matching circles of stakeholders and decision-makers; (iii) systematizing the financing of GPG; (iv) spanning borders, sectors and groups of actors.

The Neutrality Theorem

Economists are well aware of the financing problem since it is expected to be doomed by the well-known prisoner's dilemma: the free-riding strategies of each stakeholder – hoping to enjoy the benefits of public good supply without having to share the costs – leads to a sub-optimal outcome characterized by an under-supply of the global public good. Warr's theoretical work gives more support for such pessimistic views: he demonstrates that a redistribution of income among contributors to a public good has no effect on the level of the public good provided (Warr 1983). In other words, when a public good is financed by voluntary contributions, a redistributive policy that would force some higher-income countries to contribute to a multilateral fund with the view to transferring revenues to lower-income countries would not improve the quantity of public good supplied. The reason is that donor countries would then reduce their voluntary contribution to the public good proportionally to their lost income and would rely instead on contributions made by others. This phenomenon of crowding out leads to the so-called 'neutrality theorem': redistributive policies amongst voluntary contributors are useless, no matter what their preferences are in terms of public–private good ratio. This result does reduce the range of policy options available since it excludes, *de facto*, all strategies based on income transfers.

However, this result only holds for a pure public good whose technology of production is purely additive. In other words, each unit contributed to the public good adds identically and cumulatively to the overall level of public good. Contributions are therefore substitutable on a per-unit basis. The best example of an additive supply is the reduction of greenhouse gas emissions. Each country's effort will contribute proportionally, without geographical or income consideration, to the production of the GPG, that is, the curbing of global warming. We know that in such a case, collective action is doomed by two forms of free-riding: external free-riding, when countries refuse to cooperate and let others contribute; and internal free-riding, when countries have agreed to join a coalition but then do not comply with their commitments. Effectiveness in the additive case will thus very much depend on incentives for cooperation, and sanctions for non-observance.

Supply Technology and Distribution of Costs and Benefits: A Typology

Not all global public goods have this kind of additive supply technology. A number of authors, following Hirshleifer (1983) and Cornes and Sandler (1998), have designed global public good typologies based on their aggregation technologies and have then drawn conclusions on the type of collective action failure they induce (Dulbecco and Laporte 2005; Sandler 1998, Sandler and Arce 2002). Beyond the additive case, there are two other archetypal cases described in the literature. The weakest-link scenario is the situation where the overall supply of the GPG is equal to the amount provided by the contributor with the smallest effort. A well-known example is the control of epidemic diseases. Their eradication depends mostly on the effort (in terms of controls, vaccination campaigns etc.) of the least stringent country. The same reasoning applies to terrorism: the country with the weakest security policy will set the level of safety for the whole international community since that is where terrorists will find a base for their activity. The collective action issue associated with weakest link technologies is less one of free-riding than one of matching behaviour: countries have no incentives to spend more on the public good than the weakest link does, since funds paid beyond the smallest contribution yield no returns. If countries have different endowments and preferences, they may want a higher level of the public good than the one imposed by the weakest link. The challenge is then to persuade the weakest link to cooperate and increase its contribution: either by providing the means for the weakest link to do so (financial or in-kind transfers) or by changing its preferences. The issue of in-kind versus financial transfers is not a trivial one (Vicary and Sandler 2002): in-kind giving happens when a low-cost contributor chooses to supply the public good directly in the weakest link country (i.e. sending medical teams and vaccines to eradicate a disease or sending security forces to counteract terrorist action in this country), whereas income transfers increase the revenue in the recipient country, but do not necessarily guarantee an improvement in the public good supply unless tight conditionality is attached to aid. The relative performance of in-kind versus cash transfers depends on the differences in cost efficiency of the different countries.

A comparable case to the weakest link is the threshold supply, where the level of the public good must reach a set level for any benefits to be achieved. One example given by Sandler (2003) is that of peace-keeping, where the threshold is determined by the amount of firepower necessary to keep two opposing factions apart (Thoyer 2004).

The best-shot scenario, on the contrary, is the situation in which the overall quantity of the GPG is determined by the largest individual provision level; it is often the case when the supply of a public good benefits from substantial economies of scale. Investments in research to develop a new vaccine are a good example. The country/research centre that has invested the most is more likely to make a breakthrough, whereas all smaller contributions will be made redundant and will therefore yield no benefit. Gains in effectiveness then depend on the capacity to pool resources and to direct them towards the most efficient GPG producer. It can be done through specific incentive schemes (cash transfers, in-kind cooperation) or issue linkages (force the country to increase its contribution by making another advantage conditional on the provision of this GPG).

The typology of aggregation technologies can be refined by adding the generalizations of the three archetypical cases described above to the list: the weighted sum (each supplier's effort has a different weight when added to others' efforts), the weaker link (the smallest contribution has the greatest influence on provision, followed by the second smallest etc) and the better shot (the largest effort has the greatest impact on overall supply, followed by the second-largest etc). Of course, these attenuated forms lead also to less-strong conclusions concerning collective action and in some cases the fate of sub-optimality might be curtailed.

To this typology, a fourth interesting category could be added, often forgotten by the literature: the case when only one country or subset of countries can produce the global public good desired by the entire international community, because of its geographical location. This case could be named 'essential player' by analogy with vote theory. Rainforest biodiversity is a good example. All countries wish to see it preserved because it has both immediate values, and option and existence values. However, such biodiversity can only be preserved if the Amazonian forest and a small number of other primary equatorial forests are saved from deforestation and logging. In other words, such global public goods lie in the hands of the Brazilian, Congolese and Indonesian decision-makers. It both gives them a monopoly power and a dire responsibility. When the priorities of their people are different from the priorities expressed by the international community or when their political power is threatened by private interests, they find it politically difficult to fulfil the wants of other countries before the short-term needs of their constituencies. It is in this case that the debate between national sovereignty and common heritage of mankind becomes more acute. Financial transfers and aid are policy instruments that can help ease the tension.

However, such typology is often incomplete because it overlooks the distribution of benefits and costs. They are rarely shared evenly. Inequities in costs are well known: as was hinted before, some countries have a comparative advantage in the production of some global public goods because of their natural resources, their level of technology or their human capital. The CO_2 emissions rights market planned by the Kyoto Protocol is one of the ways to exploit differences in abatement costs across sectors, firms and countries, in order to reduce the overall cost of emission reduction. Less well-known – and less exploited – is the fact that some countries enjoy greater benefits from the same level of global public good provision than other countries. This can be as a result of their geographical location (and therefore the differential impact of the GPG), to their intrinsic preference for some GPGs (associated with history, culture or institutions), to their level of income, which may induce changes in taste and preferences (the elasticity of demand with respect to income is positive for a normal public good) or to joint products (efforts to supply the GPG induce also private benefits: for example, by preserving its natural assets – such as wetlands or coastal areas, a country contributes to maintain biodiversity, but at the same time, it increases revenues from tourism). This means of course that expected net benefits of contribution vary greatly from one country to another and therefore induce different strategies of participation.

For example, global warming has differentiated impacts on countries according to their geographical characteristics. Small islands or lowland countries feel more threatened by rising seawaters; Sahelian and other semi-desert countries suffer from more acute droughts. On the other hand, Nordic countries, such as Canada, benefit from rising temperatures and longer growing seasons, which improve crop yields and reduce their fossil-fuel bills. Of course, they may also face more frequent natural disasters as a result of weather instability (storms, tornados) but on the whole their benefits from curbing global warming would not be as great as for the former.

Cooperation strategies and stakes (the negotiation process, the scope for free-riding, and the forms of cooperation incentives and threats) will differ according to the nature of the GPG to be produced. One of the conclusions of course is that there is no standardized governance regime for GPG production. They require different structures of international coordination and flexibility in the way international negotiation fora are set up. Olson's *Logic of Collective Action* (1965) reminds us that the larger the group, the greater the inertia and the more difficult it becomes to overcome the free-riding issue. More homogeneity in the composition of the group's membership will help to organize reciprocal control. On the other hand, greater disparity between contributors may ensure that some countries receive sufficient gains to be willing to bear the costs of collective provision unilaterally, therefore triggering collective action. Enlarging the coalition of contributors is then often an essential step in the additive case and it can only be done through shaming, issue linkages or conditional subsidy schemes. However, it is also essential to analyse what might happen once an agreement has been signed: the incentives to defect, the means of sanction, the way non-contributors can be induced to join the coalition, etc. Risks of failures of existing coalitions depend very much on the distribution of net benefits of collective action. To circumvent these risks, redistributive policies improving equity in burden sharing can be helpful, but too much equity may bring back free-riding attitudes from the very same countries that had triggered collective action in the first place. The following four tables propose a number of recommendations for management and supply of the four types of global public good identified above: additive, weakest-link, best-shot and essential-player. They analyse the reasons for collective action failure, incentives for cooperation, the management of the signed agreement and institutional recommendations for participation.

Table 3.1   Governance of additive global public goods

Examples: reduction of greenhouse gases emissions to curb global warming; reduction of waste disposal in oceans to improve the quality of seawaters

Collective action failure	Free-riding. Prisoner's dilemma: inaction or under-supply of the GPG.
Incentives for cooperation	Very few if countries are homogeneous. If heterogeneous, then countries with high benefit-to-cost ratios are likely to start cooperating. Need to enlarge coalition to non-contributors: incentives through diplomatic pressure, issue linkage, shaming
Management of signed agreement	To prevent *ex-post* defection, improve equity in burden-sharing through two-tier contributions or interstate financial transfers. Problem of leakage (the higher the supply of the GPG, the higher the benefits of non-contributors through changes in private/public good: price ratio)*
Institutions and participation	Try to set tight agreements with easy monitoring of compliance and credible and enforceable sanctions; facilitate civil society scrutiny for monitoring and shaming

* The best example is the Kyoto-protocol leakages: reducing CO_2 emissions implies switching to clean energies, thereby reducing demand for fossil fuels, whose prices will then decline. Non-signatory countries will therefore benefit from lower costs for petrol use, and increase their emissions accordingly, thus annihilating signatory countries' efforts.

Table 3.2   Governance of weakest-link global public goods

Examples: control of an infectious disease spreading to eradicate it; surveillance of suspicious activist groups to prevent terrorist attacks worldwide

Collective action failure	Matching behaviour: all countries lower their contributions to the weakest-link's level of effort. Likely under-provision if the weakest link is unwilling or unable to increase its contribution to the desired level
Incentives for cooperation	Transfers to the weakest-link country. In kind transfers from cost-effective countries; conditional financial transfers otherwise. Can be organized also through multilateral funding financed by mandatory taxes
Management of signed agreement	Try to avoid race-to-the-bottom – where countries reduce their contribution to benefit from other countries' transfers – by making contribution commitments mandatory over a given period
Institutions and participation	Contribution of non-state actors (private firms or civil society groups) to avoid the neutrality fate

Table 3.3   Governance of best-shot global public goods

Examples: research efforts to develop a new medicine to cure infectious disease; develop an early warning system for earthquakes and tsunami worldwide

Collective action failure	Problem of coordination to identify sole provider: cost ineffectiveness most likely. Problem even more acute if it is a threshold public good
Incentives for cooperation	Concentrate resources (information, financial resources, human capital) towards the most efficient provider (with conditionality)
Management of signed agreement	Smaller coalition might be more effective than trying to enlarge cooperation If part of the public good can be made exclusive (i.e. through intellectual property rights), risk of seeing it high-jacked
Institutions and participation	Scrutiny of civil society groups Control of a multilateral institution with jurisdictional power

Table 3.4   Governance of essential-player global public goods

Examples: preserve primary rainforest in equatorial areas to improve biodiversity conservation; neutralize insecure nuclear power plants to prevent nuclear disaster

Collective action failure	Under-provision if essential player is not willing to produce it – under-reporting of the true value of the public good by essential player to get more assistance from other countries
Incentives for cooperation	Conditional financial transfers to essential player Improve the private benefits of joint products (if any)
Management of signed agreement	Problem of free-riding on who is transferring resources: if it is a normal public good, rely on highest-income contributors Ensure it does not crowd out public aid
Institutions and participation	Link with civil society groups to make preferences of essential player evolve

Coherence is also an essential dimension of global public good governance. The objective is to avoid the provision regime for one GPG competing with another. In its second book, the UNDP's office of development studies makes a number of proposals for an institutional architecture of GPG provision and governance (2003) and suggests that institutions be improved at two levels: (i) at the domestic level: UNDP emphasizes that the right conditions for GPG promotion must be encouraged at home through the creation of a national fund for global issues, the assignment of each GPG to a national lead agency in charge of promoting it both at the domestic and international levels, the appointment of a 'GPG ambassador' in charge of improving the coherence of the country's position in international forums, the revision of parliamentary committee structures in order to improve the domestic-foreign interface; (ii) at the international level: the UNDP suggests that 'issue-focussed chief executive officers' be appointed for setting up partnerships with international organizations and the private sector in order to accelerate the provision of GPG and to improve their horizontal management by overcoming bureaucratic structures. It is also highlighted that an implementation council for multilateral agreements could be created in order to improve compliance and to establish international accounts for global issues, therefore continuing the task already undertaken by the World Bank and a few national aid agencies for their own funding. These proposals are interesting pragmatic institutional reforms and should be looked at seriously by policy-makers.

Conclusion

The notion of global public goods can be useful to restructure the debate on global governance, by emphasizing that governance should be no longer conceived as the management of the balance of power between potentially competing regimes, but as the definition of an integrated, complementary system of decision at the supranational level. However, it requires that decision-makers at the national level accept the need to re-organize their diplomatic services and to improve inter-ministerial structures; it also implies that the United Nations and international institutions should undertake the necessary reforms to improve the coordination. Europe can be a driving force in this process: the European Union was successful in establishing a coherent policy programme, overcoming the difficulties associated with divergent national preferences. From this perspective, the European Union plays the role of a true institutional laboratory in which the notions of subsidiarity, political superstructures and horizontal management of cross-cutting issues have been progressively refined. Furthermore, Europe has been increasingly aware of the necessity to re-regulate its domestic markets in order better to integrate sustainable development requirements. This is where Europe could exert stronger leadership: for example, by negotiating accompanying measures and shared production of global public goods as a central component of free-trade agreements with third countries; by having greater presence in discussions led by the international financial institutions, and by demonstrating its willingness to impose at home what it recommends for others.

References

Arrow, K.J. 1951. *Social Choice and Individual Values*. New York: Wiley and Sons.

Axelrod, R. and R.O. Keohane. 1985. 'Achieving Cooperation under Anarchy: Strategies and Institutions'. *World Politics* 38: 26–49.

Barrett, S. 1990. 'The Problem of Global Environmental Protection'. *Oxford Review of Economic Policy* 6.1: pp. 68–79.

Batabyal, A. 2000. *The Economics of International Environmental Agreements*. London: Ashgate.

Carraro, C. and D. Siniscalco. 1993. 'Strategies for the International Protection of the Environment'. *Journal of Public Economics* 52.3: 309–28.

Chandler, P. and H. Tulkens. 1997. 'The Core of an Economy with Multilateral Environmental Externalities'. *International Journal of Game Theory* 26.3: 379–401.

Constantin, F., ed. 2002. *Les Biens Publics Mondiaux: Un Mythe Légitimateur pour l'Action Collective?* Paris: L'Harmattan.

Cornes, R. and T. Sandler. 1984. 'Easy Riders, Joint Production and Public Goods'. *Economic Journal* 94.3: 580–98.

Dulbecco, P. and B. Laporte. 2005. 'How Can the Security of International Trade be Financed in Developing Countries? A Global Public Good Approach'. *World Development* 33.8: 1201–14.

Hirshleifer J. 1983. 'From Weakest-link To Best-shot: The Voluntary Provision of Public Goods'. *Public Choice* 41.3: 371–86.

Kaul, I., P. Conceicao, K. Le Goulven, and R. Mendoza. 2003. *Providing Global Public Goods: Managing Globalisation*. New York: Oxford University Press.

Kaul, I., I. Grunberg, and M. Stern. 1999. *Global Public Goods: International Cooperation in the Twenty-first Century*. New York: Oxford University Press.

Kindleberger, C.P. 1986. 'International Public Goods without International Government'. *American Political Review* 76.1: 1–13.

Lamy, P. 2004. 'The Emergence of Collective Preferences in International Trade: Implications for Regulating Globalisation'. Conference on *Collective Preferences and Global Governance*, 15 September.

Neumayer, E. 2001. 'How Regime Theory and the Economic Theory of International Environmental Cooperation Can Learn from Each Other'. *Global Environmental Politics* 1.1: 122–47.

Olson, M. 1965. *The Logic of Collective Action: Public Goods and the Theory of Groups*. Cambridge, MA Harvard University Press.

———. 1969. 'The Principle of Fiscal Equivalence: The Division of Responsibilities among Different Levels of Government'. *American Economic Review*: 479–87.

Samuelson P. 1954. The Pure Theory of Public Expenditure. *Review of Economics and Statistics* 36.4: 387–96.

Sandler, T. and D. Arce. 2002. 'A Conceptual Framework for Understanding Global and Transnational Public Goods for Health'. *Fiscal Studies* 23.2: 195–222.

Sandler, T. 1998. 'Global and Regional Public Goods: A Prognosis for Collective Action?' *Fiscal Studies* 19.3: 221–47.

———. 2003. 'Collective Action and Transnational Terrorism'. *World Economy* 26.6: 779–802

Secretariat of the International Task Force on Global Public Goods. 2005. 'Strategy and Actions for Meeting Global Challenges: International Cooperation in the National Interest'. Draft Working Paper, February.

Severino, J.M. 2001. 'Réformer l'aide au développement au XXIe siècle'. *Critique internationale* 10. January: 75–99.

Thoyer, S. 2004. 'Can Conflict Management and Peace-keeping be Governed Effectively by Collective Strategies?' *The Courier ACP-EU* 202. March: 19–21.

Tubiana, L., and J.M. Severino 2002. 'Biens publics globaux, gouvernance et aide publique au développement'. In P. Jacquet, J. Pisani Ferry and L. Tubiana, *La Gouvernance Mondiale*. La Documentation Française, Les Rapports du CAE, No. 37: 349–73.

Vicary, S. and T. Sandler. 2002. 'Weakest-link Public Goods: Giving in Kind or Transferring Money'. *European Economic Review* 46: 1501–20.

Warr, P. 1983. 'The Private Provision of a Public Good is Independent of the Distribution of Incomes'. *Economic Letters* 13.2: 207–11.

World Bank. 2001. 'Effective Use of Development Finance for International Public Goods'. In *Global Development Finance 2001*. Washington DC: ch. V, 109–35.

Chapter 4

Deliberation and Democracy in Global Governance: The Role of Civil Society

Patrizia Nanz and Jens Steffek

Introduction

Global governance by international organizations (IOs) and more informal regimes is often charged with being undemocratic. These institutions are said to be remote from citizens, while decisions within them are made by non-elected diplomats, bureaucrats and experts. Their decision-making process itself is often quite secretive, and there is insufficient public debate about the resulting policy choices. Nevertheless, IOs have an increasing capacity to generate law and regulations binding democratic communities. Their only form of democratic legitimation[1] available today is a highly indirect one derived from (elected) national governments, rather than from the constituency of world citizens. In the absence of a convincing parliamentary solution to this problem, many scholars of global, and in particular EU governance, have turned to theories of deliberative democracy in order to devise some blueprint for institutional reform. In essence, many authors argue that the institutionalization of deliberative practices[2] may enhance the rationality and legitimacy of political decisions made beyond the nation state.

---

[1]   In the governance literature the empirical and normative use of 'legitimacy' is often confused. Empirically, legitimacy is understood as a general compliance of the people with decisions of a political order on the grounds that they perceive of these decisions as endowed with 'the prestige of being considered binding'. Normatively, legitimacy means that they deserve compliance according to certain normative criteria. We refer to the normative sense of legitimacy.

[2]   'Deliberation' means a discussion in which statements or positions are based on some kind of argument or reasons. Political deliberation takes place in the broader public sphere (in informal encounters, mass media etc.) as well as in organizational settings (with various degrees of openness, e.g. civic review boards, town hall meetings, parliamentary debates, advisory panels, court procedures, expert deliberation). In the literature there is often a lack of clarity about the interplay between institutionalized deliberation and broader public deliberation.

At the international or even global level of policy-making, however, it is hard to imagine how all stakeholders of governance (and this in many cases will mean citizens) could participate directly in such deliberative processes. Hence the two interrelated questions 'who deliberates?' and 'whose arguments are included in deliberation?' seem to be of crucial importance for the democratizing effects of such arrangements. We argue in this chapter that negotiation among diplomats, civil servants and experts is unlikely to secure the inclusion of all relevant concerns of the global constituency into decision-making at the global level. Moreover, what is missing is a strong link for communication between the global constituency and internationalized deliberation fora. The democratization of international governance will also depend upon the development of an appropriate public sphere. Arguments made for or against certain political proposals at the international level need to reach the citizens as ultimate stakeholders of governance.

In what follows we set out to explore the theoretical nexus between deliberation, participation and the democratic legitimacy of international governance. The first section briefly outlines the deliberative approach to the democratization of global governance. In the second section our discussion focuses on the role of civil society in democratizing global governance regimes. We argue that civil society participation in international governance holds two major promises. First, by participating in political debate at the global level, civil society organizations (CSOs) have the capacity to transport new issues, interests and concerns from (local) stakeholders to global governance arrangements. Second, their presence contributes to the emergence of a global public sphere in which policy choices are exposed to public scrutiny, thus triggering transnational debate among governance stakeholders. In the third section of this paper we engage with three critical remarks concerning the role of non-state actors in internationalized policy-making. Emanating from this discussion our conclusion identifies some avenues for empirical research on the democratizing potential of civil society involvement in global governance.

Democratizing Global Governance: the Deliberative Approach

Democracy is a political ideal that applies principally to arrangements for making binding collective decisions. Such arrangements are democratic if they ensure that any authorization to exercise public power arises from collective decisions by the citizens over whom that power is exercised. There are a variety of institutional forms of modern government that resolve this principle of democratic will formation in slightly different ways. Most Western countries have developed some form of electoral democracy. It formally secures the inclusion of citizens' interests and concerns into government by aggregating them through political parties and parliamentary bodies. For the majority of citizens, participation in this system is possible by voting in more or less frequent political elections or referenda. In addition, there are indirect and voluntary forms of participation in the political process through active citizen involvement in political parties, interest groups, social movements and civil society associations.

Along these lines, Robert Dahl (1999) has forcefully argued that international organizations cannot be democratic. He gives two reasons: first, there cannot be popular control over policy-decisions at the international level. 'The opportunities available to the ordinary citizen to participate effectively in the decisions of a world government would diminish to the vanishing point' (Dahl 1999: 22). The extent of 'delegation of authority' to international policy elites goes beyond any acceptable threshold of democracy. Second, there is no common identity and no political culture supportive of international institutions. But only a shared collective identity (a 'demos') – able to ensure societal cohesion, mutual trust and solidarity – can make policy decisions widely acceptable among the losers. In short, Dahl argues that the enormous size and heterogeneity of the global citizenry make the democratization of global governance impossible. He therefore suggests regarding international organizations as 'bureaucratic bargaining systems' without prospects for democratization.

Dahl's argument is quite convincing in its own right. International organizations are unlikely to ever resemble a democratic nation state. Yet, if global governance will ever become democratic, it will certainly not look like a national democracy writ large (Stein 2001), and it is questionable whether it should. The current state of Western mass democracy has been criticized extensively for governments being remote from citizens, for decisions not reflecting their true concerns, and for thus fostering a trend away from the active *citoyen* towards the passive *bourgeois*. In the view of its critics (Pateman 1970; Barber 1984) interest aggregation dominates over the value-oriented discussion seeking political consensus and novel solutions to problems through a cooperative and creative process of dialogical exchange.

The question hence is if there is an alternative avenue towards the democratic legitimation of global governance – one, which neither presupposes international equivalents to national electoral democracies nor a *demos*, that is, a certain (pre-political) homogeneity of the citizens of a polity. How can we devise an alternative model of democratic will formation for the emerging system of global governance? It is often argued that a deliberative understanding of democratic collective decision-making is particularly suited for global governance. Deliberation is central to democracy because it focuses political debates on the common good: Interests, preferences and aims that comprise the common good are those that 'survive' the process of deliberation. Deliberative democracy needs a framework of social and institutional conditions that facilitate the expression of citizens' concerns and rational debate about them and some mechanism to ensure the responsiveness of political power to these concerns.

In the context of international relations, the model of deliberative decision-making has taken on a vision *sui generis*. Some authors suggest well-informed and consensus-seeking discussion in expert committees that are embedded in international decision-making procedures as an effective remedy to the legitimation problems of international governance. In this perspective, political deliberation is viewed primarily in a functional fashion as a prerequisite for high levels of efficiency, efficacy and quality in political regulation. This approach to deliberation is inspired by thinking from public policy and international relations theory which has highlighted the importance of scientific expertise and consensus-seeking in the epistemic community of experts (Haas 1992; Majone 1999). This process is not designed to aggregate particularistic interests but rather to foster mutual learning, and to eventually transform actors' preferences while converging on a policy choice that is oriented towards the common good. Deliberation among experts thus becomes a key device of good governance by a responsive administration.

The presumed legitimating capacity of expert deliberation has also been grounded in empirical arguments. It has been claimed that well-informed rules are more effective because they can command voluntary assent and compliance. However, some important empirical arguments can be brought to bear against this alleged automatism. Thompson and Rayner (1998), for example, present evidence from environmental policy and risk regulation, which indicates that citizens assent to rules only if they have the impression that *their own concerns* have been treated fairly in the process of rule-making. Who has been heard and whose arguments have been included in a deliberation process seems to be extremely important for the effectiveness of the resulting rules. It is far from clear how supranational bureaucratic procedures such as 'comitology' (Joerges and Neyer 1997) can make sure that citizens' concerns will be given appropriate weight in the process of argumentation that leads to an informed decision on binding rules. Even if we trust experts and scientists to sincerely advocate norms that, in their view, serve the common good of a polity and not some particular interest, it still remains their assessment and their view. What is missing from the committee model is a mechanism that plausibly links expert governance to the concerns and interests of citizens as ultimate stakeholders of governance. Why should citizens believe that their concerns have been considered properly in comitology?

The desirability of deliberative governance by functional elites is equally questionable from a normative perspective on democratic legitimacy. As put by Cohen and Sabel (2003: 366–7)

> Deliberation, understood as reasoning about how to best address a practical problem, is not intrinsically democratic: it can be conducted within cloistered bodies that make fateful choices, but are inattentive to the views or the interests of large numbers of affected parties.

Deliberative democracy must ensure that citizens' concerns feed into the policy-making process and are taken into account when it comes to a decision on binding rules. It is therefore crucial to open the process of political deliberation within international organizations both to public scrutiny and to the input of stakeholders' concerns.

Civil Society and the Public Sphere

Many existing forms of expert consultation can be contrasted against the idea of public deliberation as a source of democratic legitimacy for governing (at the national and global level). In Habermas's theory of deliberative democracy the public sphere plays a key role. The public is understood as a collective of citizens connected by processes of communication over particular aspects of social and political life, which can, in principle, extend beyond national borders. The public sphere is a dispersed, all-encompassing, discursive network within which these citizens, connected by the means of mass communication, form their opinion about how best to resolve common problems (Habermas 1996: 360). What is important to the notion of public deliberation is that there is a warranted presumption that public opinion is formed on the basis of adequate information and that those whose interests are affected have an equal and effective opportunity to make their own interests (and their reasons for them) known. This 'public use of reason' depends on civil society as 'a network of associations that institutionalizes problem-solving discourses on questions of general interest inside the framework of organized public spheres' (Habermas 1996: 367).

Habermas's theory distinguishes between deliberation in political institutions (or decision making bodies) and deliberation in a wider, decentred public sphere. Our conception departs from this view insofar as it focuses on sites of public deliberation between policy-makers and stakeholders. We emphasize the role of organized civil society participating within governance regimes as an intermediary agent between the political institutions and the wider public. We argue that, at the international level, the public sphere – conceived as a pluralistic social realm of a variety of sometimes overlapping or contending (often sectoral) publics engaged in transnational dialogue – can provide an adequate political realm with actors and deliberative processes that help to democratize global governance practice. Deliberative participatory publics within governance regimes stimulate an exchange of arguments in which policy choices are exposed to public scrutiny.

At the national, regional and local level there are many forms of deliberative participation as a means of holding power accountable. These participatory forums have different degrees of institutionalization and impact on the political system. They come in the form of civic review boards, implementation studies and periodic official participatory hearings that follow the policy-making process or consultation of civil society. Wider public spheres can further democratic legitimacy by means of questioning, praise, criticism and judgement. What institutional mechanisms can be envisioned at the global level to serve as an institutional focus for a broader, decentred public sphere? We think of deliberative forums in which groups of social actors (e.g. national officials, scientific experts, advocacy NGOs, etc.) cooperatively address a certain global problem. Such participatory arenas have the prerogative to scrutinize and monitor policy choices of international organizations. If we conceptualize the public sphere as a communicative network where different (national and sectoral) publics partially overlap, the emerging features of global governance regimes can also be seen as offering the chance for the creation of new transnational communities of political action (Nanz 2006).

There is also some empirical evidence of an emerging transnational discourse about the faults and merits of global governance. The NGO-led campaign against the international monetary institutions, for example, was publicized through the media and triggered transnational public debate on the activities of these organizations. Global governance is questioned in a public discourse on international organizations and their policies, in which rational reasoning plays a key role (Steffek 2003: 271). As this empirical evidence suggests, non-governmental actors play a key role in triggering transnational public debates on global governance. Opening up political deliberation in international organizations to the wider public requires transcending boundaries between experts and stakeholders, functional elites and citizens. It has to be ensured that information is made available to stakeholders and that in turn stakeholder concerns reach the agenda of those political or administrative bodies that formulate the decisions to be made in international organizations. In other words, specialists and laypeople must mutually and reliably inform each other. Therefore, *deliberative procedures* in international organizations need to be complemented with *participatory practices* in order to push global governance towards democratization.

We argue that organized civil society has a high potential to act as a 'transmission belt' between specialized discourses within international organizations and an emerging transnational public sphere. Such a discursive interface operates in two directions: First, civil society organizations can give voice to citizens' concerns and channel them into the deliberative process of international organizations. Second, they can make internal decision-making processes of international organizations more transparent to the wider public and formulate technical issues in accessible terms. From a normative point of view, these civil society actors must ensure that citizens' concerns are reflected in the decision-making process of international organizations. Transnational civil society can bring together people with shared concerns, but very different national identities and considerable uncertainty of how to address their aims. Deliberative processes among them can create the basis of solidarity beyond national boundaries: through a cooperative search for the best policy practice, engaging in political (or functional) participation and sharing expertise.

Organized Civil Society and the Current Practice of Global Governance

In the last two sections we have outlined the nexus between global governance, deliberative democracy and civil society participation. At the theoretical level, there is a clear case to be made for more civil society involvement in global governance. While some authors argue that participation of civil society actors in international governance will almost automatically lead to more democratic legitimacy (e.g. Gemmill and Bamidele-Izu 2002), others have been much more sceptical. In this last part of our essay we discuss three major critical arguments that have been raised against involving civil society actors into global governance.

At present, transnational civil society interacts with virtually all international organizations. There are, however, various degrees of institutionalization and formalization of this interaction (Charnovitz 1997). The United Nations, for example, has made formal arrangements for civil society participation from the very beginning of its activity (Alger 2002; Willetts 2000). The EU also consults with a variety of civil society actors ranging from the social partners, over NGOs to religious congregations (Curtin 2002; Smismans 2004). In global economic governance, the World Bank has established extensive contacts with civil society for more than two decades, in Washington DC but also in the countries where its projects are implemented (Brown and Fox 2001; Acuña and Tuozzo 2000). The GATT/WTO and the IMF traditionally had much less interaction with civil society, but since the 1990s these organizations are slowly opening up (Scholte 2002; Woods and Narlikar 2001; Esty 1998). In sum, frequency and extent of consultation between international organizations and organized civil society are undoubtedly on the rise.

The first problem we should discuss is whether CSOs de facto have the capacity to act as interlocutors in global governance. The mere fact that civil society interacts with international public organizations does not mean that their voices are taken seriously and can be influential in determining policy outcomes. Although many international organizations consult with civil society, this does not mean that civil society actors have access to those political deliberations where crucial decisions are prepared (Khor 1999). International governance still remains to a large extent an intergovernmental affair. For example, the invitation to occasional public symposia or seminars is quite different from regular participation in political deliberation in committees or conferences. Even if access to political deliberation is granted, this does not guarantee that CSOs can influence the course of the debate significantly (Risse 2002: 265). In our view, it is certainly important to note that CSOs' influence is often limited in practice. Yet the empirical fact that their arguments are still sometimes ignored does not compromise the validity of the normative claim that they should be heard.

A second critical question is if CSOs are legitimate interlocutors in global governance. Why should they be entitled to speak on behalf of citizens? This question points at the internal democracy or 'legitimacy' of civil society organizations and their capacity to represent a global citizenry (Wahl 1998). Some authors have argued that civil society organizations cannot be representative because most of them only pursue a very limited agenda that (allegedly) matters only to very few people (Trachtman and Moremen 2003: 228). In fact, CSOs usually emerge as voluntary associations of citizens who are concerned about and rallying around certain political issues. Hence they are not representative of any constituency beyond that of their volatile group of supporters. What they represent is issues, values, or interests. We argue that precisely for this reason they complement the territorial dimension of representation that takes place in intergovernmental diplomacy. In international politics, where every state is required to speak with a single voice, this is of particular value. Governmental delegates can legitimately claim to represent a country's executive (provided it has been elected democratically). What they cannot claim to represent is the variety of political values and interests present in their national constituency. In addition, civil society organizations often add a pronouncedly critical perspective to transnational deliberation, which contributes to their functioning as a potential corrective to governmental delegation.

Yet even if we envisage the representation of transnational issues and arguments instead of territorial constituencies, we still cannot avoid the problem of representation altogether. In both its epistemic and democratic dimension the quality of political deliberation is particularly dependent upon a plurality of voices. In this respect it appears problematic that the majority of civil society organizations active at international organizations are based in the Northern hemisphere. Even if these organizations seek to be sensitive to Southern viewpoints, and it seems that at least many advocacy organizations strive to be, their perspective nevertheless remains situated. This imbalance in fact threatens the plurality of voices in international governance and raises the question if the concerns and arguments of Southern constituencies are represented adequately when they are affected by a decision.

The third group of critical remarks questions the independence of CSOs. As we said above, CSOs can offer alternative viewpoints or critical expertise that would otherwise not be included in intergovernmental policy-making. Independence from the state and its government can safeguard their capacity to function as such a corrective. As a matter of fact, some CSOs are not the result of societal self-organization but are created or 'hijacked' by ruling national elites, particularly in autocratic countries (Steinberg 2001). Non–governmental organizations that are founded and maintained by governments are known as GONGOs (government-organized NGOs). Such organizations are sometimes instrumental as governmental propaganda outlets, as the controversy over bogus CSOs such as the Sri Lankan 'University Teachers Human Rights – UTHR (J)' in the *UN Commission on Human Rights* shows.[3] However, if we take a broad

---

[3]   For the controversy see <www.tchr.net/reports_commission_2001.htm> (accessed 8 May 2005).

variety of international organizations into account this phenomenon remains the exception and not the rule. The vast majority of civil society organizations still are a genuine expression of societal self–organization. What concerns us more is the question if prolonged cooperation with international organizations might lead to a cooptation of CSOs. First, there is the 'privilege of recognition' for those CSOs that attain accreditation or some special consultative status with IOs. Fear of losing that privilege might compromise their will to criticize IOs or their policies. Close cooperation also contributes to a certain 'professionalization' of CSO staff that might insert all too well into an internationalized functional elite and lose touch with their constituency.

What is more, international organizations have become an important source of funding for CSOs (Bichsel 1996). CSOs carry out research for IOs or assist in implementing their projects. This practice is particularly widespread in the field of development assistance and humanitarian aid. Some 70 per cent of the World Bank's projects, for instance, are implemented in the target country by non–state actors.[4] This can lead to forms of financial dependency that endanger the ability of non-state actors to take a critical stance towards the IO. The need to secure money for future projects might even lead to real organizational pathologies such as reporting successes in the field that do not exist, or exaggerating prospects for future projects (Cooley and Ron 2003). Cooptation and financial dependency seem to pose a serious threat to the ability of CSOs to act as an independent voice in global policy making. Civil society is an asset to the democratic quality of global governance only if it is free to monitor and criticize the work of governmental institutions, and if it is able to mobilize public opinion through the mass media. We do not think that such possible pitfalls should lead us to deny the democratizing potential of civil society participation in global governance. What we should do, however, is to check carefully if there are empirical developments that create new obstacles to the realization of this potential.

Conclusion

In this chapter we outlined why and how civil society participation might contribute to the democratization of governance beyond the nation state. Emanating from a deliberative theory of democracy we identified two important mechanisms: First, organized civil society can channel political values, interests and concerns from the stakeholders of governance into decision-making processes. Second, organized civil society can contribute to the emergence of a global public sphere in which policy proposals and choices are debated among governance stakeholders. Thus, civil society participation can be a lever to open

---

4   Source: World Bank – Civil Society Cooperation – Progress Report for Fiscal Years 2000 and 2001 at p. 4. On file electronically at <siteresources.worldbank.org/CSO/Resources/ProgRptFY0001.pdf> (accessed 8 May 2005).

up the black box of intergovernmental negotiation, rendering internationalized decision-making more transparent and decision-makers more accountable to their stakeholders.

In the last section of this paper we have discussed three types of criticism concerning the role of non–state actors in internationalized policy–making. First, there is scepticism about the *de facto* ability of CSOs to influence international politics. Although it is important to note that CSOs' influence is often limited in practice, this does not jeopardize the validity of the normative arguments that it should be heard. Second, some critics argue that CSOs cannot or should not act as representatives of a global citizenry. We found this argument flawed inasmuch as many CSOs do not even claim to represent a geographically locatable constituency. What they do represent is issues, concerns, interests or arguments. Yet whose issues and whose concerns they represent remains an important question. If, as it is presently often the case in global governance, voices from the South are underrepresented the democratic quality of civil society involvement is at risk. Third, it has been remarked that CSOs can become dependent upon public funding and be co–opted by states or IOs. In our view, such tendencies are a source of serious concern because they compromise the ability of CSOs to act as independent voices in global deliberation.

Our conclusion is that civil society participation holds some major promises for the democratization of global governance. Whether or not this democratizing potential is realized in practice remains to be established through rigorous empirical research. In this essay we listed some major issues for future research. What needs particular scrutiny is the ability and willingness of civil society to keep a critical distance from the governmental structures in global governance and to denounce questionable practices of IOs. In addition we should carefully analyse if organized civil society is really able to secure the inclusion of all stakeholder concerns into global governance. CSOs involvement should counter, rather than reinforce existing asymmetries in global politics.

References

Acuña, C. and M.F. Tuozzo. 2000. 'Civil Society Participation in the World Bank and Inter–American Development Bank Programs: The Case of Argentina'. *Global Governance* 6.4: 443–56.

Alger, C. 2002. 'The Emerging Roles of NGOs in the UN System: From Article 71 to a People's Millennium Assembly'. *Global Governance* 8.1: 93–117.

Barber, B. 1984. *Strong Democracy: Participatory Politics for a New Age*. Berkeley: University of California Press.

Bichsel, A. 1996. 'NGOs as Agents of Public Accountability and Democratization in Intergovernmental Forums'. In W. Lafferty and J. Meadowcraft, eds. *Democracy and the Environment. Problems and Prospects*. Cheltenham: Edward Elgar: 234–55.

Brown, D.L. and J. Fox. 2001. 'Transnational Civil Society Coalitions and the World Bank: Lessons from Project and Policy Influence Campaigns'. In M. Edwards and J. Gaventa, eds. *Global Citizen Action*. Boulder, CO: Lynne Rienner: 43–58.

Charnovitz, S. 1997. 'Two Centuries of Participation: NGOs and International Governance'. *Michigan Journal of International Law* 18.1: 183–286.

Cohen J. and C. Sabel. 2003. 'Sovereignty and Solidarity: EU and US'. In J. Zeitlin and D. Trubek, eds. *Governing Work and Welfare in a New Economy. European and American Experiments*. London: Oxford University Press: 249–75.

Cooley, A. and J. Ron. 2002. 'The NGO Scramble: Organizational Insecurity and the Political Economy of Transnational Action'. *International Security* 27.1: 5–39.

Curtin, D. M. 2002. 'Integrating "Civil Society" into European Union Governance: Opening Deliberative Space Top-down and Bottom-up'. Manuscript. University of Utrecht.

Dahl, R.A. 1999. 'Can International Organizations Be Democratic? A Skeptic's View'. In I. Shapiro and C. Hacker-Cordon, eds. *Democracy's Edges*. Cambridge: Cambridge University Press: 19–36.

Esty, D. 1998. 'Non-governmental Organizations at the World Trade Organization: Cooperation, Competition, or Exclusion'. *Journal of International Economic Law* 1: 123–47.

Gemmill, B. and A. Bamidele-Izu. 2002. 'The Role of NGOs and Civil Society in Global Environmental Governance'. In D. Esty and M. Ivanova, eds. *Global Environmental Governance: Options and Opportunities*. New Haven: Yale School of Forestry and Environmental Studies: 77–100.

Haas, P.M. 1992. 'Introduction: Epistemic Communities and International Policy Coordination'. *International Organization* 46.1: 1–35.

Habermas, J. 1996. *Between Facts and Norms: Contributions to a Discourse Theory of Law and Democracy*. Cambridge, MA: MIT Press.

Joerges, C. and J. Neyer. 1997. 'From Intergovernmental Bargaining to Deliberative Political Processes: The Constitutionalisation of Comitology'. *European Law Journal* 3.3: 272–99.

Khor, M. 1999 'How the South Is Getting a Raw Deal at the WTO'. In A. Anderson, ed. *Views From the South*. San Francisco: International Forum on Globalization: 7–53.

Majone, G. 1999. 'The Regulatory State and its Legitimacy Problems'. *West European Politics* 22.1: 1–24.

Nanz, P. 2006. *Europolis. Constitutional Patriotism beyond the Nation State*. Manchester: Manchester University Press.

Pateman, C. 1970. *Participation and Democratic Theory*. Cambridge: Cambridge University Press.

Risse, T. 2002. 'Transnational Actors and World Politics'. In W. Carlsnaes, T. Risse and B.A. Simmons, eds. *Handbook of International Relations*. London: Sage: 255–74.

Scholte, J.A. 2002. 'Civil Society and the Governance of Global Finance'. In J.A. Scholte with A. Schnabel, eds. *Civil Society and Global Finance*. London: Routledge: 11–32.

Smismans, S. 2004. *Law, Legitimacy and European Governance: Functional Participation in Social Regulation*. Oxford: Oxford University Press.

Steffek, J. 2003. 'The Legitimation of International Governance: a Discourse Approach'. *European Journal of International Relations* 9.2: 287–313.

Stein, E. 2001. 'International Integration and Democracy: No Love at First Sight'. *American Journal of International Law* 95.3: 489–534.

Thompson, M. and S. Rayner. 1998. 'Risk and Governance Part I: The Discourses of Climate Change'. *Government and Opposition* 33.2: 139–66.

Trachtman, J. and P. Moremen. 2003. 'Costs and Benefits of Private Participation in WTO Dispute Settlement. Whose Right Is It Anyway?' *Harvard International Law Journal* 44.1: 221–50.

Tussie, D. and M.P. Riggirozzi. 2001. 'Pressing Ahead with New Procedures for Old Machinery: Global Governance and Civil Society'. In V. Rittberger, ed. *Global Governance and the United Nations System*. Tokyo: United Nations University Press: 158–80.

Wahl, P. 1998. 'NGO – Multis, McGreenpeace und Netzwerk-Guerilla. Zu einigen Trends in der internationalen Zivilgesellschaft'. *Peripherie* 71: 55–68.

Willets, P. 2000. 'From "Consultative Arrangements" to "Partnership": The Changing Status of NGOs in Diplomacy at the UN'. *Global Governance* 6.2: 191–212.

Woods, N. and A. Narlikar. 2001. 'Governance and the Limits of Accountability: the WTO, the IMF and the World Bank'. *International Social Science Journal* 53.4: 569–84.

Chapter 5

Assessing Civil Society Participation: An Evaluative Framework

Jessica F. Green

Introduction

It has become a truism that the participation of civil society in international governance is occurring at unprecedented levels. In the last decade especially, there has been a huge growth in the number of civil society organizations worldwide (Clark, Friedman and Hochstetler 1998; Smith 1997). This has been mirrored by a parallel surge in the number of civil society organizations affiliated and accredited with the United Nations (UN). In 2004, there were 1,514 non-governmental organizations accredited to the Department of Public Information, and 2,418 to the Economic and Social Council, the latter reflecting more than a threefold increase in a dozen years (UN DPI/NGO n.d.; UN DESA n.d.). Not only are there more civil society actors, there are more than ever active within the UN system.

This growth in civil society is coupled with a growing recognition among policy-makers and the public at large that civil society plays an integral role in international governance for sustainable development. This realization is evidenced by the growing body of international legal instruments that identify public participation as a prerequisite for promoting the goals of sustainable development. As a result, the importance of broad-based public participation – often achieved through civil society involvement – has emerged as a consistent theme in many international agreements for sustainable development – from the Stockholm Declaration (Part I, paragraph 7) all the way through to the Johannesburg Declaration on Sustainable Development (paragraph 26). The Convention on Access to Information, Public Participation in Decision-making and Access to Justice in Environmental Matters (the Aarhus Convention) represents a new precedent for participation. The Convention, which entered into force in October 2001, has been signed by forty states within the Economic Commission on Europe, and among other things, requires all Parties to abide by specific procedures to ensure public participation for a number of activities with potential environmental impact.

Despite new instruments such as the Aarhus Convention, and the emerging legal and normative consensus that civil society is a key force in sustainable development, some civil society actors have become vocal critics of the current workings of international governance systems. Many maintain that they are marginalized from decision-making processes. The growth of parallel fora and other civil society activities that take place outside official international negotiations is one indication of this discontent. Many civil society groups have shifted from protesting outside official meetings to holding their own summits, thus shaping their own agenda (Pianta 2002). The number of protesters outside key meetings of international financial institutions, the G8 and others serves to emphasize the sentiment among civil society that voices of the citizenry are not being heard in policy discussions.

This presents a confused picture: is civil society a key player in international governance, as the law mandates and rhetoric often highlights, or does it remain disenfranchised from international policy-making? This chapter will address this question by offering a framework for understanding how to evaluate civil society participation in governance for sustainable development – both from the perspective of civil society actors, and through assessing institutional rules. It will proceed in four parts. First, I will review the terms of the discussion: who constitutes civil society and what roles does it play in sustainable development governance? Then, I will discuss the institutional aspects of civil society engagement, reviewing the improvements that have been made in institutional mechanisms, and highlighting the problems that remain. The second section will address the actor-based attributes that affect civil society participation. This section will describe the dimensions that influence civil society's ability to engage in international policy-making – and disaggregate this concept into three constituent dimensions. These dimensions describe the characteristics of civil society actors that can either promote or impede their participation in the multilateral process. The third and final section will compare the current institutional mechanisms with the actor-based attributes perceived to affect engagement, and examine the extent to which civil society can be considered disenfranchised – or, lacking the ability to participate and influence the policy-making process – from international policy-making for sustainable development (for a full discussion of this concept, see Green 2004).

Who is Civil Society, and Why is its Participation Important?

Before moving forward, it is important to clarify the term 'civil society', and its roles in international governance for sustainable development. In this chapter, civil society will be used in its most general form, as the social sphere separate from the state and the market (Cohen and Arato 1992: ix). Thus, although policy discussions about civil society participation tend to focus on non-governmental organizations (NGOs), I will use the term more expansively, to include local and grassroots organizations, social movements, transnational advocacy networks and campaigns. However, I do *not* include representatives of business in this definition. Given the differences between the access of business groups and civil society sectors to resources that affect the state – and as a result, their influence within the policy-making process – the distinction between these two groups is important to maintain. Along with scientific organizations, business is an important non-state actor with a growing role in international sustainable development governance, but one that should be considered separately from civil society. The roles of these two groups will be addressed briefly in the latter part of the chapter.

Much has been written on the roles and functions of civil society in international policy-making (see e.g. Betsill and Corell 2001; Corell and Betsill 2001; Fox and Brown 1998; Keck and Sikkink 1998; Smith 1997, 2001; Tarrow 2001; von Moltke 2002) and in particular, of NGOs (see Finger and Princen 1994; Gemmill and Bamidele-Izu 2002; Raustiala 1997; Wapner 1996). Civil society actors perform a variety of different functions in international governance for sustainable development. In a recent discussion about environmental governance in the context of sustainable development, Haas, Kanie and Murphy put forth a number of these functions, including: agenda setting, developing usable knowledge, monitoring, rule-making (through principled standards), policy verification, enforcement and capacity building (Haas, Kanie and Murphy 2004: 267). Two other commonly cited functions include implementation or service provision (Tussie and Riggirozzi 2001; Weiss 1999) and norm setting (Florini 2000, Wapner 2000). Clearly, this variety of functions means that civil society organizations (CSOs) will have different inputs to offer different international processes.

In addition, the involvement of civil society lends legitimacy to international policy-making. That is, legitimacy is enhanced through deliberation and discussion, which bolster the 'normative belief by an actor that a rule or institution ought to be obeyed' (Hurd, 1999: 381). Thus, by allowing the input and opinions of civil society, the policy-making process becomes legitimate. Lastly, as mentioned above, broad-based participation is a fundamental tenet of sustainable development; therefore, civil society involvement is recognized by international law as a necessary and desirable part of the policy-making process. Civil society engagement in sustainable development governance is therefore important for a number of reasons. Yet such engagement will not be uniform; different actors will engage in different ways, and involvement will vary across regime. In the following section, I put forth some of the ways that the notion of engagement has been operationalized within the United Nations through mechanisms for participation. Yet, as will be discussed, these mechanisms for participation may not necessarily translate to political engagement in policy-making.

Institutional Mechanisms for Civil Society Participation

Progress ...

A brief historical review of civil society's participation in international governance reveals the tremendous progress that has been made since the creation of the United Nations. The mandate for civil society involvement in international policy-making comes from Article 71 of the UN Charter, which states that

> The Economic and Social Council may make suitable arrangements for consultation with non-governmental organizations which are concerned with matters within its competence. Such arrangements may be made with international organizations and, where appropriate, with national organizations after consultation with the Member of the United Nations concerned.

These 'suitable arrangements' became the basis for the accreditation of non-governmental organizations with the Economic and Social Council (ECOSOC). Yet, at the outset, there were few NGOs affiliated with ECOSOC. The number of accredited NGOs began to grow and gained real global attention at the 1992 Earth Summit in Rio, where 1,400 accredited NGOs were estimated to have been directly involved with the negotiations, and thousands more attended parallel events and sessions (Kakabadse and Burns 1994). Indeed, ECOSOC accreditation has reflected this change: the total number of non-governmental organizations accredited has jumped from 744 in 1992 to 2,418 in 2004 (UN DESA n.d.).

Agenda 21, which came out of the Rio Summit, was another important landmark for civil society participation; it identifies the 'commitment and genuine involvement of all social groups' as an integral component of the effective implementation of the agreement (Chapter 23, paragraph 1). The legal mandate for civil society participation in sustainable development regimes only expanded after Rio: The Commission on Sustainable Development (CSD) is required to solicit the input of civil society with respect to the implementation of Agenda 21. The nine Major Groups recognized in Agenda 21 participate in the CSD, and interact with delegates and UN agencies in discussions about implementation. Other treaties, such as the Convention on Biological Diversity, and the Convention on International Trade in Endangered Species of Wild Fauna and Flora (CITES) also name non-governmental actors as having a role in promoting sustainable development. Indeed, a number depend on civil society to implement decisions taken by the parties. It is important to note, however, that this increased involvement occurs at the behest of states, the final arbiters of civil society involvement (see especially, Clark, Friedman and Hochstetler 1995).

Irrespective of the political impetus, the growth in the number of civil society actors, and the increasing recognition of their role in global governance has in turn given rise to some modifications in the mechanisms developed for their participation. The Non-Governmental Liaison Service (NGLS) was created in

1975 to 'promote dynamic partnerships between the United Nations and non-governmental organizations' (UN NGLS 1998). In 1996, an ECOSOC Resolution standardized and streamlined accreditation procedures for NGOs wishing to participate in UN conferences, and opened the process to NGOs on the sub-global level (UN ECOSOC 1996). The last decade has seen a number of institutional innovations in mechanisms within existing processes, such as multi-stakeholder dialogues (Financing for Development) and Type II Partnerships (Johannesburg Plan of Implementation). And there have been altogether new bodies formed, such as the Permanent Forum on Indigenous Issues, which was created to provide a new place to discuss and promote indigenous peoples' concerns related to economic and social development (UN ECOSOC 2000). Thus, the formal system is taking steps to accommodate the growth in civil society participation. Of course, the existence of these mechanisms does not ensure effective engagement; therefore, the following section will turn to a more careful assessment of these and other mechanisms for civil society participation.

... and Problems

Despite these changes and improvements, there are still a number of problems with the current institutional mechanisms for civil society participation. First, the rules governing civil society participation are often determined on a regime-by-regime basis. Thus, there is wide variation in the level of engagement across regimes. This is not inherently problematic, for the role of civil society will also vary by regime; however, without some standardized baseline for participation, each regime is free to restrict civil society involvement to the extent its parties collectively agree to do so. In addition, rules can be changed according to the political winds. If pressed, states can and have chosen to restrict civil society access to intergovernmental discussions (Florini 2000: 214–16). Thus, although it may be appropriate for participation mechanisms to vary with the differing needs and activities of a given regime, the potential cost of this approach is the lack of safeguards to ensure a minimum of civil society engagement.

Second, and related to the first problem, is the inconsistency between rules and practice. Some UN bodies do not allow CSOs to participate or even observe negotiations and proceedings, yet occasionally do invite them for briefings. The General Assembly, for example, does not allow CSOs to attend its proceedings, but has invited them to give briefings on occasion. The same is true of the Security Council, which has invited human rights and relief organizations to discuss Iraq, the Middle East and other humanitarian crises (see Globalpolicy.org 2004). This practice is problematic on two fronts. First, this 'a la carte' approach has given rise to the critique that rules of engagement are sometimes ad-hoc and arbitrary (Oberthur et al. 2002). If civil society can only participate by invitation, then who is invited and why? Second, this practice suggests that there is a potential role for CSO input into institutions that currently do not permit it. Again, the appropriate level of civil society involvement will vary by organizational body and regime, but that level should be publicly discussed. Rules should be transparent and made to reflect the consensus, and practice should conform to the rules.

The third problem with current mechanisms for civil society engagement is the fragmentation in the accreditation structures. While the aforementioned ECOSOC resolution improved coherence in accreditation practices for ECOSOC and related global conferences and regional processes, there are a number of other international processes that have their own separate procedures. CSOs wishing to participate in the climate or biodiversity negotiations, for example, must be accredited through the secretariats of the Conventions, and according to their rules. This patchwork of accreditation processes and requirements is not only confusing, but also very labour intensive for groups with limited resources.

Moreover, accreditation processes are targeted toward NGOs. Though NGOs are the primary civil society actor involved in international policy-making processes, they are one of many different types of civil society actors. Transnational advocacy networks, social movements, issue coalitions, grassroots organizations and others all work on issues of sustainable development, and at times, their work is relevant on the international level. Yet, because accreditation structures are almost singularly focused on NGOs, these other organizational forms face additional obstacles to participation. Other types of non-state actors, such as business and scientists, experience a similar challenge of organizational representation. In order to participate in international policy-making processes, they must find a way to represent their group – either informally, such as through caucus groups, or through the formal accreditation of one or more members.

In addition to the procedural problems with current mechanisms for civil society engagement, there are some more significant substantive criticisms. First, some civil society organizations maintain that despite formalized processes for participation, they cannot meaningfully engage in the policy-making process. Their opinions are not taken into account, or are considered too late into the process, once most of the serious decisions have been taken. Even when there are opportunities to participate through interventions, some assert that their input is symbolic, since real decision-making often occurs in backroom discussions. That is, they note a difference between the ability to participate and the ability to influence policy discussions, with the latter being their desired goal (Green 2005). This disjunct alleged by some civil society actors is particularly problematic given the fact that public participation is one of the fundamental tenets of sustainable development. It should be noted here, however, that the goal of removing barriers to civil society participation, and understanding the conditions that enable their input – are ways to promote their engagement through the roles and activities enumerated above. Providing the opportunities for civil society both to participate and potentially influence policy-making does not mean endowing them with greater legal rights or putting them on a par with states. Rather, proposed reforms would allow civil society organizations of all types and sizes to undertake the activities and assume the roles now commonly assigned to them.

Thus, sceptics maintain that opportunities for influencing outcomes are minimal, yet this is a difficult claim to assess. Few scholars have put forward ways to evaluate the level of influence exercised by civil society in intergovernmental processes. Zurn (1998) and Betsill and Corell (2001) have made some progress in this endeavour, through methodologies such as process tracing and counterfactual analysis, though again, they remain focused exclusively on NGOs. These are useful frameworks; however, they do not take into account influence exercised through 'informal pathways' outside official policy-making processes, nor of civil society actors who fall outside of the NGO category. These non-institutional avenues of participation – such as attracting media coverage, agenda setting, lobbying and mobilizing constituencies to pressure governments – must also be considered when analysing civil society influence. Yet, there are relatively few comparative assessments of the impact of transnational civil society on international policy (but see, for example, Florini 2000; Fox and Brown 1998; Keck and Sikkink 1998).

The second substantive criticism of current CSO involvement in international policy-making is the significant imbalance between civil society participation from the developed and developing worlds. Though there has been a dramatic increase in the number of CSOs active in international governance for sustainable development, much of this increase is due to the growing presence of large international NGOs, generally based in the developed world. This imbalance raises a host of questions about whom civil society represents, and to whom they are accountable. Indeed, as the role of civil society in international governance has grown, so too has the importance of demonstrating its accountability. Brown and Moore (2001) offer a useful framework for understanding civil society accountability, pointing to four different types – legal, moral, prudential and strategic – where each type privileges a different group of constituents. Thus for a civil society actor to be accountable, it must fulfill its obligations to these diverse constituencies. If future civil society engagement in international policy-making is to be credible, CSOs must develop transparent mechanisms to hold them accountable to their constituencies. Thus, CSOs, and particularly transnational networks of CSOs, must be able to point to internal mechanisms and procedures that affirm their legitimacy and accountability.

Greater parity of participation between CSOs of the developed and developing worlds will also help address the legitimacy problem. Input from civil society would not appear one-sided, and there would be greater probably of acceptance of and compliance with international policies for sustainable development. Some have argued that progress toward better balance is already being made (Florini 2000), but this assertion is subject to debate (Shaw 1999). However, this goal cannot be achieved through institutional reform alone; clearly, there are actor-based attributes which contribute to the degree of participation of civil society actors. Therefore, the chapter will now turn to an actor-based explanation of participation.

Enfranchising Civil Society: Dimensions of Participation

Institutional mechanisms are not the only determinant of civil society engagement in international governance for sustainable development; the organizational attributes of each CSO also have an important impact. This section will offer a framework for considering the characteristics that determine the level of participation of civil society actors, and in some cases, limit their capability to participate and influence agenda setting and decision-making in the international policy-making process. Each of the three dimensions – endogenous resources, transnational connectivity and geopolitical standing – will be described in turn.[1]

'Endogenous resources' describes those resources that come from within the CSO, or the nation within which is it is based, that equip it to participate and influence international policy-making for sustainable development. This dimension encompasses human resources, including the people, training and knowledge needed to engage with international governance. Civil society organizations must have knowledge and understanding of the issues being debated, as well as of the policy implications of proposals and decisions. They must be able to speak and understand English, which is often the default language of unofficial lobbying sessions, late-night negotiations and contact groups. And they must be able to travel to and attend international meetings and sessions. Many of these endogenous resources can be reduced, quite simply, to an endowment of financial resources. Training people, sending them to meetings and allowing them to invest the time to understand the issues being discussed and carry out their programmes requires ample funding. Another important aspect of endogenous resources is the political system of the country in which a CSO is located. Autocratic nations may not permit civil society to organize and advocate on specific issues. Civil society groups in politically unstable nations may choose instead to direct their focus to more urgent domestic matters.

Transnational connectivity can also contribute to civil society organizations' ability to participate and influence policy-making for sustainable development. Transnational connectivity describes the means through which civil society actors receive and transmit information that promotes engagement. Information is essential for participation and influence in international policy-making. CSOs who wish to be involved must follow international processes and discussions. They must stay abreast of when meetings are held, and where; what issues are being discussed, and what the implications are of decisions being taken. This requires understanding relevant natural and environmental processes, emerging research and consensus, and other policy-relevant information. Gathering and distilling this information can be both difficult and time-consuming. Transnational connectivity not only facilitates CSO access to this information, it may also provide the analysis of this information. That is, instead of having to obtain and analyse

---

[1]   This section is based on Fisher and Green, 2004.

all of the necessary information in-house, transnational connectivity can provide links to other CSOs and international actors who can furnish the relevant policy information in a format that is easy to understand and to act upon. Such links to other actors obviate the need to undertake extensive analysis, and perhaps, therefore, for large amounts of endogenous resources, because information in user-friendly format is already available.

Of course, to be effective, CSOs cannot simply be informed about policy discussions, they must also contribute to them. Through connections to other civil society actors, epistemic communities and policy-makers, CSOs can circulate their work and opinions, and find out about the work and activities of other civil society actors. The Internet has been a particularly important tool for facilitating these types of contacts and interactions. Thus, transnational connectivity can be especially important in contributing to CSO engagement when other endogenous resources are lacking.

The final dimension that determines the level and degree of civil society participation and influence in international governance for sustainable development is geopolitical standing. This dimension acknowledges the fact that there are always key players in international governance. Geopolitical standing stems from political reality: certain actors (state or non-state) have more clout than others due to their wealth, endowments of natural resources, their military power, political alliances with other important actors or some combination thereof. To the extent that civil society actors derive influence from geopolitical standing, it is largely because of their national context. That is, though some have maintained that there is a global civil society (see for example, Glasius, Kaldor and Anheier 2001; Lipschutz 1992; Wapner 1996), geopolitical standing recognizes that civil society actors derive some power from their national context (see Tarrow 2001b).

For example, some developed nations, such as Canada, Norway and the United Kingdom, have begun inviting civil society representatives to serve on delegations on a regular basis. Those CSOs that are selected (and perhaps, transitively, others that are affiliated with them) enjoy more influence in a negotiating setting compared to other civil society actors; at the very least, they have the ear of their government. The fact that they are now key players is because of their national context – governments' recognition that civil society representation is of value to the government and its positions – and to their strategic alliance with the home government. Of course, there are those who question whether their inclusion can be considered meaningful, arguing that civil society representation on delegations is sometimes a form of 'tokenism' (Simpson 2004).[2] However, others note that civil society actors who enjoy this type of geopolitical standing have the potential to

---

[2]   Indeed, some have argued that only those closely aligned with government positions are invited to serve on the delegation, whereas more radical points of view would not be welcomed.

create new types of leadership – in concert with states – and facilitate agreement (Kanie 2004).

These three dimensions of participation all affect the level of engagement and impact of CSOs on international policy-making processes. Though this framework is as yet untested, it is likely that there are thresholds for each dimension. That is, at a certain point, additional endogenous resources or transnational connectivity no longer result in increased levels of participation and influence. Moreover, the dynamics of the relationships between these dimensions make the thresholds unclear. That is, a high level of geopolitical standing, for example, may compensate for a dearth of endogenous resources, or vice versa. Only further empirical research can clarify the nature of these relationships.

Assessing the Level of Civil Society Participation

Now we have traversed both sides of the participation debate. A review of institutional mechanisms reveals that there have been improvements in civil society engagement over time, but that a number of procedural and more serious substantive problems remain. As pointed out earlier, empirical work assessing NGO influence is scarce, but institutional mechanisms and the participation of certain civil society actors suggest that current avenues for engagement do an adequate job of obtaining the input of a certain sector of civil society. These civil society actors are mostly NGOs, and a large proportion is from the developed world. Yet the quality of this input is a matter of debate, and the empirical evidence to support a conclusion on either side is scant. Deconstructing the actor-based attributes that affect civil society participation and influence shows that three different dimensions must be considered. Different endowments of endogenous resources, transnational connectivity and geopolitical standing will affect CSOs' ability to participate in and influence international policy-making. At the same time, this capacity cannot be assessed in a vacuum; these dimensions must be considered in tandem with the opportunities and constraints on participation, which differ by institution. When these two factors are considered jointly, does civil society appear to be disenfranchised from international governance for sustainable development?

The first response to this question must be a clarification of terms. A single answer does not apply to all of civil society. As noted earlier, civil society consists of many different types of actors who assume myriad organizational forms and perform many different functions. Despite this fact, many discussions of civil society and international governance fail to differentiate between these types of actors, 'and do not adequately specify their relations with each other or with states and international institutions' (Tarrow 2001a: 2). Indeed, instead of examining the important and sometimes significant differences between civil society actors, some scholars have chosen to refer to a global civil society, which is often assumed to have shared values and goals (Anheier 2001: 224). Yet, it is debated whether global society does share norms, or whether it is rather, 'a contested political terrain where different social and political forces vie for hegemony' (Munck 2002: 357). The debate about global civil society is an important one, for it has considerable implications for the types of participation mechanisms that are used. Global civil society suggests a certain shared identity. However, this chapter has argued that civil society actors take on many different forms and perform many roles in international governance for sustainable development; as such, each will best contribute in different ways. In sum, if the task is to measure civil society engagement, we must be clear about what and whom we are measuring.

When one does distinguish, even on a basic level, between the different actors that comprise civil society, the answer to the question about their level of engagement becomes clearer: some civil society actors are very well integrated into international policy-making, while others remain marginalized. This fact is evidenced by the imbalance between civil society actors participating from the North and South, and by the 'organizational' biases of accreditation systems toward professionalized and international NGOs. Clearly, some CSOs from both the developed and developing worlds are both participating and influencing international governance for sustainable development. Invitations to sit on state delegations to intergovernmental negotiations, the 'revolving door' phenomenon that moves high-level bureaucrats between government and civil society organizations, and the increasing trend toward subcontracting service provision to CSOs have all afforded certain actors within civil society a greater voice in and impact on policy-making.

At the same time, many voices, often from the developing world, are not being heard at all. This is in part because institutional mechanisms may not work in their favour, in the sense that these mechanisms are most available to those with the resources to utilize them. Moreover, the fact that current UN pathways for engagement emphasize NGOs as the primary actor within civil society may also work against CSOs that assume other organizational forms, such as grassroots groups or issue coalitions. As one author has pointed out, 'it is indicative of the power of the non-governmental sector that civil society has come to be identified with NGO activism ... in policy prescriptions of international institutions' (Chandhoke 2002: 38). According to this view, it follows logically that UN mechanisms for civil society input should focus almost exclusively on NGOs, yet this is clearly to the detriment of other non-NGO civil society actors.

CSOs with small endowments of the three dimensions of participation described in the previous section are also likely to be at a disadvantage. Because participation is hypothesized to have a direct relationship with these three types of resources – endogenous resources, transnational connectivity and geopolitical standing – it appears that developing countries are likely to be on the lower end of the endowment spectrum. They are likely to have lesser endowments of endogenous resources, particularly financial resources, than their developed counterparts. Transnational connectivity, which may be realized through Internet availability, membership in epistemic communities or connections with like-minded academics, activists or practitioners in other nations, may also be dependent on human and financial resources, and therefore limited. In addition, lack of legal frameworks and political disposition to enable civil society to come together and act on a national level will preclude the usefulness of any transnational connections (Florini 2000). This is more often the case in less democratic societies of the developing world. Lastly, only a few developing nations enjoy considerable geopolitical standing, and even those civil society organizations with close ties to their home government may find that this relationship does not significantly boost their influence in the international arena.[3]

Those civil society actors without the endowments in the dimensions that promote engagement, those who do not conform to the 'ideal' organizational type of the UN, many of whom are likely based in the developing world – can be considered disenfranchised from international policy-making. They lack the tools to access the mechanisms that would allow them the most basic level of input. Proposals for reform, therefore, must be targeted specifically at these actors, not at 'global civil society'.

Institutional reforms must begin by focusing on those civil society actors already participating in international governance. Changes should enhance standards of accountability and transparency of all civil society organizations participating in international governance. The systematic imbalances threaten to undermine future civil society participation by calling into question the legitimacy of those civil society actors currently engaged in international policy-making processes. In discussing how transnational coalitions, for example, must deal with these problems, Jordan and van Tuijl call for a focus on 'political responsibility' to the coalition's members, to ensure that all members are responsive to the others' needs and goals (Jordan and van Tuijl 2000). Others concur that responsibility, and not broad representation of many actors, is the best outcome that coalitions of such diverse members can achieve (Tarrow 2001a).

This distinction – between responsibility and representation – is a useful concept in considering institutional reforms, particularly for complex organizational forms. It implies that certain standards of transparency and internal democratic or consensus-based governance are needed, and at the same time, expands the concept of legitimacy to a much broader group of civil society actors. Thus, transnational advocacy networks, issue-based coalitions, or even partnership initiatives, could be recognized and accredited actors in international processes, as long as they meet agreed-upon standards set by the intergovernmental process. This shift to broader accreditation scheme would be beneficial in two ways. First, it would build in transparency and 'good governance' principles into accreditation. Establishing norms about acceptable types of

---

[3]   It is important to point out that geopolitical standing may vary by regime; for example, some of the small developing countries that are members of the Like-Minded Megadiverse Countries of the biodiversity regime are important players in these policy discussions because of the high concentrations of biodiversity within their borders.

internal governance is vital. If certain behaviours or practices are a prerequisite for official recognition and participation, incentives to comply will be created, and more importantly, transparent principles of conduct will eventually become an accepted norm. Second, good governance requirements would change the current bias toward recognizing NGOs as the primary legitimate representative of civil society. Allowing multi-actor civil society groups to be officially recognized would also alter the prevailing practice of representing multi-group civil society actors, such as transnational networks, with one organization – which is often a large, professionalized NGO from the developed world.

Other changes to institutional mechanisms for civil society engagement are also needed. First, as pointed out by many civil society groups consulted by the High Level Panel on UN-Civil Society Relations, the current accreditation procedures are fragmented, spanning across a number of different bodies and processes.[4] Streamlining the system, so that accreditation comes from one body and provides access to all processes, is one proposal to reduce demands on CSOs who wish to participate in various policy processes. Consolidating fragmented accreditation processes would be a good first step, so too, would the careful documentation of rules of procedures and engagement for civil society in different processes. Clearly, it would be unreasonable to expect the Security Council to allow civil society interventions in the same way that the Commission on Sustainable Development does. Nonetheless, the precedent for their participation in each institution has been set, and should not continue on an ad-hoc basis. These practices should be codified, and made available and transparent to all who wish to participate.

From the actor side, improved participation must begin with a better understanding of its constituent dimensions. We must advance beyond the simple explanation that 'more capacity' will yield better engagement. From the framework put forward above, which dimension most strongly predicts participation and influence? And what thresholds must be met? Understanding the constituent dimensions of engagement may also be important for promoting basic improvement in participation. If, for instance, access to transnational networks and international communities strongly predict greater engagement, this may be an effective, low-cost way to promote capacity in CSOs. Moreover, such a finding would also be critical in directing the policies and programmatic work of UN agencies and intergovernmental agencies that work with CSOs on all levels. In order to help develop the civil society sector to become an effective advocate for and implementer of sustainable development programmes, an important first step would then be to facilitate communication with similar actors in other countries. However, further research is needed to understand how these dimensions affect different types of civil society actors' engagement.

Lastly, there are a number of emerging discussions in international governance for sustainable development that will be important in understanding the impact

---

[4]   See the individual reports of the consultations on the High Level Panel's website, <www.un.org/reform/panel.htm>.

of actor-based attributes on participation. First, partnerships, which emerged as one of the main outcomes of the Johannesburg Summit, are attracting increased attention from scholars and practitioners. Sceptics wonder, are they truly partnerships, or simply a re-labelling of traditional hierarchical relationships? Though they have the potential to engage civil society in constructive and inclusive ways, some preliminary findings suggest that this is not the current trend among Type II partnerships (Andonova and Levy 2004). Moreover, the proliferation of partnerships has sparked discussions among participants of the struggles and successes of democratic governance structures within them. As stated earlier, this is a significant issue for the future role of civil society in international governance; thus, these discussions may provide some useful insights and/or solutions. And finally, though this chapter has evaluated the role of civil society in international governance, partnership arrangements may raise precisely the opposite question: must civil society be incorporated into pre-established institutions for international governance, or does its potential for effective change lie in creating new institutional arrangements? Recent pairings of NGOs with private companies indicate that some civil society actors have changed tactics. Instead of pressuring governments to regulate the private sector, they are going straight to the private sector themselves, to come up with workable solutions to problems such as climate change and sustainable forestry management. (See, for example, the World Resources Institute's work with the World Business Council for Sustainable Development to develop reporting standards for companies' greenhouse gas emissions, or the Forest Stewardship Council's certification of sustainably managed forests.)

Another important development for civil society participation in international governance is the entry into force of the Aarhus Convention, which promotes access to information, public participation and access to justice in environmental matters. The Convention has not only codified rules, procedures and rights concerning participation (Article 6), but also specifies the events and activities that trigger them (Annex I). Although it is a new treaty, it has the potential to set a meaningful precedent for civil society involvement in decision-making at the regional and sub-regional levels. In addition, its recent 'Draft Guidelines on Promoting the Application of the Principles of the Aarhus Convention in International Forums' may help provide both the political impetus and policy know-how to create better public participation procedures in a variety of international processes.

Lastly, the findings of the High Level Panel on UN-Civil Society Relations, which was assembled at the request of the Secretary General, made recommendations for reforming the institutional mechanisms now in place in the UN system. The Panel acknowledged the fragmentation of the current system, and as a remedy, proposed merging all existing accreditation procedures into one, to be overseen by the General Assembly. It also proposed to 'widen access of civil society organizations beyond the Economic and Social Council forums' (United Nations 2004: 54). The Panel's report has provided the political space to address the changing nature of governance in the multilateral system, and could significantly impact the perceived role of civil society in international policy-making. This will depend on the extent to which its recommendations are implemented through further actions taken by the General Assembly.

In examining the challenges of civil society participation, the High Level Panel wisely noted that it must avoid a 'one-size fits all' approach to civil society engagement. Policy-makers and academics working on this issue must also realize institutional mechanisms should at the least, be cognizant and accommodate the many forms and functions of civil society, and ideally, be tailored to them. Even in those regimes where civil society is much more involved, their level of engagement will necessarily vary by function and by organizational form. By highlighting the diversity of actors that comprise civil society, and the many services and benefits its participation offers, understanding and collaborative efforts can only improve. If future efforts to integrate civil society more fully into the United Nations are to be successful, the international community must first recognize this fact, and use it to society's collective advantage.

References

Andonova, Lilliana B., and Marc A. Levy. 2004. 'Franchising Global Governance: Making Sense of the Johannesburg Type II Partnerships'. *Yearbook of International Cooperation on Environment and Development 2003–04*: 19–31.

Anheier, Helmut. 2001. 'Measuring Global Civil Society'. In H. Anheier, M. Glasius and M. Kaldor, eds. *Global Civil Society Yearbook 2001*. Oxford: Oxford University Press.

Betsill, Michele, and Elisabeth Corell. 2001. 'NGO Influence in International Environmental Negotiations: A Framework for Analysis'. *Global Environmental Politics* 1.4: 65–85.

Brown, L. David, and Mark H. Moore. 2001. 'Accountability, Strategy and International Non-Governmental Organizations'. *Working Paper, The Hauser Center for Nonprofit Organizations, The Kennedy School of Government, Harvard University.* Working Paper No. 7.

Chandhoke, Neera. 2002. 'The Limits of Global Civil Society'. In Marlies Glasius, Mary Kaldor and Helmut Anheier, ed. *Global Civil Society 2002*. Oxford: Oxford University Press: 35–53.

Clark, Ann Marie, Elisabeth J. Friedman, and Kathryn Hochstetler. 1998. 'The Sovereign Limits of Global Civil Society: A Comparison of NGO Participation in UN World Conferences on the Environment, Human Rights and Women'. *World Politics* 51.1: 1–35.

Cohen, Jean, and Andrew Arato. 1992. *Civil Society and Political Theory*. Cambridge, MA: MIT Press.

Correll, Elisabeth, and Michele Betsill. 2001. 'A Comparative Look at NGO Influence in International Environmental Negotiations: Desertification and Climate Change'. *Global Environmental Politics* 1.4: 86–107.

Earth Negotiations Bulletin. 2004. 'Summary of the Twelfth Session of the Commission on Sustainable Development'. <www.iisd.ca/vol05/enb05211e.html> (7 May 2004).

Edwards, Michael. 2001. 'Global Civil Society and Community Exchanges: A Different Form of Movement'. *Environment and Urbanization* 13.2: 145–9.

Finger, M. and Princen T. 1994. *Environmental NGOs in World Politics*. London: Routledge.

Fisher, Dana R. and Jessica F. Green. 2004. 'Understanding Disenfranchisement: Civil Society and Developing Countries' Influence and Participation in Global Governance for Sustainable Development'. *Global Environmental Politics* 4.3.

Florini, Ann, ed. 2000. *The Third Force: the Rise of Transnational Civil Society* Tokyo: Japan Center for International Exchange and Washington DC: Carnegie Endowment for International Peace.

Fox, Jonathan A., and L. David Brown, eds. 1998. *The Struggle for Accountability: The World Bank, NGOs and Grassroots Movements*. Cambridge, MA: MIT Press.

Gemmill, Barbara, and Abimbola Bamidele-Izu. 2002. 'The Role of NGOs and Civil Society in Global Environmental Governance'. In Daniel Esty and Maria Ivanova, eds. *Global Environmental Governance: Options and Opportunities*. New Haven: Yale School of Forestry and Environmental Studies: 77–101.

Glasius, Marlies, Mary Kaldor and Helmut Anheier, eds. 2001. *Global Civil Society Yearbook*. Oxford: Oxford University Press.

Global Policy Forum. 2004. 'Special Meetings between NGOs and Security Council Members'. <www.globalpolicy.org/security/mtgsetc/brieindx.htm> (7 May 2004).

Green, Jessica F. 2005. 'Promoting Enfranchisement: Toward Inclusion and Influence in Sustainable Development Governance'. United Nations University-Institute of Advanced Studies, January.

———. 2004. 'Engaging the Disenfranchised: Developing Countries and Civil Society in International Governance for Sustainable Development'. United Nations University-Institute of Advanced Studies, February.

Haas, Peter, Norichika Kanie and Craig Murphy. 2004. 'Institutional Design and Institutional Reform for Sustainable Development'. In Norichika Kanie and Peter Haas, eds. *Emerging Forces in Environmental Governance*. Tokyo: United Nations University Press.

Hurd, Ian. 1999. 'Legitimacy and Authority in International Politics'. *International Organization* 53.2: 379–408.

Jordan, Lisa and Peter Van Tuijl. 2000. 'Political Responsibility in Transnational NGO Advocacy'. *World Development* 28.12: 2051–65.

Kakabadse, Yolanda N. and Sarah Burns. 1994. *Movers and Shapers: NGOs in International Affairs*. Washington DC: World Resources Institute.

Kanie, Norichika. 2004. 'NGO Participation in Global Climate Change Decision-making Process: A Key for Facilitating Negotiation'. IIASA Working Paper, September. On file with the author.

Keck, Margaret E. and Kathryn Sikkink. 1998. *Activists Beyond Borders: Advocacy Networks in International Politics*. Ithaca, NY: Cornell University Press.

Lipschutz, Ronnie. 1992. 'Restructuring World Politics: The Emergence of Global Civil Society'. *Millennium* 21.3: 389–420.

Munck, Ronaldo. 2002. 'Global Civil Society: Myths and Prospects'. *Voluntas: International Journal of Voluntary and Nonprofit Organizations* 13.4: 349–61.

Oberthur, Sebastian, Matthias Buck, Sebastian Muller, Stefanie Pfahl and Richard Tarasofsky. 2002. *Participation of Non-Governmental Organisations in International Environmental Governance: Legal Basis and Practical Experience*. Berlin: Ecologic.

Pianta, Mario. 2002. 'Parallel Summits of Global Civil Society: An Update'. In Marlies Glasius, Mary Kaldor and Helmut Anheier, eds. *Global Civil Society 2002.* Oxford: Oxford University Press: 371–6.

Raustiala, Kal. 1997. 'States, NGOs and International Environmental Institutions'. *International Studies Quarterly* 41: 719–40.

Shaw, Martin. 1999. 'Global Voices: Civil Society and Media in Global Crises'. In Timothy Dunne and Nicholas Wheeler, eds. *Human Rights in Global Politics.* Cambridge: Cambridge University Press: 214–32.

Simpson, Leanne. 2004. 'The Legacy of Deskaheh: Decolonizing Indigenous Participation in Global Governance Regarding Sustainable Development'. United Nations University-Institute of Advanced Studies, Working Paper, September.

Smith, Jackie. 1997. 'Characteristics of the Modern Transnational Social Movement Sector'. In Jackie Smith, Charles Chatfield and Ron Pagnucco, eds. *Transnational Social Movements and World Politics: Solidarity Beyond the State.* Syracuse, NY: Syracuse University Press: 42–58.

———. 2001. 'Globalizing Resistance: The Battle of Seattle and the Future of Social Movements'. *Mobilization* 6.1: 1–21.

Tarrow, Sidney. 2001a. 'Transnational Politics: Contention and Institutions in International Politics'. *Annual Review of Political Science* 4: 1–20.

———. 2001b. 'Rooted Cosmopolitans: Transnational Activists in a World of States'. Paper presented at the Cornell Workshop on Transnational Contention, University of Wisconsin. 2 November 2001.

Tussie, Diana, and Maria Pia Riggirozzi. 2001. 'Pressing Ahead with New Procedures for Old Machinery: Global Governance and Civil Society'. In Volker Rittberger, ed. *Global Governance and the United Nations System.* New York: United Nations University Press: 158–80.

UN Department of Public Information. 2004. 'Non-Governmental Organizations'. <www.un.org/dpi/ngosection/asp/form.asp> (3 May 2004).

UN DESA. 2004. 'Number of NGOs in Consultative Status by Category'. <www.un.org/esa/coordination/ngo/> (3 May 2004).

UN Non-governmental Liaison Service. 1998. 'Mission Statement'. <www.un-ngls.org/aboutusjm.htm> (3 May 2004).

United Nations Economic and Social Council. 1996. 'Consultative Relationship between the United Nations and Non-governmental Organizations'. E/RES/1996/31.

———. 2000. 'Establishment of a Permanent Forum on Indigenous Issues'. E/RES/2000/22.

United Nations Economic Commission for Europe. 2004. 'Report of the Second Meeting of the Expert Group on Public Participation in International Forums. Addendum: Draft Guidelines on Promoting the Application of the Principles of the Aarhus Convention in International Forums'. ECE/MP.PP/WG.1/2005/8/Add.1, 23 November.

United Nations. 2004. 'We the Peoples: Civil Society, the United Nations and Global Governance. Report of the Panel of Eminent Persons on United Nations–Civil Society Relations'. A/58/817, 11 June.

Von Moltke, Konrad. 2002. 'Governments and International Civil Society in Sustainable Development: A Framework'. *International Environmental Agreements: Politics, Law and Economics* 2: 341–59.

Wapner, Paul. 1996. *Environmental Activism and World Civic Politics.* Albany, NY: State University of New York Press.

Wapner, Paul. 2000. 'The Transnational Politics of Environmental NGOs: Governmental, Economic and Social Activism'. In Pamela Chasek, ed. *The Global Environment in the Twenty-first Century: Prospects for International Cooperation*. Tokyo, Japan: United Nations University Press: 87–107.

Weiss, Thomas George. 1999. *International NGOs, Global Governance and Social Policy in the UN System*. Helsinki : STAKES.

Zurn, Michael. 1998. 'The Rise of International Environmental Politics: A Review of Current Research'. *World Politics* 50.4: 617–49.

PART 2
Participation in International Agenda-setting and Decision-making

Chapter 6

The International Agenda
for Sustainable Development:
International Contestatory Movements

Carlos R.S. Milani and Chloé Keraghel

Introduction

The notion of sustainable development was already on the agenda of the United Nations Conference on the Human Environment held in Stockholm in 1972. It was then taken up by several economists and sociologists including Sachs, Riddell and Glaeser, and reworked at United Nations agencies and by several NGOs. Sustainable development has received multiple definitions, almost as numerous as the stakeholders speaking in its name. There is, however, a certain consensus with regard to the necessary balance between the three spheres formed by *society*, *economy* and *environment*, and also with regard to the relations between present and future generations. The development model founded on pushing the physical limits of the planet to the infinite would seem to have had its day and its continuation at the various scales of space and time would be clearly impracticable and insupportable for mankind as a whole (Sachs 1993).

The evolution of the sustainable development concept since the 1970s and in particular its implementation at the global level since the Rio de Janeiro conference in 1992 both reveal many contradictions in local and international political action. 'From garden to planet', sustainable development requires political actors both to think globally to act locally and to think locally to act globally, but also to handle its three dimensions – ecological, social and economic – symmetrically (Lipietz 1993). Since as was underlined by Edgar Morin and Anne-Brigitte Kern (1993),

the private individual becomes abstract when he is isolated from his context, isolated from the whole that he is part of. Likewise, what is global becomes abstract when it is just an entity without its components. The formation of the sustainable development concept contributes to the formation of planetary thinking that is ceasing to oppose the universal and the concrete, the general and the specific: the universe has become both singular – the cosmic universe – and concrete – the terrestrial universe.

Bearing very varied labels, such as sustainable livelihoods (United Nations), human development (UNDP) or socially sustainable development (UNEP), sustainable development has thus become a political watchword at the beginning of the twenty-first century. It is considered as a fundamental feature in the various international political agendas. With the growth of economic and financial globalization, the links between sustainable development, international trade and financial globalization have been strongly highlighted and discussed at the international level (Anderson 1992; Arden-Clarke 1992; Bartlett, Kurian and Malik 1995; Milani 1995). But nevertheless, as we demonstrate in this chapter, the precise definition of sustainable development remains particularly difficult to qualify in detail and to dissect in terms of political action.

In spite of all the efforts made by governments and non-governmental organizations, political negotiations at the Rio conference in 1992 were already at the conceptual and semantic level of the definition of sustainable development. The divergences between North and South were carried over in the preparation of the documents. Beyond traditional divisions between protection of the environment in the North and the need for development of the southern countries, between international regulation of common goods and the exercising of national sovereignty, between financial conditionality and additional funding earmarked for the protection of the environment, the countries in the North favoured the inclusion of the polluter-pays principle, the precautionary principle, the conservation of natural resources and birth control in the various conference documents. In contrast, the southern countries were in favour of the principle of shared responsibility (especially in financial questions), the transfer of new technologies on a more favourable basis than that of the market and an increase in public aid for development.

During the institutional negotiations that followed the Rio conference, North-South discussions were repeated without the serious addressing of the complementary role of international funding within the framework of increasingly globalized economies. On the one hand the southern countries were reluctant to recognize the capital importance of the mobilization of local resources for funding sustainable development. On the other, the northern countries did not make the necessary distinctions between the different forms of financial cooperation. They put all kinds of international funding in the *aid* for development category. The 'Rio discussions' were unable to address these fundamental questions of international cooperation and so the average public aid for development (calculated by OECD) is today hardly more than half of the threshold of 0.7 per cent GDP established by the United Nations in the 1970s.

The political results of the intergovernmental conferences in Rio, New York (Rio+5) and Johannesburg (Rio+10) have placed little constraint on the countries in the North and the South. For it must finally be recognized that the existing economic model is incapable of solving the social and environmental problems that it engenders. This means that the current crisis cannot be identified simply as the result of predatory action by the North. The existing economic systems in southern countries are also responsible for environmental degradation and failure to meet the needs of most of the populations of these countries. Corruption, misuse of public funds and the implementation of policies that do not take the social and environmental effects into account are also factors. It is true that in most cases the structural adjustment policies required by international financial authorities play a major role in the maintaining of this situation, but this does not totally eliminate the national responsibility of politicians in the running of the southern countries.

As a result, it is not surprising that the international protest movements should appropriate sustainable development as a subject since they go deeper into the political discussion of the very definition of sustainability according to the various geographic, cultural or historical contexts. Talk of sustainable development is heard within the framework of international protest particularly when alterglobalists discuss access to water supplies, the solidarity-based economy or, from an even more critical viewpoint, sustainably flat growth. Alterglobalists call sustainable development into question through their position with regard to the neoliberal development model, which they say tends to ignore the diversity of culture and the special features of local history. As we wish to demonstrate in this chapter, the question that is central to the strategic future of sustainable development is closely related to the political legitimacy of the actors who speak in the name of *projects for a sustainable society*.[1] The content of so-called actions for sustainable development refers to projects for a society that bear a risk of once again dividing development players in the North and the South. In order to meet the challenge of political analysis of the world sustainable development agenda, we address the three following series of questions:

1 How is international protest organized? Who are the actors? (Part 1)
2 How is sustainable development envisaged at the World Social Forum (WSF)? What are the main discussions with the WSF that are directly related to sustainable development? (Part 2)
3 Why and how may the definition of sustainable development interest WSF actors? How is the issue of political participation closely associated with that of sustainable development for the international protesters? (Part 3)

International Protest and the World Social Forum

As a process, the World Social Forum can be viewed as an integral part of a larger, broader movement commonly referred to as the alterglobalist movement, a name

---

[1]   When John Pezzey selected definitions of sustainable development (over 25 in the economic literature), he put forward that most of these definitions understand sustainability as a way of improving the quality of life and not as a means of maintaining existence in the world (Pezzey 1989).

that recently replaced the term 'antiglobalist', thus marking a major switch from the *anti* to the *alter* position. The roots of the movement lie in the 1990s with the emergence of the Zapatista movement in Mexico, which can be considered to be the first insurrection against neoliberal globalization, particularly with regard to its position on 1 January 2004 when the North American Free Trade Agreement (NAFTA) came into force. The Zapatistas stated their rejection of neoliberalism and decided to focus the movement on the increase of international trade and private investment at the expense of local cultures. Action started in July and August 1996 when the Zapatistas held a first intercontinental meeting against neoliberalism and called for the setting-up of a network of resistance (Le Bot 2003).

Since the end of the 1990s, the protest movement has used *mobilizations* in the form of counter-summits and assemblies in Seattle, Prague, Nice and the first counter-summit to the Davos economic forum, which then led to the first World Social Forum held in Porto Alegre (Brazil) in January 2001. In 1999, Seattle was marked by continuous demonstrations from 30 November to 3 December with the participation of some 350 organizations facing up to the World Trade Organization (WTO) and, according to statements by alterglobalists, to the liberal system of which it is part. The Seattle demonstrations clearly expressed protests participating in a broader anti-neoliberal movement. It was not an isolated event but a process that used new planned actions or actions to be planned to tend to strengthen participation in decision-making by civil society at different political scales (Coburn 2003). The July 2001 demonstrations in Genoa against the G-8 summit meeting were considered at the time to be the largest mobilization of antiglobalists (Caramel 2001).

The question raised after the events in Seattle and Genoa is that of the organization of protest in order to develop concrete proposals. The leaders of the movements formed the habit of seeing each other by holding strategic meetings to discuss the mobilization calendar and to link the networks in the North and those of the South. The importance of the International Forum on Globalisation can be noted; this defines itself as an alliance of economists and activists (including Maude Barlow of the Council of Canadians, Vandana Shiva of the Research Foundation for Science, Technology and Ecology, Walden Bello of the Focus on the Global South and Martin Khor of the Third World Network). This Forum plays a leading role in the protest against the neoliberal economy. Discussions in alliances such as this are centred on the four main campaigns:

1   writing off the debts of developing countries;
2   reforming international financial institutions;
3   taxing movements of capital;
4   new rules for world trade that award importance to sustainable development.

Each of these is set in a large network of actions. Although the campaign centred on the regulation of world trade was initially less organized, the militants of the NGO Friends of the Earth, of Via Campesina and consumer associations profited from the non-adoption of the Multilateral Investment Agreement (MIA) in 1998 to make public their concern with regard to food security, genetically modified organisms (GMOs) and environmental protection. Furthermore, these organizations started another kind of 'political combat' by condemning the excessive protection awarded to the investments of multinational corporations through the clause on the expropriation of capital.[2]

In this particular case, these social movements came up against the difficulty of taking a position as a coherent joint force for proposals. Nevertheless, their diversity is seen as an advantage thanks to the mingling of ideas and experiences in the setting-up of political alliances with certain representatives of institutions and governments during international trade negotiations. In the case of the MIA, for example, the French government supported the alliance. This system of forming political alliances with certain governments became a strategy of the alterglobalist groups. An alliance was formed at the WTO ministerial meeting in Cancun in September 2003 between the governments of Brazil and India (among others) on the one hand and the alterglobalists on the other against the maintaining of non-egalitarian rules for trade in agricultural products between countries in the North and the South.

Thus the multiplicity of speakers and actors and the diversity of sometimes contrasting objectives did not prevent the emergence of a more constructive image of the alterglobalist movement at the first WSF at Porto Alegre in January 2001, where more than 15,000 people assembled to oppose the Davos World Economic Forum (WEF). Priority was given to drawing-up proposals on which to found an alternative project to the neoliberal model. The Forum thus became 'a place where the anti-globalist movements demonstrated their globalisation' (Hardt and Negri 2003). Indeed, the WSF as a process developed according to its own

---

[2]   The MIA established that each part of the Agreement should treat the investors of other member countries and their investments as favourably as its own investors and their investments (national treatment clause) or the investors and investments of third countries (most-favoured nation clause) in similar circumstances. Each party to the Agreement would be obliged to guarantee the most favourable regime between the national treatment clause and the most-favoured nation clause (this is taken up in Articles 11, 1102 and 1103 of NAFTA, for example). It is important to note that in both of these documents the notion of investment applies to goods and services, transactions and financial holdings (stocks, shares, options, etc.), to natural resources, to real estate, land and agricultural and intellectual property. Laws requiring fair prior compensation exist in practically all countries in the case of the seizure of the property or holdings of a domestic or foreign company; MIA and NAFTA add the notion of measures 'tantamount to expropriation' that would give the right to compensation for 'loss of future profits', for example in the case of a new regulation concerning the environment or public health. This clause might prevent the member states party to the agreement from making any sovereign effort in social or environmental policies as these policies can be considered by businesses as a barrier to the free expansion of investment.

logic in parallel with numerous counter-summits. The creation of this area in which civil society groups attempt to develop alternatives was first suggested as a counter-summit at Davos and set up in 1999. Then Oded Grajew (a Brazilian entrepreneur and president of the Ethos Institute for Social Responsibility), Francisco Whitaker (of the Brazilian Justice and Peace Commission) and Bernard Cassen (of ATTAC, the French NGO) expressed their determination to hold the first forum in a southern country (in Porto Alegre) and to call it the World *Social* Forum in opposition to the World *Economic* Forum in Davos. The WSF was to be held on the same dates as the WEF to symbolically mark its opposition to the liberal world. The city of Porto Alegre gave its approval in March 2000. It already seemed to be the most appropriate place for hosting the meeting because of its innovative experience in renewing local democracy, including the participative budget established by the Workers Party (Fisher and Ponniah 2003).

The WSF broadened as many other forums were held at various scales (regional, local, continental and thematic). The Social Forums thus provide a platform suitable for discussion and reflection on the possible alternatives to the neoliberal globalization model and can be considered as open areas for meetings, discussions and proposals or, as suggested by Fisher and Ponniah, 'a pedagogical space enabling learning, networking and political organisation' (Fisher and Ponniah 2003).

The main subjects discussed at the first Forum in 2001 and then in 2002 were twofold: some participants defended their views in opposition to neoliberal globalization, while others looked for possible alternatives in order to make a better world accepting the idea of *another* globalization. In 2003, a new stage in the political process marked the start of a movement away from reflection towards the specific proposal of alternatives to the existing world political and economic system. The various actors in international protests were already succeeding in establishing a global political space in opposition to the Davos Economic Forum and henceforth questioned traditional political power, as was demonstrated at the WTO meeting in Cancun in September 2003. Although there is much convergence in struggles and discussions, management diversity in this network of networks is still difficult, as is the question of a consensus on projects for a sustainable society that remain to be defined (Rojo, Milani and Arturi 2004).

Furthermore, the process of critical reflection of the movement by itself also intensified. The trend was seen at the second European Social Forum held in Paris, Saint-Denis and Bobigny just before the WSF in Mumbai (India) in November 2003 – held outside Brazil for the first time. Activists and Forum participants thus tended to favour the refocusing of discussions on the strategies and identity of the alterglobalist movement, which was no longer supporting an antiglobalization strategy, but which sought alternatives in order to achieve a more human globalization, another form of globalization. The second European Social Forum thus revealed the need for further analysis and discussion of the nature and identity of the movement itself as a *sine qua non* in order to produce a better definition of political strategies and in the search for alliances, and pathways for changing world society.

There is no doubt that the alterglobalist movement has gained political maturity and that the question of its identity as an open space is increasingly raised, and is necessary for the extension of the WSF to other regions of the world, as was seen in 2004 with Mumbai. Alterglobalists portray themselves as an emancipation movement aiming to uncovering the lies of neoliberalism and provide information on the political issues of globalization. It is a movement in which cultural and social diversity is considered by militants to be a vital force in the way in which democracy is conceived and practised. Even if the political orientations of the participants (both individuals and associations) diverge, their union is based on the shared conviction that right should outweigh profit and profitability. The political consensus, defined as both the recognition by all of the existence of different visions of the world and also as agreement on a common denominator of strategic action, is based on the Charter of Principles of the Forum in an approach that refuses both neoliberalism and imperialism and the politics of violence.

Indeed, as time went by and in particular in the world context immediately following the founding of the WSF in 2001, opposition to war and the struggle against militarism were incorporated in the discourse of the Forum leaders. Then, as the most recent meeting was held in India in 2004, this vocabulary was considerably extended to the point of including opposition to the caste system and to the splitting of society into communities and ghettos. After many discussions at the meeting in Miami (June 2003), the international council of the Forum finally approved this enrichment and broadening of the vocabulary. Furthermore, the Forum leaders then made two important revisions to the original (April 2001) version of the Charter of Principles, producing a revised, finalised version (June 2001). These revisions marked a radical change in the thinking and politics of the Forum. The World Social Forum also became more restrictive at the Indian edition. Following a decision made by the international council in 2003, the organizations wishing to become full members of the decision-making body of the Forum should now formally support the Charter of Principles. The Charter thus states clearly that the World Forum is essentially open to 'groups and movements of civil society that are opposed to neoliberalism and to domination of the world by capital and any form of imperialism, and are committed to building a planetary society centred on the human person'.

The significant changes that took place in 2004 in India (the extension to other subjects of struggle, opposition to the caste system and to religious fundamentalism and the massive, broader participation of women) strengthened the objectives drawn up at the 2003 WSF. These were aimed at considering the best ways of promoting justice, solidarity and democracy as global values, at serious reflection on the practice of alternatives to neoliberal globalization and to considering putting into practice the issues discussed at the Forum. Questions nonetheless remain for the organizers: how can the format of the Forum succeed in meeting the challenge of diversity and all these changes? The management of the Forum (international secretariat and international council) that is gaining a considerable scope seems to be changing a symbolic arena into an international political actor. Although it calls itself the World *Social* Forum, the movement is *a priori* a political idea and its founders have clearly set out a certain political culture for running it (Keraghel and Sen 2004).

Now aware of its own globalization as much as of the switch from its position from that of *anti* to *alter*, the alterglobalist movement calls sustainable development into question in particular through its position with regard to the homogenizing model imposed by neoliberal global model. As a result, it is essential to know the content of the debates on sustainable development that mark the players in international protest, in both the North and the South, in comparison with the institutional actors who negotiate agreements and implement international programmes related to sustainable development.

Sustainable Development within the World Social Forum: a Critical and Radical Debate

Sustainable development is at the heart of the discussions of the WSF and its thematic and regional ramifications. These discussions are not of the same kind as those of the intergovernmental and institutional negotiations held within the United Nations system since Stockholm-72 and especially since Rio-92. In Porto Alegre in 2001, sustainable development incorporated the Forum's second thematic area, entitled access to wealth and sustainability. The subjects of the workshops held on the theme included social control of the environment, environmental protection, the democratization of scientific knowledge and the privatization of knowledge within the framework of intellectual property. The same thematic area was maintained in 2002, with the workshops placing more stress on the links between techno-science, ecology and capitalism, agro-ecology and intellectual property rights, green, ethical and sustainable consumption and cities as areas of sustainability. The thematic areas changed in 2003, with the first devoted to democratic, sustainable development. It is interesting to note the link now established between sustainability and democracy, with the latter being considered as a prerequisite for the former. Alterglobalists hold, for example, that the management of natural resources requires first and foremost the implementation of democratic mechanisms for the social control of access to these goods.

At the fourth WSF held in Mumbai, a set of organizations (Asia Pacific Movement on Debt and Development, Public Citizen, Sweetwater Alliance, Council of Canadians and Cry of the Water) set up a global Peoples' Water Forum. Internationally known activists such as Vandana Shiva, Ricardo Petrella and Tony Clarke participated in these discussions. At the meetings of the Pan-Amazonian Social Forum in January 2002 (in Belém du Pará, Brazil), January

2003 (also in Belém) and February 2004 (Ciudad Guayana, Venezuela), activists and participants analysed sustainable development from the angle of ecological sovereignty, sustainable management of areas by the people, the conservation of protected forest zones (the reserves known as *reservas extrativistas*), food security, biodiversity, agro-ecological production by rural families, the geopolitics of water and water resource management.[3]

Furthermore, reading the articles presented in the Library of Alternatives of the official WSF website and analysis of some of the speeches made at the various Forums by the main leaders of the movements and organizations that form part of it (Francisco Whitaker, Arundhati Roy and Walden Bello among others), it is possible to identify a series of criticisms levelled by alterglobalists at both the increasing institutionalization of the sustainable development debate and the resulting political hijacking of strategies (programmes, projects and action plans).

The starting-point for these criticisms is at the level of the report entitled *Our Common Future* and Agenda 21, the two documents most cited by the international agencies working on sustainable development (UNEP, UNESCO, UNDP, the World Bank and all the bilateral cooperation agencies) and that serve as the philosophical basis for countless international initiatives. These documents were drafted by teams consisting of diplomats, international civil servants and specialists from the North, South, East and West of the world. This global editorial team is doubtless apparent proof of diversity of opinion and is a great political advantage but led to a consensus and compromise such that their content has no precise meaning. The main defect of the Brundtland Report and of Agenda 21 is thus the result of one of their strengths: they try to attain a consensus and avoid political oppositions. The attempt made at all costs to link development and environment, ecology and the expansion of international trade, protection of the environment and the neutrality of techniques, outward-looking development (exports) and inward-looking development (the domestic market) leads to the production of formulae that are frequently very vague or that require somewhat unrealistic financial contributions. Furthermore, the Brundtland Report does not draw attention to the real costs and the different cultural visions of sustainable development.

Another example of serious criticism is that in this process of institutionalization of the debate on sustainable development international cooperation agencies tend to encourage a degree of confusion between the different levels of the economic

---

[3]   The coordination of this regional forum (AWSF) is handled by the NGO Caritas, the Conselho Indigenista Missionário (CIMI), the Coordination of the Indigenous Organisations of the Brazilian Amazon (COIAB), the Central Workers' Union Confederation (CUT), the Amazon Working Group (GTA) and the Brazilian Writers' Union. AWSF is the first regional forum organized in the historic process of the World Social Forum. More than 10,000 people attended the second AWSF held on the central theme of 'All against the free trade zone of the Americas'.

value of the environment. Now, the total economic value of the environment should be the sum of its direct and indirect use value, its option value and its existence value. Its use value is awarded by the individuals or groups who benefit from the endangered environment. The option value is the setting aside of an environment for the benefit of future generations according to a value structure that is not focused on the primary consumption of goods and services. Lastly, the existence value is the result of an environmental right that is independent of the present or future use of resources. How can these values be measured without ranking them and considering them as fungible?

Furthermore, with regard to the first stirrings of sustainable development, how is it possible not to touch on the question of the distribution of wealth? For example, the Brundtland Report only mentions increased wealth for future redistribution. At the international level, calling into question the distribution of existing income would mean not accepting the flagrant inequality between the developed countries and the least-developed countries (and inequality within the countries themselves). What basic income would be necessary for the advent of sustainable development in each country? In the 1970s, this question was at the origin of discussions on the new world economic order, but its foundations were not taken up in intergovernmental discussion of sustainable development; this was once again midway between political compromises and intellectual and theoretical rigour.

At the national level, how is it possible not to touch on productive capital and natural resources with a view to the reform of land ownership in discussion of the change in the paradigm of development, as encouraged by the sustainable development concept? In Brazil, for example, the question of access to productive land (simultaneously providing market access for production) is at the heart of political negotiations and conflicts between government officials, landowners and social movements (especially the Landless Movement, one of the pillars of the WSF in Brazil). It would be precarious to discuss sustainable development in Brazil without including the key question of historically constructed social inequalities.

In the field of nuclear power, the economic strategies for sustainable development taken up in the Brundtland Report and Agenda 21 do not seem to be in contradiction with the energy choices made by certain countries such as Japan and France. So why not therefore criticize these choices or show their ecological or even economic defects? Furthermore, how can one avoid talking about the concrete difficulties encountered by the development of a sustainable society? Do we believe that technology will prevent growth from damaging nature and the environment? But how could technological innovation alone prevent the damage caused by excessive consumption or poor consumption?

As Arundhati Roy pointed out, some 40 million people have been displaced by large dams in India in the past 50 years (Roy 2003). It was estimated in 1979 that slightly more than 6,000 families would be displaced by the Sardar Sarovar dam project on the Narmada alone. In 1992, the government admitted that 40,000 families were affected and the official figures fluctuated around 45,000 families in 2000. According to Roy, it is clear that sustainable development cannot reconcile protection of the environment and the culture of these populations with the idea of the exponential increase in the number of dams in the world. She therefore raises the question of whether the construction of large dams that flood natural zones in India where very old cultural identities have evolved for hundreds of years is not contrary to the principles of sustainable development.

There are many questions and only a few answers. In the eyes of the alterglobalist movements, the limits of the discussions of sustainable development in institutional agencies are thus of several kinds: temporal (are sustainable development times the same everywhere?), spatial (what degree of contextual variation is possible in the implementation of sustainable development?), political (defining the sustainability of development), economic (what position has the market economy in relation to the immaterial value of the environment?) and cultural (what are the rankings between the various forms of knowledge defining the basis of sustainable development?). We have only listed a few here. In the final analysis, the concept as presented in intergovernmental reports does not seem to draw a clear distinction between strong and weak sustainability.[4] As Beckerman emphasized, intergovernmental agencies try to make a market economy approach compatible with the promotion of weak sustainability, even though they sometimes take a radical conservation position (Beckerman 1994). The justification offered for this mixed approach is manifestly economic, even if ethical, aesthetic and scientific values are frequently mentioned as factors in supporting conservation reasoning. For example, it is stated in the Brundtland Report that economic reasons are not the only ones to justify the conservation of species but, for those who insist on having accounts, the potential economic value of the genetic material contained in all the species should amply justify their conservation. This reasoning is followed by the recipe for activities that are economically promising with regard to the conservation of natural resources: the pharmaceutical industry, medicine and agriculture (the genetic *revolution*), fields that the economic sector could draw on in order to ensure both the conservation of species and considerable profits. But alterglobalists, and especially the ecologists

---

[4]   Weak sustainability tends to enhance support of growth whereas strong sustainability gives priority to the conservation of the environment. Weak sustainability is based on a rule of distribution of capital (natural, manufactured, human and social) among the generations. The types of capital are perfectly substitutable and the important thing is to increase the potential for well-being as time goes by. This concept leaves many questions unanswered: a) how can the price of the different capitals be compared; b) does technical progress alone make it possible to find substitute solutions to lost natural capital; c) can the substitution of natural goods and services by material goods and services – when this is technically feasible – always be envisaged from an ethical point of view? Strong sustainability applies two further constraints: a) the identification of a critical natural capital that could neither be used nor replaced by productive capital; and b) a requirement of non-decrease of natural capital (the principle of precaution and inter-generation responsibility).

who are part of the movement, wonder about the price to be paid for this. How far will the limit of the privatization of living material and the merchandization of life be pushed?

We could simplify the question and say that three schools of thought are looking for the right definition of sustainable development. First the neoclassical, liberal approach: using the notion of the externalization of ecological costs and the polluter-pays principle, some economists propose the privatization of ecological goods or the establishment of rights to pollute. Then come the neo-Keynesian approaches, with increased protection of the environment by means of economic growth and job creation in the environment industry. Lastly, the radical approach in which the economy follows the example of nature and must organize itself according to the principle of closed circuits that regulate themselves perfectly; the economic sphere is located in the heart of the social sphere which is in turn in the sphere of nature (Passet 1979, 2001). Of these three models – which are in fact different projects for society and very varied conceptions of sustainability – only the first accepts that ecological rationality could emerge from the economy and that the man-nature contradiction would be solved by the economic system itself. It is precisely this first current of thinking that is targeted by most of the criticism levelled by the alterglobalist movements. Might there be other ways of regulating economy-society-environment relations other than via the market?

Boaventura de Sousa Santos reminds us that a political response must be made to ecological dangers. In addition to systemic forms of regulation – by the market or by state power alone – the response could also come from making citizens aware and their active participation and vigilance. In the absence of a single system capable of promoting the necessary changes in society-economy-environment relations, mobilized citizens and the sectors affected by ecological dangers would be the only actors capable of playing the role of a social body that would perceive ecological interdependence and would give priority to protection of the environment. Now, it is certain that this trend in sustainable development must be founded on democratic participation and an ideal of social justice that are far from being shared by all citizens but that the WSF is attempting to initiate (De Sousa Santos 2002).

Sustainable Development and the Demand for Closer Political Participation

From the perspective of the political protest that the WSF wishes to express or even represent on a global scale, thinking concerning sustainable development can contribute to deep-seated changes in international political economics. First, this is because this thinking could be interpreted as the condemning of the *laissez faire* typical of economic liberalism. The ecological stalemate would oblige liberal capitalism to undergo structural changes. *Homo oeconomicus* – used as a model for traditional economic reasoning – displays the feature of not consuming or of over-consuming what he produces and not producing what he needs to consume.

This means that classical and neoliberal economic thought does not take into account questions of quality, attractiveness, beauty, happiness, freedom of choice and moral standards, but only questions of trade value, flows, quantities, planned obsolescence and global balance. Deregulation in favour of the market runs up against needs to protect nature and to conserve increasingly depleted resources. There is no doubt that the ecological crisis shows that while everybody is trying to increase their comfort and quality of life, the situation of society as a whole does not improve at all. Deregulation and the satisfaction of individual interests encouraged by an 'invisible hand' have disastrous results in terms of protection of the environment.

In this respect, the problems of sustainable development can enable contemporary man finally to cease the trial of strength that he had set up with nature. This is a second 'revolutionary' aspect of thinking on sustainable development that has been received favourably in the alterglobalist movement (Rousset 2002). The question is not that of knowing what man can still do to change and conquer nature, but of what nature can stand. The promise of technology – an essential basis of the twentieth-century liberal and socialist ideologies – has turned into a threat, or at least the two go together. This makes it necessary to anticipate the threat itself, what Jonas calls the 'heuristics of fear' (Jonas 1979).

Furthermore, by encouraging critical analysis of the relations between man and nature, thinking on sustainable development can lead political players to take increasing account of the urgent need to protect the common goods of the planet. As is underlined by Badie, the taking into account of the definition of common goods by the international community should also suggest the importance of the regulatory mechanisms that they probably bear, since these goods touch on the primordial conditions for the survival of humanity. By tracing the outline of a world society, the hypothesis underlying the idea of common goods would transcend the factors of division and create a regulation potential in international relations because of the common destiny shared by all (Badie 1995). The question of the mechanisms for the regulation of common global goods is obviously at the centre of the alterglobalist movement's discussions and proposals.

A fundamental point is that of how to define common goods. What resources should be subjected to non-trade political regulation at the global level? Which stakeholders should participate in negotiations? These questions reveal a dimension of thinking on sustainable development that appears to us to be essential to understand how and why alterglobalists are interested in the concept. The definition of sustainability is a highly political question that unveils plans for societies, social representation, economic ambitions and numerous, but sometimes contradictory, ways of viewing relations between nature, society, man and the market.

As a result, protesters claim the radicalization of democracy on the world scale and increased political participation in the forming of public opinions and in decision processes. For example, Teivanem underlines the need to make clearer the political dimension of democracy at the WSF, and above all to make visible those players who are traditionally invisible on the world scene. He considers that it is possible to construct a new social emancipation project on the following four pillars: the universalization of access to the goods and services required for a dignified life, the non-merchandization of life, the refusal of war and violence and the extension of sovereignty of the people, including coverage of international economic relations (Teivanem 2004).

Part of the philosophical base that justifies this request by alterglobalists for political participation is related to the present crisis in intergovernmentalism and multilateralism. North-American unilateralism and the partiality of the rules of the international system are making a decisive contribution to calling into question the idea of international community. Furthermore, this crisis is also the result of the change in a model of international society in which nation states would play an exclusive role in the regulation of the world's affairs. Intergovernmentalism is under pressure from the emergence of a powerful quest for legitimacy in relation to the world's consumers and citizens of a series of new stakeholders (multinational corporations, financial agencies, the international media, NGOs and also protest movements). These new players in world politics do not necessarily have a national territorial base in the defining of their strategies; in most cases they operate independently of national sovereignty. Their field of action is a transnational area of projects, practices, symbols and utopias.

It is clear that the plans of these various transnational stakeholders are not necessarily complementary. What transnational economic capital wants, for example, is opposed to the desires of the alterglobalists. They nevertheless share the same transnational zone, use the same technological resources and call into question the monopoly of the state in international relations. The political strategies of these transnational players are virtually 'deterritorialized'. This does not mean that they do not use a territory, but they occupy a territorial continuum running from local to national to global (Amiraux 1999). Their political identity is therefore located beyond the national frontier (this differs, for example, from the social movements of the nineteenth century) and can be explained by a triple shift in international power: from the public to the private, from the national to the transnational and from the nation state to international financial and trade institutions.

The alterglobalists already oppose these shifts of power, and try in their own way to participate in the management of world affairs. Even if they use a modern set of collective actions that are typical of the nineteenth century (as identified by Charles Tilly: demonstrations, strikes and petitions), at least three new strategies are used. First, their action must always be a happening in the tradition of the 1968 movements, and protests increase as the neoliberal plans spread. Second, they use second expert evaluations through reports, meeting and alternative media. Third, they make their actions a media event, and include acts of civil disobedience (Dufour 2005; Salée, Harvey and Murphy 2005). The media visibility of alterglobalist meetings has given these movements an opportunity to make themselves known at the world scale, especially in the early days of their protests (Seattle, Nice and Prague). As Susan George said at one of these meetings, referring to their direct opposition to the Davos Forum, WTO, the World Bank and the IMF: 'wherever "They" are, some of "Us" will be also' (Fougier 2002). Seeking media coverage also helps in the process of the construction of the identity of the alterglobalist movement.

In addition, the way in which political participation in the international system is envisaged among alterglobalists is influenced by the diversity of organizations, trade unions, social movements, social and solidarity groups, NGOs and research centres, among others, that attend the social forums. Some are organizations that militate for global causes (Action contre la Faim, Amnesty International, Greenpeace, Médecins sans Frontières), others that have a very clear political vocation (Global Trade Watch, ATTAC, Public Citizen) but also social anarchist movements that are in favour of violence (Black Block, Third Position) or against the use of violence (Direct Network Action, Tute Bianche, Reclaim the Streets). There are mass organizations (the AFL-CIO, for example, America's union movement with 13 million members in the United States), international NGOs (Greenpeace, Friends of the Earth, Oxfam, Christian Aid, Misereor), small farmers' movements (Via Campesina, the Landless Movement) and groups of experts specialized in monitoring economic globalization, such as WTO Watch, Corporate Watch and ATTAC (Fougier 2001, 2002).

The tension that can be generated between the 'reformist alterglobalists' (for example, the organizations that are part of the UNO Economic and Social Council and that attended the Millennium Summit in May 2000) and the 'radicals' (internationalists or nationalists) results from a twofold strategy whose political result is not clearly defined. How can one choose a common position between playing on the balance of power, opposing the financial agencies and the neoliberal principles of the economic system on the one hand, and entering international negotiation and attempting to change the world order through breaches in the institutional structure on the other?

It seems that the limits placed on political participation of the players in protest are found in the very heart of the alterglobalist movement. Deep-seated features of the WSF include avoiding unified statements, recognition of difference as a common denominator, defining oneself as an area/movement in which the different cultures meet each other, avoiding the emergence of a spokesman for the movement, using confusion as a tactic, refusing urgency and working on a long-term basis. These features contrast clearly with those of the institutional stakeholders in international cooperation and international relations.

The challenge that the alterglobalists seem to wish to set also concerns representations of globalization. They know that the unequal structure of political representation at the world level is a reflection of the inequalities in social forces; the alterglobalists are therefore slowly trying to change this unequal structure in their favour by working, for example, on symbols and culture.

Conclusion

Although numerous militant alterglobalists describe the WSF as a new stakeholder on the international scene, above all its role as a tool for teaching and its ability to provide an open political arena are important. The Forum is a place for discussion, for networking and for the development of collective projects in the name of those who participate. It thus plays an important role in the development of a pedagogy of participation aimed first and foremost at militants in international political activism.

The WSF must nevertheless face several obstacles in order to remain plural (in the diversity of the movements of which it consists) while conserving its cohesion centred on values and strategic choices. One of the questions that is unanswered so far is that of the sustainability of the political approach based on diversity within the Forum. Will this multiplicity of actors and opinions survive in the long term once concrete proposals must be set out on the negotiating table devoted to issues of sustainable development? In other words, diversity without critical recognition and awareness of what makes internal players different one from another can lead to future political and strategic problems. The management of the tensions set up between the multiplicity of positions (of activitists, movements and organizations) and the collective drafting of proposals leads to a risk. According to the alterglobalists themselves, the latter is not related to the variety of players within the movement but to an attempt to promote a false consensus (a 'soft consensus') and not to discuss the subjects that cause problems. The etymology of the word 'dialogue' (from the Greek *dia*, meaning 'between' and *logos*, 'reason') reminds us that a dialogue means seeking other (intermediate) reasons from reasons that are discussed and gone over. Therefore, a pathway for future analyses could be set out as follows: how can the players in international protest conserve the unity and diversity of the WSF but also build their capacity to develop new *plural reasons* in order to understand relations between mankind and nature and to draw up proposals for an in-depth change to the economic system?

References

Amiraux, Valérie. 1999. 'Les limites du transnational comme espace de mobilisation'. *Cultures and Conflicts* 33–4. Fall: 25–50.
Anderson, Kym. 1992. *Commerce mondial et environnement*. Paris: Economica.
Arden-Clarke, Charles. 1992. *South-North Terms of Trade, Environmental Protection and Sustainable Development*. WWF International Discussion Paper, Geneva: WWF.
Badie, Bertrand. 1995. *La fin des territoires – essai sur le désordre international et sur l'utilité sociale du respect*. Paris: Fayard, Collection L'Espace du Politique.
Bartlett, Robert, Kurian Priva and Malik Madhu. 1995. *International Organisations and Environmental Policy*. London: Greenwood Press.
Beckerman, Wilfred. 1994. 'Sustainable Development: Is it a Useful Concept?' *Environmental Value* 3.3. Fall.

Caramel, Laurence. 2001. 'Les réseaux de l'antimondialisation'. *Critique Internationale* 13: 153–61.

Coburn, Elaine. 2003. 'La bataille de Seattle'. In Michel Wieviorka, ed. *Un autre monde ...: Contestations, dérives et surprises de l'antimondialisation*. Paris: Balland.

De Sousa Santos, Boaventura, ed. 2002. *Produzir para viver. Os caminhos da produção não capitalista*. Rio de Janeiro: Civilização Brasileira.

Dufour, Pascale. 2005. 'Globalisation as a New Political Space: The End of the Quebec-Quebec Debate?' In *The State of the Federation. Quebec and Canada in the New Century: New Dynamics, New Opportunities*. Queen's: Queen's University Press.

Fisher, William and Thomas Ponniah. 2003. *Un autre monde est possible*. Paris: Parangon.

Fougier, Eddy. 2001. 'Mondialisation: radiographie de la contestation'. *Sociétal (L'analyse trimestrielle des réalités économiques et sociales)* 34. Winter.

———. 2002. 'Le Mouvement de Contestation de la Mondialisation'. *Annuaire Français des Relations Internationales*. Bruxelles. III.

Hardt, Michael and Antonio Negri. 2003. 'Préface'. In Michel Wieviorka, ed. *Un autre monde ...: Contestations, dérives et surprises de l'antimondialisation*. Paris: Balland.

Jonas, Hans. 1979. *Le Principe Responsabilité: une éthique pour la civilisation technologique*. Paris: Editions du Cerf.

Keraghel, Chloé and Jai Sen. 2004. 'Explorations in Open Space, The World Social Forum and Cultures of Politics'. *International Social Science Journal* 182: 483–93.

Le Bot, Yvon. 2003. 'Le zapatisme, première insurrection contre la mondialisation néolibérale'. In Michel Wieviorka, ed. *Un autre monde ...: Contestations, dérives et surprises de l'antimondialisation*. Paris: Balland.

Lipietz, Alain. 1993. *Vert espérance, l'avenir de l'écologie politique*. Paris: La Découverte.

Milani, Carlos. 1995. 'Les rapports commerce-environnement et les dangers de l'écoprotectionnisme'. *Cahiers des Amériques Latines* 20: 5–28.

Morin, Edgar and Anne-Brigitte Kern. 1993. *Terre Patrie*. Paris: Editions du Seuil.

Passet, René. 1979. *L'Economique et le vivant*. Paris: Payot.

———. 2001. *L'Eloge du mondialisme*. Paris: Fayard.

Pezzey, John. 1989. *Economic Analysis of Sustainable Development*. The World Bank Discussion Paper Series, Washington DC.

Rojo, Raúl, Carlos Milani and Carlos Arturi. 2004. 'Expressions of Political Contestation and Mechanisms of Democratic Control'. *International Social Science Journal* 182: 615–28.

Rousset, Pierre. 2002. 'Lo ecológico y lo social: combates, problemas, marxismos'. *Library of Alternatives* <www.forumsocialmundial.org.br> (15 November 2004).

Roy, Arundhati. 2003. *L'écrivain-militant*. Paris: Gallimard, Folio Documents.

Sachs, Ignacy. 1993. *L'écodéveloppement, Stratégies de transition vers le XXIe siècle*. Paris: Syros.

Salée, Daniel, Lazar Harvey and Michael Murphy, eds. 2005. *The State of the Federation. Quebec and Canada in the New Century: New Dynamics, New Opportunities*. Montreal: McGill-Queen's University Press.

Teivanem, Teivo. 2004. 'Twenty-two Theses on the Problems of democracy in the World Social Fórum'. *Library of Alternatives* <www.forumsocialmundial.org.br> (15 November 2004).

Wieviorka, Michel, ed. 2003. *Un autre monde ...: Contestations, dérives et surprises de l'antimondialisation*. Paris: Balland.

Chapter 7

Epistemic Community and International Governance of Biological Diversity: A Reinterpretation of the Role of IUCN

Sélim Louafi

Introduction

This chapter focuses on the role of the International Union for the Conservation of Nature and Natural Resources (IUCN) in the design of the United Nations Framework Convention on Biological Diversity (CBD), concluded on 5 June 1992 at the Rio de Janeiro Earth Summit. The CBD is a multilateral convention ratified by 180 parties. The three main objectives of this Convention, are the conservation of biological diversity, the sustainable use of its components and the fair and equitable sharing of the benefits arising out of the utilization of genetic resources, including by appropriate access to genetic resources and by appropriate transfer of relevant technologies, taking into account all rights over those resources and to technologies, and by appropriate funding (CBD art. 1).

Since the beginning of the 1980s, four types of semantic discourse used by the various stakeholders in the international negotiations on biological diversity could be identified:

1 the environmentalist discourse, associated with ecological science;
2 the agronomic discourse, associated with agriculture-related science, which was the first to incorporate the advances related to genomics;
3 the economic discourse, founded on the theory of property rights;
4 the culturalist discourse, founded on ethno-sciences.

This chapter shows how the International Union for the Conservation of Nature has influenced the international debate on biodiversity by trying to mix, at least partially, these various discourses. Based on the inadequacy of the conventional, intergovernmental forms of coordination, IUCN has sought to take in the multi-dimensional complexity of the biodiversity issue. For this purpose, it has relied upon scientific evidence, provided by its own scientists. This learning process has even found expression at the institutional level via a redefinition of the principles guiding IUCN's actions.

While IUCN has traditionally been seen as an interest group linked to the conservationist movement, this chapter demonstrates that it is in fact a genuine 'epistemic community', with a double dynamics largely based on a participative process, both at the level of the scientific actors and of the institution itself.

Traditional Interpretation of IUCN as an Interest Group

The IUCN has traditionally been seen as a simple interest group, developing out of the conservationist movement for nature protection (Mc Donald 2002). What are the elements that make it possible to interpret IUCN's role this way?

IUCN's Institutional Structure

IUCN is made up of three 'pillars'; the scientific commissions, the secretariat and the members. The scientific commissions are commissions of experts responsible for drawing up lists of endangered species (the famous 'red list', which made IUCN famous to the general public), identifying the principles of healthy ecological management, improving awareness of risks associated with poor environmental management and drawing up criteria and guidelines for good management. There are six commissions: the Commission on Ecosystem Management (CEM), the Commission on Education and Communication, the Commission on Environmental Law (formerly CEPLA), the Commission on Environmental, Economic, and Social Policy (CEESP), the Species Survival Commission (SSC) and the World Commission on Protected Areas (formerly CNPPA).

A secretariat takes care of the management of certain agreements (like Antarctica, Ramsar or CITES for instance) and manages crises situations or environmental emergencies (near-extinction of the panda, civil war in Uganda that threatens the national parks, re-introduction of endangered species into their biotope).

The members include at the same time non-governmental and governmental institutions who aims are to promote nature conservation, and governments/states from a total of 130 countries. Nonetheless, their role is often restricted to the one of pressure groups that alert the IUCN staff.

Institutional Changes

The problem that arose at IUCN at the end of the 1970s was finding out how to work alongside the United Nations agencies (UNEP, UNESCO, FAO) and more broadly with all the intergovernmental or non-governmental international organizations involved in environmental issues, either directly or indirectly (such as Council of Europe, Arab League, International Council for Science – ICSU).

These organizations developed rapidly in the 1980s, in parallel with an increase in multilateral agreements and treaties related to the environment, and they even sometimes developed their own expertise, which risked marginalizing IUCN as an international organization. The stakes were all the higher because IUCN suffered a serious financial crisis at the end of the 1970s.

Under the leadership of Maurice Strong, chairman of the United Nations Conference On The Human Environment conference (Stockholm 1972), IUCN launched a work programme in 1976 entitled 'Conservation for Development', intended to link the IUCN's scientific expertise in conservation to the work of development aid agencies. The 'Conservation for Development Centre' (CDC) was created in 1981 and was in charge of being the link for fieldwork projects between IUCN, the principles decreed in the World Conservation Strategy (see below) and the development aid agencies. It is tempting to analyse the creation of the CDC in strategic terms (Christoffersen 1997) and to view it as a result of a desire to take a stand as a development cooperation agency on environmental matters, in order to try to bring in extra funds and set up national conservation strategies:

> In addition to the Commission's work and the central policy development work of the Secretariat, IUCN was going to develop and implement field programmes in collaboration with its members. The ambition was ultimately to build a massive global force for conservation, turning the outputs of the Commissions into action on the ground. (Michael Cockerell, first Director of the CDC, letter to M.W. Holdgate 1998)

There were two concrete effects of this reorientation (Christoffersen 1997; Holdgate 1999): the introduction of financing from bilateral development cooperation organizations that had been practically absent from the list of IUCN donors (then essentially financed by WWF and the UNEP) and greater decentralization of IUCN operations, along with the establishment of regional and local representations of the CDC. This decentralization was associated with an increase in governmental and non-governmental members from developing countries and a significant decrease in the influence of the scientific commissions. The CDC was thus seen as the lynchpin between the bilateral or multilateral development cooperation agencies (the donors), the commissions (that wanted to keep intellectual leadership over the developing of projects) and the secretariat (that makes it an additional tool for action).

Furthermore, the strong institutional link between IUCN and the secretariats of several international organizations (mainly UNEP, but also UNESCO and even FAO via the Ecosystem Conservation Group in the 1980s) is generally perceived as a privileged means of exerting direct influence on the international discussions; through putting issues on the agenda, formulating solutions through participation in the international conferences and through scientific technical cooperation with the international institutions.

For example, in the field of biodiversity, IUCN's Commission on Environmental Policy, Law and Administration (CEPLA), aided by the Environmental Law Centre (ELC), prepared successive agreement drafts between 1984 and 1989. Based on these drafts, the IUCN/WWF/WRI triumvirate participated in the August 1988 meeting of the working group, which was responsible for setting up the first meeting of the expert group (held in November 1988).

The World Conservation Strategy

The two orthodox approaches in the beginning of the 1980s at IUCN were that of protected areas and national parks, and of conservation of species (symbolized by the two flagship commissions, the SSC and the CNPPA, see above).

It was observed that there were neither substantial nor institutional links between conservation and development. This was the reason for the decision to write a document that could both give coherency to the various themes developed by IUCN and improve the impact of conservation policies in development projects (Christoffersen 1997). It was this need for coherency between the themes that meant that the preparation of the document, entrusted to Robert Prescott-Allen (scientific writer at IUCN and trained biologist) involved as much internal consultation with the various commissions, the various members, and the General Assembly, as with the external partners, particularly the two co-financers WWF and UNEP, but also UNESCO and FAO. The beginnings of collaboration were organized at the end of the 1970s with UNEP, FAO, UNESCO, and WWF among others; for IUCN the issue was to take on the *intellectual leadership* on environmental matters at the international level. Between 1977 and 1980, this document gave rise to numerous work seminars and distribution of drafts to the partner institutions (Holdgate 1999: 149–51). The result, published in 1980 as *World Conservation Strategy* (published by IUCN, WWF and UNEP) represented the first document linking human well-being to the environmentalist movement's traditional vision of the management of natural heritage (Reed 1996). In addition, it contained major principles of action for establishing national conservation strategies.

The World Conservation Strategy (WCS) led to a new notion of conservation, covering three objectives belonging to different scientific disciplines and communities that had never been associated before:

1   the upkeep of essential ecological processes and of life-maintaining systems;
2   the preservation of genetic diversity;
3   concern for the sustainable use of species and ecosystems.

Even if the wording is not the same, those three objectives appear again in the text of the Convention on Biological Diversity.

Conservation therefore went beyond the concept of wild nature, to incorporate all biological resources including forests, agriculture and fishing, for example – three biomes where human activity is central. It also includes genetic diversity, a scientific domain at the extreme opposite – and not just in terms of observation scale – of ecological science.[1] Furthermore, all trace of conservation promotion on a purely ethical or emotional basis disappeared.

By succeeding in satisfying both the conservationist community revolving around IUCN (and to a lesser degree UNESCO) and the community of developmentalists (around UNEP and FAO), IUCN succeeded in achieving international recognition, by reaching out particularly to public actors (governmental or development practitioners).

Despite the great substantial innovation of the notion of sustainable use, WCS thus remains a compromise text. As Vivien emphasizes:

> stress is put on action at the international level, and especially on international law. It is planning and regional development at the global level that are being considered with in-situ conservation areas, such as the UNESCO biosphere reservations or the IUCN protected parks or areas, and the ex-situ conservation areas, in zoos or botanical gardens. This way of thinking is found in the 'World Program in Favor of Regions Rich in Genetic Resources', which is presented in Point 17 of the WSC. (Vivien 2001)

Furthermore, we retain a functionalist approach to solving problems that are determined in substance by scientists: for example the principle of sustainable optimal yield – improving the living conditions of human communities while remaining within the limits of what the ecosystems can handle.

Evolution of the IUCN: Learning Process of the Actors and Institutional Learning Process

The evolution between 1980 and 1992 of substantial content of the various texts published by IUCN on conservation matters indicates that a certain form of accumulation of knowledge occurred.[2] In a very fluid international system undergoing rapid growth, the success of the WCS risked being only short-lived, and the designers of this text conceived it from the beginning as an evolving document to be continuously revised and improved as knowledge deepened (Holdgate 1999). It is therefore tempting, based on the findings of Ernst and

---

[1] For geneticists, a living being is the product of a natural selection in that it is programmed to be optimized for its reproduction, whereas for the biologist a living being is a coordinated group of flows of matter and energy.

[2] 'Caring for the Earth', published in 1991 by the same consortium (IUCN/UNEP/WWF) has been presented as a revision and the successor to the 'World Conservation Strategy' published in 1980.

Peter Haas (1995), to see to what extent we can qualify IUCN as an *epistemic community*.

The Learning Process of Scientific Actors

With regards to this purely strategic challenge of maintaining intellectual leadership and the significant challenge of deepening the concept of sustainable use, what collective coordination measures were devised? How did the actors who make up IUCN take new stands with regards to the change that occurred?

In terms of measures, the learning process of actors within IUCN was carried out around three elements:

1 *Increased involvement by the scientific world and emphasis on information exchange.* The objective was to increase the learning process of the scientific actors by getting more experts from other disciplines[3] to work in the commissions, through the organization of global conferences and workshops that attracted scientists, practitioners and decision-makers.

2 *Support to the UN organizations.* Creation of the 'Ecosystem Conservation Group', a multi-organization structure that facilitated the coordination of the various multilateral agencies of the United Nations and reinforced IUCN's scientific expertise and intellectual leadership.

3 *Participation in implementing development projects.* The interpretation of the creation of the Conservation for Development Centre to work with the secretariat as a simple agency intended to bring in extra funds, by focusing its action on development projects, has already been discussed. However, this institutional innovation also enabled information feedback from the field that further increased in knowledge within IUCN. CDC moved from project design (centralized at the secretariat) to on-the-ground implementation that required an on-location professional staff: decentralization with a considerably increased presence in the developing countries. National committees and regional advisory committees that include IUCN members, scientists and practitioners of the Commissions and regional representatives of the IUCN staff, were set up, giving the members the opportunity to be directly involved in the perfecting of the IUCN programme.

---

[3]   'One of the most notable features of the new programme was its emphasis on "the social sciences", including economics. If conservation policies were to work in the real world, it was clearly essential to understand the human dimension of development. The Director-General was worried about a lack of social science expertise in the secretariat, and wondered whether the Commission on Sustainable Development (as the Commission on Environmental Planning had been renamed) might provide linking philosophy' (Holdgate 1999: 204).

The IUCN scientific actors joined forces and took action from the 1980s in defining strategies for the international community of donors, with a definite emphasis on the programme and project activities related to sustainable use of biological resources.

We can thus see a use of knowledge for reinforcing in-house skills and for increasing the responsibility and will of the actors and institutions to manage, plan, conserve and use natural resources in a sustainable and equitable way. Furthermore, we can also see use of the lessons from the IUCN's fieldwork experiences to attract other experts and to extend the spectrum of knowledge.

This scientific community within IUCN goes beyond the simple context of community of experts – looking for and sharing the relationships of cause and effect – and responds to the very definition of epistemic community, through its desire to share the evaluation of probable effects of certain solutions that it has itself selected. Indeed, through the creation of the CDC, we see a veritable taking charge of the social implications of the political actions that the organization suggests. This is primordial, in that it enables validation and feedback on its own knowledge.

To sum up, IUCN moved from a coming together based on shared values (the model of a transnational interest group) to a mechanism of coordination based on the increase of knowledge, making IUCN what Ernst and Peter Haas (1995) have called an 'epistemic community'.

Institutional Learning Process

The change for IUCN from being an advisory organ for decision-makers to becoming an operational agency can be interpreted as a desire to take charge of the social consequences of what are decreed as guiding principles. In terms of the learning process of the scientific actors, this is obviously essential, but this also doubles as a learning process at the institutional level, with a return to the content of these guiding principles and objectives: As M. Holdgate notes (1999), 'as CDC evolved, it set up its own machinery for steering field projects, and separate advisory committees were appointed to guide the new theme programmes'. This change led to a reduction in the predominance of the commissions in elaborating new conservation matters in favor of other sources of knowledge – not necessarily scientific.

The increase of IUCN's participation in various levels of policy definition led to empowerment of the expertise. According to a participative model of co-regulation, IUCN evolve gradually from a network of multi-disciplinary experts who aims to increase knowledge to the development of practical solutions negotiated between stakeholders. The stress put on the learning process through the interaction of social actors enabled the creation of new collective skills that generate new forms of cooperation.

In terms of measures, this is illustrated by three elements:

1   The division for coordinating IUCN policy in biodiversity matters that organizes multi-actor forums.
2   The Global Biodiversity forum, designed as a mechanism that is continuous, independent and constructive, and that enables a broad range of interest groups to discuss biological diversity.
3   Social Policies Programme (SPP), which has a horizontal role with regards to the members and the secretariat of IUCN, for learning about the objectives of the organization via emerging themes such as social equity, demographics, co-management or relations with industry.

The Significant Innovations Enabled by this Form of Operating

The epistemic community-type mechanism of operating has enabled disciplinary decompartmentalization, which has corrected the fragmented, biocentric and often specific focus of the problems. It has enabled the emergence of innovative solutions, especially in terms of positive incitement to sustainable use, thereby furthering conservation – in direct contrast to coercive measures that were the form of traditional regulation for environmental interests.

First of all, there was been scientific evolution. On the one hand, there was the shift from a vision by species or by sector – fishing, forestry, fauna, flora – to a broader and fuller vision of biological diversity along with measures such as the incorporation of science and politics, knowledge management and dwelling conservation (ecosystem-based approach). On the other hand, there was the taking into account of the human dimension in conservation as a factor for enriching biological diversity: introducing new species, new landscapes and new agro-ecosystems.

Then, there was socio-political evolution, along with the inclusion of the human component in its socio-economic dimension. The measures for conserving biodiversity depend less on the intrinsic value of this diversity than on the costs and economic advantages of conservation compared to the minimum needs of human communities. This evolution also includes recognition of the international macro-political and macro-economic context, along with issues such as the pioneer fronts, perverse economic incentives, indebtedness of developing countries, access to land, forms of consumption, climatic change, the effects of globalization and of trade and population growth, among others. All of these factors play against sustainable and equitable use of natural resources.

This evolution is concretized in the forms of regulation proposed in the various documents published by IUCN, through:

1   setting up measures that make protected zones operations that are economically profitable for the local populations concerned and financially balanced for the states. At the local level, for example, this involves guaranteeing communities and individuals rights of access to, and use of, resources via land reforms and the establishment of property rights.

2 variation in the types of protected areas. IUCN lists at least eight:
   a) full reserve;
   b) national parks (tourism, education, research);
   c) natural monuments;
   d) planned natural reserves (human intervention required to keep the reserve going);
   e) protected landscapes (complex agro-ecosystems);
   f) reserves for restricted use (hunting, forest);
   g) anthropological reserves (area of traditional use reserved for indigenous peoples;
   h) areas of multiple use in which some resources can be subject to specific protection.
3 a bio-regional approach consisting in redefining appropriate borders of protected areas that take into account the complexity of the dynamics of the systems concerned (dynamics of landscapes, spread of agricultural land, pollution, climatic change), but that are small enough for those concerned to be able to negotiate solutions to conflicts that arise.
4 setting up national conservation strategies. These strategies initially – between the WCS in 1980 and up to the Brundtland report in 1987 – stressed above all the development of consensus between the various governmental sectors that have impact on the environment and insist on the need for better knowledge of ecological processes (education, research, training). Along with the McNeely text in 1988, taking into account the economic and institutional context of resource management came to the fore, and there was also the question of involvement by local communities. But this theme did not become central, and only acquired institutional legitimacy from 1996, when a resolution on participative management was adopted at the Montreal Congress.

Conclusion

By emphasizing the learning processes and the substantial evolutions that resulted, an interpretation of IUCN has been given in other terms than those of a strategic alliance with its donors or in terms of interest group linked to the conservationist movement. IUCN enabled a real increase of knowledge through i) the learning process of scientific actors in formulating and implementing public policies of economic and social development or ii) the institutional learning processes that made possible a return to the objectives peculiar to IUCN. This generated evolutions in understanding the complexity of biodiversity and regarding the tools required to manage it.

On the other hand, the limit can be seen to a system in which incentive measures remain functional and limited to the economic level. Natural resource users and managers are, for the first time, taken into account, but are concerned only with the application phase of the measures. The results of their own experiences and studies in the field of sustainable use do not show through IUCN operates at any time. While there has been decentralization in functional terms, there has not been any decentralization of knowledge: no opportunities for validating the knowledge and know-how of the actors concerned. Instrumental conception of knowledge is possessed by an international scientific and intellectual community made up of experts of organizations, scientists, and consultants who, at the international level, determine the subjects to cover, define the priority issues and sketch out solutions.

While IUCN did represent a framework for learning for its scientific actors at a given moment of its history, it has not changed into a framework of transformation of practices, either for its members or for those who are increasingly concerned by sustainable use but are not IUCN members, such as private businesses or indigenous and local communities.

References

Christoffersen, L.E. 1997. 'IUCN: A Bridge-builder for Nature Conservation'. In *Green Globe Yearbook 1997*. Norway: Fridtjof Nansens Insitutt.

Haas, Ernst B. and Peter M. Haas. 1995. 'Learning to Learn: Improving International Governance'. *Global Governance* 1.3: 255–85.

Holdgate, M. 1999. *The Green Web, A Union for World Conservation*. London: IUCN, Earthscan.

IUCN. 1989. *From Strategy to Action: The IUCN Response to the Report of the World Commission on Environment and Development*. IUCN, Gland, and Cambridge, UK.

IUCN/UNEP/WWF. 1980. *World Conservation Strategy*. Gland, Switzerland.

IUCN/UNEP/WWF. 1991. *Caring for the Earth, A Strategy for Sustainable Living*. Gland, Switzerland.

LePrestre, P.G., ed. *Governing Global Biodiversity*. Burlington, VT : Ashgate, 2002.

Mc Donald, K. 2002. 'IUCN: A History of Constraint'. Presentation to the Permanent workshop of the Centre for Philosophy of Law, Higher Institute for Philosophy of the Catholic University of Louvain (UCL), Louvain-la-neuve, Belgium.

Reed, D. 1996. 'Sustainable Development'. In D. Reed, ed. *Structural Adjustment, the Environment and Sustainable Development*. Washington, DC: WWF International.

Vivien, F.-D. 2001. 'Biodiversité et développement durable: retour sur la stratégie de l'IUCN'. Presentation at the PEVS/CNRS seminar, *Les ONG dans le champ de la biodiversité*. 15 November 2002, Montpellier.

Chapter 8

Emerging Corporate Actors in Environment and Trade Governance: New Vision and Challenge for Norm-setting Processes

Isabelle Biagiotti[1]

This chapter explores the changes that have come about following the emergence of corporate actors as governance actors, and their actions within the sphere of trade and environmental norms setting. It describes how corporations have adopted a new attitude based on social responsibility. It then presents the new mechanisms created to activate the contribution of private actors, which has led to a privatization of governance processes. In conclusion, it suggests new avenues to investigate further the strategies used by corporations to gain influence in international negotiations on global environmental and trade governance.

The environmental governance scene is changing rapidly and deeply, mainly as a result of the evolution of non-state actors. This change has been brought about, not by the creation of new institutions, but by the evolution of the strategies of actors towards the already-old processes of decision-making: the corporate actor enters the political arena leading other actors – NGOs and scholars, but also municipalities and regions – to adapt their strategy. There is, as a result, a quality shift in environmental governance processes, and particularly when this environment is subjected to trade. This shift has to be assessed.

The existence of non-state actors in the realm of environmental and trade governance is itself a challenge for an 'architectural' approach to governance. No architectural words – such as 'pillars', 'roof', 'floor', 'foundations' and so on – fit with the characteristics of the strategies of non-state actors in environmental governance. Lobbying is maybe the only etymological exception. Indeed, the words describing their actions are of a more informal nature – such as 'networking',

---

[1] This text has benefited from the inputs from Hélène Ilbert (Institut Agronomique Méditerranéen de Montpellier), François Lerin (Institut Agronomique Méditerranéen de Montpellier, *Courrier de la planète*), Stéphane Guéneau (Institut du développement durable et des relations internationales) and Benoît Martimort-Asso (Institut du développement durable et des relations internationales).

'influence', 'advocating' and the like. This informality is also what their efficiency relies on. They are constituencies of the environmental public policy community, as Rhodes and Marsh (1995) have described them. They share values, are stable over time, have numerous interactions and so on.

However, these common features cover a strong heterogeneity of the group of non-state actors in environmental and trade governance. They come from three main sources – civil society organizations, corporate actors and scientists – combining to form the so-called epistemic community. Until recently, these actors considered themselves opposed to each other. The scientists and the NGOs have been the first to build a common agenda on specific issues – species protection, nature conservation, pollution, climate and so on. This alliance has proved to be efficient and powerful in many cases. On the one hand, scientific works have supported political claim and action. Political demand has revealed and highlighted, on the other hand, new routes for scientific research.

Since then, corporations have begun to appear as 'full-rights' actors of environmental and trade governance. This is not to say that corporations had not influenced environmental policies before. However, what was new was the claim by corporate actors to have an active share in policy building and implementation. Part of this new trend is the corporate willingness to account for their actions and their engagement. In many cases, they thus call for NGOs to watch and assess their actions, and even to become full partners in the initiation and management of environmental corporate policies. The promise of efficiency, founded on the corporate financing and *savoir-faire* in scaling-up, has been powerful enough to bring NGOs, researchers, states and intergovernmental organizations round to this point of view.

This chapter explores the changes brought about by the emergence of corporate actors as governance actors, and their actions in trade and environmental norms setting. The first part of the paper describes how corporations have adopted a new attitude based on social responsibility. The second discusses new mechanisms so-created and leading to a privatization of governance processes. The final part suggests new routes to investigate further the strategies used by corporations to gain momentum in international negotiations on global environmental and trade governance.

From Private Interest to Global Social Responsibility

The 2002 Johannesburg Summit, designed to build a sustainable development agenda for the twenty-first century, has endorsed a long-lasting trend in environment and trade governance, that is, the emerging of corporate actors as plain stakeholder and contributor in negotiation, norm-setting and implementation of governance instruments. Corporate strategies to enter the public environment and trade arenas reveal a shift of paradigm.

For years, corporations have pleaded for the state and public actors to stay out of their production, investment and location policies. Environmental and social concerns would be best pursued, they claimed, if the public authorities let them set their own objectives, and their own ways to achieve them. This demand has accompanied a posture of covert lobbying and discrete interactions with other actors – state, NGOs, research, municipalities and so on. What can be seen currently is different: corporations no longer go to environmental or social fora as 'observers', but as actors; presenting projects, building alliances with other groups, making claims for transparency, accountability and equity. What are the forces and rationales at stake behind this new posture?

Making Private Goods a Matter of Public Interest

Firms have for decades repeatedly been accused of privatizing the tools of local, national and international governance. In this very common view, they are presented as being driven by pure market forces, pursuing their best interests regardless of borders, long-term development or environmental impacts (Ohmae 1990; Reich 1993). They are presented as the main promoters of an unregulated liberal globalization. Their influence has then been linked with their action in a public arena determined by governmental negotiations, scientific expertise and public pressure. Corporate actors have thus tried these different elements of the definition of public policies and influenced them in their own favour.

It is also assumed (and often verified) that corporations have constantly been lobbying for national and international legislation favouring their interests. This behaviour has been described as the most-often achieved form of their influence (Gill 1999; Underhill 2000), and has been extensively documented. At the global level, Sell and May have, for instance, demonstrated how a cluster of twelve US private firms operating in the pharmaceutical, computer or entertainment industries has largely contributed to defining the content of what is now known as the Trade Related Intellectual Property Rights (TRIPs) agreement in the World Trade Organization (WTO) (Sell and May 2001). These twelve corporations have been able to convince the US government that they were really endangered by the existent patent patterns. Their representatives have been enrolled in the US negotiation team for the Uruguay round. The twenty-year monopoly given to the landlord of any intellectual discovery (including medicines) has been evaluated as the most pro-corporation ruling ever given by international law.[2]

Corporate actors entered into university administrations long ago, and contracted with research institutions in order to redirect public research to profit-oriented paths or to limit the economic impact of developing norms. Olivier Godard (2004) has documented a number of cases when economic actors have

---

[2]   This result was later moderated by the Doha Agreement in November 2001 and the official recognition of the State right to issue compulsory licences, in order to produce and distribute needed medicines to their population, in spite of patent rights.

had a significant impact on the hypothesis and directions of research. The most dramatic example is the changing position of the firm Dupont de Nemours, with reference to chlorofluorocarbon (CFC) gases. In the 1970s, the Dupont de Nemours funded research aimed at proving the harmlessness of the CFCs. In the 1980s, in the meantime having developed a substitute for CFCs, Dupont de Nemours has joined forces with environmentalist groups to press for the signing of the Montreal Treaty, in order to enjoy the competitive advantage that its innovation would guarantee to the firm. This shows the long-term and ambiguous interaction between corporate interest, expertise and governance.

This behaviour has attracted a great deal of criticism, particularly from NGOs. Major environmental catastrophes (Bhopal, Exxon-Valdès ...), growing de-localizations of production together with reports of child labour, bad working conditions and bans on unions have fuelled an image of corporate irresponsibility and opportunistic exploitation of resources and labour. The Permanent Peoples' Tribunal (PPT)[3] sat in judgement cases such as the Amazon or the Bhopal catastrophes. The role of transnational corporations in the disruption of democratic regimes like Chile in 1972 has also been emphasized (Rigeaux 2002: 138). The economic performance of companies such as Nike or Shell has been jeopardized by NGOs campaigns, documenting for the former the low wages of their workers and for the latter their abuse of human rights in Nigeria (Van den Hove 2003: 65). And this image has grown powerful enough to become costly. In the last ten years, more and more corporations have taken a stance on their commitment in favour of the environment and sustainable development. But the greening of the corporate actors has been marred by their refusal to accept any process of genuine accountability. They have been repeatedly – and still are – accused of 'greenwashing' their activities through a change of discourse instead of a change of practice (Bruno and Karliner 2002). If it seems difficult to totally discard these accusations, it is worth emphasizing that things may have recently changed in this area, with the development of discourse and the practice of Global Social Responsibility.

Corporate actors today seem ready to accept more transparency. This is mainly the doing of large multinational firms able to set up philanthropic foundations, and projects like the Bill and Melinda Gates Foundation providing money for the Global Fund for Children's vaccines, or French company Suez financing the

---

[3]   The Permanent Peoples' Tribunal grew out of the Bertrand Russell War Crimes Tribunal and the anti-imperialist movement that produced the Algiers Declaration on the Rights of Peoples, 1976. Supported by the Italian foundation Lelio Besso for the Rights and the Freedom of Peoples, the Tribunal has ruled: (1) on the wrongs resulting from industrial hazards (1994); (2) on the Chernobyl nuclear 'accident' (1996); (3) on the violations committed by the international garment industries (1998); (4) on the crimes committed by the French oil and energy corporation Elf-Aquitaine in collusion with the French state in the former territories of French colonial rule (1999); and (5) on Global Corporation and Human Wrongs. Rulings can be found at: <www.grisnet.it/filb/sentenze%20_fre.html>.

UNESCO Water Research Project and so on, and the shift is still in its infancy. But the capacity of transnationals to contribute to the financing and scaling-up of large social and environmental projects such as access to water, sanitation, protection of coastal areas, endangered species and other priorities on the environmental agenda is so great that the question should not be considered as marginal too quickly.

A corpus of definitions and behaviours is now known as Corporate Social Responsibility (CSR). Spread by corporate organizations such as the World Business Council for Sustainable Development,[4] CSR is expected to contribute to sustainable development at local, national and now global level.[5] It is worth remembering here that one of the purposes of the Davos World Economic Forum is 'the reintroduction of the notion of social responsibility in the corporate world' (Klaus Schwab in Balanya et al. 2000: 19).

First Attempts at Institutionalization

State actors – that is, governments and intergovernmental organizations – have a clear responsibility in the emergence of corporations as full-rights actors. They have not only mainly accepted the corporate claim to economic independence for decades, but they have also encouraged corporations to enter and to replace state agencies in an increasing number of domains, including environmental protection and development, which is traditionally an area of public responsibility. This positive pressure can be partly explained by the participation mantra that has spread in the governance realm for almost twenty years (see first chapter of this book). It is emphatically stated that no governance can be achieved without the participation of actors concerned at all stages in the decision-making process – definition of the question, of the ways of action and of the assessment procedures. This doctrine has enabled trade unions, then NGOs, to enter the governance fora as experts, undertakers and assessors of environmental policies. These fora are now opening to the participation of corporate actors, reflecting once more the dynamics already in use at local and national levels. The partial renouncement of state actors can also be explained by the fact that they are increasingly aware of their own limits (including budgetary constraints) and are looking for fresh alternatives to provide public goods.

---

[4]   The World Business Council for Sustainable Development convenes some 170 companies around the world with the commitment to work and promote what they understand as the three pillars of sustainable development namely economic growth, environmental balance and social progress. See <www.wbcsd.ch/>.

[5]   Authors (Caroll, Lantos, Van den Hove) enumerate four components of CSR: economic, judicial, ethical and philanthropic responsibility. If these four components are more or less present in most of the countries where the corporate has its activity, the judicial component is clearly the weaker at the global level.

Corporate participation to the global agenda has been recognized at the highest level. The UN Secretary-General, Kofi Annan, asked corporations in July 2000 to join the UN initiative Global Compact – an informal group of multinationals, NGOs and trade unions. The idea presented in 1999 at the Davos World Economic Forum was to encourage corporations to accept and respect nine UN principles[6] in their business strategies, in exchange for a UN label. The objective was 'to anchor the global market in a shared-values network' (Annan 1999: 4). Kofi Annan's proposal documents the fact that the UN is constantly lacking resources and authority to implement the international legal corpus. Since its inception, the UN has suffered from erratic financing by member states, and is therefore calling for the voluntary assistance of corporations in the implementation of the social, economic and environmental rights that appears to be recognized by the international community of states as a functional option.

The Global Compact is based on four instruments: learning fora, a multistakeholder dialogue, projects for developing the Global Compact principles and communication tools.[7] When a firm has endorsed the nine principles of the Global Compact, it must report every year on its action in these domains and post its result on the Global Compact website. The initiative, like several other UN tools promoting human rights, relies on image and fame (Ruggie 2000). NGOs and trade unions that have been invited into dialogue with corporations in this forum have already expressed doubts about the efficiency of the project. They are afraid of being used to legitimate global corporate policies. Others are using the Global Compact Principles as a legal reference to judge corporate actions. Corporate Watch, for example, has launched a campaign against the World Business Council for not respecting principles 8 and 9 of the Global Compact – namely 'adopting a precautionary approach towards environmental challenges' and 'promoting a better social responsibility (Biagiotti 2001).[8]

The Global Compact initiative is certainly too recent to be assessed fairly. It is particularly difficult to forecast what it can achieve in the area of global

---

[6]   These nine principles are derived from: The Universal Declaration of Human Rights, The International Labour Organization's Declaration on Fundamental Principles and Rights at Work and The Rio Declaration on Environment and Development.

The principles are as follows: (1) businesses should support and respect the protection of internationally proclaimed human rights; and (2) make sure that they are not complicit in human rights abuses. (3) Businesses should uphold the freedom of association and the effective recognition of the right to collective bargaining; (4) the elimination of all forms of forced and compulsory labour; (5) the effective abolition of child labour; and (6) the elimination of discrimination in respect of employment and occupation. (7) Businesses should support a precautionary approach to environmental challenges; (8) undertake initiatives to promote greater environmental responsibility; and (9) encourage the development and diffusion of environmentally friendly technologies.

[7]   The main window to Global Compact is a website where tools, principles, references and some results reports are available. It can be found at <www.unglobalcompact.org>.

[8]   <www.corporatewatch.org>.

corporate responsibility. Social learning and transparency have already proved to be more complicated than expected. But, at the same time, the Global Compact constitutes a forum of promotion of social and environmental values that are scarcely promoted in a world liberal economy (Utting 2003). Meanwhile, the more interesting, challenging attempts to organize interactions between corporations, NGOs, international organizations and states are much less institutionalized.

Rise of Partnerships

The hundreds of public-private partnerships (PPP) signed on the occasion of the Johannesburg Summit are testament to the openness of state actors to accept corporate contribution,[9] as well as to the pressure from transnational firms to enter the scene.[10] They are presented by the UN as a positive outcome of Johannesburg and a contribution to the implementation of Agenda 21 and the Johannesburg Plan of Implementation (UN General Assembly December 2003, Resolution 58/129). Among the many impressive examples that could be cited is the UNESCO–SUEZ Partnership on Water.[11] Signed for five years, bringing a $12 billion-a-year budget to the less market-oriented UN agency, this contract shows more than words what is at stake: on the public actor's side, the incentive comes from decreasing public financing and the need for new means of action. On the corporate side, it is fuelled by the need for recognition and increased legitimacy.[12] But this trend did not start at the Johannesburg Summit. In the last decade, there have been several interesting partnerships for public common goods, particularly in the health sector. Several immunization campaigns and AIDS prevention programmes could only have been initiated because of the constitution of funds supported by multinationals. Examples include the Global Alliance for TB Drug Development financing immunization against tuberculosis,

---

[9] A list of major PPPs – starting well before Johannesburg – can be found at <www.transnationale.org/transnationale/information/ppp.htm>.
More than 250 projects of partnership have been submitted to the World Summit on Sustainable Development. Their list can be found at: <www.un.org/esa/sustdev/partnerships/list_partnerships.htm>.

[10] In advance of the Johannesburg Summit, the World Business Council and the International Chamber of Commerce joined to form the Business Action for Sustainable Development (BASD). The claim of this lobby has been clear: 'business is part of the solution' (BASD 2001).

[11] The terms of the contract can be found at <www.unesco.org/water/news/agreement_141002.shtml>.

[12] It is here worth comparing this need to the results of the 2001 Edelman PR Worldwide study on NGOs influence on the behalf of the Global Compact. This study shows clearly that citizens around the world have no confidence in corporate actors and that large firms encounter increasing difficulties in creating direct links with consumers. This assessment, among other converging assessments, explains why new corporate firms have resolved to take a stance on global governance.

or the International AIDS Vaccine Initiative and the Malaria Vaccine Initiative supporting research into new vaccines. These PPPs are clearly considered as a serious way of promoting the global public good constituted by health (Arhin-Tenkorang and Conçeicao 2003).

In the corporate world there is a real potential for financing public goods, and some already worry that it may encourage the UN to overvalue the relationships with business and to pay less attention to other non-state actors, namely the NGOs (Utting 2002). The relationships between NGOs and corporations are not new: there have been privately funded citizen actions for centuries (Charnovitz 1997; Scholte 1999). Partnerships have emerged in different environmental domains in recent years: Greenpeace has labelled the Schlumberger fridge, WWF has agreed to assess several corporate environmental policies – such as that of Lafarge in France. It seems that room for PPPs does to exist, but who will ensure that these partnerships will effectively serve to promote global public goods?[13] Many NGOs, on the contrary, express their fear of seeing partnerships been 'used' by developed countries as substitutes for formal commitments on their part to improve the current abject situation in both environment and development spheres. These so-called 'partnerships' and private-sector projects are also likely to be driven by private corporations' drive for profits rather than by the goal of meeting public interests (Tan 2002). Just before the Johannesburg Summit, Corporate Watch launched a campaign to free the UN from transnational influences.[14] So far, no solution has been found other than the proposal that the negotiation capacity of each partner should act as a counterweight.

Today's innovation is fuelled by the exponentially growing number of partnerships merging NGOs and corporations, sometimes with the participation of states, municipalities or universities. This trend divides the NGOs into two groups: those who accept and follow the corporate proposal as a realistic answer to the difficult problem of financing, and those who refuse it because of the risk of compromising. Both will have to adapt their strategies. The former will have to learn to work with corporations, to set limits to keep their autonomy, to lobby them (not exactly the same as denouncing them), to lean on their orientations. This is a lot of work, and difficulties can already be anticipated. The latter group will also have to learn to consider corporations as actors. Denunciation and opposition can only be their strategies if they have the materials to fuel them.

---

[13] Global public goods have been central in the international political debate on cooperation as a powerful rational to raise governments' compliance to finance development. This debate has been institutionalized by the UNDP, which has supported research and publications on the subject, illustrated by the books edited by Inge Kaul's team – *Global Public Goods: International Cooperation in the 21st Century* and *Providing Global Public Goods: Managing Globalization* <www.undp.org/globalpublicgoods/globalization>.

[14] <www.corpwatch.org>.

Therefore, there is a lot of investigation work to do on strategies in progress – by nature difficult to assess.

Privatization of Norms

Parallel to this merging of interests and practice, there is also an increase in private norms, especially in the environmental domain. Each is specific to an activity and created by an *ad hoc* group of actors, from NGOs to corporations, including municipalities and regional actors. Most of them result from a compromise between different interests – the protection of forest and the research for profit for instance – and are implemented and assessed by the actors themselves, or by organizations recognized by all parties. The certification of forest exploitation by the Forest Stewardship Council is perhaps one of the most successful private management systems of a natural resource, merging NGOs and corporations. More recently, a partnership has been created between the World Business Council for Sustainable Development (WBCSD) and Greenpeace, on greenhouse gas emissions. These examples give evidence of very active alternative norm-setting processes geared by corporate and citizen actors. They culminated in Johannesburg with the demonstration of hundreds of 'Type II Partnerships', grouping NGOs, states, corporations, municipalities, research centres and so on, under all possible layouts. Each of them may fuel the creation of private norms, while the states have encountered severe difficulties in endorsing a common framework for all these initiatives. Some social or environmental agreements convene corporations and local public actors – municipalities, regions and so on, and may relate to an ecological label for forest exploitation or an agreement for benefit-sharing for the use of phyto-genetic resources. Few of these contracts are transparent; it is most likely that the negotiations are secret, and the rules of assessment and benefit-sharing unknown. If reports are made, they are not distributed. But here again, soft law[15] is created. The Merck-INBio agreement, bringing together one of the biggest pharmaceutical corporations, Merck, and a Costa-Rican research institute on biodiversity (INBio), was signed in 1991. It has quickly become a model for bio-prospecting contracting between biotech corporations and governments. Ten years later, it is still the exception to the rule in Central America (Majano 2003).

Another emerging trend is the direct negotiation of bio-prospection rights between corporate firms and local authorities outside of the mediation of national states. Already present in Amazonia, Biodivalor, created by the NGO Pro-Natura, and financed partly by the French Foreign Affairs Ministry, is directly contracting with municipalities for prospecting rights in Central Africa's genetically rich forests, access to local traditional knowledge connected with forest plants and benefit-sharing. Most of the time, municipalities are negotiating alone, without

---

[15] 'Soft law' is the law created by contracts, as opposed to 'hard law', which is created by legislation.

support from the national administration, without information on already signed contracts and the like. As a result, all studies that have been conducted so far have identified user measures as a 'key capacity-building need' (Tobin and Zakri 2003: 3). The same authors conclude that the construction of an international regime on the use and benefit sharing of genetic resources is necessary.

These norms clearly respond to a social demand for regulation, but their impact and their legitimacy are different from those of universal public norms that have been the mark of the emerging environmental governance system in the second half of the twentieth century.[16] If this process has first been guided and controlled by states and intergovernmental actors, it is increasingly marked by the intervention of non-state actors. This trend reveals two kinds of problem: the legitimacy of these norms created and implemented by private actors, and their articulation with the national and international norms created and implemented by public actors.

Compliance to the Law

Creation of partnerships, of funds and of environmental initiative has successfully raised the support of public authorities, particularly when they appear to fill a gap in environmental or social law. They are always tolerated. This clearly shows that public authorities consider voluntary regulation as the best instrument to induce the corporations to adopt cooperative behaviour. It also shows that they do not feel legitimate enough to make legislation on corporation policies (Laville 2002). Moreover, the global trend towards liberalization and protection of private investments gives less and less room for individual states to rule corporate behaviours.

The question, therefore, is to understand under what conditions private norms may constitute the basis for the development of universal public norms and enter the international public law. Here again the question is less one of architectural choices than of actor strategies. Such a step implies, on the one hand, the recognition of the soft law by the only legitimate international actors to date – the states. It seems very doubtful that state actors will give away what remains as their main source of power easily (Biagiotti 2003). On the other hand, it is unclear whether the corporate actors are really committed to the building of constraining universal norms. Their participation in the constitution of private norms seems on the contrary to indicate their preference to an *ad hoc* regulation

---

16   The different public norm-setters in the environmental realm, according to Charnovitz (2002), include: the UNEP, more than 200 Multilateral Environmental Agreements, the World Meteorological Organisation, the Global Environment Facility (GEF), the pollution control programmes of the World Sea Organisation, the International Tropical Timber Organisation, the UN Forest Forum, the forest and fishing programmes of the FAO, the Intergovernmental Panel on Climate Change and the Intergovernmental Oceanographic Commission.

of their activities. Bruno and Karliner (2002: 9) go as far as suggesting that the corporate stance for partnership 'revolves around avoiding new regulations and promoting voluntary measures and self-regulation'.

Another set of questions deals with the articulation between private and public norms. Partnership agreements are often activity-oriented, and more and more often limited territorially – a region, municipalities and so on. No one knows exactly which laws may apply on this kind of contract. Should they comply with national laws? Should they observe international norms – for example, the WTO rules? Which court or forum may be referred to when there is a conflict? Thus, the proliferation of norms blurs the authority of traditional powers and adds to the confusion of local actors – which is commonly held as contrary to 'good governance'.

There is an underlying assumption under the *laissez-faire* attitude surrounding partnerships and private initiatives. It is as if states are assuming that, by working with other actors, corporations are going to adopt different behaviours. But what has been learnt at the global level about the process enabling social learning to occur is that a certain amount of constraint is necessary in order for all the actors to acquire a common language and common view of the objectives (Utting 2003). There is a strong need for long-term discussion and guidance forums, for places to share and learn from first initiatives taken, and it is not sure that the Global Compact will be able to assume this role.

In conclusion, it is difficult to regret the opening-up of environmental regulation to corporations. The governance of environment, in term of representation and efficiency, should be ameliorated by their participation. Questions arise when one wonders about the effectiveness of corporate participation in the formulation of norms or about its willingness to comply with these norms. In other words, the question is to assess what kind of rationality will guide corporate actors in this arena. Will they accept a real partnership with other actors, will they enter efficient and public-good oriented policy network or will they – as their opponent think they will – pursue only their own interests, accepting public debate only to further direct it?

Thus, the future of environmental governance is less a question of architecture than one of the capacity of other actors (states, NGO, scholars, municipalities ...) to make the new entrants accept common rules of negotiation and behaviour. No one can assume that this acceptance will be easily given. Growing instability in the discussion should be expected, because every actor will need to adapt the others. The explosion of traditional grouping in relation to the question of corporate participation in global governance can already be seen.

Underlying Motives of Corporate Actions

There are clearly quality changes in environmental governance processes. Noticing this trend encourages a focus on actors' representation and strategy.

NGOs and states are now traditional study objects for researchers. Business is less studied by researchers, particularly by scholars interested by environmental governance. This should change with the growing participation of businesses in governance processes.

In the same way, it is important to assess the recombination of the other major Non-state group – that is, NGOs – in response to this change. Lastly, since we expect the governance system to enter an area of instability with the participation of corporate actors, we should research the conditions for a new equilibrium.

The Motivation of Firms

The potential involvement of corporate actors in the environmental governance scene clearly demonstrates their will to participate in the setting of the rules. This position can not be understood without taking into account the growing pressures on their economic results and public relations. Increasingly, transnational corporations cannot hope to keep their hegemonic position unless they build themselves a 'citizen image', created out of social and environmental responsibility. Whatever the base rationale of this change may be, it raises at least three types of questioning.

The first set of questions is directed at corporate motivation: why are corporations collectively accepting transparency and responsibility now? We have already suggested that they may have responded to several types of pressure (Flaherty and Rappaport 1999), but this has to be verified through qualitative inquiries. But why are some multinationals not joining this movement? Do they have different strategies to escape pressures? Are these pressures only oriented toward a defined type of corporation? Is it possible that this trend will grow further, and begin to affect small businesses or enterprises in developing countries? If not, will this barrier not limit the potential of change of corporate participation by itself? Some observers insist on the marketing component of the current business commitment to environment. For them (Flaherty and Rappaport 1999; Utting 2000 2003), corporations are positioning themselves to take advantage of growing markets for environmental goods and services in both industrialized and developing countries. This assumption is another avenue for corporate-oriented research.

The second line of inquiry on the link between firms and trade and environmental governance is concerned with understanding how far corporations will be prepared to participate. Will they go as far as accepting restricting rules and, even, respecting them? If they will, what kind of social control will they endure? The first hints given in Johannesburg express their continuous rejection of legally binding norms, in favour of self-expressed ethics and practical projects. In the same vein, corporations always appear keen to choose the assessors of their actions themselves, preferring to contract with human rights and environmental NGOs, rather than with states or public authorities.

The third line of questioning is the scope of change to be expected from the emergence of corporate actors in public environmental arenas. So far, very little progress has been made in term of adopting ecologically and socially sustainable production processes. The most successful attempt was proposed in Sweden, by Natural Step,[17] but remains an isolated case. Qualitative studies may thus try to assess whether corporate managers have – or have not – changed their perception in their role when they choose cooperative governance.

Recombination of Civil Society

There have always been two kinds of NGOs' demand, supported by different organizations. Some organizations have asked for more protection of the environment, in its plainer sense. Others have pressed for more regulation between the environment and other interests – mainly trade and corporate interests. An alternative, and minority, view has linked the protection of the environment with the promotion of human beings. Doing so has clearly set them on the path to of sustainable development. In the new context described above, the challenge for NGOs in terms of governance is clearly to ask for – maybe to provide – regulation between public and private interests in environmental governance.

Another challenge would be to keep their role of advocacy for the less listened-to, who in this case are the actors – non-governmental as well as governmental – from the South. The debate on environmental governance is too-often reduced to Northern priorities (Scholte 2002). In the context of a rising participation of corporate actors to environmental policies worldwide, they will also have to make sure the issue is well addressed. There is a need for information and experience sharing in every aspect of cooperation with corporate actors.

Here there is clearly dimension for a renewed active role for the NGOs. This recombination in itself is of interest for scholars. There is a lot of investigation to do on the processes of contracting between corporations and NGOs, or between corporations and state actors, or between corporations, NGOs and state actors. There is also a large field of work on the impacts of the projects initiated under this structure. Thus, there is also the theme of corporate rationale to explore. The size of the potential market for sustainable development may be a part of the explanation of the corporate commitment. But this has to be verified and discussed.

Towards a New Equilibrium?

The emergence of a new simple actor in public international environmental fora, plus the increase in private norm-setting processes, thus form the new striking

---

[17]   Natural Step has since developed similar programmes in other countries. More information can be found at <www.naturalstep.org>.

features of global environmental and trade governance. This will clearly force changes in traditional governance processes.

One way to start to assess these changes is to look for the impacts on actors and on their legitimacy. One common fear after Johannesburg was seeing the corporations becoming such central actors that other non-state actors, and even state actors, might loose their legitimacy and their leverage (Utting 2002). It therefore seems necessary to explore the new equilibrium of power that will come out of partnerships. How will the agendas of partners change? Whose values will be better listened to? How will the new partnerships affect the capacity of different actors to influence decision-making processes?

A second strand of research should assess the impact of this change on the hierarchy of norms. All observers insist on the need for universal frameworks that guide all initiatives, partnerships and codes of conduct. The idea is to make businesses comply, not only with national and international law, or with their own norms and standards, but also with those determined to a large extent by civil-society organizations (Murphy and Bendell 1999). This assumption comes with a number of questions: Will private norms become increasingly recognized? What guarantees of independent verification can be given? Will they enter the public norm hierarchy? If they do, under what conditions? Will they prevent the formulation of new public norms? Will they, on the contrary, under the pressures exerted by other actors, introduce references to universal standards such as Agenda 21 or the International Labour Organization (ILO) and Human Rights Conventions?

The last set of questions concerns the impact of institutional architecture on global environmental governance. The qualitative changes in processes may add weight to the institutional forums. Some observers consider the Global Compact as such a new forum, dedicated to the expression of business (Utting 2002). They also plead for its reform in order to allow effective NGO participation. The rise of a new non-state actor may thus be conducive to the emergence of new fora better adapted for the participation of corporate and non-state actors. Such a change can only be imagined with the consent of state actors. Will they initiate such a change? Will such a forum be, by nature, unbalanced? What would be the conditions for equilibrium?

In the guise of a conclusion, should not current research in environmental and trade governance take these changes more into account? In addition to the important question of the architecture of governance, this should lead the setting of such an architecture (WTO/ Multilateral Environmental Agreements, relations, the creation of a World Environmental Organization and so on) and the study of the articulation of the different levels of trade and environment governance.

References

Annan, Kofi. 1999. 'Secretary General Proposes Global Compact on Human Rights, Labour, Environment in Address to World Economic Forum in Davos'. UN Press Release SG/SM/6881.

Arhin-Tenkorang, Dyna and Pedro Conçeicao. 2002. 'Beyond Communicable Disease Control: Health in the Age of Globalization'. In Inge Kaul, Pedro Conceiçao, Katell Le Goulven, Ronald U. Mendoza, eds. *Providing Global Public Goods. Managing Globalization.* UNDP, Oxford: Oxford University Press.

Balanya, Belen, Ann Doherty, Olivier Hoedeman, Adam Ma'anit and Erik Wesselius. 2000. *Europe Inc. Regional and Global Restructuring and the Rise of Corporate Power.* Pluto: London.

Biagiotti, Isabelle. 2001. 'Le Global Compact'. *Le Courrier de la planète* Société civile mondiale: la montée en puissance. 63.

―――. 2003. 'Gouvernance mondiale: discours, acteurs et processus de négociation – l'exemple du protocole de biosécurité'. *Cahier du Gemdev* 29. 'Développement durable: quelles dynamiques?'. Paris (October): 45–60.

Bruno, Kenny and Karliner, Joshua. 2002. *Greenwash+10. The UN's Global Compact, Corporate Accountability and the Earth Johannesburg Summit.* San Francisco: Corporate Watch.

Business Action for Sustainable Development. 2001. 'What is BASD?' <www.basdaction. net/about/index.html>.

Charnovitz, Steve. 1997. 'Two Centuries of Participation: NGOs and International Governance'. *Michigan Journal of International Law* 18: 183–286.

―――. 2002. 'A World Environment Organisation'. *Columbia Journal of Environmental Law* 27.2: 101–40.

Edelman PR Worldwide. 2001. *Annual Trust Barometer.* Annual versions are online at <www.edelman.com/events/Trust/startwm.html>.

Flaherty, M and D. Rappaport. 1999. 'Corporate Environmentalism: From Rhetoric to Result's. Mimeo. Geneva: UNRISD.

Gill, S. 1999. 'La Nouvelle Constitution Libérale'. *Economie Politique* 2.

Godard, Olivier. 2004. 'A la recherche de la précaution'. *Courrier de la planète* 71: 54–60.

Kaul, Inge, Pedro Conceiçao, Katell Le Goulven, and Ronald U. Mendoza, eds. 2002. *Providing Global Public Goods. Managing Globalization.* UNDP, Oxford: Oxford University Press.

Kaul Inge, Isabella Grunberg and Marc A. Stern, eds. 1999. *Global Public Goods. International Cooperation in the Twenty-first Century.* New York: Oxford University Press.

Laville, Elisabeth. 2002. 'Entreprises: l'apprentissage permanent'. *Le Courrier de la planète* 68: 61–63.

Majano, Ana Maria. 2003. 'The Role of the Private Sector in Capacity Building for Environmental and Biodiversity Management: Lessons from Central America'. Paper prepared for the Norway/UN Conference on Technology Transfer and Capacity Building, Trondheim Conferences on Biodiversity, 23–27 June.

Murphy, D. and J. Bendell. 1999. 'Partners in Time? Business, NGOs and Sustainable Development'. Discussion Paper 109. UNRISD, Geneva.

Ohmae, K. 1990. *The Borderless World: Power and Strategy in the Interlinked Economy*. London: Fontana.

Reich, R. 1993. *L'économie mondialisée*. Paris: Dunod.

Rhodes, R.-A.-W. and D. Marsh. 1995. 'Les réseaux d'action publique en Grande Bretagne'. In P. Le Galès and M. Thatcher, *Les réseaux de politique publique. Débat autour des policy networks*. Paris: L'Harmattan.

Rigaux, François. 2002. 'Towards an International Criminal Tribunal to Adjudicate upon Corporate Wrongs'. *Transnational Associations/Associations transational* 2: 128–42.

Ruggie, John G. 2000. 'Globalisation, the Global Compact and Corporate Social Responsibility'. *Union of International Association* 52.6: 291–94.

Scholte, Jan Aart. 2000. *Globalization: A Critical Introduction*. New York: St Martin Press.

———. 2002. 'Société civile et gouvernance mondiale'. In Pierre Jacquet, Jean Pisani-Ferry and Laurence Tubiana, *Gouvernance mondiale*, Rapport au Conseil d'Analyse Economique. Paris: La documentation française: 211–32.

Sell S.K. and C. May. 2001. 'Moment in Law: Contestation and Settlement in the History of Intellectual Property'. *Review of International Political Economy* 10.

Tan, Celine. 2002. *Why Trade and Finance Groups should get involved in the World Summit Process?* Malaysia: Third World Network.

Tobin, Brendan and A.H. Zakri. 2003. 'Benefit Sharing – a Cooperative Enterprise between Providers and Users of Genetic Resources'. Paper prepared for the Norway/UN Conference on Technology Transfer and Capacity Building, Trondheim Conferences on Biodiversity, 23–27 June.

Underhill, G.D.R. 2000. ‚The Public Good versus Private Interest in the Global Monatory and Financial System'. *International and Comparative Corporate Law Journal* 2.3: 335–59.

United Nations General Assembly. 2003. Resolution 58/129. December.

Utting, Peter. 2000. 'Business Responsibility for Sustainable Development'. UNRISD Occasional Paper 2. Geneva: UNRISD.

———. 2002. 'The Global Compact and Civil Society: Averting a Collision Course'. *Development in Practice* 12.5.

———. 2003. 'The Global Compact: Why All the Fuss?' *UN Chronicle* 1.

Van den Hove, Sybille. 2003. 'Approches institutionnelles de la responsabilité sociale des entreprises'. *Cahier du Gemdev*, 29. 'Développement durable: quelles dynamiques?': 63–81.

Chapter 9

Transparency and Participation of Civil Society in International Institutions Related to Biotechnology

Jona Razzaque[1]

Introduction

The advent of biotechnology has provoked a wide array of reactions ranging from optimism to profound scepticism. Despite an enthusiastic reception from some in the USA and elsewhere, biotechnology has encountered significant resistance in many parts of the world. In particular, biotechnology has raised concerns about the impact of the introduction of genetically modified organisms (GMOs) on human health and the environment. In addition to the scientific controversy relating to the assessment of potential risks of consumption of GMO products or the introduction of GMOs into the environment, there are also societal controversies causing some civil society groups – including public interest non-governmental organizations (NGOs) (such as environmental groups and consumer associations) and trade associations – to mobilize either against or in favour of GMOs. There is also an economic risk associated with biotech firms that might exploit their monopoly advantage in the market, and appropriate genes and genetic diversity for their own benefit. The participation of civil society could help decision-makers responsible for regulating biotechnology to better understand the diverse concerns of the community and to formulate policies reflecting the needs of society. Decision-making processes responsive to public demands for transparency are likely to lead to more credible and legitimate results. Civil society can contribute essential information or insights, and civil society participation can build public confidence in decisions related to biotechnology and biotech products. However, with relatively little capacity for preparation and participation in these

[1]   This chapter is part of FIELD's research project on 'Transparency and participation of developing countries and civil society in the international institutions', funded by the United Nations University. Earlier drafts of this chapter received comments from Ruth Mackenzie, Alice Palmer, Maria Vardeva and Sophie Thoyer. The chapter is up to date as of August 2004.

processes, some sections of civil society can find their interests affected by rules adopted through processes in which they have played little or no part.

The move of GMOs from the laboratory to the market has accelerated the need for better regulation. There has been growing activity in the area of international policy making on modern biotechnology. New instruments have been developed, and existing organizations have turned their attention to the development of rules and standards to regulate GMOs. The result is a complex framework of relevant international regulations, many of which are still under development. While the primary focus and objective of the instruments administered by these institutions differ, each represents an effort towards international harmonization of standards and procedures related to bio-safety. Discussion in this chapter will show that rules or standards promulgated in one forum could affect the content of rules in another.

This chapter aims to explore the level of participation of civil society, identify commonalities and assess transparency in the decision-making processes in three international institutions related to biotechnology: the bodies constituted under the Cartagena Protocol on Bio-Safety (the Bio-Safety Protocol); the Codex Alimentarius (Codex); and the World Trade Organization (WTO). Within the context of these institutions, this paper examines three issues: the normative structure for accommodating participation and inputs from civil society; transparency in the decision-making processes; and the role civil society plays in decision-making and regime formation.

The term 'civil society' includes individuals and organizations in a society that are independent of the government (defined by Webster's *New Millennium Dictionary of English* as public interest groups, professional associations, trades unions, business associations). However, there is a lack of a common definition of 'civil society'. Similarly, a definition of NGOs might include public interest groups and private sectors that are not formed or controlled by the government (Holloway 1997). In the absence of any common definition, the term 'civil society', for the purpose of this paper, will include private sectors (e.g. industry groups, business associations, trade unions) and NGOs (i.e. public interest groups such as environmental groups and consumer associations).

Cartagena Protocol on Bio-Safety

The Bio-Safety Protocol, a legally binding instrument, seeks to protect biological diversity from the potential risks posed by living modified organisms resulting from modern biotechnology (LMOs) and issues related to the impact of LMOs on the environment and human health (Article 1). The Protocol was negotiated under the 1992 Convention on Biological Diversity (CBD) and entered into force in 2003. The governing body of the Bio-Safety Protocol is the Conference of the Parties (COP) serving as the Meeting of the Parties to this Protocol (COP/MOP) (Article 29). The COP/MOP promotes effective implementation of the Protocol, seeking cooperation and information from competent international organizations and intergovernmental and non-governmental bodies (Article 29 (4) (c)). The COP developed an open-ended *ad hoc* working group on bio-safety (BSWG) to draft a Protocol on bio-safety (Decision II/5), which completed its work in 1998. BSWG, during its six meetings, convened several contact groups to consider definitions of key terms and produce a consolidated draft text for negotiations of a Protocol. The COP also established an Open-ended *Ad Hoc* Intergovernmental Committee for the Cartagena Protocol on Biosafety (ICCP). Its mandate was to undertake, with the support of the CBD Executive Secretary, the preparations necessary for the first meeting of the Parties to the Protocol, at which time the ICCP ceased to exist (Decision EM-I/3).

Though the Bio-Safety Protocol does not explicitly recognize a right of public access, it states that the parties should endeavour to increase public awareness and education, and improve access to information on imported LMOs identified in the Protocol (Article 23). The regionally balanced roster of experts[2] includes a number of public interest groups and coalitions of industries. Public interest groups and industries can also participate in the experts meeting of the Biosafety Clearing House (BCH), which facilitates the exchange of information on LMOs and assists countries in the implementation of the Protocol. Parties to the CBD that are not parties to the Protocol can participate as observers in the proceedings of any meetings of the COP/MOP (Article 29(2)). However, they do not have any right to vote, and decisions are made only by those who are parties to the Protocol (Article 29 (2) and Article 32 (2)).

Participation of Civil Society During the Negotiation of the Protocol

The negotiations of the Protocol marked a sharp division between different countries' positions on bio-safety. This led to the formation of several negotiating groups, such as the so-called 'Miami Group', a US-led group of countries sharing the interest of major agricultural exporters and backed by Argentina, Chile and Uruguay. This group expressed views in support of the commercial agricultural business, and did not support the formulation of a bio-safety agreement at all (Arts and Mack 2003; Newell and Glover 2003).[3] From the very outset,[4] public interest

---

[2]   As of the end of June 2002, the roster contained 443 experts nominated by 60 governments. The regional breakdown was 26 per cent Africa, 18 per cent Asia and Pacific, 22 per cent Central and Eastern Europe, 14 per cent Latin America and the Caribbean and 20 per cent Western Europe and others.

[3]   The Miami Group (and the industries whose interests this group shared) unconditionally favoured the development of genetic modification technology and considered the WTO regime to be the 'main benchmark for deliberations over biosafety'.

[4]   Even before the COP1 of CBD, Third World Network, GRAIN, RAFI and Greenpeace convinced the G7 and China for work to begin on an internationally binding Protocol and for the COP to endorse their request.

groups were very resolute in their views on bio-safety and on the formation of the Protocol. Environmental groups pushed forward several agenda issues, such as:

- inclusion of the precautionary principle as the overriding objective and the basis for all decision-making under the Protocol;
- non-subordination of the Protocol to the WTO;
- advanced informed agreement, ensuring that countries are provided with the information necessary to make informed decisions before agreeing to the import of such organisms into their territory;
- labelling and segregating GMOs;
- liability.

Following the rules of the CBD, NGOs participated as observers in the bio-safety negotiations (Article 23(5) of the CBD). According to Gale (2002), Greenpeace and other environmental NGOs followed two strategies: (i) they shared with delegates their knowledge of scientific, legal, technical, and current market and political development. This was especially helpful to the developing country delegations as they contained a small number of delegates at the negotiations; (ii) they informed members of the public about the ongoing negotiation, the issue at stake and the positions of the respective governments. Moreover, national and local NGOs organized a series of events to inform further the public and media about the negotiations (Gale 2002).

During the negotiation stage, biotechnology industry representatives interacted with NGOs and government delegates. After an apprehensive start, the private sector organized themselves under the banner of the Global Industry Coalition (GIC) in 1998 (Reifschneider 2002). They provided delegates with practical information about the state of biotechnology research and development, and the commercial movement of LMOs. By 1999, in Cartagena, the members of the GIC included industry representatives from developed and developing countries, and from a broad spectrum of related industries and sectors, including: the farming community, the commercial forestry sector, seed companies, pharmaceutical companies, forestry industry, commodity traders and shippers, and some food manufacturers (Reifschneider 2002). Many commentators noted that the 'global' coalitions prioritized and represented the concerns of European and North-American firms, and that issues related to firms from developing countries were generally disregarded (Newell and Glover 2003). It is claimed that although representation from developing countries has increased over time, the GIC was led by association leaders from Canada, the USA and Europe (Reifschneider 2002). Smaller firms and small and medium-sized enterprises were underrepresented in these global coalitions and they lacked resources to participate in international decision-making processes (Newell and Glover 2003).

Participation in the Working Group on Biosafety

Both industry groups and NGOs played a prominent role in the work of the Participation in the Working Group on Biosafety[5] by providing information to the delegates. At the first BSWG meeting in Denmark (1996), private-sector participation was extremely limited, and companies and associations were unsure about the level of resources to commit to the process. Once industry groups became aware of the potential impact of the Protocol on international trade in agriculture, medicine and other important products of modern biotechnology, they became more organized. In order to shape the negotiation, industry groups brought in experts who participated in other environmental negotiations (Newell and Glover 2003). Although NGOs were permitted to have broad access to meetings, including contact groups, their participation seemed to have been limited during the work of the BSWG 4 and 5. During BSWG 5 (1998), the BSWG Bureau decided that NGOs should be allowed to participate as observers, but that they had no right to intervene, negotiate or participate, and that they could be removed from any meeting at the request of any government. The Chair of the BSWG explained that it was necessary to maintain such a closed system because NGOs were not supposed to directly influence delegates from other countries during the meetings (Para. 20, UNEP/CBD/BSWG/5/3, 1998). Participation by NGOs was further restricted in BSWG 6, where NGOs could participate as observers in the initial phase of the discussion of the working groups and contact groups, but with no right to speak, except at the invitation of the Chair (Para 23, UNEP/CBD/ExCOP/1/2, 1999).

Participation in the Intergovernmental Committee for the Cartagena Protocol

Approximately 575 participants from 83 countries and 131 intergovernmental, non-governmental and industry organizations participated in the first meeting of the Participation in the Intergovernmental Committee for the Cartagena Protocol in 2000. Delegates met in two working groups to discuss six issues: information sharing and the BCH; capacity building; the roster of experts; decision-making procedures; handling, transport, packaging and identification; and compliance. During this meeting, the GIC highlighted capacity building as a key priority for the private sector. During the concluding session of ICCP-1,[6] a group of NGOs produced a statement outlining their views on different areas of the Protocol, including capacity building, roster of experts and compliance mechanisms. While NGO views of compliance tended to focus on the commitments of exporters,

---

[5]   The work of the BSWG is well documented by the *Earth Negotiations Bulletin*, available at <www.iisd.ca/linkages>.

[6]   NGO Statement at ICCP 1 (Montpellier, 15 December 2000). More than 25 groups from Europe, North America, Latin America and Asia signed the statement. <161.200.41.3/SPR/soprun/report/biosaf.htm>

developing countries highlighted their concern over not being able to comply with their obligations under the Protocol because of a lack of national capacity. During ICCP-3 in 2002, approximately 580 participants from 147 countries (representing a much larger participation than in 2000) and 100 intergovernmental, non-governmental and industry organizations attended. In this meeting, NGOs collaborated to produce a statement[7] in which they urged the countries to speedily ratify the Protocol so that an MOP would finalize some of the contentious issues. The statement called for:

- an immediate moratorium on all releases of LMOs until a rigorous bio-safety regime was in place;
- an international regime of strict liability and redress;
- adequate risk assessment;
- an inclusive identification system;
- transforming the BCH into an equitable, reliable, transparent and user-friendly system;
- greater financial support from industrialized countries to help developing countries to participate in the bio-safety process.

NGOs emphasized the need for the application of precautionary principle to refuse imports until countries have developed capacity at the national level.

Of primary concern for NGOs was access to information considered necessary for the proper functioning of the BCH. According to some public interest groups, the BCH was not a transparent and user-friendly system, both of which were critical for the effective implementation of the Protocol and for public participation. Concerns were raised that some developing countries and NGOs would not be able to use the electronic BCH fully and would therefore be disadvantaged (Burrows and Lin 2002). As the information in the BCH came from many sources, and much of the information might only be in the form of summaries or might come from other databases, there was a concern that it might not be possible to ensure accuracy and comprehensiveness of information.

Conclusion

Civil society participated at various stages in the making of the Protocol. At the pre-negotiation stage, a small number of NGOs, such as Greenpeace and Third World Network, endorsed the need for a Protocol. During the negotiation of the Protocol, public interest groups participated at different levels of consultation and in decision-making processes. NGOs formed a coalition, disseminated complex scientific information and related safety and ethical implications to delegates in an easy, accessible manner. At the same time, they identified a need for better access to documents and for partnership between the private sector, NGOs and

---

[7]　The Hague, 26 April 2002. <www.gene.ch/genet/2002/May/msg00024.html>.

developing-country governments. Outside the formal forum, they also organized demonstrations to attract media and public attention. From negotiation to adoption of the Protocol, the influence of large industry groups and business associations was apparent, while insufficient capacity and ability to address bio-safety issues restricted the participation of public interest groups. Though the Protocol does not address all concerns related to modern biotechnology, the simple fact that it exists against strong resistance from GMO producer/exporter countries and the biotechnology industry can be seen as an achievement for public interest groups.

After the Protocol came into force in September 2003, the emphasis of COP/MOP-1 (Malaysia 2004) was the implementation of the Protocol at the national level. Private-sector groups and NGOs have already joined their efforts in building the capacity of developing country governments to engage in biosafety-related issues. An example of this is the United Nations Environment Programme/Global Environment Facility (UNEP/GEF) global project on the development of National Biosafety Frameworks (NBFs).[8] The UNEP/GEF global project began in 2001 and is assisting up to 123 countries to develop their NBFs so that they can comply with the Protocol. The UNEP/GEF project promotes regional and sub-regional cooperation on bio-safety and has the following objectives: assisting eligible countries to prepare their NBFs; promoting regional and sub-regional collaboration and exchange of experience on issues of relevance to the NBFs; providing advice and support to countries throughout the development of their NBFs.[9] The UNEP/GEF project envisages active participation of NGOs, the private sector and other stakeholders in the implementation of the programme, mostly through the involvement of such organizations in the regional workshops on bio-safety organized around the world. A strong emphasis is set on the role of NGOs, industry and other non-governmental representatives with regard to information and data gathering, presentation, dissemination and exchange.[10]

World Trade Organization

The WTO has 149 members, accounting for over 97 per cent of world trade, and committed to a process of encouraging global trade, reducing trade barriers and

---

[8]   The NBFs are a combination of policy, legal, administrative and technical instruments to speed up implementation of the Protocol at the national level, and to address safety for the environment and human health in relation to modern biotechnology. See: <www.unep.ch/biosafety/about.htm>.

[9]   For additional information on the characteristics and the objectives of the project see <www.unep.ch/biosafety>.

[10]   For additional information on the role of NGOs and the private sector in the UNEP/GEF project as well as for facts on NGO and industry participation in national bio-safety workshops and framework developments, see <www.unep.ch/biosafety>.

ensuring that the benefits of liberalization also accrue to developing countries. The main WTO agreements of relevance to the regulation of biotechnology are the 1994 General Agreement on Tariffs and Trade (GATT), the Agreement on Technical Barriers to Trade (TBT Agreement), the Agreement on the Application of Sanitary and Phytosanitary Measures (SPS Agreement) and the Agreement on Agriculture. These agreements share the common purpose of ensuring that measures that affect the trade in products do not discriminate on the basis of a product's country of origin, and that these measures are no more trade-restrictive than is necessary to achieve the purpose for which they were designed. Each agreement has detailed rules, and a growing body of practice that develops these disciplines further. Successful implementation of each of these agreements depends on the participation of all members and civil society.

The WTO's highest decision-making body, the Ministerial Conference, meets at least once every two years. Below this is the General Council, which meets several times a year in the WTO's Geneva headquarters (normally ambassadors and heads of delegation in Geneva, but sometimes officials sent from members' capitals). The General Council also meets as the Trade Policy Review Body and the Dispute Settlement Body. At the General Council level of the WTO, decisions are taken by the entire membership by consensus and members can vote on the basis of 'one country one vote'. Civil society does not participate and has no right to vote. At the next level, the Council for Trade in Goods (overseeing GATT), a Council for Trade in Services (overseeing GATS) and the Council for Trade-Related Aspects of Intellectual Property (overseeing the TRIPS Agreement) report to the General Council. Each of the higher-level councils has subsidiary bodies, and there are several specialized committees and working groups that deal with the individual WTO agreements, and other areas such as the environment, development and regional trade agreements. Membership at the committee level is open only to members and intergovernmental organisations (IGOs).

The WTO does not make any distinction between various components of civil society (Ecologic and FIELD 2003). Representatives of business, trade unions, farmers, environment and consumer associations are all placed on the same footing with respect to arrangements made for NGOs. It should be noted that wide-ranging debates have taken place on issues of internal and external transparency in the WTO, and are the subject of extensive literature and recommendations (Cameron and Ramsay 2000; Esty 1998; Narlikar 2001; Steffek 2007). Despite its limited participation, civil society plays an influential role in providing technical expertise, disseminating information, initiating debate and representing diverse interests such as human rights and the environment (Halle 2002). The WTO's relationship with civil society is managed in an *ad hoc* way and there is no long-term strategy for increasing openness and transparency (OECD 2000). Some developing countries fear that increasing access for well-resourced NGOs and private sectors of the developed countries to WTO policy-making processes, particularly to the dispute settlement system, may further reduce their own ability to influence WTO outcomes, especially on environmental and labour issues (World Civil Society Forum 2002). In recent years, there have been some initiatives to increase the WTO's engagement with NGOs and private sectors, such as the Guidelines for Arrangements on Relations with Non-Governmental Organisations (WT/L/162 (23 July 1996)). This was based on Article V:2 of the 1994 Marrakesh Agreement establishing the WTO, which states that 'The General Council may make appropriate arrangements for consultation and cooperation with non-governmental organisations concerned with matters related to those of the WTO'. The guidelines included provisions related to de-restriction of WTO documents (WT/L/160/Rev.1, 26 July 1996), the creation of an NGO section on the WTO website containing information of particular interest to civil society (WT/INF/30, 12 April 2001), NGO symposia and NGO briefings on WTO council and committee work. In 2002, a procedure for accelerated de-restriction of official WTO documents was finally reached (WT/L/452, 15 May 2002). Though these initiatives increased the flow of information, there is no mechanism yet through which the civil society can directly affect WTO decisions. According to many NGOs, the WTO needs to: grant NGOs observer status at the WTO committee level, have regular regional symposia with civil society, initiate regular meeting with the WTO on trade and environment issues and adopt measures to expedite participation of southern NGOs in WTO sessions (Mason 2003).

Participation in WTO Ministerial Conferences

In the GATT, there was no official recognition of NGOs, nor was any facility provided for them at ministerial conferences and meetings. Many NGOs attending the closing of the Uruguay Round negotiations gained access by securing press credentials. Since 1996, NGOs with direct links to trade issues have been able to gain accreditation to ministerial conferences. This accreditation, however, provides for only very limited access to plenary sessions. Outside ministerial conferences, civil society groups have no access to the day-to-day WTO administrative committees, either as observers or for the purpose of distributing information. The symposia organized by the WTO Secretariat and side events at Ministerial Conferences provide a channel of communication between civil society groups and trade diplomats. The main objectives of the symposia are to keep civil society informed of the work underway in the WTO on trade and environment, and to allow experts in the field to examine and debate the interlinkages between trade, environment and sustainable development. No attempt was made to summarize the views of civil society or to identify consensus positions (Werksman 2000).

During the first Ministerial Conference (Singapore 1996), the WTO General Council decided that a system of accreditation would be set up whereby NGOs could have limited participation in the conference. However, at this Conference, there was hardly any interaction between NGOs and the government delegates, and NGOs were unable to observe the actual discussions and negotiations. The WTO Secretariat gave a daily briefing at the NGO centre on what was happening at the conference. However, the real negotiations were held behind closed doors and the Secretariat official could not provide information on what was happening. NGO representatives were not allowed in the 'informal meetings' where the real negotiations on the text of the Ministerial Declaration took place (Werksman 2000). At the second Ministerial Conference (Geneva 1998), the participation of NGOs was even more limited. Around 362 delegates from 128 NGOs participated. Among them, twenty-two were environmental NGOs, forty-six business NGOs, twenty-one trade unions, twenty-six development NGOs, three farming-related NGOs and six consumer-related NGOs (WTO 2004). The same procedure for accreditation as in 1996 was followed and, once again, NGOs had no access to the meetings (formal or informal) of the delegates: they could observe only the opening and closing ceremonies (Werksman 2000).

The Third WTO Ministerial Conference (Seattle 1999), however, showed a dramatic increase in the number of public interest organizations, because of the early planning for the launch of the new-millennium round of trade negotiations. Of the 686 NGOs that participated, 101 were from developing countries. While the immediate cause of the failure of the Third Ministerial Conference was the inability of the USA and the European Union to bridge their differences, civil society considered that they had also contributed to the collapse (Third World Resurgence 2000). Massive street demonstrations were held by public interest groups to voice their concerns about the negative aspects of globalization, and the lack of participation in the decision-making processes of international institutions such as the World Bank, IMF and the WTO. The Fourth WTO Ministerial Conference (Doha 2001) saw a substantial decrease in the number of attending NGOs, with 651 NGOs deemed eligible to participate, of which 370 were represented at the meeting and 370 registered participants (WTO 2003). This low level of participation was because only one person per NGO was allowed to register. Various NGOs later spoke out about the difficulty and inefficiency of obtaining visas for Qatar, as well as the deliberate separation of government officials and NGO delegates, hindering association and discussion, and the inability to collect documents after the conference (World Civil Society Forum 2002). NGO participation in the Fifth Ministerial Conference (Cancun 2003) was the largest so far, with around 800 NGOs and private-sector organizations, and almost 1,600 of their representatives attending the Conference. The NGO network that evolved during the Doha Ministerial Conference was useful in making NGOs more aware of the social and environmental impact of the decisions being taken at the WTO, and that fact partly influenced the rise in the number of NGOs in Cancun.

However, the increase in participation of civil society in the Fifth Ministerial Conference (Cancun 2003) did not ensure transparency in the decision-making process. Long before the conference, NGOs and other civil-society representatives had undertaken various actions to highlight the fact that the WTO's decision-making processes remained non-transparent, that civil society's participation was still too limited and that the situation was unlikely to undergo satisfactory change during the Cancun Ministerial Conference (CIEL, 2003). The General

Council's decision on procedures for registration and attendance of NGOs at the Cancun Conference (WT/MIN(03)/INF/1) restricted participation of NGOs. The decision provided that NGOs would be allowed to attend plenary sessions of the meeting, without making interventions. NGOs were required to apply with documents showing that they were 'concerned with matters related to those of the WTO'. Similar procedures were applied for NGOs to attend the Doha Ministerial Conference (WT/MIN(01)/INF/3). Strict limits were placed on both the number of representatives an NGO could register, and the number of these registered representatives that were permitted to enter the convention centre where the conference took place. Each accredited NGO was allowed to register three representatives. Of these three, only one was to be allowed into the convention centre at any given time. Once inside the conference centre, NGO representatives and members of the press were to have access to the main plenary and briefing rooms only if there was enough space. Neither NGOs nor the press were allowed in the areas reserved for ministers and delegations. As in preceding ministerial conferences, the WTO Secretariat published briefings for NGOs and seats were reserved for NGO representatives wishing to attend the opening and closing ceremonies. It appears that, despite NGOs' prior efforts to enhance participation in the Cancun Ministerial Conference, the actual participation of NGOs was similar to previous WTO ministerial conferences.

Access to the Dispute Settlement Process

NGOs do not have any access to documents submitted to a dispute settlement panel and the Appellate Body (AB) in the course of dispute-settlement proceedings as they are, in principle, confidential. Nothing in the Dispute Settlement Understanding (DSU), however, precludes a party to a dispute from disclosing statements of its own position to the public. Moreover, in order to increase transparency, a party to a dispute that submits a written submission to the panel must, upon request of another party to the dispute, provide a non-confidential summary of this text that could be disclosed to the public (Article 18.2 of the DSU).

Moreover, NGOs have no formal access to WTO dispute settlement panel or AB hearings, or the meetings of the Dispute Settlement Body. Article 13 of the DSU gives a panel the 'right to seek information and technical advice from any individual or body which it deems appropriate' and it provides that panels 'may consult experts to obtain their opinion on certain aspects of the matter'. In the *Shrimp Turtle* case,[11] the AB ruled that the right to seek information under Article 13 of the DSU included the discretionary power of a panel to accept

---

[11]   Appellate Body Report on United States–Import Prohibition of Certain Shrimp and Shrimp Products, Appellate Body Report, WT/DS58/AB/R, adopted 6 November 1998.

non-requested information from non-governmental sources.[12] It considered that the DSU accords a panel 'ample and extensive authority to undertake and to control the process by which it informs itself both of the relevant facts of the dispute and of the legal norms and principles applicable to such facts' (paragraph 106). In the *British Steel* case,[13] the AB found that it had the authority, under Article 17.9 of the DSU, to decide whether it may accept unsolicited submissions. After emphasizing that non-members have no legal right to make submissions, and that it has no duty to consider them, the AB held that it has the legal authority to consider *amicus curiae* briefs[14] (paragraph 39). In practice, however, NGO contributions have been considered in very few instances.[15] A number of international dispute-settlement bodies provide representatives of civil society with the opportunity to observe the process of decision-making and to contribute arguments relevant to the cases at hand. Other international tribunals, such as the International Court of Justice, and human rights tribunals, hold their sessions in public without invading sovereign privilege or interfering with the course of justice (Razzaque 2001). The underlying rationale for this is that panels should be able to consider a wide range of information and arguments in order to make the best decision possible.

There are proposals by some NGOs, and now by some governments, that NGOs should be allowed to participate in the dispute settlement hearings of

------

[12]   The Appellate Body specified that: '[i]n the present context, authority to seek information is not properly equated with a prohibition on accepting information which has been submitted without having been requested by a panel. A panel has the discretionary authority either to accept-and-consider or to reject information and advice submitted to it, whether requested by a panel or not'. Appellate Body Report on United States – Import Prohibition of Certain Shrimp and Shrimp Products, WT/DS58/AB/R, circulated on 12 October 1998, paras 106–107.

[13]   United States – Imposition of Countervailing Duties on Certain Hot-Rolled Lead and Bismuth Carbon Steel Products Originating in the United Kingdom, AB-2000-1, WT/DS138/AB/R (00-1896), adopted by Dispute Settlement Body, 7 June 2000.

[14]   *Amicus curiae*, known as the 'friends of the court', submits arguments independently of the parties to the dispute. An '*amicus curiae*' brief generally contains materials submitted to the courts and is additional to that submitted by any other parties. An *amicus* can submit information as to the broader implications of decisions beyond the immediate interests of parties, serving to enhance public participation in international decision-making.

[15]   For example: Canada and the EU regarding the French ban on the import of asbestos (*amicus* brief submitted by a coalition of environment and health NGOs), *BRIDGES Weekly*, 13 February 2001 (<www.ictsd.org/html/weekly/story5.13-02-01.htm>). In the asbestos case, the Appellate Body outlined specific procedures for the admission of *amicus* briefs and was later curtailed by the DSB/General Council. Therefore, consideration of *amicus* briefs by the Panel and Appellate Body remains to be discretionary. In the European Communities – Trade description of Sardines case (WT/DS231/AB/R- 26 September 2002) – the Appellate Body stated that it has the authority to accept amicus from a private individual. *BRIDGES Weekly*, 2 October 2002 (<www.ictsd.org/weekly/02-10-02/story2.htm>).

the WTO and also to submit *amicus curiae* briefs at the hearings. In 2002, in a special (negotiating) session of the WTO Dispute Settlement Body, the USA (TN/DS/W/13) tabled a proposal outlining its ideas on how to achieve a 'more open and transparent process' by opening dispute settlement procedures to the public, providing timely access to submissions and reports, as well as formalizing the handling of *amicus curiae* briefs. The European Union (TN/DS/W/1 and TN/DS/W/7) also tabled a similar proposal supporting the USA's submission. Some developing countries, such as Brazil, Chile, India, Indonesia, Mexico, Malaysia, The Philippines and Uruguay however, rejected the US proposal on the grounds that it would undermine the intergovernmental character of the WTO (TN/DS/W/18 and Add.1). The criticism of developing countries centred on the issue of allowing unsolicited submissions by non-parties to a dispute, arguing that this would provide third parties with more rights in dispute settlement proceedings than members themselves. In a separate submission, calling the dispute settlement mechanism 'complicated and overly expensive', the African Group tabled a proposal (TN/DS/W/42) that suggested setting-up a permanent fund, financed by members, to enable developing countries to better engage in dispute settlement proceedings. According to the present WTO rules, only official delegates can attend these hearings, and submissions are to be made by governments, especially those who are parties to the dispute.

Concluding Remarks

Despite the fact that two-thirds of WTO members are from developing countries, industrialized countries dominate the WTO agenda. The developing countries feel that they do not have the capacity, or the human and financial resources to match the negotiating machinery of the developed country (Figueres-Olsen, Salazar-Xirinachs and Araya, 2000; Khor 1999). Though developing countries have access to official documents at the policy-making level, informal documents stay out of reach of many developing countries and NGOs. Moreover, not all meetings are open to NGOs, and accredited NGOs can participate in the ministerial conferences in a very limited manner. Because of their extensive reliance on informal processes to reach decisions, and the nature of the consensus-based decision-making process, developing countries and NGOs are often sidelined. Although civil society plays a very important role, and there have been some initiatives by the WTO to promote civil society participation, there is no effective institutionalized structure to accommodate and integrate them in the processes of the WTO.

Participation in WTO dispute settlement has also given rise to a concern regarding transparency and, in particular, the right of NGOs to make written submissions to the dispute settlement panels and AB. Some NGOs have been the most ardent critics of the deficiencies of the institutional arrangements and the lack of transparency of its dispute settlement process. To many environmental NGOs, the WTO's dispute settlement body is an inappropriate forum to resolve environment-related disputes. Some NGOs, such as Greenpeace, assert that the

WTO cannot and should not be used to undermine environmental agreements, especially where public-health issues are at stake, such as the trade in GMOs. The WTO dispute settlement body deals with more complex disputes as new multilateral environmental agreements and related obligations come into force. This creates an expectation that the dispute settlement body will modernize its procedure to take account of all relevant interests, and promote equitable participation of developing countries and civil society.

Codex Alimentarius

Created in 1963, the Codex Alimentarius (Codex) is a joint programme of the Food and Agriculture Organization (FAO) and World Health Organization (WHO). The governing body of Codex, the Codex Alimentarius Commission (CAC), establishes food-safety and quality standards in order to protect the health of consumers and ensure fair practices in food trade, including standards for additives, pesticide residues, contaminants and labelling (FAO and WHO 1999). The Commission is an intergovernmental forum where food safety and standards of different countries are discussed, and which promotes equal participation of the North and the South (Lassalle de Salins 2001). Codex standards are more important now, given the fact that these standards 'have become the benchmarks against which national food measures and regulations are evaluated within the legal parameters of the Uruguay Round Agreements' (FAO and WHO 1999). Stakes within Codex are higher since the adoption of the WTO Agreements, as governments seek to have their own national approaches reflected in international standards that would benefit from a presumption of WTO-consistency (Kennedy 2000; Victor 2000).

With the new role granted to them by SPS and TBT Agreements of the WTO – which encourage the international harmonisation of food standards (Annex A, para. 3 of the SPS agreement, and Article 2.6 of the TBT Agreement) – Codex standards have gained a major status in food trade, both directly for international food trade, and indirectly through their potential impact on national regulations. National SPS measures are presumed to be consistent with the WTO SPS Agreement if they conform to Codex standards, recommendations or guidelines (Article 3.2 of the SPS Agreement). The TBT Agreement does not contain a list of international organizations whose standards are considered international standards, but requires the use of international standards by members except where the international standard would be ineffective or inappropriate in the national situation (Article 2.4 of the TBT Agreement).

The 11th Session of the Conference of FAO in 1961 and the 16th World Health Assembly in 1963 passed resolutions to establish the CAC, and adopted the Statutes and Rules of Procedure for the CAC.[16] The CAC's executive and

---

[16] <www.fao.org/documents/show_cdr.asp?url_file=/DOCREP/005/Y2200E/y2200e02.htm>

administrative organs are the Executive Committee and the Secretariat. A number of specific subsidiary bodies carry out preparatory work on the elaboration of Codex standards. There are two categories of subsidiary bodies: Codex committees (general subject and commodity committees) and coordinating committees (regional committees). There are nine general subject committees (including Food Labelling, General Principles, and Food Additives and Contaminants), twelve commodity committees, and six regional coordinating committees (which correspond to seven regional groups). In additional, there are three *ad hoc* intergovernmental task forces, including the Task Force on Foods Derived from Biotechnology (FDB).[17]

Membership of the CAC is open only to member states and associate members of FAO and WHO (Article 2, Statutes of CAC 1966, Rule 1 of the Rules of Procedure of the CAC). The 171 Members of the CAC are divided into several regional groups, such as Africa, Asia and Europe.[18] The CAC follows two procedures: full and accelerated,[19] to elaborate Codex standards. Under both procedures, international organizations, including NGOs, have an opportunity to comment on the draft standard. The CAC meets every two years, and delegations may, and often do, include representatives of industry, consumers' organizations and academic institutes. Countries that are not yet members of the CAC and a number of IGOs and NGOs, including consumer groups and industry associations, may attend in an observer capacity (Rule 8 of the Rules of Procedure of the CAC).[20] As observers, NGOs are entitled to participate in the sessions of the CAC and may be accompanied by advisers. According to the rules, the observers do not have any right to vote, but they receive all working documents and discussion papers, and can circulate their views in writing (Rule 5, Section II, Procedural Manual). The CAC should allow such organizations to put forward their suggestions at every stage except the final decision, which is the exclusive prerogative of member states. In order to facilitate continuous contact

---

[17]   The objectives of the Task Force on FDB are to elaborate standards, guidelines, or other principles, as appropriate, for foods derived from biotechnology. <www.codexalimentarius.net>.

[18]   See members listed by regional group in <www.codexalimentarius.net/web/index_en.jsp>.

[19]   See Annex I or Rules of Procedure of the Codex Alimentarius Commission (Procedural Manual, 11th Edition, FAO and WHO 2000), <www.codexalimentarius.net/web/procedural_manual.jsp>.

[20]   The international NGOs permitted as 'observers' must (i) be international in structure and scope of activity, (ii) be concerned with matters covering a part or all of the Commission's field of activity, (iii) have aims and purposes in conformity with the Statutes of the CAC and (iv) have a permanent directing body, authorized representatives and systematic procedures for communicating with its membership in various countries. Rule 3, Section II (Principles concerning the participation of international non-governmental organisation in the work of the Codex Alimentarius Commission), Procedural Manual. Full text: <ftp://ftp.fao.org/codex/PM/Manual14e.pdf>.

with members, the CAC in collaboration with governments, has established Codex contact points at the national level. NGOs and academics, as members of National Codex Committees, can play an active role in coordinating activities at the national level.[21] NGOs, as observers, have also gained access to the sessions of the Task Force on FDB, the Committee on General Principles and the Committee on Food Labelling, to voice their opinion and ideas.

Currently, there are 158 organizations listed as observers: industry groups (71 per cent) top the list, with professional associations (22 per cent) and public interest organizations (8 per cent) next.[22] NGOs, as observers, have sent written comments and made oral statements during the sessions. However, the number of written comments, for example, in the area of FDB, has been insignificant and mostly from international trade associations or consumer groups.[23] Some of these NGOs and industry groups also have a visible role through the national Codex Contact Points. Moreover, public interest groups have participated in several regional Codex meetings.[24] However, there have been complaints from public interest groups that Codex committees are non-transparent. During the twenty-third session of the CAC, the International Association of Consumer Food Organisations firmly stated that public support towards what Codex does depends on whether all Codex activities, including the work of the Executive Committee, are conducted in an open and transparent manner (ALINORM 99/37).

Procedures to Improve Participation

At present, the CAC is discussing ways to increase the participation of NGOs and has asked the Codex Committee on General Principles to revise the Principles

---

[21]   Questionnaire sent to all members in 2002 by CAC shows that around seventeen low-income countries out of thirty respondents have national codex committees and thirteen are without committees. Of eighteen low-income countries (out of thirty-five), only two countries say that their national codex committee has very little influence on the government's position in the codex committee. Seven countries, however, believe that they play a greater role in influencing the government, and nine countries believe that they play some role in the government's position in the CAC.: <www.codexalimentarius.net>.

[22]   Full list available at: <www.codexalimentarius.net/organizations_ngo.stm>.

[23]   At least, three groups sent written comments before the 1st session of the Task Force on FDB: the International Association of Plant Breeders for the Protection of Plant Varieties – a trade union of seed producers; the Council for Responsible Nutrition – a trade association of companies in the dietary supplements industry; and the International Association of Consumer Food Organisations – a consumer group.

[24]   For example, Report of the 4th Session of the Codex *Ad Hoc* Intergovernmental Task Force on Food Derived from Biotechnology (Japan 2003) (ALINORM 03/34A), Report of the 32nd Session of the Codex Committee on Food Labelling (Montréal, May 2004) (ALINORM 04/27/22) and Report of the 20th Session of the Codex Committee on General Principles (Paris 2004) (ALINORM 04/27/33A) indicate that a large number of representatives from consumer and business groups were present at the meetings.

Concerning the Participation of International Non-Governmental Organisations in the Work of the CAC by 2005 (para. 175, ALINORM 03/41).[25] In the past, there had been two initiatives, the Chairman's Action Plan 2000 and Codex Strategic Framework 2003–2007, where the executive arm of the Codex put forward a number of strategies to make Codex meetings more transparent. One of the six action plans by the Chairman of the CAC was to increase transparency and participation by NGOs. As the meetings of the Executive Committee are closed to civil society, the action plan reiterated the intention to have a new group to replace the Executive Committee, which would include all committee chairpersons, and could act as an advisory body to the CAC. Consumer groups and other public interest groups could select representatives to participate in the deliberations of this proposed new group, which would increase transparency of the work of the group (Billy 2000). According to the action plan, the CAC should meet once a year and NGOs would continue to be involved at CAC's meetings. This would provide a forum for the exchange of information on how food regulatory problems are addressed domestically and should be addressed internationally, including common public health, nutrition and trade issues. Moreover, it would offer NGOs an opportunity to influence the work of the CAC on the development of standards upon which their respective national standards would ultimately be based, and which impact their nations' participation in global food trade. According to the action plan, such a CAC meeting would provide interest groups with an existing internationally recognized forum for their deliberations and recommendations, and their involvement would add relevancy and credibility to Codex's deliberations.

The Codex Strategic Framework 2003–2007 sets out the strategic priorities for the CAC. Objective Five (Promoting Maximum Membership and Participation) of the Strategic Framework affirms the full participation by all Codex members and other interested parties in the work of the CAC. More importantly, it emphasizes that the 'participation of all members and relevant intergovernmental and non-governmental organisations is critical to sound decision-making and ensuring that Codex standards and related texts take account of the full range of interest and viewpoints' (Codex Strategic Framework, paras 16–17). This framework identifies two major constraints – resource constraints and capacity building (para. 16) – in participation in Codex activities by developing countries and civil society. The CAC hopes for more involvement and input of consumers and NGOs, which it considers 'essential to build public confidence in international standards and assure the strong public input, acceptance and support for Codex standards, guidelines and recommendations as a basis for domestic regulation and trade' (para. 17). This Strategic Framework takes up

---

[25] This issue is still under consideration. See: Proposed Amendment to the Rules of Procedure of the Codex Alimentarius Commission, Appendix-III, Report of the 20th Session of the Codex Committee on General Principles (Paris 2004) (ALINORM 04/27/33A).

the issue of external transparency, stressing that the CAC needs to promote and facilitate the participation of consumers and public interest groups in its processes at the international level, in order to build public confidence in international standards (paras 16–17).

The Report of the Evaluation of the Codex Alimentarius and other FAO and WHO Food Standards has assessed the transparency and inclusiveness of Codex work. The report states that the consumer groups have found the level of inclusiveness and transparency of the CAC unsatisfactory and they have a very low opinion (100 per cent) of the accountability and governance of the Codex (Codex Alimentarius Commission 2002, Tables 24 and 25). The report comments that while consumer groups believe that they have too little influence in Codex, industry observers believe consumers have slightly too much influence in Codex (para. 146). The report recommends that Codex should review its principles and procedures for observer status and should consider applying stricter criteria to ensure that observers are genuinely international (Recommendation 27).

Participation of Industry and Business Groups

The current rules of participation allow such a broad definition of NGOs that business groups can also join as part of civil society. When FAO and WHO jointly set up the Codex to establish food-safety and quality standards, it was to help developing countries improve health and environmental safety. Over the years, some commentators have considered Codex's decision-making processes to have become dominated by transnational companies using Codex to legitimize standards, definitions and the composition of their own products (Krut et al. 1997). Noting the associated business opportunity Codex offers, Newell and Glover state:

> standard-setting [in the biotechnology sector] is increasingly conducted by corporate representatives, working alongside other governmental and non-governmental specialists. For example, industry groups have played a key role in the work of the Codex Alimentarius Commission ... Multinational corporations and trade associations are aware of the role that Codex has been given by the WTO agreements as the organisation through which disputes over trade in food products may be resolved. (Newell and Glover 2003)

At the twenty-third session of CAC (Italy 1999), some delegations from industrialized nations had a very large number of industry representatives. For example, 40 per cent of delegates from the USA, 40 per cent from Switzerland, 38 per cent from France and 38 per cent from Germany, were industry representatives. In contrast, only around ten NGOs were invited as participants in national delegations. However, a large number of NGO observers attended that meeting (FOE International 2001). Recently, at the 27th Session of the CAC (2004), only around five out of twenty-eight NGOs were public interest groups.[26] It creates a concern among public interest groups that Codex is dominated by industry interests.

Participation of Consumers' Association

Since the beginning of Codex in 1965, consumer organizations have participated in its various sessions as observers. The involvement of consumers in the CAC's work has been the subject of explicit discussions within the CAC (Codex Alimentarius Commission 2002). Consumers' participation in decision-making in relation to food standards and the Joint FAO/WHO Food Standards Programme, for instance, was an item on the agenda of the 20th Session of the CAC (1993) where Members agreed to continue working in close cooperation with consumer organizations. The Codex Secretariat disseminates Codex documents to international consumers organizations relating both to its own activities and to those of its subsidiary committees to Codex Contact Points in member states, with the expectation that they will be forwarded to nationally based consumer organizations for comment as appropriate. In the 23rd Session of the FAO/WHO Co-ordinating Committee for Europe (CCEURO) in 2002, Consumers International proposed the following measures: involve consumers in national Codex Committees; provide feedback information following Codex meetings; and fund the participation of consumer representatives in national delegations. It added that the CCEURO should develop guidelines for enhancing consumer participation and compile information on measurable objectives. Furthermore, FAO and WHO were asked to identify the main obstacles to the participation of consumer groups and provide training and funding for their representatives (ALINORM 03/19). It was added that consumer participation in Codex can be improved by not only opening meetings of the Codex Executive Committees to observers, but also encouraging consumer representation on national Codex delegations. During the 13th Session of the FAO/WHO Regional Co-ordinating Committee for Asia (Malaysia 2002), consumer groups suggested that national Codex committees should be open to all consumer groups, and that national delegates to Codex meetings should also include members of consumer groups (ALINORM 03/15). Despite several calls to the CAC, the numbers of consumer associations attending CAC meetings are still low. Of the thirty-seven NGOs that participated in 26th CAC (2003), only around ten of them were public interest groups (ALINORM 03/41). Although availability of Codex documents has been improving steadily through use of the Internet, and importance of online documents has recently been emphasized in the 27th session of CAC (Appendix

---

[26]   Joint FAO/WHO Standards Programme: Codex Alimentarius Commission (27th Session 2004, Geneva, Switzerland), ALINORM 04/27/41. Available online: <www.codexalimentarius.net/web/reports.jsp?lang=en>.

II, ALINORM 04/27/41 (2004)), many consumer organizations have only limited access to the Internet.

Conclusion

Codex has become an extremely important body for the food industry because of the impact of its regulations on international food trade, and because of its potential impact on national regulations. As an intergovernmental organization and an international standard-setting organization, Codex has established its place in the developing regime governing biotechnology. It is imperative to note that the standards and guidelines set by Codex are voluntary. Though a high number of developing countries participate in the Codex meetings, questions have been raised as to the type of national delegates participating in these meetings. The trend also shows an increasing number of industry groups joining Codex meetings. In most cases, developing countries and public interest groups do not have the capacity to understand the issue under discussion. Both public interest NGOs and industry groups can participate in CAC meetings as delegates or observers. However, there is no dividing line between industry groups and consumer groups and, as the recent CAC Evaluation Report (Codex Alimentarius Commission 2002) shows, there are some concerns about the dominant role of industry groups in the meetings. The Executive Committee meetings are closed to NGOs, and many NGOs, along with developing countries, do not have any access to information or translated materials.

Conclusion

The concept of transparency includes the right to information and the equal participation of all parties that could be affected by the consequences of such decision in the decision-making processes. The need for better participation of civil society is well recognized and emphasized in the mandate of all three international institutions considered in this paper: the Bio-Safety Protocol, the WTO and the Codex Alimentarius. However, there is a further need to increase the level of transparency in their decision-making processes, without impinging on their status as intergovernmental organizations. Increased transparency would ensure that the agreements reflect the widest possible range of affected interests, and adopt decisions that are sustainable and forward-looking. Though the WTO and the Codex have gone through reforms at the institutional level, this is not enough to ensure a legitimate and transparent process. Public interest groups fear that all three institutions are at risk of being captured by industry and lobby groups. The refined notion of participation and transparency has raised the need for an elaborate definition of public participation and effective consultation. The experience in the three institutions has shown that structure and demand for substantive inputs are as important as the participation of various interest groups.

There is also concern about the participation of a higher number of industries in all three institutions. Observers representing trade associations and consumer groups have been present in the Codex meetings for many years. However, the number of industries participating is significantly higher than consumer bodies. Time and again, consumer associations have called for guidelines for consumer participation and in deliberations. Many NGOs also believe that observers should be permitted to attend working group meetings and drafting sessions of Codex committees. Numbers of participating industry groups are also high in the WTO, and the Protocol showed the active participation of industries at all levels of negotiation. Therefore, an added challenge for all these institutions would be to regularize industry participation.

In all three institutions, lack of information hinders effective participation by civil society. Although civil society representatives participate as observers at meetings of parties, and more actively at the committee and sub-committee level in all three institutions, these do not ensure transparency in the decision-making processes. At Codex meetings, many NGOs do not have access to translated documents, and in many cases, translation is not available. Codex negotiations are usually held in English, and non-English speakers and non-native English speakers often comment that their proposals are not translated (Suppan and Leonard 2002). There is also a concern about transparency in Codex consultations, and about the groups that are chosen for to take part in consultation. There should be a procedure to reach all relevant stakeholders, not just a narrow circle of interested groups.

Official NGO consultation mechanisms are expensive, and are most likely to be undertaken by the countries that can afford them. Therefore, NGOs that are based in industrialized countries, or with good access to decision-makers, are likely to be able to get their concerns across (Werksman 2000). Although all three institutions recognize that civil society has a role to play in increasing awareness of activities related to biotechnology, there is as yet no mechanism in any of them by which public interest groups can directly affect the decision-making process. Moreover, financial support is needed to assist developing countries and public interest groups to participate in various conferences and to follow the process more generally. NGOs have already emphasized this issue in various civil society forums, and in Codex and WTO meetings. Because of the existing informal ways in which these three institutions manage their relationship with civil society, NGOs wishing to influence policy decisions may need to forge close cooperation with their national governments. They need to work together and exchange their knowledge in order to identify priority issues. NGOs need to participate more at the national level and work closely with the government, as many of the higher-level committees at the international level are closed to them.

Although there are signs of increased transparency within the WTO, the Codex and the Protocol, NGOs along with many developing countries lack capacity to understand and to critically analyse the issue under discussion. Therefore, it is necessary to build capacity at the national level and among the trade negotiators of the developing countries. Civil society organizations working on trade-related subjects have a responsibility to increase public awareness of the relevance of international trade policy to their constituencies, thereby raising the level of national debate (Werksman 2000). Members of civil society can play a greater role by campaigning in their home countries so that the issues come to the attention of the national media and are also discussed in national parliaments. The development of defined and structured processes of participation by civil society would encourage better decision-making processes in the three institutions, revitalizing sustainable environmental governance.

References

Arts, B. and S. Mack. 2003. 'Environmental NGOs and the Biosafety Protocol: a Case Study on Political Influence'. *European Environment* 13: 19–33.
Billy, T.J. 2000. Speech to the Codex Alimentarius Commission Executive Committee Meeting. June 28 2000, Geneva. <www.fsis.usda.gov/OA/speeches/2000/tb_exec. htm>.
Burrows, B. and L. Li Lin. 2002. 'The Biosafety Clearing House – Safe, Clear and Friendly?' <www.twnside.org.sg/title/bch.htm>.
Cameron, J. and R. Ramsay. 2000. 'Integrating Dissident Voices Through International Institutional law: Participation by Non-Governmental Organisation in the World Trade Organisation'. <www.gets.org/Library/Listcontent.cfm?SelectedCategories=44>.
CIEL 2003. 'Memorandum on the Need to Improve Internal Transparency and Participation in the WTO'. Available at <www.ciel.org/Publications/Cancun_21July03_ ExecSum.pdf>.
Codex Alimentarius Commission 2002. 'Report of the Evaluation of the Codex Alimentarius and Other FAO and WHO Food Standard Work'. <www.fao.org/docrep/ meeting/005/y7871e/y7871e00.htm#E12E4>.
———, 2004. *Procedural Manual*. <www.codexalimentarius.net/web/procedural_manual. jsp>.
———. *Procedural Manual*. Twelfth Edition. <www.fao.org/DOCREP/005/Y2200E/ y2200e00.htm#Contents>.
Ecologic and FIELD 2003. 'Participation of Non-Governmental Organisations in International Environmental Governance'. <www.ecologic.de/modules.php?name= News&file=article&sid=773>.
Esty, D.C. 1998. 'Non-Governmental Organisation at the World Trade Organisation: Cooperation, Competition, or Exclusion'. *Journal of International Economic Law* 1.1: 123–48.
FAO and WHO 1999. 'Understanding Codex Alimentarius' (Preface). www. codexalimentarius.net>.
———. 2001. 'Procedures for the Elaboration of Codex Standards and Related Texts'.
Faulkner, R. 2000. 'Regulating Biotech Trade: the Cartagena Protocol on Biosafety'. *International Affairs* 76.2: 299–313.

Figueres-Olsen, J., M. Salazar-Xirinachs and M. Araya. 2000. 'Trade and Environment at the World Trade Organisation: The Need for Constructive Dialogue'. <www.unu.edu/news/wto/ch08.pdf>.

FOE International 2001. 'WTO-Transparency, Democracy and Power'. <www.foei.org/trade/activistguide/democ.htm>.

Gale, L. 2002. 'Environmental NGOs: Greenpeace International'. In C. Bail, R. Falkner and H. Marquad, eds. *The Cartagena Protocol on Biosafety: Reconciling Trade in Biotechnology with Environment and Development?* London: RIIA/Earthscan: 251–62.

Halle, M. 2002. 'WTO and Civil Society in Developing Countries' (July 2002, ICCG 18). <www.worldcivilsociety.org/pages/147/en/quest.php>.

Holloway, R. 1997. 'NGOs: Loosing the Moral High Ground-Corruption and Misrepresentation'. Paper presented at the 8th International Anti-Corruption Conference, 7–11 September (Lima, Peru). <www.transparency.org/iacc/8th_iacc/papers/holloway.html>.

Kennedy, K.C. 2000. ,Resolving International Sanitary and Phytosanitary Disputes in the WTO: Lessons and Future Directions'. *Food and Drug Law Journal* 55: 81.

Khor, M. 1999. 'Civil Society's Interaction with the WTO'. www.fimcivilsociety.org/etud_khor_english_text.html>.

Krut, R., K. Howard, E. Howard, H. Gleckman and D. Pattison. 1997. 'Globalisation and civil society: NGO influence in International Decision Making'. Discussion Paper No. 83 (April 1997). Available online: <www.rrojasdatabank.org/toc83.htm>.

Lassalle de Salins, M. 2001. 'Foods Derived from Biotechnology in the Codex Alimentarius'. Paper presented at *European and American Perspectives on Regulating Genetically Engineered Food*, organized by INSEAD and Berkeley-University of California, INSEAD Fontainebleau, 8–9 June. <www.insead.fr/events/gmoworkshop/papers/4a_Lassalle.pdf>.

Marrakech Agreement Establishing the World Trade Organisation 1994. Final Act Embodying the Results of the Uruguay Round of Multilateral Trade Negotiations, Results of the Uruguay Round, 33 I.L.M. 1140, 1144–1153.

Mason, M. 2003. 'The World Trade Regime and Non-Governmental Organisations: Addressing Transnational Environmental Concerns'. <www.lse.ac.uk/collections/geographyAndEnvironment/pdf/rp84.pdf>.

Narlikar, A. 2001. 'WTO Decision-Making and Developing Countries. South Centre'. Working Paper No. 11, November. <www.southcentre.org/publications/pubindex.htm>.

Newell, P. and D. Glover. 2003. 'Business and Biotechnology: Regulation and the Politics of Influence'. IDS Working Paper 192. <www.ids.ac.uk/ids/bookshop/wp/wp192.pdf>.

Nijar, G.S. 2002. 'Environmental NGOs: Third World Network'. In C. Bail, R. Falkner and H. Marquad, eds. *The Cartagena Protocol on Biosafety: Reconciling Trade in Biotechnology with Environment and Development?* London: RIIA/Earthscan.

OECD. 2000. 'Transparency and Consultation on trade and Environment in Five International Organisations, Joint Working Party on Trade and Environment'. COM/ENV/TD(99)96/FINAL18 August 2000. <www.olis.oecd.org/olis/1999doc.nsf/linkto/com-env-td(99)96-final>.

Razzaque, J. 2001. 'Changing Role of Friends of the Court in the International Courts and Tribunals'. *Journal on Non-State Actors in International Law* 1.3: 169–200.

Reifschneider, L.M. 2002. ,Industry: Global Industry Coalition'. In C. Bail, R. Falkner and H. Marquad, eds. *The Cartagena Protocol on Biosafety: Reconciling Trade in Biotechnology with Environment and Development?* London: RIIA/Earthscan.

Steffek, J., C. Kissling and P. Nanz, eds. 2007. *Civil Society Participation in European and Global Governance: A Cure for the Democratic Deficit?* Houndmills: Palgrave Macmillan.

Suppan, S. and R. Leonard. 2002. Comments submitted to the Independent Evaluation of the Codex Alimentarius and Other FAO-WHO Work on Food Standards. <www.tradeobservatory.org/>.

Third World Resurgence 2000. 'NGOs Voice their Views at Seattle'. <www.twnside.org.sg/title/deb11-cn.htm>.

Victor, D.G. 2000. 'The Sanitary and Phytosanitary Agreement of the World Trade Organisation: An Assessment after Five Years'. *New York University Journal of International Law and Politics* 32: 865.

Werksman, J. 2000. 'Institutional Reform of the WTO'. Oxfam GB Discussion Paper 3/00. <www.oxfam.org.uk/what_we_do/issues/trade/wto_reform.htm>.

World Civil Society Forum. 2002. 'WTO and Civil Society in Developing Countries'. 18 July 2002, ICCG 18. <www.worldcivilsociety.org/>.

WTO. 2003. 'NGO's Participation in Ministerial Conference was Largest Ever'. <www.wto.org/english/news_e/news03_e/ngo_minconf_6oct03_e.htm>.

———. 2004. 'Relations with Non-Governmental Organizations/Civil Society'. <www.wto.org/english/forums_e/ngo_e/ngo_e.htm>.

Chapter 10

Global Forest Governance: Effectiveness, Fairness and Legitimacy of Market-driven Approaches

Stephen Bass and Stéphane Guéneau

Introduction

Traditionally, international environmental governance has focused on the issue of global public goods that states cannot provide individually, with intergovernmental cooperation being aimed at the creation of an international regime (Krasner 1983; Young 1997 2001). Over the past decade, this governance 'model' has been marked by a crisis of multilateralism that is notable for the refusal of certain large countries, such as the United States, to engage in international collective action on environmental protection. In addition, other multilateral agreements, notably on trade and production sectors, are struggling to meet objectives that are ecologically acceptable. This crisis has given rise to new forms of global environmental governance.

Alongside mechanisms for international coordination between sovereign states, a hybrid form of governance is gradually emerging: it is characterized by global policy networks (Reinike 1998; Streck 2002) where public and private actors share authority and a common goal. At the same time, a third 'non-state market-driven governance' (NSMD) model, where authority is diffuse and based in the marketplace (Cashore 2002; Bernstein and Cashore 2003), has asserted itself.

This new order raises questions on the nature of international collective action and on the legitimacy of these governance systems, their comparative effectiveness – their ability to provide solutions to global environmental problems – and their complementarity. These questions are particularly pointed where global forest governance is concerned.

So far, no form of international coordination focusing specifically on forest conservation and management has really materialized. Although global forest governance is a topic that continues to prompt heated intergovernmental negotiations, the relevance and legitimacy of a multilateral approach are now being addressed: at the same time as these diplomatic efforts, other governance systems are bringing non-governmental actors into play – NGOs, the private sector, local institutions – actors who have had very little influence over the globalization process up until now.

Do these newer systems represent a viable solution? Do they make it possible to overcome the constraints associated with a classical governance system in the form of a legally binding multilateral agreement on forests? This chapter attempts to answer these questions. After reviewing the evolution of global forest governance, we will analyse the main points of contention surrounding the new forms of governance.

Ineffectiveness of State Forest Governance Systems

Before 1992, particularly during negotiations leading up to the Earth Summit, the international community was extremely attentive to forest matters. When it discussed ways of fighting global warming, it often stressed the impact of the world's forests on carbon storage. It also pointed out repeatedly that tropical deforestation represented the greatest threat to biodiversity. As a result, governments became actively involved in talks to put together a legally binding multilateral agreement on forests.

As early as 1985, the Ninth World Forestry Congress, held in Mexico City, concluded with a manifesto urging 'all human beings of all nations and their governments, within the framework of their own sovereignty, to recognize the importance of forest resources for the biosphere and the survival of humanity'. A few years later, in 1991, Edouard Saouma, Director-General of the Food and Agriculture Organisation of the United Nations, opened the Tenth World Forestry Congress with the following remarks: 'climate change, the imperilled environment and the North/South interchange are of concern to the whole world. Preserving and developing the essential functions of the forest must therefore be tackled as a worldwide undertaking on three fronts: the ecological, the economic and the social'.

At the time, global diplomacy was working to strengthen international environmental law, and the preservation of forest ecosystems – those of the tropical rainforest in particular – was generally considered to be a matter deserving of greater international collective action.

The Bogging Down of Intergovernmental Negotiation Processes

Right from the start, multilateral negotiations on forests were marked by intense North–South divisions. Broadly speaking, developed countries considered that forests were part of our global heritage and required international protection. They argued that the lack of global rules for forests could lead to the rapid disappearance of rich forest ecosystems. At the same time, developing countries contended that forests were natural resources over which they had sovereignty, and that their development depended in part on those resources. Consequently, at the 1992 Earth Summit in Rio, the international community was unable to reach a consensus on the substance of a global forest agreement. The vastly different goals of developed countries and developing countries stood in the way of any positive outcome. Diverse interests in forest environmental services were also overlaid by differing trade interests, with timber importers and exporters seeking a range of international provisions – not all consistent with environmental requirements.

Despite this persistent North–South impasse, specific negotiations for forests were not abandoned. Based on the Rio Declaration and Statement of Forest Principles, and Chapter 11 of Agenda 21 ('Combating Deforestation'), these carried on under the auspices of the United Nations Commission on Sustainable Development (CSD). In 1995, CSD decided to set up a special body – the Intergovernmental Panel on Forests (IPF) – to develop consensual proposals to strengthen the management, preservation and sustainable development of all types of forests. In February 1997, IPF approved a set of over one hundred proposals for action designed to take up the challenge of global forest management. The delegates were unable to agree, however, on a number of vital matters; for instance those to do with financial assistance, the trade/environment relationship and the opportunity for beginning talks on a global forest agreement.

In June 1997, the governments at a UN General Assembly Special Session adopted IPF's proposals. Their commitment to implement these proposals represented an important decision on forest policy at the very highest level, without actually constituting an international forest agreement per se. IPF's successor, the Intergovernmental Forum on Forests (IFF), was mandated to facilitate implementation of the IPF proposals. In concrete terms, this new body looked at how well the different countries were getting on with implementing IPF's recommendations, based on the annual progress reports they submitted. IFF was also supposed to 'identify the possible elements of and work towards a consensus on international arrangements and mechanisms, for example a legally binding instrument on all types of forests' – the key stumbling block in negotiations.

In its final report presented in 2000, IFF proposed an International Arrangement on Forests (IAF), a successor mechanism providing for two bodies. First, there was IFF's direct successor, officially instated in October 2000: the United Nations Forum on Forests (UNFF). A subsidiary body of the Economic and Social Council (ECOSOC), UNFF was supposed, among other things, to 'consider, within five years, the parameters of a mandate for developing a legal framework on all types of forests' – wording that was vague enough to satisfy those for and those against a legally binding instrument.

The second IAF component, the Collaborative Partnership on Forests (CPF) – a means for collaboration between the main international organizations involved in forest governance – was created in April 2001 to assist UNFF. CPF's fourteen founding members include intergovernmental institutions (UNEP, UNDP, World Bank, FAO, ITTO), the Secretariat of UNFF and Rio's key environmental agreements (UNFCCC, CBD, CCD), international research bodies (ICRAF, CIFOR, IUFRO), the GEF Secretariat and IUCN. The CPF network was also supposed to help implement the 280 or so proposals for action coming under these successive negotiation processes.

With UNFF coming to the end of its mandate and IAF to be evaluated in the near future, the question of a legally binding agreement on forests remains very controversial. Government participation is decreasing – witness the low number of progress reports the UNFF Secretariat has received from different countries on the implementation of the proposals for action.[1] Influential players internationally with significant forests, such as Brazil, Malaysia and Sweden, are still fiercely opposed to a legally binding agreement. Even Canada, a major advocate of an international forest agreement, is beginning to express doubts regarding the possibilities of reaching that objective.

One of the ideas suggested for getting around the obstacles was moving towards a legally binding multilateral agreement in discrete stages. With this approach, an 'umbrella' agreement would contain a number of broad principles, or guidelines, and include regional protocols that would have a certain amount of autonomy, while abiding by these principles. This way, each forest region would be able to promote its own interests and progress, independently from the others, in terms of implementing legally binding instruments. This idea was not acted on, however, once again, because of continued opposition to the multilateral challenges, less significant though they were, to this proposal.

Lack of Consensus on International Architecture

The debate on international forest governance is also wrapped up with the need to clarify the international institutional architecture, which many people consider complex and fragmentary. One of the motives for opening international negotiations on forests is therefore tackling the fragmentation of the global forest regime, including its many legal and institutional overlaps. In addition to UNFF, there are two multilateral instruments devoted to forests specifically: the International Tropical Timber Agreement (ITTA) and the FAO Committee on Forestry. Other non-specific international mechanisms also incorporate provisions that are essential for forests. For example, the Kyoto Protocol attached to the United Nations Framework Convention on Climate Change (UNFCCC) addresses the role played by forests as carbon sinks. The last Conference of the Parties (COP) of the Convention on Biological Diversity (CBD) developed a special work programme on forest biodiversity. The Unesco World Heritage Convention deals in part with protection of the world's most remarkable forest ecosystems. The CITES convention regulates trade in certain species of wood. The Convention to Combat Desertification contains provisions on the role played by forests in the preservation of arid and semi-arid ecosystems. International Labour Organization (ILO) Convention 169 deals with the issue of indigenous peoples, which is so important in tropical forested areas.

---

[1]   *Forest Watch*, Issue 91, FERN, December 2004.

The divisions over forestry issues with these many multilateral legal instruments have led governments to debate two different options for global forest governance. The first has been discussed above: a new instrument that would be more or less legally binding and would aim, among other things, at improving coordination between these different mechanisms. The second option is less ambitious: strengthening existing institutional frameworks in order to implement the many measures currently proposed by different international authorities, in particular the IPF/IFF and CBD proposals for action.

This strictly institutional debate came to a head in April 2002, at the sixth Conference of the Parties to the CBD, where CBD addressed the forestry issue specifically for the first time. The scientific community had estimated that the world's forests contained one half to three-quarters of terrestrial biodiversity. An expanded work programme on forest biological diversity was adopted (Decision VI 22) and the Parties were urged to implement it on a voluntary basis, in keeping with their countries' priorities and needs.

To give this programme a more operational dimension, negotiations were suggested to create an additional CBD protocol. With this option, the Parties could be forced to implement the CBD forest program measures. It was opposed on two fronts, however – by those in favour of strengthening IAF with a view to a legally binding multilateral agreement on forests, and by those from developing countries who refused to see forestry issues treated from the angle of biodiversity preservation specifically and insisted that the contribution of their forests to their economic development be given greater consideration by negotiators from rich countries.

International negotiations are not the only level affected by this wrangling. In some countries, ministries in charge of forestry support one option over another based on their own trade or environmental sensibilities, sometimes to the extent that it is impossible to detect a clear position in talks.

Lack of NGO Support

At the Earth Summit, NGOs held great hopes for the international negotiation. Since then, however, they have become somewhat sceptical about the potential of multilateral talks on the environment to produce regulatory instruments that are truly legally binding and are effective, with good rules of observance, monitoring and sanction mechanisms. They base this position on several arguments (Guéneau and Wilson 2003).

NGOs alert political decision-makers regularly to the slowness of multilateral talks on the environment and the risk of ending up with a consensus that reflects the lowest common denominator. They point out that a lack of political will leads to non-implementation – despite the fact that the issues are fundamental and pressing. They cite the Convention on Climate Change as an example: how long it is taking for the Kyoto Protocol to come into force, the weakness of its objectives, shortcomings in monitoring and evaluation, the red tape involved in and compliance procedures applied to the Parties' commitments (annual progress reports), and the lack of financial means and technical assistance. Lastly, they note the problems with equity in international negotiations, which result in delegations from developed countries having more influence than those from developing countries.

NGOs also point out the lack of government openness to civil society representatives in negotiations – the UNFF talks especially. Most large NGOs are therefore not very inclined to support a new international instrument. Others consider that certain conditions must be met for IAF to play its role fully as a coordinator of international collective action aimed at forests (Mankin 2004), without actually turning it into their key concern.

Increasing Influence of Approaches Based on Public–Private Partnerships

In relation to the weaknesses of multilateral solutions, a pragmatic view of forest governance is emerging. This view entails forming 'coalitions of the willing' that include public actors (governments and international organizations) as well as private actors with different viewpoints (NGOs and private sector) for the purpose of reaching a common goal. There is by no means universal support for this view, however.

Regional Partnerships

The heterogeneous nature of forest resources, exploitation methods and social, cultural and environmental issues have prompted governments to decide that it is a good idea to deal with some forestry issues regionally. Forest management standards, for instance, were the subject of a dozen or so regional negotiation proceedings, or 'processes', which defined criteria and indicators for sustainable forest management that are now widely recognized by producers: the Helsinki Process for Europe (1993), Montreal Process for North America (1993), Tarapoto Process for the Amazon (1995) and the African Timber Organization's Criteria and Indicators (1996), to name a few.

In parallel with this strictly standard-based approach, more ambitious attempts were made to strengthen regional forest governance. For example, the heads of state of Central African countries organized a summit in 1999 on the conservation and sustainable management of tropical forests. The summit was followed by the creation of the Conference of Ministers in charge of Forests in Central Africa (Comifac), which met for the second time early in 2005. This new institution, which was charged with the tasks of boosting regional cooperation and facilitating dialogue with donor countries, is still financially strapped. For Comifac's action plan to be implemented, member states would have to make a real financial contribution and donor countries would have to provide better support – and these things are far from happening. Financial considerations aside, there is also internal wrangling over leadership.

Designed to get around such recurrent institutional problems, a number of governance innovations came into being at the World Summit on Sustainable Development held in Johannesburg in 2002. Three regional public–private partnerships devoted specifically to tropical forests – referred to as Type II Initiatives – were set up. Composed of governments, international organizations and NGOs, these partnerships were created to raise funds and implement programmes for the conservation and sustainable management of forests in the world's three tropical regions.

For Central Africa's forests, the Congo Basin Forest Partnership was put together by the South African and United States governments in collaboration with a number of other governments, international institutions, large NGOs (such as the Wildlife Conservation Society, WWF and Conservation International), and representatives from the private sector. In all, there are twenty-nine partners associated with this original initiative. A similar initiative, the Asian Forest Partnership, was launched by the Japanese government. Lastly – on a more modest scale – a network of model forests in Latin America was confirmed by Canada, a number of partner countries and UNDP.

These new forms of governance reflect two fundamental trends. First, there is the increase in private- and government-sector intervention in forest governance systems, particularly in regions where attempts to re-establish the rule of law have failed. Second, the global approach to the world's forests that prevailed in the late 1980s and early 1990s is apparently being supplanted by more pragmatic regional approaches. Could global forest governance be the result of the addition of such coalitions of the willing, focusing on the planet's most endangered forest areas?

Industry-based Approaches: Example of the Fight against Illegal Logging

Another way to tackle forest governance is to develop industry-based regional approaches. The fight against illegal logging and illegal trade is an example of this recent type of approach. In effect, international treatment of forestry matters involves a prioritization of problems – and illegal logging,[2] or delinquent forestry practices, has gradually moved up just about to the top.

This all began in 1998 when the G8 Summit concluded with a plea for governments to join forces and fight illegal logging. More recently, this objective, along with the reinforcement of capacities and improvement of dialogue between Central African actors, was advocated by France, when it took on the leadership of the Congo Basin Forest Partnership.[3] NGOs have also made illegal logging one of their campaign themes, pointing out the role played by illegal logging and

---

[2]   By illegal, we mean non-compliant with the laws of the country of origin (Brack and Hayman, 2001).
[3]   Cf. Speech by French President Jacques Chirac at the opening of the 2nd Heads of State Summit on the conservation of Central Africa's forest ecosystems, Brazzaville, 5 February 2005.

trade in deforestation, loss of tax revenue and increased poverty. According to WWF, 50 per cent of Cameroon's logging operations are illegal and 80 per cent of Brazil's lumber is produced illegally.[4]

In 2001, World Bank organized a conference on illegal logging that brought together thirteen countries, including the United Kingdom, the United States and a number of East Asian countries; NGOs; and representatives from the private sector. This conference gave birth to the FLEG (Forest Law Enforcement and Governance) process. In April 2002, the European Union organized a multi-stakeholder workshop to develop its own plan for fighting illegal logging: the Forest Law Enforcement, Governance and Trade (FLEGT) Action Plan.[5] The plan aimed to increase the ability of developing countries to control illegal logging and reduce trade in illegal wood between these countries and the European Union. In Africa, a Ministerial Conference in October 2003 launched a similar process: the Africa Forest Law Enforcement and Governance (AFLEG) process.[6] These regional processes for fighting illegal logging and trade represent a concrete application of broader-based public–private partnerships such as the Congo Basin Forest Partnership.

The key measures of the action plans created by these regional processes are geared towards strengthening the laws of producing countries and improving bilateral, regional and international cooperation in the fight against illegal logging and trade. These processes result in bilateral partnership agreements, such as the agreement signed between the United Kingdom and Indonesia in April 2002 to reduce British imports of wood products and timber produced illegally in Indonesia. Among other things, this agreement provides for verification of legality through greater civil society involvement, joint examination of the legislative reforms needed to combat forest crimes, incentives for 'serious' manufacturers, mechanisms for tracking timber movement and so on.

Through such examples of bilateral and regional cooperation, the first stirrings can be seen of new forms of governance, where organized civil society, the private sector and importing countries play a central role in dealing with the failings of the countries unable to govern forest resources. These industry-based, multi-actor forms of governance already appear to yield better results than classical intergovernmental processes.

For example, the legality requirement can be included in conditionalities imposed on suppliers when public timber procurement policy is designed in consumer countries. Manufacturers also become involved in legality by developing independent verification systems with NGOs. This is the case with the Congo

---

4   WWF, The Timber Footprint of the G8 and China, <www.panda.org>.

5   Cf. European Commission External Relations Directorate General, Forest Law Enforcement, Governance and Trade (FLEGT), Brussels Workshop, 22–24 April 2002, Summary of Discussions.

6   Cf. Declaration of the Africa Forest Law Enforcement and Governance (AFLEG) Ministerial Conference, October 2003.

Basin forest concession monitoring system developed by IFIA in collaboration with several NGOs, including Global Forest Watch, the World Resources Institute (WRI), IUCN and WWF (Achancho 2004). This system is designed to single out countries that comply with the laws in force by means of legality certification. Companies participate voluntarily in complying with laws and commitments to sustainable forest development, set out by a multi-party steering committee composed of representatives from regional organizations (Comifac), NGOs and the private sector. WRI is responsible for auditing how these requirements are met. Mediation procedures are provided for any offenders it finds, creating reputation incentives (or disincentives) for the company in question. If the company still fails to comply at the end of a one-month time limit, its certificate of legality can be taken away. The certificate attesting to the legality of the logging operation is attached to the other documents required to export products. Certifiers have developed certification and control systems that vary somewhat, such as the 'timber origin and legality certificate' created by Eurocertifor in 2004.

In spite of some criticisms, NGOs – including the hardliners – consider the FLEG(T) process to be a possible way of creating an international sustainable forest management standard. They therefore suggest using FLEG(T) processes and partnership agreements to progress rapidly at the bilateral and regional levels with countries that hope to agree on the definition of a high standard of sustainable forest management and benefit from the support of the European Union and other G8 members. According to the NGOs Greenpeace, FERN and WWF, once a critical mass of producing countries and consumer countries have agreed on guidelines for a sustainable forest management standard, it will be possible to return to a multilateral option – an option for which the EU and G8 will have laid the groundwork at the same time as bilateral, regional negotiations.[7] A set of regional approaches directed in participatory fashion by coalitions of the willing could therefore be a viable alternative to global forest governance systems stemming from intergovernmental negotiations based entirely on nation-state participants.

Non-state Network Governance Systems

NGOs active in the international forest policy debate have markedly improved their ability to influence forest governance systems (Bass 1996; 2003; Haufler 2003; Meidinger 2003). During the 1980s, several NGOs, frustrated with government inaction and the absence of clear agreement at the intergovernmental level, called for a tropical timber boycott. Although some governments, such as those of the Netherlands and Austria, were ready to follow suit with official bans, this strategy was not very successful.

---

[7]   Illegal Logging and the Global Trade in Illegally Sourced Timber; a Crime Against Forests and Peoples, NGO Statement, April 2002. Available at: <www.fern.org/pubs/ngostats/logging.pdf>.

The failure of attempts to boycott tropical timber is fairly indicative of the limited latitude for action as a result of the trade policies of consumer countries. When these countries wanted to ban tropical timber exports, they were faced with the threat of trade sanctions. Differences in forest management standards between countries are generally as a result of the heterogeneous nature of natural endowments, development status and community preferences, and therefore do not justify resorting to such trade policy instruments as import bans, quotas or taxes. Any attempts at arbitrary trade restrictions that are not justified on exceptional grounds, such as public health protection, could infringe World Trade Organization (WTO) rules and be the subject of a Dispute Settlement Body case.

Thus, regarding the forest sector, governing trade and environment issues within the WTO rules is obviously incomplete. And the chances of arriving at a forest agreement that is truly effective and legally binding are very low. This therefore brings us back to the well-worn question of how to govern global forestry without an international coordination mechanism playing the role of world government. It is in response to this question that NGOs supported a new network-based form of world governance.

As for the timber distribution companies, they looked for new ways to protect their activities from boycott threats, which they took very seriously. They realized that they would have problems giving consumers guarantees that the products they sold came from sustainably managed forests. They recognized that they could arrive at the most credible alternative to boycotts through greater collaboration with NGOs on the joint development of a non-state network-based governance system. Thus the Forest Stewardship Council (FSC) was born in 1993.

The FSC Case

The FSC is an international association that provides standard-setting, trademark assurance and accreditation services for companies and organizations interested in responsible forestry. FSC's mission is to promote environmentally appropriate, socially beneficial and economically viable management of the world's forests. Its role is both to determine good international forest management standards and to provide accreditation services to certifiers and National Initiatives.

The FSC Accreditation Program provides for three types of services: accreditation of certifiers, FSC National Initiatives, and FSC National Standards. FSC-accredited organizations certify forest owners and managers in accordance with criteria and indicators that meet FSC guidelines. The certification process is voluntary.

FSC has a unique governance structure that is founded on sustainable development principles (Bass 2002). Since 1993, FSC has distinguished itself through its:

1 *Sustainable development based organization:* Members (primarily NGOs, forest producers and traders) are divided among three 'chambers' – economic, environmental and social – reflecting the three pillars of sustainable development.

2 *Equity/fairness:* Within each chamber, there is voting parity between North and South member countries. However, some regions are overrepresented, particularly the countries of the North. Others, such as African countries, are underrepresented.

3 *Multi-stakeholder participation:* Members are a diverse mixture of representatives from environmental and social groups, the timber trade and forestry profession, indigenous peoples' organizations, responsible corporations, community forestry groups and forest product certification organizations from around the world. Membership does not include government, however. This is because FSC wanted to be a voluntary initiative and avoid falling foul of trade laws, and because it did not want to duplicate the 'lowest common denominator' positions of (inter)governmental forest initiatives.

4 *Global standard setting: The FSC has ten Principles of Forest Stewardship that* apply to all tropical, temperate and boreal forests. These Principles and fifty-six associated Criteria (P&C) form the basis for all FSC forest management standards. They cover economic, environmental and social factors. They were arrived at as a result of a great deal of consultation; they could be said to embody 'the spirit of Rio'; and they are regularly reviewed and revised. They can be applied to all types of forests around the world.

5 *Global presence:* FSC is a global network with an international centre in Bonn, regional offices in all parts of the globe, National Initiatives in thirty-four countries and certified forests in sixty-two countries. FSC operates through its network of National Initiatives in over thirty countries.

6 *Local implementation and flexibility:* National multi-stakeholder working groups translate FSC's Principles and Criteria into national and subnational standards relevant to the forest type. These are evaluated for certification purposes by certifiers and other involved and affected parties on a case-by-case basis. As a result, standards differ from one country to the next, but are considered compatible internationally. The standards include implementation of all relevant legislation, but tend to set a higher benchmark.

7 *Independence and credibility:* Standards are independently verified on site in the forest (and on the basis of the logging company's documented forest management system) by accredited auditors, resulting in a certificate and labelled timber.

8 *Relationships with major retailers/wholesalers:* WWF has organized buyers' groups (usually retailers, mostly in countries of the North) that have pledged to stock FSC-certified timber only.

9 *Incentive impact:* Labelled timber offers an incentive to producers. The reward tends to be market access, but in some areas includes a price premium.

Because of its demanding requirements, FSC has not managed to impose a harmonized system for the standardization and encouragement of sustainable forest development that is acceptable to all actors worldwide. All the same, 50 million hectares have been certified over the past ten years in over sixty countries as complying with FSC standards, and several thousand products bear the FSC trademark.[8] More important still: FSC has undeniable influence over negotiations and practices in different parts of the world.

FSC's Influence over Forest Policy

According to Rezende de Azevedo (2004), although the FSC certification programme only applies to a fairly limited percentage of Brazilian forests, it has had a significant impact. It has contributed to improve working conditions in forest activities, to change forest management practices and to enhance community relations with indigenous people in areas where there are forest activities. Tollefson (2004) highlights the important role of forest certification as a precursor to public regulation focused on indigenous rights in British Columbia.

FSC's rapid success prompted certain economic operators and states with sensitive forestry interests to react by developing their own market-driven regulation systems. National certification programmes were introduced in several large countries, such as Malaysia, Brazil and Indonesia, and private initiatives were born in North America, Europe and Africa. Although less restrictive than FSC's system, these certification schemes nevertheless structured and codified forest management practices.

At the same time, in order to promote FSC's system worldwide, WWF set up a network of buyers' groups, now known as the Global Forest and Trade Network (GFTN) – a partnership between different stakeholders, NGOs, local institutions, negotiators and retailers in the timber, paper, and manufactured wood products industries. The first buyers' group was created in the UK in 1991. Now this group is made up of large chains of home renovation, furniture and carpentry stores, paper firms, newspaper and magazine publishers amongst others. Other groups were set up in Europe, North America and Australia, and then the trend hit Southern Europe, Asia (Japan, Taiwan, Hong Kong), Brazil and Africa. Most of the major markets are now covered by these buyers' groups. Many local institutions (municipalities, regions, etc) have adopted procurement policies requiring wood from certified or locally logged forests – for example, the Nord-Pas-de-Calais regional council and municipalities (Lille, Rennes) in France.[9] At the beginning of 2001, Germany's North Rhine-Westphalia government decided to buy only FSC-certified timber.[10] By promoting voluntary certification

---

[8]   See <www.fsc.org>.

[9]   Bâtir sans détruire. Les collectivités locales protègent les forêts tropicales. Campaign led by Les Amis de la Terre and Robin des Bois, 2000.

[10]   FSC Arbeitsgruppe Deutschland e.V., Press Release, 19 January 2001.

at different forest governance levels, FSC provided leverage for local actors who, in the case of timber consumer countries, felt excluded from the international forest regulation process.

At the national level, the most significant governance impact has derived from the FSC national certification working groups. Multi-stakeholder in nature, and including government at this level, in many countries they are the only forum for reviewing forest matters. They have focused on such critical issues as 'What is good forestry? How should we recognize it? How can we hold managers accountable? How can we encourage improvement? And how can we reward them?' Even when certification does not itself prove to be the answer to these questions, the debate has been effective. There are cases of working group deliberations being taken into other policy arenas. At the very least, the work of such groups has had an excellent capacity development effect (Bass 2002).

Contestability of New Non-State Forms of Governance

Public–private coalitions and network governance systems are 'competing' more and more with inter-state international governance processes, challenging the very need for a legally binding instrument on forests. The obvious popularity of these new forms of forest governance must not, however, obscure a number of questions (Guéneau 2002). First of all, the effectiveness of market-driven regulation systems using instruments such as certification or the monitoring of illegal logging and trade is being questioned. Do these systems make it possible to fight deforestation effectively? Second, despite its organizational model favouring balanced representation of different categories of actors, some of the arguments against the FSC system are based on its unfairness, or inequity. Lastly, there is debate on the legitimacy of forms of governance that involve organized civil society as opposed to being based on government intervention.

Effectiveness of Non-state Governance Instruments

Considering the certification boom around the world and the exponential increase in certified forest surface area, there is no doubt that the FSC system has achieved a high profile and has had successes. These have already inspired an extension of this market-driven regulation system to other sectors, such as the seafood industry. Plans are also under way for similar systems for the agricultural, tourism and mining industries. These outcomes are certainly significant, but should be viewed from a variety of perspectives. First, as a result of fears on the part of manufacturers and forest owners that environmentalists would force management requirements on them that would be too strict and/or irrelevant, competing certification programs have rapidly sprung up. These include the Canadian Standards Association (CSA) programme, Sustainable Forestry Initiative (SFI), Pan-European Forest Certification Scheme (PEFC), Pan-African Forest

Certification Scheme (PAFC), and national certification programmes in Brazil, Chile, Malaysia and Indonesia. While FSC's standards apply to forests worldwide, these other programmes are primarily of a regional or national nature. What we are witnessing then, is a race between programmes to impose their own criteria on the market by increasing the certified surface area they control. Considering how heated the debate over certification has been between the private sector and the non-governmental sector, it is likely that network governance systems will end up weakened by this battle for standard control, in part because of loss of credibility amongst confused consumers and state authorities.

Second, although the development of these programs has certainly regulated the timber industry – in particular, allowing 'good' producers to be distinguished from the 'bad', especially in countries where controls are difficult – there are signs that certification could merely entrench management practices suited to 'good' producers and their business models – which will not always produce desirable results. In other words, what will be the real incentives associated with market-driven governance systems?

Two things need to be pointed out here. First, the NGOs supporting FSC advocate its high performance standards, while other certification programmes emphasize flexibility through procedural standards. Second, it seems obvious that market-driven governance systems will only be able to have an impact on a very limited portion of tropical forests: the part that exports timber to the European and North American markets, which discriminate in favour of 'green' products.

The following observation seems to apply to certification systems as well as programmes for fighting illegal logging and trade: only large companies exporting most of their output to developed countries with strong environmental sensibilities subject themselves voluntarily to forest management and/or legality verification measures. However, neither the timber destined for the large booming consumer markets of Southern countries, with China leading the way, or the timber sold on the domestic markets of tropical countries, led by Brazil, appear at this point to be influenced by market-driven governance systems. And yet it is precisely these countries that are making the tropical timber markets so dynamic: according to ITTO, Chinese imports of tropical timber increased by 33 per cent between 2003 and 2004 (Ze Meka 2005) and China is soon to be the biggest timber importer. What is more, certification of good forest management does not have any significant influence over crucial issues of 'asset stripping' forms of logging or forest conversion into farmland – the leading causes of deforestation. Certification appears to offer no incentive or sanction for 'poor' producers.

Market-driven governance systems are therefore having difficulties gaining recognition in places with weak local governance systems. Kern (2003) stresses the case of Indonesia, where illegal logging accounts for 70 per cent and where FSC withdrew the certification of a large teak plantation subsequent to finding that its standards and procedures were not being complied with. Local governance systems, calling on local policies and controls, would therefore appear to be necessary to fight illegal logging. Despite the enthusiasm of private producers,

NGOs and governments for improved forest governance systems, a number of authors (Karsenty 2002) also feel that – more than the fight against illegal logging by repressive action – it is the fight against the underlying causes of illegal activities that needs to be given priority, i.e. fighting underdevelopment.

Are the New Forms of Forest Governance Fair?

Questions of equity, or fairness, are a central issue in discussions on market-driven forest governance systems (Thornber 2003; Thornber, Plouvier and Bass 1999). The statistics speak for themselves: according to the International Tropical Timber Organization, tropical forests represent only 7 per cent of certified forests worldwide (Ze Meka 2005). The FSC system itself, which is organized internally around the equitable distribution of responsibilities between North and South, shows uneven results: over half of its certified forest surface area is concentrated in Europe and less than a quarter in tropical regions, where the forests are the most abundant. Out of the 50 million hectares of forest certified by FSC, only a little less than 2 million hectares are in Africa – no certificates have been issued for any countries in the Congo Basin – and less than 400,000 hectares are in Asia, half in Japan alone. Plantations account for a large proportion of FSC-certified tropical forest.

It is a fact that it is easier to certify the forests that are the most homogeneous, that is, plantations and temperate forests, where resource inventories and development plans are also well established; there are less land-ownership problems; practices are recorded clearly; forestry employees are competent and well-trained, laws are obeyed and controls facilitated; and the political regimes are stable. In some countries – those of Central Africa, for instance – the implementation of sustainable development plans, which should inevitably lead to certification, necessarily takes longer and is more costly than in the countries of the North, even though most tropical timber is in competition with certified temperate and boreal forest products. In addition, the threat of reducing non-certified timber imports for public markets or industrial lumber markets is very real in Europe. The risk is that part of the flow of tropical timber will be redirected towards markets where legality controls are limited and/or the demand for certified timber is low.

Problems of fairness are also related to company size. The costs of certification, which include the cost of the preliminary certification evaluation, making the management changes required to obtain certification, and the annual audits, effectively limit the certification prospects of small producers. A portion of these costs are fixed costs, and consequently induce scale effects: the bigger the forestry operation, the smaller the proportion of the overall cost of the certified product, and the more competitive advantages forest certification generates. Small operations, on the other hand, have the most difficulty bearing these costs. Even though FSC addressed this problem a while ago by setting up a special certification programme for small owners and producers, most of the companies certified to date are bigger and well-resourced – or are small tropical community groups whose certification was funded by donors. Certification has therefore had the initial effect of recognizing the best producers and making good ones even better – with little impact on the real forest problem of the asset-stripping behaviour of the bad producers.

How Legitimate are Non-state Governance Systems?

Traditional global governance systems are based on relationships between states, with the outcome being the creation of institutions responsible for organizing cooperation so that states can pursue common or shared goals. Opting for this kind of regime gives states a number of rights and obligations to guide their public policy. With these systems, governance is founded on democratic legitimacy in sovereign countries.

The source of legitimacy with the new forest governance systems is completely different, however. The institutions created under these systems are based on markets rather than territory. International pressure from NGOs makes it possible to govern at least some forestry matters independently of states, on political terrain that is different from that of intergovernmental relations (Bernstein and Cashore 2003). What are the underlying reasons for legitimacy with these governance systems? How are they more legitimate than systems based on the democratic legitimacy of states? These questions are vital insofar as certain actors contest the legitimacy of non-state actors to play what they see as the state's role. In addition, the privatization of a number of the sovereign functions of states, such as creating standards and implementing or enforcing them, is problematic. If companies pay for access to the regulation system, and specialized bodies or organizations are remunerated for monitoring compliance with standards, how can the system's neutrality and independence be guaranteed?

In the opinion of Bernstein and Cashore (2003), actor participation and responsibility is more important than democratic legitimacy in judging a system's legitimacy. In other words, a rule or an institution is legitimate if the different groups of actors concerned by this question consider it to be relevant and appropriate.

From this angle, transparency, better participation, and the way interests are allocated and distributed both by FSC's decision-making power structure and national working groups in the forest industry are indications of legitimacy. FSC's openness to the private sector, and companies' attempts at self-regulation through certification or voluntary codes of conduct, also back up this system's legitimacy (Kern 2003). Lastly, civil society participation in decision-making processes in places where the rule of law is difficult to enforce is another argument used to demonstrate the legitimate nature of non-state governance systems.

At the national level, FSC working groups are created wherever possible. When this is not possible, however, procedures are provided to assure the system's legitimacy locally. They include mandatory consultation of local actors and mechanisms for communities and local NGOs to lodge complaints. Kern therefore considers that, in some countries, the rights granted to local people via FSC can be better than those they are granted by national laws. This statement needs to be put into perspective, however, considering the lack of means and deterioration in government services in many forestry countries. Should the improvement of local forest governance be prompted by outside intervention or, conversely, should it be founded on the development and support of an indigenous vision embraced by local actors?

Conclusion

We can conclude that non-state forest governance systems will have increasingly significant effects on how forestry is treated at different levels, from the local to the global. They 'compete' with the international governance process and call into question the need for a legally binding instrument on forests. If the legitimacy of market-driven systems has gained growing recognition locally and internationally, their effectiveness remains to be proven – particularly with regard to the more vulnerable actors, the majority of whom are found in tropical forested areas under highest pressure.

What seems to impress most observers about FSC is its role as a catalyst for change in forest practices and policy. This influence, which is considerable, revolves around its role in reinforcing the articulation between public and private spheres in the development of global forest governance mechanisms. Forest governance cannot be dogmatically based on one approach alone, but rather requires better articulation between different systems.

We would not advocate a swing too far towards NSMD forms of governance. Excessive attention to NSMD, at the cost of basic state processes and capacities, runs the risk of establishing two-tier governance. Evaluating market-driven governance systems through the lenses of effectiveness, fairness and legitimacy has begun to reveal their incompleteness, as well as their potential.

References

Achancho, Valantine. 2004. 'Final Report of the Workshop on Voluntary Independent Forest Concession Monitoring in Central Africa'. Douala, March. <www.ifiasite.com/pdf/ifi>.

Bass, Stephen. 2002. 'Global Forest Governance: Emerging impacts of the Forest Stewardship Council. International Institute for Environment and Development'. Brief Paper for International Sustra Workshop, 'Architecture of the Global System of Governance of Trade and Sustainable Development', 9–10 December, Berlin.

———. 1996. 'Certification as a Manifestation of Changing Roles in Forestry'. Presentation for the short course 'Making Forest Policy Work', Oxford Forestry Institute, July.

————. 2003. 'Certification in the Forest Political Landscape'. In Errol Meidinger, Chris Elliott and Gerhard Oesten, eds., *Social and Political Dimensions of Forest Certification*. Germany: Remagen-Oberwinter. <www.forstbuch.de>.

Bernstein, Steven and Benjamin Cashore. 2004. 'Non-state Global Governance: Is Forest Certification a Legitimate Alternative to a Global Forest Convention?' In John J. Kirton and Michael J. Trebilcock, eds. *Hard Choices, Soft Law: Combining Trade, Environment and Social Cohesion in Global Governance*. Aldershot: Ashgate.

Brack, Duncan and Gavin Hayman. 2001. 'Intergovernmental Actions on Illegal Logging'. RIIA, March.

Cashore, Benjamin. 2002. 'Legitimacy and the Privatization of Environmental Governance: How Non-state Market-driven (NSMD) Governance Systems Gain Rule-making Authority'. *Governance: An International Journal of Policy, Administration and Institutions* 15.4: 503–29.

European Commission. 2003. 'Communication from the Commission to the Council and the European Parliament'. FLEGT Proposal for an EU Action Plan. Brussels: European Commission.

Guéneau, Stéphane. 2002. 'La forêt tropicale: entre fourniture de bien public global et régulation privée, quelle place pour l'instrument certification?' In *L'outil économique en droit international et européen de l'environnement*. La Documentation française, Collection Monde européen et international.

Guéneau, Stéphane and Anne-Marie Wilson. 2003. 'Gouvernance mondiale des forêts: Une évaluation à partir de l'analyse de la position des organisations non gouvernementales'. Iddri, October. <www.iddri.org>.

Haufler, Virginia. 2003. 'New Forms of Governance: Certification Regimes as Social Regulations of the Global Market'. In Errol Meidinger, Chris Elliott and Gerhard Oesten (eds.), *Social and Political Dimensions of Forest Certification*. Remagen-Oberwinter, Germany. <www.forstbuch.de>.

Karsenty, Alain. 2002. 'Pour une hiérarchie des causes et manifestations de l'exploitation illégale des bois tropicaux, Cirad-Forêt'. Paper presented to the French Working Group for Tropical Rainforests, April.

Kern, Kristine. 2003. 'Global Governance Through Transnational Network Organizations: the Scope and Limitations of Civil Society Self-organisation'. WZB discussion paper. Berlin 2003.

Krasner, Stephen D. 1983. 'Structural Causes and Regime Consequences: Regimes as Intervening Variables'. In Stephen D. Krasner, ed., *International Regimes*. Ithaca: Cornell University Press: 1–21.

Mankin, Bill. 2004. 'The IAF at the Crossroads: Tough Choices Ahead'. WWF Forests for Life Program, September. WWF International, Gland, Switzerland

Meidinger, Errol. 2003. 'Forest Certification as a Global Civil Society Regulatory Institution'. In Errol Meidinger, Chris Elliott and Gerhard Oesten, eds. *Social and Political Dimensions of Forest Certification*. Remagen-Oberwinter, Germany. <www.forstbuch.de>.

Reinecke, Wolfgang. 1998. *Global Public Policy: Governing without Government?* Washington, DC: Brookings Institution Press.

Rezende de Azevedo, Tasso. 2004. 'The Forest Stewardship Council: a Developing Country Perspective'. In John J. Kirton and Michael J. Trebilcock, eds. *Hard Choices, Soft Law: Combining Trade, Environment and Social Cohesion in Global Governance*. Aldershot: Ashgate.

Streck, Charlotte. 2002. 'Global Public Policy Networks as Coalitions for Change'. In Daniel C. Esty and Maria H. Ivanova, eds. *Global Environmental Governance: Options and Opportunities*. New Haven: Yale School of Forestry and Environmental Studies.

Tollefson, Chris. 2004. 'Indigenous Rights and Forest Certification in British Columbia'. In John J. Kirton and Michael J. Trebilcock, eds. *Hard Choices, Soft Law: Combining Trade, Environment and Social Cohesion in Global Governance*. Ashgate

Thornber, Kirsti. 2003. Certification: A Discussion of Equity Issues. In Errol Meidinger, Chris Elliott and Gerhard Oesten (eds.), *Social and Political Dimensions of Forest Certification*. Remagen-Oberwinter, Germany. <www.forstbuch.de>.

Thornber, Kirsti, Dominiek Plouvier and Stephen Bass. 1999. 'Certification: Barriers to Benefits – A Discussion of Equity Implications'. European Forest Institute Discussion Paper, 8, EFI, Joensuu, Finland.

WWF. 'The Timber Footprint of the G8 and China'. <www.panda.org>

Young, Oran, ed. 1997. *Global Governance. Drawing Insights from the Environmental Experience*. Cambridge, MA and London: MIT Press.

———. 2001. 'Inferences and Indices. Evaluating the Effectiveness of International Environmental Regimes'. *Global Environmental Politics* 1.1: 99–121.

Ze Meka, Emmanuel. 2005. 'Impact écologique de la demande internationale des bois tropicaux'. Communication à l'atelier 'Gérer durablement la biodiversité tropicale et subtropicale: île et forêts' de la Conférence internationale 'Biodiversité: science et gouvernance'. Paris, 26 January.

PART 3
Participation in Implementation and Evaluation

The Role of Scientific Expertise in Assessing Sustainability under Uncertainty and Controversy – Lessons from the Case of Climate Change

Olivier Godard

Introduction

Integrated assessment of policy impact is a highly demanded and a highly demanding approach. Its aim is to increase the coherence and efficiency of public policies, but also their transparency and communication. Recently, the European Commission (2002) committed itself to developing integrated impact assessment of major policy initiatives. One unique framework is to be used for catching business, environmental, gender and trade impacts. This demand for integrated impact assessment highlights a frequent claim that previous public policies were ill-designed, had unintended side effects or were incapable of reaching the assigned goals. It also depends on one assumption: sources of weakness are to be found mainly in insufficient information used for policy design. In other words, weakness of expertise and lack of appropriate framing of expertise would explain policy failures.

This is a highly contentious assumption, one that is not confirmed, for instance, by the huge investment in scientific expertise on the issues of climate change. There have been unprecedented efforts to organize at a global level, through the Intergovernmental Panel of experts on Climate Change (IPCC), a regular updating of scientific knowledge on climate change from all concerned disciplines and active research and development, using all sorts of models designed to enlighten policy issues, for at least twenty years. In spite of all this, and the eventual enforcement of the Kyoto Protocol by February 2005,[1] allowed by the Russian ratification,

---

[1]   The practical relevance of the Kyoto Protocol has been devalued by the withdrawal of the United States and Australia. Only one-third of world emissions are covered by quantified objectives of control of greenhouse gases. The Protocol ends in 2012 and nothing is planned for the post-Kyoto period. In 2006, the issue is still at the stage of preliminary discussions.

national policies still do not really exist, or lack strength. Even in the European Union (EU), the only region where a political will was claimed and significant policy initiatives were taken, there is a gap between statements of intentions and goals and achievements. The most significant initiative, the development of an EU CO_2 market for stationary sources of big emitters from the industry and energy sectors,[2] has had a tough start. Since no EU member wants to hurt its industry with constraining measures, national allocation plans for the first period (2005 –2007) are lax: quotas are allocated for free; the amounts given have been based on business predictions of future needs; new capacities and new entrants will also receive the quotas they need, for free.[3] All this demonstrates that the main preoccupation of national governments is to do their national industrial champions no harm, not to use a new tool to promote cost-effective abatement solutions in line with the claimed goals and commitments. Fifteen years of international negotiations have ultimately achieved rather poor results. Can we really say that such a somewhat wasteful expenditure of time, effort and confidence in public governance is the result of a lack of integrated assessment of the issues at stake?

The aim of integrated assessment is to gather a variety of information sources and analytical pieces into one unique framework, in order to authorize a broad look at a specific issue of concern in a policy context, such as new trade agreements within the World Trade Organization (WTO). Beyond legitimate doubt about the real source of policy failure, an increasing use of impact assessment practices in the context of policy choice raises several questions in relation to sustainable development (SD). Can SD be included in that framework; that is, can we assess impact on SD in the same way as impacts on business or trade? What conditions should be met to make sustainability impact assessment (SIA) a useful tool to promote coherent and ambitious SD policies? The first question is related to the status of SD. If we agree that SD cannot be measured as a physical characteristic (see Chapter 2), to assess impact on SD promises to be a complex endeavour, since it would be necessary to follow the various ways through which SD conceptions (values, goals, tests) are elaborated, and to see to what extent these various conceptions are supported by stakeholders. The second question leads to a reconsideration of the manner in which scientific expertise and decision-making are articulated in a neo-corporatist decision-making process based on openness to various stakeholders for consultation and lobbying.

This chapter is devoted to expertise. It aims to explain what happens to scientific results when they are used in a context of expertise, that is, a context framed by goals and constraints of decision-making (see Box 11.1 below). Often,

---

2   See Directive 2003/87/EC of 13 October 2003 establishing a scheme for greenhouse gas emission allowance trading within the Community and amending Council Directive 96/61/EC.

3   For an assessment of the final French national allocation plan of first period accepted by the EU Commission in December 2004, see Godard (2005).

Box 11.1: Scientific Research and Scientific Expertise

Scientific expertise is a science-based activity that differs from scientific research, even if it is researchers who take the role of experts from time to time. Differences are manifold. They are related to:

1. the source and nature of questions raised: they are made endogenous in scientific research, they come from the society in expertise;
2. the time-frame of the activity: there is a scientific competition, particularly in the context of techno-sciences having a huge intellectual property dimension, but there is no *a priori* time limit for scientific research, whereas there are huge time constraints for expertise, which are imposed by the management or policy agenda;
3. the nature of activity: experts are not doing research, they critically analyse and synthesize available scientific work and output, and qualify existing scientific uncertainties in relation to practical policy issues;
4. the procedures of validating a statement or an opinion: peer discussion of specific proof elements (methods) for a given result are at the core of scientific activity; discussions within groups of experts aim at checking that an overview of a scientific domain is correct in relation to a practical issue; expert judgements have to be based on sound argumentation beyond what can be scientifically proven.

---

decision-makers misunderstand the nature of scientific analyses and misuse expert opinions; sometimes, however, they tend to use the results strategically or even cynically, either putting weight on them beyond their scientific validity, or suggesting that they mean the opposite of what the experts concluded or of data they presented to back their opinion. To neutralize such attempts, the least that can be done is to obtain that expert opinions are made public through modern medias of communication (the web) for a large dissemination through society.

Meanwhile, under uncertainty and controversy, it is clear that experts are taking roles in practice that go beyond their official status. Such roles emerge from the situation created in a context of scientific uncertainty and controversy, and specific ways of organizing interrelationships between experts and decision-makers. The international and national arena for climate change policies provides the empirical background from which the description has been obtained. It confirms it is worth understanding what is at stake when impact assessment exercises are developed.

The first section details the key questions related to the use of scientific expertise for integrated assessment. The second section is devoted to an examination of models of scientific expertise, and the third takes the case of climate change to show how a standard framing adopted by a discipline may be changed by its use in a situation of expertise. The fourth explains the implicit roles taken by experts in context of uncertain and controversial science, and the

fifth recounts a typical anecdote from French energy policy, illustrating possible
tensions and strategic misuse of experts opinions by policy-makers.

Scientific Expertise and Integrated Assessment

Looking at scientific expertise (see Box 11.1) from a technical viewpoint, two basic
issues are raised by the project of integrated assessment. The first one is related to
the insertion of heterogeneous information on heterogeneous matters within one
unique framework. The standard response from economists is well known, and
is aimed at finding some balance between various 'items': cost-benefit analysis
provides the needed framework. It implies the use of prices or, more generally, of
marginal rates of substitution between compensating marginal changes in various
types of impacts of projected policy. Following that view, integrated assessment
calls for the use of an objective function embodying all the marginal rates of
substitution responding to policy preferences. How should we proceed, when such
an objective function cannot be formulated by governing bodies? The idea of a
coexistence of several justification orders relevant for public decision-making (see
Chapter 2) makes it pointless to assume one unique objective function.

The second issue is related to the interrelationship of the various aspects
and dimensions that are separated for analytical reasons, but linked to some
extent in real life. In scientific terms, it raises the problem of interdisciplinary
communication and exchange of data, in spite of different scientific backgrounds
and different semantics. One current solution is to find a common interface
variable between economic and physical models, such as greenhouse gas emissions
(GHG), although the conditions of use and the level of aggregation of data are not
the same for economic modelling as for atmospheric or biological ones. Moreover,
such a focus on one or a few variables does not fit the plurality of policy goals and
relevant considerations; in the case of climate change, mitigating GHG emissions
is not the only objective; adaptation, carbon sinks and sequestration, climate
engineering and distributive dimensions of abatement efforts and physical damage
between income classes and between regions and countries are important matters
too. In multidisciplinary contexts, each disciplinary compartment or block is a
black box for experts belonging to other disciplines. This raises a specific problem
regarding a trans-disciplinary use of results (how to assess the level of confidence
of the results of other disciplines?) and the management of the overall level of
uncertainty of mixed results obtained from the coupling of several specialized
models, taking into account disciplinary sources of uncertainty produced in each
block. One of the challenges of integrated assessment is to provide an explicit tool
to perform uncertainty analysis (Dowlatabadi and Morgan 1993). In this regard
it may be useful to distinguish the various types of uncertainty, since they call
for different solutions. According to Yohe (2003), we should consider differences
between model uncertainty, derived from the structure of a model, calibration
uncertainty linked to statistical limits, prediction uncertainty (which occurs when

a specific parameterization is used to produce predictions), projection uncertainty linked to the assumed trajectories of key variables and contextual uncertainty resulting from the gap between a calibrated model and a future reality that will incorporate structural change.

At this stage of development of integrated assessment, fewer efforts have been devoted to the ways of establishing links between scientific expertise, relevant tests of justification and the diverse concerns of stakeholders taking part to the policy process. Developing such links should allow the avoidance of integrated assessment becoming a new black box, strategically instrumentalized by social actors or political leaders. Typical environmental issues are not only affected by extensive uncertainty about critical variables for decision-making, which is acknowledged by most scholars, but also by long-lasting scientific and social controversies based on an indecisive confrontation of different theories of the world (Godard 1997, and this volume, Chapter 2). Not enough consideration has been given to the consequences of this controversial state of knowledge with respect to the organization of expertise and impact assessment.

Models of Expertise

According to a standard position[4] linked to an ideal representation of democratic functioning, experts recount the facts and the science that gives the facts their meaning, whereas political leaders prioritize values and make decisions. Such a division of labour is clear-cut, but in fact too much so to be quite honest. Without pleading for a technocratic mode of decision, it is clear that committees of experts do not limit their role to the collection and synthesis of data. They are doing that and more. And more is expected from them.

In their fundamental and official role, experts are indirectly the spokesmen of a reality; indirectly, because they do it through the specific mediation of scientific knowledge. When policy decisions are at stake, this reality is a mixture of physical and social data and behaviours. Here, a specific issue is linked to the normalization of human behaviours and beliefs. Experts are committed to a process of objectification aiming at predictive statements. The social effect of this role deserves attention. Objectivity is often confused with uniqueness of views or figures, which is misleading. Within a given discipline, scientific controversies contrast different ways in order to represent a phenomenon, whereas different disciplines build different objective representations of the same complex reality. Once they are commissioned, experts are unable to wait for the end to all controversy or a harmonization of different disciplinary approaches before giving an informed and sound opinion, since their time horizon is derived from

---

[4] The Communication of the EU Commission on impact assessment (2002) recalls that impact assessment is an aid to decision-making, not a substitute for political judgement.

the constraints and requirements of the decision-making calendar. Already, at the first level, pluralism is a key, inescapable, feature of expertise. There cannot be one unique image of reality, a conclusion that applies to impact assessment.

A second issue is related to the possibility of experts working towards the production of objectively based opinions without introducing uncontrolled normative elements. Involving some normative elements is inescapable, to the extent that experts are tackling phenomena involving the behaviour and beliefs of human beings; those behaviours and beliefs are shaped or influenced by normative benchmarks, whatever their nature (self-conscious, moral values, social rules, legal norms) and raise the classical issue of individual freedom versus social order. In this respect, experts are obliged to adopt hypotheses on the extent to which human behaviours and beliefs will let a space of freedom in responding to social and legal norms or the extent to which good practice requirements are to be followed, on who is going to see his risk exposure significantly affected, about the probability of frauds or poor implementation of rules and their incidence on damage prevalence and so on. For any analysis, there is a gap between what can be said in cases where everybody is assumed to apply all regulatory requirements strictly and cases in which it is assumed that, in different countries, the regulatory culture will lead to different levels of enforcement. Beyond that, choices regarding the relative weight given to various elements, and implicit judgements about what is important and should be documented, and what is not, are of a normative sort.

When experts are asked to give a diagnosis, they have to relate data and knowledge of facts to a perception of values in society. Expertise is always issue driven. This implies that experts are informed about social interests and rights, the viewpoints of various stakeholders and liability rules. When experts pretend to assign a relationship in objective terms between certain phenomena and a type of social interaction that is a source of conflict or controversy within society, the result is quite ambiguous because of liability issues: are they still neutral or part of the social conflict? It is therefore important to ask who takes part in the definition of issues and the framing of problems for action. Positivist approaches assume that reality imposes its own definition of issues, and experts are just revealing what the objective problems are. Constructivist approaches consider that an image of reality can be built from various viewpoints, and that social actors are actively framing issues and defining the problems in which they find interest. Which of the suggested framings of issues takes precedence in the public arena is then seen as a key issue for a democratic approach of SD. To expect the delivery of the correct framing from experts alone is misleading, as is the opposite statement that asks experts to be banned from this operation: framing cannot be at odds with reality, but framing cannot be deduced from reality. A key role of experts is to delimit the core of framings that are compatible with what they know of reality, and to put aside clearly inadequate ones.

As a result of this situation, several models have been proposed and implemented in order to organize the activity of experts. The two extremes are the so-called 'traditional French model' and 'American model' (Godard 2001). In the 'traditional French model',[5] public authorities have a monopoly over launching and organizing a legitimate expertise for public policy-making. Experts called by the public authorities are supposed to be the best scientists and to give an objective picture of facts and needs of public initiatives. Cost-benefit analysis or other forms of public economic and financial assessments are the procedures to be followed under this model in order to give an evaluation of technical data. Choices relative to framing or socio-political weights remain veiled, since public action is presented as a simple deduction of an objective state of reality. The opposite, so-called 'American model', stresses conditions of a pluralist and contradictory expression of reality by experts within an advocacy public procedure. Advocacy experts do represent identified stakeholders; they take from reality what is useful to defend the interest or viewpoint of their client. At the same time, they tend to use the authority of science to dress-up their specific positions as statements directly coming from reality. It is through the competition between alternative claims that an instance of judgement is able to shape its own view on what reality is or may be. This model mixes scientific issues and confrontation of conflicting interests. Final arbitration or judgements will decide the reality and the balance of interests at the same time. This model immediately raises the issue of equal access for various social groups to experts capable of helping those groups to discover where their interest lies and how to present solutions favourable to them as an objective requirement of the situation revealed by scientific works.

The opposition between these two models is nothing new. In the 1970s, it fed debates about technology assessment (Godard et al. 1975; Hetman 1973). Since then, intermediate solutions have frequently been found. For instance, in France, a Parliamentary Office for Scientific and Technological Choices Assessment was created in July 1983, commissioned to help elected representatives to get access to expertise independent of the government executive. More recently, in 1999, public independent agencies for expertise in the field of safety (food safety, medicines, environmentally based health hazards) were set up to replace internal expertise drawn from within the administrative services. The latter had been accused of lacking transparency, and even of being driven by the economic interests of influential producers more that promoting responsible care regarding the protection of public health and the environment.

Behind the choice between models of organization of expertise lies the issue of the type of reality to tackle. Under stabilized universes (Godard 1997), the first model may be appropriate, inasmuch there are no basic social controversies fed by scientific ones; distributive conflicts may exist, but they develop against the background of a shared view about reality and the problems to solve. Expertise on

---

[5]   This French model is an 'ideal-type'; it captures some basic features that once were underlying French practices in certain dominant civil services (transportation infrastructures, energy production). In other parts of public life (agriculture, health care, for instance) expertise was shared with involved professions. The policy field of environmental protection has always given a significant role to dialogue with NGOs.

the one hand, and negotiation to solve conflicts and conciliate opposite interests on the other hand, can be settled as two clearly separated phases. Such situations are not the norm when environmental issues are at stake. They are even less frequent for SD; the higher level of hesitation and competing views on its content make it more appropriate to refer to controversial universes.

In controversial universes, roles empirically taken by experts are enriched. Most of the time this enrichment is implicit since the distinction between stabilized and controversial universes is not currently acknowledged by public institutions. This very fact generates an illusion that experts are just objective spokesmen of facts, whereas they actively contribute to shaping the definition of problems and the frames of collective action in those fuzzy contexts. They are also disseminating views that become social conventions. Through the framing of data, they produce pre-standards, reputed to be science-based, that give directions to action and pave the way for burden sharing. Eventually, they disseminate to the public a feeling of safety or unease that goes beyond what can be objectively extracted from scientific knowledge.[6]

The role of experts in framing social issues and the importance of a mobilization of scientific results to justify social positions has led various economic and social stakeholders to invest in scientific expertise in order to push their own interests, through a dissemination of their own vision of the world. Expert controversies are now a structural component of any public debate. Meanwhile, this indirect confrontation of interests through expertise has some positive consequences: each party has to find scientific arguments to back its views, and has to explain why arguments and data presented by other parties have to be dismissed. If debates are well organized, the logic of deliberation and the constraint of having to show the scientific foundation of arguments may lead some stakeholders far from their initial views. This is the reason why stakeholders sometimes withdraw from collective exercise of expertise before the stage of writing an opinion, just to avoid becoming a prisoner of an opinion that would not be in line with their interests, and to preserve their political capability to attack that opinion vigorously.

All these elements can be found in the case of global climate change; an issue that has been covered by intense activity of expertise, but that still remains full of uncertainty and controversy.

-----

[6]   Surely, it is most frequently in an involuntary manner that experts contribute to social amplification of certain risks, whereas it is generally expected from them to restore a 'reasonable' approach of issues against an emotional one. However, the very fact that an expertise is commanded and that sources of uncertainty are identified and publicly noticed, may be understood in some circumstances by lay people as the very signal of a pervasive danger, which then contributes to raise or amplify emotion.

The Case of Climate Change: From Standard Cost-Benefit Analysis Towards Sequential Approaches

Climate change is one of the major global environmental threats that humanity will have to address during the twenty-first century. The problems raised are typical of SD issues. In spite of huge investment in scientific investigations, modelling and other studies, governments and economic agents have to make decisions in a context where science gives rather few ascertained benchmarks on key variables relevant for decision-making. For instance there is no clear scientific evidence that one given target should be chosen instead of any other, as regards the final concentrations of GHG in the atmosphere and the correct trajectory of emissions.

Another key factor is that all human activities are involved, because all human activities – industry, agriculture, forestry, housing and transportation – use fossil energy. In order to mitigate climate change, actions are needed throughout the whole economy, not just in delimited sectors. Therefore, patterns of economic and social development do matter, which leads to an enlargement of the scope of analysis, beyond a switching of techniques in production for a same output: policy-makers have to consider structural determinants of demand, such as the shapes of human settlements and the development of communication infrastructures, but also the sharing of productivity gains between income and free time. In this respect, climate policy is an issue of shifting lifestyles and styles of development, not just an issue that can be solved by a technological fix.[7]

Lastly, all the countries of the world have to find an agreement on a common set of goals, rules and burden sharing to protect the climate, in spite of huge differences in all possible criteria: wealth, population, geographical situation, access to resources, institutions able to instigate mitigation and adaptation and so on. This highlights the fact that it does not mean a lot for a community or a country to want to be sustainable alone, as far as global public goods are concerned. Ultimately, SD can only be a common endeavour on a global scale. Meanwhile, countries persist in disagreeing on what the basis of a fair international climate regime of protection, including fair burden sharing, should be.

To what extent can expertise be useful in overcoming drawbacks and obstacles? Climate change is the contemporary environmental issue to which the most intense efforts of collective expertise worldwide have been devoted for twenty years. Following experience of what had been achieved for the protection of the atmospheric ozone layer since the Vienna Convention and the Montreal Protocol, the rise of global warming on the international agenda has been prepared,

---

[7]   Quite evidently this does not mean that technological change is useless for mitigation or adaptation strategies! Challenges such as an abatement of 75 per cent of world business-as-usual emission scenarios of greenhouse gases by 2050 can only be successful by combining deep technological change and huge economic structural change in styles of development, including changes in lifestyles.

accompanied and reinforced by the creation of a central platform of expertise, the IPCC. With variations during the first fifteen years of its activity, IPCC has been organized around three main topics:

1   fundamental science of global climate (functioning of exchanges between the atmosphere, the oceans and the terrestrial biomass; climate modelling);
2   impacts on ecosystems, vulnerability and technological responses allowing adaptation;
3   socio-economic aspects (determinants of GHG emissions trajectories, damage and abatement costs estimates, policy issues for mitigation, such as the choice of instruments and equity considerations).

The general mission of IPCC is to produce up-to-date state-of-the-art reports based on a critical examination of all scientific published materials related to various aspects of climate change. Four main assessment reports have been made as a result of this process, in 1990, 1995, 2001 and 2006.

Economics has an interesting standing as a discipline, since its very constitution led it to combine positive and normative approaches of reality, which is also a key feature of expertise as a social practice. What has been learned from the investment of economists on the climate change issue and their participation to the IPCC process?

The initial mandate of Group III of IPCC was to elaborate a cost-benefit analysis of all relevant aspects, because governments asked for that, wanting to get hard facts and figures. Natural scientists had the same genuine demand: they expected from economists that they gave strong cost-benefit analysis of all aspects of concern, to make everything clear and controversy-free.

Prominent standard economic models used for assessment generally assumed that it was meaningful for decision-making to develop long-run optimization models to identify optimal economic development and emissions trajectories within the framework of classical growth theory or the cost-benefit rationale (Cline 1992; Fankhauser 1995; Manne and Richels 1995; Nordhaus 1991; Tol 1995). Such approaches do have positive analytical contributions, particularly in clarifying the logical structure of some issues: identifying the trade-off involved as regards intertemporal consumption flows; stating 'impossibility theorems' (for instance: with unsubstitutable critical natural assets and no margin for technical progress, any consumption path is unsustainable); showing the importance and controversy surrounding of the choice of the discounting factor (every value between 1 per cent and 8 per cent has been justified by rational arguments) (Birdsall and Steer 1993; Bruce et al. 1995; Cline 1992, 1993; Philibert 1999; Portney and Weyant, 1999), which leads to valuations differing by several order of magnitudes; or revealing the implicit or shadow value of marketable natural assets and so on. Empirically, it forced the identification and description of all known relevant impacts of climate change, taking account of huge regional differences, and the linking of impacts to economic processes (income generation and distribution) through their economic evaluation.

In spite of these achievements, the surprise has been that in the IPCC process, cost-benefit analysis did not bring about peace and agreement. On the contrary, cost-benefit analysis involuntarily brought more arguments over conflicts of interest between North and South, Europe and the USA. The core of disputes was to be found in both methodological and legitimacy aspects of economic evaluations. One critical topic has been the question of assessment of losses of human lives: the strict application of economic concepts to loss of statistical human lives suggested the result that an individual Indian's death was worth 50 to 100 times less in terms of loss output than the death of an American individual, because the income earned by these two individuals, if they had the chance to live, would have been in that proportion. When scientific input is introduced into an international arena of negotiation framed by a North–South conflict, it is supposed to inform and help the diplomatic process of negotiation by providing an objective view of problems, not just to achieve an academic exercise. Several NGO observers attended IPCC meetings along with governmental representatives. Both types of actors joined in a strong protest against these results, as being evidently unfair and unacceptable from an ethical viewpoint. In a United Nations context, each human being is supposed to have the same 'value'. Consequently, it was claimed that the same level of resources had to be devoted to save one human life whatever the region at stake, and the same value had to be used in damage assessment. This would have resulted in amplifying the figures of damage from which developing countries would have to suffer as a result of the 'inconsequent' behaviour of industrial nations. This claim had no economic positive foundation in real-life situations: the same resources are not seen to be allocated to reduce the risk of death of one statistical person all around the world. The claim relies on a tension between a general abstract ethical statement (all human beings are ethically equals) from which formal rights are derived, and an economic, contextualized valuation of damage measuring the opportunity cost for a given society of the death of a person who is an economic actor within this society. Is it possible to formulate an assessment of damage without a previous agreement on the ethical dimension of the exercise and on the way to approach it?

As a result of this controversy, the part of the assessment dealing with damages to individuals has been dismissed from the policy viewpoint as a fragile one, and has not been incorporated in the executive summary for decision-makers, which had to be approved in detail by governments. Economists in charge of this assessment have been surprised at this result, because they had followed the general guidelines given for reviewing existing international literature and used academically accepted concepts, tools and techniques. It was not bad economics, it was just economics. But this economics has not been able to bring what was expected in a broad hybrid context where scientific assessments aim at supporting efforts to come to an agreement between various stakeholders, in this instance in the context of international political negotiations.

More generally, modelling exercises that used the cost-benefit analysis framework were not able to give reliable results for making practical decisions in controversial contexts. They are made of so many assumptions and approximations that they can only be judged impressive or decisive by people who accept the end results without questioning the means used to obtain them. As was written in the 1995 IPCC WGIII report (Bruce et al. 1995: ch. 8): 'Although researchers attempt to incorporate their best understanding of development processes into the studies, neither the baseline nor the intervention scenarios should be interpreted as representing likely future conditions, especially more than a decade into the future'. So, to what sort of social use are these exercises devoted? Quite often, such economic assessments are given a rhetorical role in order to force some framing of social issues well beyond what they can legitimately provide in terms of validated results. What seems to matter in developing this role is the appropriateness of results and conclusions to the preconceptions that some prominent social actors (governments, lobbies) want to disseminate. In these cases, instead of being a way to achieve a sound social agreement, they take part in the very process of controversy, and may even amplify it by raising new points of dissent, as highlighted by the previously mentioned issue of valuing human lives in the North–South context.

Following the 1995 IPCC assessment report, the scientific community realized that it was not at hand to solve every issue by economic analysis, because of questions related to framing, values and uncertainties. So a shift began to be introduced regarding the decision-making approach to climate change. Instead of the once-and-for-all intertemporal optimization developed in a cost-benefit analysis framework, it has been suggested that the huge scientific and structural uncertainty should be addressed by promoting a sequential approach to decision-making (Bruce et al. 1995; Hourcade 1997). A sequential approach means that the present generation is not expected to optimize emissions trajectories during a period as long as 200 years. The responsibility of present decision-makers is just to decide what should be done in the next twenty or thirty years, and then other people will reconsider the problem and find their ways on the basis of new information on climate issues and available technologies for mitigation and adaptation. To make such a revision possible and meaningful, immediate decisions should be calibrated so as to preserve future margins of manoeuvre and avoid huge, irreversible commitments in relation to the policy issue under consideration.

In that framework, the main questions become: what is the best timing of action combining mitigation and adaptation for the next twenty or thirty years? Should the main polluters postpone any effort to control GHG emissions during the period, or launch crash programmes right now to get a significant abatement against business-as-usual trends? With what intensity? Arguments for early action generally put forward the huge inertia of physical processes underlying climate change and the possibility of existence of some zone of catastrophic danger, which would be of ethical relevance regarding future generations that may be exposed to catastrophic events without compensation from present generations. Under this assumption, inertia of economic and technological systems combine in such a manner that delaying mitigation actions too much makes it impossible to avoid entering the danger zone (Lecocq et al. 1998). To maintain compatibility of emissions trajectories with the avoidance of a future entry in the danger zone, early action is needed that will smooth the abatement and adaptation efforts that may be required in the future, at the same time developing the technological capability of response that future generations will inherit. This shift in the framing of the decision problem is clearly a step forward that has been accomplished by economists who accepted facing limitations of knowledge when dealing with risks such as global climate change.

Either with cost-benefit analysis or with a sequential approach to collective choices to make, building a broad social agreement requires the basic framing of issues to become a largely accepted social convention among leaders and stakeholders, not just among economists. The use of a cost-benefit analysis framework would require that welfare utilitarianism be generally accepted as delivering the right principles for identifying the public interest. Such requirements are not well-suited to a decision universe where controversies on basic framings are unresolved within the community of economists, and several justification orders coexist within society (see Chapter 2), with at least the practical result that welfare considerations mix with concerns for moral obligations and rights. To contribute positively to the social process of decision, economic expertise should then be adapted to controversial contexts.

To this end, a sequential approach to decision-making is less demanding in terms of information and commitment, since it preserves flexibility about the courses of action that will be followed for the next steps in the future.[8] It also changes the focus. The main challenge is not to assess and evaluate all possible future damage, but once the possibility of a catastrophic evolution is acknowledged, to increase the future capacity of efficient reaction to new events or new progress of scientific information. It means that different targets are assigned to assessment of policy impact. It is no longer the ultimate impact on welfare that is of concern, but the impact on the systemic resilience of technological and economic systems and the capabilities of various groups and settlements to sustain unforeseen events and possible radical change of priorities of investment. Action is not directly designed to prevent a well-identified risk, but to develop

---

[8]   Asking for less commitment is a source of weakness of the regime, since long-run expectations on the future trajectory that will be followed by the international community cannot be ensured; moreover, the concept of periodical revisions of commitments associated with a sequential approach also means that each party can look at its abatement and compliance strategy during a given period in light of the prospects of gaining a less-demanding effort in the next burden-sharing game. But when asking for long-run commitment is demanding too much and may be severely inappropriate, the alternative is no agreement at all, right from the beginning!

the capacity to prevent a set of risks linked to climate change in the future in such conditions that would be acceptable to the people who may be dramatically concerned. Such a switch in the targets of assessment is certainly something of general intellectual interest for sustainability impact assessment.

Under scientific controversy, and taking due account of the intrinsic pluralism of the sustainability concept, integrated assessment should be posited as a framework focusing on the articulation of the various time dimensions involved both in natural and social processes, with a particular attention to the delays needed to develop new technologies and set up new institutions. It should allow the connection of the assessment exercises to the concerns of various social groups, without assuming that the latter share common 'visions of the world', values and priorities, or an agreed social preference function. At the same time, tests should be built to allow a judgement on claims of different stakeholders, which cannot be accepted as relevant or acceptable just because these groups have formulated them.

The climate change scene is also very rich in opportunities to show the role of expert committees in uncertain and controversial contexts. Let us identify these roles.

The Roles of Experts in Tackling Uncertain and Controversial Risks: Lessons from Climate Change

Beyond the symbolic role of maintaining an apparently intangible frontier between objective facts and normative choices, collective scientific expertise takes several roles, implicitly or explicitly, according to circumstances. The following topics continue to be extracted from the climate change issue.

Framing Issues and Defining Problems to Solve

In stabilized contexts, public authorities provide the framing, and scientific experts are only asked to fill it with data and facts. But in complex and fuzzy contexts, the first role expected from experts is to ensure an initial framing of issues and to help define the problems to consider. This involves gathering data in such a way to give form to the idea of potential damage affecting targets (social groups, the environment). Meanwhile they also have to separate real scientific controversies from artificial conflicts built up by some stakeholders.

In the context of climate change, a huge scientific investment has been made to identify and calibrate possible damages of various scenarios of emissions of GHG and alert on the original features of the threat (global nature; huge inertia of the climate system ...). IPCC has also been conceived as a means to identify a core of representations of issues compatible with scientific results and dismiss pure fantasy or negation.

Identifying Alternative Schemes of Action

Since experts are mobilized in the context of a policy process, they are frequently asked to go further, and identify and assess various courses of action from between which decision-makers can choose. One key issue for experts is then to delineate what is possible and under which conditions it is possible, and what looks impossible anyway. The controversial and partial features of scientific knowledge make it a subtle task.[9] It is nevertheless useful to know where the borderline in the partition is, since this will influence the sort of actions that will have to be considered. For instance, if an event or a change is taken as inescapable, the main issues are about helping or compensating victims, or delivering symbolic rituals to give a cultural meaning to unavoidable catastrophes. If dangers and risks can be prevented, it is important to know as far as possible how long such an opportunity will exist for.

If experts conclude that it is possible to act to deal with the problem, they consequently have to draw up a bundle of possible actions. To develop possible strategies of action, experts need to concentrate on parts of problems for which causal links can reasonably be set. This allows the problem to be reformulated around the most solid elements. For example, because the link between GHG emissions and the impact of climate change is complex, but emissions can be measured (assessed, monitored) relatively easily compared to other parts of the problem, experts have focused attention first on the link between human activities and the level of GHG emissions, and second, between GHG emissions and GHG atmospheric concentrations. So the initial problem, 'mitigating climate change so as to prevent a dramatic change' is translated into 'how can we stabilize GHG atmospheric concentrations at some level?' and then 'which targets of emissions should we fix at different terms?'. There are clearly missing links between the different statements, but it is not possible to conceive of preventing actions directly in terms of the localized impacts of the latter on ecosystems and economies. So the gap between the initial issues raised and the design of action cannot be filled on a pure scientific basis, and depends on a framing activity. Experts and stakeholders should jointly have a key role to this regard.

---

[9]   Interestingly, Nordhaus (1994) organized an opinion survey of twenty-two recognized experts professionally active into national or international assessment of global climate change. This poll included both social scientists, mainly economists, and natural scientists. Asked about the magnitude and probability of loss resulting from climate change as a percentage of Gross World Product (GWP) in three scenarios (3° Celsius rise by 2090, 6° rise by 2175, 6° rise by 2090) results show an enormous dispersion of estimations: for the least catastrophic scenario, the range goes from 0 to 21 per cent of GWP; it is much larger in the other scenarios. This dispersion particularly reflects disciplinary differences. Natural scientists estimates of damage are much bigger than those of economists. One explanation given by Nordhaus is that 'the economists know little about the intricate web of natural ecosystems, whereas scientists know equally little about the incredible adaptability of human economies' (ibid.: 48).

This task of identification of possible courses of action cannot escape from impacting on the composition and status of committees of experts. Since public action is at stake, public authorities generally want to keep the process under control. At the same time, purely administrative or business expertise has lost a lot of credibility because the public has been convinced that experts tied to decision-makers may defend economic and political interests more than an objective account of scientific knowledge and public health. At the junction of these two requirements, a concept of independent public agencies has emerged whose top management is still nominated by government, or mixed solutions such as IPCC.

IPCC was created to mobilize the authority of science and to facilitate the emergence of a consensus on the directions to take. Its credibility depended largely on the fame and scientific authority of the main scientists in charge of its management, on the extensive cross-examination of scientific literature worldwide and on the involvement of scientists coming from all regions of the world. At the same time, as an intergovernmental body, IPCC was submitted to a certain amount of political logic: proposed members were nominated by governments after a pre-selection by scientific communities and an agreement of IPCC staff, a balanced representation of each region has been sought for the allocation of various tasks and some sessions were open to active NGOs. In practice, all this resulted, during final discussions preceding the adoption of an assessment report, in a hybrid confrontation of very high-level scientists, diplomats with scientific background, civil servants belonging to national administrations and the advocacy of NGOs. But scientists kept control over the content of scientific reports: confrontation was not to lead to allegiance to ideological and political games and interests.

Indirect Testing of Positions of Parties

Particularly in international contexts, groups of experts give the opportunity to various social actors, mainly governments, to examine the position of others, in order to see where the borderline between acceptable and unacceptable solutions for the other parties might lie. These expectations have an influence on the choice of experts and the organization of their work. Such a game is subject to two constraints: (a) in most cases, the borderline is not well-defined *ex ante* but will result as an end-product of the process of expertise and negotiations organized around it; (b) each party wants to know more about the others, but does not want its ultimate positions being made transparent to others. So dissimulation and tactics regarding exchange of information can be expected. The picture that some parties may think they have obtained about others may be revealed as wrong when the process switches to direct political negotiations. Meanwhile, the political advantages of this approach of international coordination through scientific expertise are, first, to preserve the political autonomy of governments and avoid premature commitment, and second to progressively shape an acceptable framework for collective action. Many IPCC workshops on policy economic instruments (carbon taxation, emission trading) were of this sort and have been instrumental in acculturating tradable permits in international, EU and national circles, with the paradoxical end result that the preferred instrument of the United States has eventually been adopted by the Kyoto Protocol without the United States, whereas EU governments that were more inclined to adopt policies and measures, and to verbally supported carbon taxes, are now implementing a directive creating a European market of CO_2 quotas!

Preparing an Attribution of Obligations and Rights

An important part of the activity of scientific experts is devoted, not to collecting facts or synthesising results of basic research, but to looking for and organizing data in order to prepare an attribution of obligations, rights and liabilities to solve a problem and to settle accounts on this basis. For example, much effort is being made towards achieving inventories of emissions by source (countries, plants). On the climate change issue, data on GHG emissions have been shaped per country and, for each country, per inhabitant. These most simple ratios (for example one American citizen emits 6 tonnes of carbon (tC) yearly from CO_2 producing activities and one French citizen only 2 tonnes) serve as implicit normative benchmarks for imputing a moral and political responsibility, before any explicit political or legal judgement is made. Such work adds nothing to the basic understanding of processes of climate change, but is decisive for the purpose of action. In the case considered, other framings were possible, for instance the one that would frame data according to economic sectors (world agriculture, oil refining, iron and steel industry and so on). Such an alternative would have fitted to an organization of action based, not on states, but on international business branch organizations.

Enhancing Rational Decision-Making

Any rational approach involves defining equivalence relationships, making comparisons, setting hierarchies and producing assessments according to some scale of value. Specific operators and statistical formats are needed to shape data into a useful form. The choice of appropriate indicators and methodological standards are key elements that, in uncertain and controversial contexts, demonstrate a subtle interference with social or ideological inputs within the process of producing objective data.

So, in the case of climate change, two steps were required to establish a perfect rational framework for decision-making: (a) to find a common unit for measuring all the costs; (b) to find a general index of equivalence between all types of actions as regards their effect on climate change. Using these two elements, a complete classification of mitigation and adaptation strategies could be established, at least in theory, in order to allow the choice of the best option on the basis of a cost-effectiveness ratio. This programme was not available from the very beginning.

A key step was made when IPCC responded to the political demand of governments to elaborate one index setting equivalencies between the various GHGs (CO_2, CH_4, CFCs, N_2O and so on). In its 1990 report (Houghton, Jenkins and Ephraums 1990), IPCC gave such an index, the Global Warming Potential Index (GWPI). To the extent that gases do not all have the same lifetime in the atmosphere, these equivalencies have been set for two time-periods: twenty years and one hundred years. These values have been used for numerous calculations, and have since been accepted for accounting the abatement actions taken by governments to address their obligations under the Kyoto Protocol. Such an index incorporates a degree of convention, and has not been given by scientists without reluctance, which reveals the gap between the real state of knowledge and the type of information ideally needed to get a rational framework of action.

Key points about the GWPI were the following:

1 indirect effects were voluntarily not taken into account because of deficiencies of basic knowledge, although they could be significant in real climate machinery;
2 the index did not take account of phenomena of mutual dependency of the values selected for each gas: as a matter of fact, the climatic incidence of a given concentration of one gas depends on the concentration of other GHGs; pure scientific soundness would have required each unit value to be replaced by a multi-factorial function or a vector;
3 a time instability of the values taken for each sort of gas, as a result of the progress of the understanding of the climate machinery.

However imperfect this index is, its practical value for organizing an international regime of protection of global climate took over and led to its adoption.

Concluding Lessons

Climate change is a very rich field of investigation, and a source of lessons regarding the roles and significance of expertise. It allows us to see the gap between scientific methods and results and the sort of activity implied by expertise. Specialist scientists know that their results are contingent results from models, and depend on a handful of critical assumptions: scientific results are not a direct expression of reality. Changing assumptions and adding new variables changes the results but, from a scientific viewpoint, this is not a threat to the credibility of scientists. Meanwhile, in controversial contexts, the profusion of modelling exercises with all sorts of uncoordinated assumptions and a great dispersion of results makes one dizzy, and opens the way to various and opposite conclusions in relation to the choice of a strategy of action. Science being inconclusive, collective action has to be based on other justifications, be they moral, political or economic.

In that context, a critical virtue of expertise is to allow an identification of points of scientific consensus or dissent and to deliver a contradictory assessment of the pros and cons of each opposing theory. Another is to find a precise articulation of the work of experts to deal with the questions raised by different stakeholders.

In this regard, misunderstandings of what scientific results actually mean are not infrequent. When they are placed in positions as experts, scientists are often listened to as if they were expressing the rough reality, not an indirect image obtained through the contingent results of human constructs. Even if they do not personally express themselves as speaking in the name of reality, what they write and disseminate will tend to be interpreted as such by non-scientists. All the qualifications and restrictions about assumptions and specific methods tend to be forgotten. The circulation of scientific results in larger circles tends to generate an ossification of contingent statements into illusory 'hard facts'. When scientific statements are in accordance with pre-existing beliefs, they are even more easily selected by non-specialists as true and direct expressions of reality. This is reinforced by the implicit idea that an uncertain science is a bad science. As a consequence, an identical state of scientific knowledge can result in opposite but equally strong convictions about the real state of the world, at least for a while.

Thus, the value of collective expertise should not be placed mainly in the quality of specific results at one moment, but in the open process of informed debate among specialists and stakeholders, with feedback to research. Such a process is very valuable, not because it is expected to lead to consensus – it may on some points, not on others – but because the key issues, variables and sources of uncertainty are made apparent through the debate. Helping to pose some useful questions and to give a useful framing to a fuzzy set of issues is what groups of experts and open debates can do best. This process needs time – several years – and may be contradictory to the desire of policy-makers to get clear-cut advice within a short period.

Difficult Relationship between Experts and Political Leaders: One Typical Anecdote from French Energy Policy

Ambiguity of relationships between experts in economics and policy-makers can be illustrated with an example from French energy and environment policy. This instance arose from the publication in 1998 of an official forecast study on energy futures in France. The forecast was made by the Commissariat général du Plan, on behalf of the Minister of Industry (Commissariat général du Plan 1998). It consisted of energy scenarios for France into 2010 and 2020. I took part in the exercise as a general rapporteur of the Experts Group in charge of building those energy scenarios. We built three scenarios according to social and political assumptions on the possible evolution and priorities of French society: 'Market society' (S1), 'Industrial State' (S2) and 'a State prioritizing health and environmental protection' (S3). What must be noted from Table 11.1 is that only one scenario, S3, was roughly compatible with the stabilization of emissions of CO_2 in the years 2010 and 2020 at their 1990 level, which was then the commitment of France in the context of the Kyoto Protocol and the EU bubble.[10]

Variants V40 and V30 correspond to two assumptions on the useful lifetime of existing nuclear power plants: forty and thirty years. In S1-V30, nuclear plants are progressively replaced by combined-cycle gas-fired turbines (CCGTs), even for base production, hence a sharp increase in CO_2 emissions (30 MtC). In S3-V30, old nuclear plants are replaced by new European pressurized reactor (EPR)[11] plant for 30 GW (gigawatts) of generating capacity.

Scenario S1 had two variants. In variant V30, there was an assumption that existing nuclear power plants could not, for safety reasons, go beyond a lifetime of thirty years, and that CCGT plants would be substituted for them. The latter assumption was based on the fact that with a discount rate nearer to the standard used by private investors (12 per cent instead of 8 per cent, net of inflation), switching to gas would be more profitable. The consequence of this variant is that France would dramatically cut the share of power generation coming from nuclear plants between 2010 and 2020: from 65 per cent of electricity demand in 2010 to 12.5 per cent in 2020. Impact on CO_2 emissions would be a sharp increase of emissions, of around 30 million tonnes more of carbon. The more environmentally oriented scenario, S3, did achieve stabilization of emissions, but this was made possible only because it assumed a strong demand-side management, and that 30 GW of capacity from existing nuclear power stations would be replaced by new EPR-type nuclear power stations, so that nuclear power would still provide 60 per cent of power generation in France. If in that same scenario S3 a progressive, but complete, withdrawal from nuclear power generation by 2020 had been considered, it would have meant 33 million more tonnes of carbon, which would represent an increase of approximately 33 per cent in French emissions from 1990 levels of fossil energy use, whereas the French target under the Kyoto Protocol and the EU bubble is 0 per cent for all GHGs covered by the Protocol.

Following the dissemination of results in the media, the then French Minister of the Environment, Mme Voynet (1998), explained in the press that the main result of the Commissariat général du Plan's study was that it was possible to stop generating power from nuclear plants, to withdraw from this technology, to

---

[10]   In the framework of the Kyoto Protocol, all EU countries have accepted a legally binding target of – 8 per cent of the yearly mean level of GHGs emissions during the period 2008 -2012 as compared to 1990 emissions. They did so under the provision that countries could join their efforts and redistribute targets among themselves by a separate agreement, the outcome of which will be the same on the whole as with the initial distribution of targets. EU countries have negotiated such a separate agreement; this is the EU bubble. It requires that France has a zero growth rate of GHGs emissions during the 1990–2012 period.

[11]   EPR is the new vintage of nuclear reactor for power generation. The French government decided in 2004 to build an EPR pilot in order to be able to redevelop productive capacity on a large scale with this new technology by 2020.

Table 11.1 Future CO_2 emissions from energy use in France by 2010 and 2020 (total of direct and indirect emissions)

Year	Sectors	CO₂ Emissions total in MtC and % (in parentheses)					
		Market society (S1)		Industrial state (S2)		State prioritizing environmental protection (S3)	
1990	Industry	32 (30.8%)					
	Domestic/Services	30 (28.7%)					
	Transportation	39.7 (38%)					
All sectors (MtC)		104.5					
2010	Scenarios total (MtC) and %						
	Industry	33.3 (25.4%)		29.6 (24.9%)		21.5 (21.2%)	
	Domestic/Services	37.6 (28.7%)		32.7 (27.5%)		31 (30.6%)	
	Transportation	57.5 (43.9%)		54 (45.4%)		46.2 (45.6%)	
All sectors (MtC)		131.1		119.0		101.4	
2020	total (MtC)	V40	V30	V40	V30	V40	V30
	Industry	34.8	44.5	30.5	30.5	23	25.9
	Domestic/Services	43.3	64.1	36	36.4	31.4	33.4
	Transportation	69.2	69.4	62.2	62.2	48.9	49
All sectors (MtC)		150.2	180.7	131.5	131.8	106.1	111.0

Source: Commissariat général du Plan (1998).

Note: results obtained by imputing emissions from primary production of energy (oil refinement, power generation) to sectors in proportion with their consumption of power and refined oil products.

diversify the energy system and to comply with strict implementation of Kyoto targets on French territory, without using the international market for GHGs quotas! Though formally compatible with the main parameters of the situation,[12] the focus of the statement was a long way from the conclusions of the expert group showing that closing all the nuclear power plants and replacing them mainly with CCGTs was only possible through a large-scale usage of international emissions trading, the so-called Kyoto flexibility mechanisms. If France had been willing to stop using nuclear power by 2020, it should have the possibility to buy a large amount of CO_2 quotas from other countries, a solution to which Mme Voynet was strongly opposed, having joined other EU governments to back the proposal of imposing a stringent ceiling on the capability of a country to use emissions trading (around 2.5 per cent of 1990 emissions level): in fact France would need to buy an amount ten times higher than such a ceiling or it would be definitely - at least for many decades (sixty years?) – prevented from withdrawing from nuclear technology, just because Kyoto-type flexibility mechanisms would have been refused and impeded for ideological motives.

This is a minor anecdote, but typical of the tensions between experts and decision-makers who try to accommodate experts opinion into their political projects and discourses. What should be the response of experts in such contexts? My personal reaction was to publish an article in the same newspaper as the Minister (Godard 1998) to explain what results our work really obtained and why, because of the Kyoto-type constraints, it demonstrated the existence of a basic contradiction between two goals: achieving the French 'Kyoto and beyond' CO_2 target of abatement at home, without using emissions trading, and withdrawing from nuclear power generation. This article had notably two effects: I received a letter of support from the President of the CNRS[13] and convocation for a discussion with the cabinet of the Minister.

Following international negotiations on the implementation of the Kyoto Protocol led signatories to confirm the flexibility mechanisms (emissions trading), and European countries, including France, eventually abandoned the requirement to impose a ceiling on international trading. It remains the formulation of the

---

[12] The term of the commitments embodied in the Kyoto Protocol is the year 2012. Nobody in France, and specifically not the Commissariat général du Plan, has suggested withdrawing from nuclear energy by this date. The discussion on a possible withdrawal was only relevant for achievements in the post-Kyoto periods. However, there is a strong presumption that the post-Kyoto arrangements will ask developed countries, including France, to further decrease their level of net emissions of GHGs against 1990 levels. Without buying CO_2 quotas on the international carbon market, France will then be condemned to continue with nuclear generation of electricity, even if a new majority of citizens wish to withdraw. The contradiction for France between a withdrawal from nuclear power generation and non-tradable CO_2 quotas would be fully exacerbated.

[13] CNRS is the acronym of *Centre national de la recherche scientifique*, the huge organization in charge of general and fundamental scientific research in France since World War II.

Protocol that emissions trading should only be additional to domestic action. Regarding France, the latest Plan for Climate (MEDD, 2004) still defines a list of measures announced to allow France to achieve its objective of stabilisation of GHGs emissions by 2010 on its own territory, whatever doubts are formulated by observers and NGOs regarding the realism of figures put on the paper and the credibility of several measures.

This story shows the kind of voluntary misuse of the work of experts political leaders may attempt, in the service of preconceived ideas and goals. Similar examples in other countries could easily be found. Here lies one important source of the scepticism of many scientists regarding the actual use of their expertise by public authorities. In those cases, it is important that experts are able to disseminate their results through the media to inform the public and various stakeholders, without being misrepresented by the single interpretation given by public authorities.

Conclusion: Some Consequences for Integrated Modelling and Sustainability Impact Assessment

At first sight, the target of developing integrated models that would be able to catch the whole set of interactions between society and environment underlying SD is attractive. It gives rise to the hope of transforming situations of conflicts into a rational, objectively informed resolution of problems. As a matter of fact, it is repeatedly claimed by scholars working in modelling, and by managers of science policy, that integrated modelling is currently the right response to the challenge of setting up interdisciplinary research and synthesizing information for policy purpose (Guesnerie 2003). Meanwhile, we have good reason to see this way as less promising than claimed, as far as SD is concerned. Not that I am suggesting we forego modelling, but that we reconsider integrated modelling by scrutinizing the expectations it raised and the achievements it can obtain more precisely.

Up to now, integrated modelling has been a strategic means for a community of climate and economic modellers to impose themselves as key partners of policy-making at a time when decision-makers may be tempted to reduce their support for such work. Other reasons related to social tactics within national or European bureaucracies may explain the expectations placed on these approaches. It is possible that the unspoken project is to put an authoritarian end to social controversies that are perceived as an obstacle on the way of some political projects. The general purpose of getting objective data to inform public deliberation is welcome. Thus, in uncertain and controversial contexts, objectivity calls for an organized pluralism of viewpoints and ways to link the scientific work to the concerns of stakeholders. On the contrary, the idea that figures resulting from integrated quantitative modelling would allow policy-makers to impose policy developments in the name of a claimed demonstrated superiority regarding SD should be open to discussion.

The development of transversal modelling exercises organized from specific polar viewpoints would be quite different. 'Integrated' approaches do not mean 'all-inclusive' ones. Each integrated approach has to choose a viewpoint, and cannot escape partiality; at some point, it has to switch to another type of modelling before being able to obtain results. Specific tools would have to be built for establishing translation interfaces, that is, tools for switching from one semantic system to another one on the basis of conventions that are only valuable for a specific context (see chapter 2).

At this stage, it should be acknowledged that the definition of problems and relevant issues is as much a responsibility for decision-makers and social actors as for scientists. This should be reflected in the way of organizing the patterns of relationship between those three categories of actors. An agreement on framing would be a useful achievement in helping the process of expertise (Godard 2003). The requirement to build context-specific tools also means that the validation of these tools does not exclusively belong to strictly scientific procedures, any more than procedures coming out of one unique discipline. As a genre, tools being used belong to the realm of 'future studies' more than the one of pure scientific models. Statements that can be legitimately derived from such exercises are conjectural and conditional, not strictly predictive. Acknowledgement and qualification of uncertainty would have to be placed on a central position. Nevertheless, due attention would have to be given to minimum requirements of coherence and an identification of possible orders of magnitude. In spite of what could be meant at first by the expression 'sustainability impact assessment', this approach could not just be an assessment of the impact of a policy on sustainability of development.

References

Birdsall, Nancy and Andrew Steer. 1993. 'Act Now on Global Warming – But Don't Cook the Books'. *Finance and Development* 3: 6–8.
Bruce, James P., Hoesung Lee and Erik F. Haites, eds. 1995. 'Climate Change 1995. Economic and Social Dimensions of Climate Change'. Contribution of Working Group III to the second assessment report of the IPCC. Cambridge: Cambridge University Press.
Cline, William. 1992. *The Economics of Global Warming*. Washington, DC: Institute for International Economics.
———. 1993. 'Give Greenhouse Abatement a Fair Chance'. *Finance and Development* 3: 3–5.
Commissariat général du Plan. 1998. 'Énergie 2010–2020 – Rapport de l'atelier Trois scénarios énergétiques pour la France'. Paris, September.
Dowlatabadi, Hadi and M. Granger Morgan. 1993. 'A Model Framework for Integrated Studies of the Climate Problem'. *Energy Policy* 21.3: 209–22.
European Commission. 2002. *Communication on Impact Assessment*. Brussels, COM (2002) 276 final, 5 June.

European Parliament and Council of the EU. 2003. Directive 2003/87/EC of 13 October 2003 establishing a scheme for greenhouse gas emission allowance trading within the Community and amending Council Directive 96/61/EC. *Official Journal of the European Union* L. 275. 25.10: 32–46.

Fankhauser, Samuel. 1995. *Valuing Climate Change*. London: Earthscan.

Godard, Olivier. 1997. 'Social Decision-making under Scientific Controversy, Expertise and the Precautionary Principle.' In Christian Joerges, Karl-Heinz Ladeur and Ellen Vos, eds. *Integrating Scientific Expertise into Regulatory Decision-making – National Experiences and European Innovations*. Baden-Baden: Nomos Verlagsgesellschaft: 39–73.

———. 1998. 'L'atome ou le CO_2'. *Libération* 5449. 25 November.

———. 2001. 'L'expertise économique du changement climatique planétaire – 1. Modèles d'organisation de l'expertise. – 2. Sur la scène internationale, le GIEC. – 3. Sur la scène française, autour du Commissariat général du Plan'. *Annales des Mines – Série Responsabilité et environnement* 21: 23–65.

———. 2003. 'Comment organiser l'expertise scientifique sous l'égide du principe de précaution?' *Revue de l'Électricité et de l'Électronique* 11: 38–47.

———. 2005. 'Politique de l'effet de serre – Une évaluation du plan français d'affectation des quotas d'émission de CO_2'. *Revue française d'économie* XIX.4: 147–86.

Godard, Olivier, Patrick Lagadec, Solange Passaris et Ignacy Sachs. 1975. 'Environnement et politique scientifique'. *Le progrès scientifique* 176: 21–51.

Guesnerie, R. (président). 2003. *La recherche au service du développement durable*. Rapport intermédiaire du Groupe de travail installé par Mme Haigneré, ministre déléguée à la Recherche et aux Nouvelles Technologies. Paris: May.

Hetman, François. 1973. *Society and the Assessment of Technology: Premises, Concepts, Methodology, Experiments, Areas of Application*. Paris: OECD Publications.

Houghton, John T., Geoff J. Jenkins and J.J. Ephraums, eds. 1990. *Climate Change: the IPCC Scientific Assessment*. Cambridge: Cambridge University Press.

Hourcade, Jean-Charles. 1997. 'Précaution et approche séquentielle de la décision face aux risques climatiques de l'effet de serre'. In Olivier Godard, ed. *Le principe de précaution dans la conduite des affaires humaines*. Paris: Ed. de la Maison des sciences de l'homme et INRA-Editions: 259–94.

Lecocq Franck, Jean-Charles Hourcade and Minh Ha-Duong. 1998. 'Decision-making under Uncertainty and Inertia Constraints: Sectoral Implications of the When Flexibility'. *Energy Economics* 20.5/6: 539–55.

Manne, Alan and Richard Richels. 1995. 'The Greenhouse Debate: Economic Efficiency, Burden Sharing and Hedging Strategies'. *The Energy Journal* 16.4: 1–37.

Ministère de l'écologie et du développement durable (MEDD). 2004. *Plan Climat 2004*. Paris. 22 July.

Nordhaus, William D. 1991. 'To Slow or not Slow. The Economics of the Greenhouse Effect'. *The Economic Journal* 101.6: 920–37.

Nordhaus, William D. 1994. 'Expert Opinion on Climatic Change'. *American Scientist* 82(1): 45–51.

Philibert, Cédric. 1999. 'The Economics of Climate Change and the Theory of Discounting'. *Energy Policy* 27: 913–29.

Portney Paul R. and John P. Weyant, eds. 1999. *Discounting and Intergenerational Equity*. Washington, DC: Resources for the Future.

Tol, Richard S.J. 1995. 'The Damage Costs of Climate Change. Towards More Comprehensive Calculations'. *Environmental and Resource Economics* 5.4: 353–74.

Yohe, Gary. 2003. 'Estimating Benefits: Other Issues Concerning Market Impacts'. OECD Workshop on the Benefits of Climate Policy. Paris: OECD Environment Directorate. 12 September.

Chapter 12

The Contribution of Network Governance to Sustainability Impact Assessment

Tom Dedeurwaerdere[1]

Introduction

Network governance has been extensively studied in the literature.[2] It can be characterized by an attempt to take into account the increasing importance of non-government organizations (NGOs), the private sector, scientific networks and international institutions in the performance of various functions of governance. From a functional point of view, the aim of network governance is to create a synergy between different competences and sources of knowledge in order to deal with complex and interlinked problems. From this functional perspective, governance is accomplished through decentralized networks of private and public actors associated with international, national and regional institutions. As the study by Reinicke and Deng states, 'a typical network (if there is such a thing) combines the voluntary energy and legitimacy of the civil society sector with the financial muscle and interest of businesses and the enforcement and rule-making power and coordination and capacity-building skills of states and international organisations' (Reinicke and Deng 2000: 29). Prominent examples of such networks that have been instrumental in forging

[1]   A first draft of this chapter was presented at the International Environmental Governance Conference in Paris organized by Iddri (Centre Kleber 2004) and at the *Séminaire de développement durable et économie de l'environnement* de l'Iddri/Ecole Polytechnique-EDF (Iddri 2004). The case study benefited from a seminar on SIA organized within the Sustra network at the Université Catholique de Louvain (Louvain-la-Neuve 2003). We would like to thank the participants at these meetings for their input and comments on this work. We acknowledge the financial support for our research of the Belgian Federal Government (IAPV) and the European Commission (HPSE-CT-2002-50023 and Sustra).
[2]   For an overview, see for example Diani and McAdam 2003; P.M. Haas 2004b; Ostrom 2001; Reinicke and Deng 2000; Hajer and Wagenaar 2003: 33–59. Cambridge, Cambridge University Press.

successful working arrangements are the World Commission on Dams, the Global Environment Facility and the flexible mechanisms of the Kyoto Protocol (Streck 2002). Another ongoing initiative is the United Nations Global Compact, which combines multiple stakeholders within a trilateral structure that includes representatives from governments, the private sector and the NGO community (Haas 2004b: 6).

From a theoretical point of view, the concept of network governance is characterized by a profound ambiguity. According to the analysis of the concept of network governance by Schout and Jordan, there are two models of network governance: one that focuses on networks as self-organizing systems, and one involving active steering (Schout and Jordan 2003: 9).

The network governance approach adopted in the European Commission's White Paper on governance (Commission of the European Communities 2001) relies on self-organization. This approach does in fact aim to reform our modes of governance, by delegating a number of tasks to networks of self-regulated actors who negotiate their own collective coordination agreements.[3]

However, to some extent, this approach presupposes what it wants to achieve: the existence of a set of actors linked by sufficiently strong interdependences that allow for the emergence of decentralized solutions to coordination problems. Moreover, in the specific case of European governance, the institutional context is made up of heterogeneous actors and a complex hierarchy composed of different levels of interaction.

The absence of any reflexivity on the institutional conditions for the emergence of collective action by self-organization has condemned the policy of environmental policy integration through network governance to go unheeded. For instance, in spite of the high-level support for environmental policy integration

---

[3]   Generally speaking, a network is made up of a set of interconnected units (agents, organizations, computers, etc.) – the nodes – and a set of connections transmitting a signal (information, energy, etc.) from one node to another, with a certain connection strength. The network concept has been studied both as a form of collective organization and as an information processing device:

1   as an information-processing device its main property is to be able to decentralize problem-solving and information acquisition to the different individual information processing units or nodes of the network. For example, in the Water Sacramento forum, different stakeholders were able to enhance their knowledge – and thus their problem-solving capacity – through network interaction, without, however, having recourse to a centralized water governance agency (Innes and Booher 2003).

2   as a form of collective organization the focus is on the self-organizing capacities of a highly interconnected network. In this case, through the interaction dynamics between the different nodes, a form of coordination emerges that is an overall property of the network. For instance, in the so-called e-economy, a heterogeneous set of actors – both private and public – are interconnected in a new form of economic coordination through the Internet (Brousseau and Curien 2001: 28–9).

through self-regulation,[4] no supplementary capacity has been created for building a common information base, or for common agenda setting between different sectoral officials (Schout and Jordan 2003: 16–19). As a consequence, very little horizontal articulation has been created between sectoral Directorates General of the Commission or between national experts. Ultimately, the policy of integration through self-regulation has remained limited to some temporary bursts of coordination activity by the Council of Ministers, driven by short-term crises or intense lobbying by pressure groups (Lenschow 1999).

Nevertheless, as Schout and Jordan (2003) demonstrate, another perspective is possible, which is not based on the assumption of an automatic institutionalization of self-regulated networks of activity, but which explicitly addresses the question of the appropriate institutional framework for network operation. Accordingly, in his analysis, Jordan proposes that networks should be supplemented with institutions that help to steer the network design, carry out audits, adopt a critical stance and formulate management alternatives (ibid.: 12). Such institutions could also monitor the creation of coordination capacities between the different nodes in the network, in order to permit the integration of common objectives into the network as a whole (ibid.: 18–19).

Several questions are raised by the network governance approach: to what extent are networks self-organizing? Under what conditions can the iterative process of institution-building lead to effective governance systems? And when, and to what extent, is there a need for institutional regulation of self-regulation? In order to study these questions, we shall start from concrete examples where self-organized networks were mobilized to perform various functions of governance, and analyse the conditions under which concrete examples of self-organized networks were able to function effectively.

We first argue for the incompleteness of forms of network governance that rely only on self-organization. In order to do this, we shall focus on extensive research on self-organization in the context of the management of common pool resources. Second, we analyse the possible contribution of organizational learning to a more complete approach of network governance. Lastly, we shall apply our analysis to the case of sustainability impact assessment.

The Limits of Network Governance

In the current literature on theories of governance (Black 2001; Steward 2001), there is a growing interest in self-regulatory solutions to the problem of collective management of our natural resources. Recourse to self-organized collective

---

[4]   Environmental policy integration is the only integration requirement to be explicitly mentioned in the founding Treaties (initially the 1987 Single European Act; more recently in Article 6 of the 1997 Amsterdam Treaty). It has also been the subject of numerous European Council Resolutions over the last decade (cf. Schout and Jordan 2003).

action is not, however, limited to community self-regulation, but also occurs in forms of market self-regulation such as labelling practices addressed at user communities, or technical self-regulation through standardization agencies. The term self-regulation thus stands for a diverse set of arrangements, including forms of spontaneous self-regulation in particular communities, as well as forms of self-regulation by delegation, which are based on a delegation of power by government to a self-regulatory agency (Gunningham and Grabosky 1998). Accordingly, the prefix 'self' in self-regulation should not be understood literally, but points to a certain degree of collective constraint, other than that emanating directly from government, and making it possible to realize objectives that cannot be attained through individual market behaviour alone. The current use of the term also implies that collective constraint includes a series of well-established rules, be it in the form of customs, or of written rules, through which activities are regulated (Ogus 2000).

In order to analyse the limitation of recourse to self-organizing collective action in governance networks, we shall first study the question of the emergence of collective action in relation to the well-documented case of self-regulatory solutions to the *in situ* conservation of biological diversity.

Self-Regulation and Polycentric Governance

Current field research on self-regulation in the area of biodiversity governance highlights the emergence of collective action through experimentation with local rules, enabling the sustainable management of the ecosystem on which a community relies.

An example of such mechanisms is the collective management of *refugia* such as sacred ponds and groves as prevalent elements in indigenous resource-management systems (Gadgil, Berkes and Folke 1993). These systems might have evolved through a process involving an implicit trade-off between the benefits of the use of the natural resource and the necessity to minimize the risk of its depletion or extinction (Joshi and Gadgil 1991).

In another important case study, the emergence of such self-regulatory mechanisms results from the accumulation of information about the important role that species play in generating ecological services and natural resources. In his long-term field research in the Amazon basin, Posey discovered the role of *apete* or forest islands in producing a range of useful products while enhancing biodiversity. During the life span of the *apete*, management rules evolve from maintenance of a diverse productive zone, lasting a couple of years, to its transformation into a savannah-like open clearing, managed for its fruit and nut trees, and 'game farms' that attract wildlife (Posey 1985). This type of management is in sharp contrast with the slash-and-burn practices that merely result in temporary clearings within the forest landscape.

The evolution of such self-regulatory mechanisms is not, however, limited to indigenous people or communities of subsistence farmers. For example, a case study on coastal fisheries in Sweden shows how different local communities have developed dynamic, self-regulating patterns in order to adapt to natural fluctuations in fish resources (Hammer, Jansson and Jansson 1993).

This first type of field research shows the importance of experimentation with rules and the accumulation of local knowledge about effective rules that enable cooperative solutions to emerge. However, this mechanism does not consider the appropriate institutional conditions for the sustainable operation of these cooperative processes, such as effective monitoring and the use of graduated sanctions to ensure compliance with the rules.

A second type of field research aims at going beyond this insufficiency. This second kind of research has shown that sustainable self-organized management can only be successful in a context where efficient communication and social control is possible, allowing clear mechanisms for monitoring conformance with rules, and graduated sanctions for enforcing compliance (Ostrom 1998: 8). This can be the case both in small-scale communities where direct communication enhances the possibility of the emergence of norms of reciprocity, reputation and trust (Ostrom 1998: 13–14), and in larger communities, such as certain Internet-user communities, where the possibilities of coordination and control are increased by modern technology (E. Ostrom et al. 1999: 279).[5]

However, in spite of social control, the self-regulatory institutions remain subject to takeover by opportunistic individuals, and to potentially perverse dynamics. In particular, self-organized governance systems can be dominated by a local leader, or by a power elite, only accepting changes that are to their advantage. Some appropriators will not organize because of the presence of low-cost alternative sources of income and thus a reduced dependency on the resource (Ostrom 1999: 527).

This problem of network opportunism can be addressed in 'larger, general-purpose units that are responsible for protecting the rights of all citizens and for the oversight of appropriate exercises of authority within smaller units of government' (Ostrom 1999: 528). Indeed, according to research on self-organization in common pool resource management, a polycentric governance system involving higher levels of government as well as local self-regulatory units is more likely to provide incentives leading to self-organized, self-corrective institutional change (Ostrom 2000: 42).

Self-Regulated Systems as Complex Adaptive Systems

The behaviour model that emerges from empirical research on self-organization has received broad confirmation within the more general theoretical framework of complex adaptive systems (Holland 1995). Such systems are characterized by

---

[5]   The opportunistic appropriation of some 'common good' by certain Internet users can be sanctioned through management of the mailing lists and the means of access to the network (Brousseau 2001: 358).

a large number of active elements, which produce emergent collective properties that do not exist at the level of the elements, but only exist at the level of the combined effects of their interaction.

A much-discussed example of such emergent collective properties within a decentralized organization is the analysis by Hutchins (1995) of the navigation of a sailing ship. It shows that successful navigation does not require a specified centralized scenario for all situations. Instead, when a member of the crew detects a failure in the organization, he communicates this to the closest competent person. This person executes a corrective task, which has consequences in the further chain of interactions. In that manner, collective behaviour emerges through a history of local adaptations to a common environment (ibid.).[6] In this example, we find the mechanisms that are also mentioned in research on self-regulation, that is, experimentation with a decentralized set of rules through a process of trial and error on the one hand, and accumulation of knowledge about effective rules on the other.

Moreover, research on complex adaptive systems identifies some more specific mechanisms that also play a prominent part in the study of self-organization (Ostrom 1999: 521–3). These are:

1   the role of tags[7] in the categorization of the relevant properties of the environment;
2   internal models, including scenarios adapted to particular situations and partial cognitive maps of the environment;
3   clusters of distributed rules allowing a progressive adaptation to changing conditions in the environment through what have been called context-transforming generalizations (Clark 1993).

Modelling collective action in terms of complex adaptive systems has epistemological consequences (Dedeurwaerdere 2001). First of all, the effect of the rules and mechanisms will vary according to the way the system itself constructs an interpretation of its operational context through tagging and internal modelling. Second, we also have to reconsider the role of the environment in a different way. In fact, stabilization of the dynamics of self-organized systems depends on the asymmetrical evolution of the autonomous environment of the system. Even simple adaptationist models have to acknowledge this fact (Suppe 1989: 165). Stabilization of the competition between species in an ecosystem depends on the sources of nutrition in the environment. If a disturbance modifies those sources, then the system will evolve to another state of equilibrium. The

---

6   This is also the principle of 'loose coupled systems', as it is developed in the organizational literature (cf. Weick and Roberts 1993).

7   Tags are used to mark agents or objects that would otherwise be indistinguishable. For example, uniform, country of residence or personal characteristics can be used as a tag for identifying different crew members in the example of the sailing ship.

consequence of this interaction with the dynamics of the environment is that the collective behaviour resulting from a certain set of rules should be evaluated, not only in terms of its short-term consequences as a solution to a particular problem, but also in terms of its capacity to penetrate the self-organization of its environment. In that sense, a certain type of behaviour also has an explorative function, in provoking and processing adequate feedback information from the environment.

Combining these two limits, it can be said that the same type of behaviour has a reversible and an asymmetrical effect: it is a behaviour adapted to a particular problem in the environment, framed in a certain manner, and it is information provoking adequate feedback from the environment (Maesschalck 2001: 185). An example of this effect in cognitive ethology is the way fishes explore the autonomous flow dynamics of the stream through which they are navigating, and, in particular, the way they generate whirlpools and use the autonomous feedback of these whirlpools to swim faster (Triantafyllou and Triantafyllou 1995). This kind of modelling was only made possible as a result of rethinking the broader epistemological framework through which we approach dynamic systems in general.

Once we understand collective action from the point of view of the asymmetry of the evolution of its environment, we have to take into account some specific limitations on the modelling of self-regulation (Dedeurwaerdere 2001). Indeed, because of the necessity of taking into account the asymmetry of the evolution of the context, and in order to account for the stabilization of a particular system, the models have to include a hypothesis on the long-term behaviour of the environment.

In the context of research on common pool resources, it is the notion of polycentric political systems that accounts for the role of the broader environment. This notion was introduced by Vincent Ostrom in the context of his study of metropolitan governance, and connotes a system of 'many centres of decision-making which are formally independent of each other' (V. Ostrom, Tiebout and Warren 1961: 831). This environment composed of interacting units can be said to function as a whole to the extent that these 'take each other into account in competitive relationships, enter into various contractual and cooperative undertakings or have recourse to central mechanisms to resolve conflicts' (ibid.). According to the analysis of Elinor Ostrom, this research demonstrates that 'the study of the performance of a local public economy should be addressed at an interorganisational level of analysis rather than at the level of a single unit' (E. Ostrom 2000: 35). It is this 'modified form of competition' that can be viewed as a 'method for reducing opportunistic behaviour'. An example in the context of metropolitan governance is the creation of a larger consumption unit, making it possible to curb the strategic behaviour of the wealthy or to control the distribution of the costs of urban goods and services that do have large-scale effects (ibid.). In the context of global governance, examples that spring to mind are the United Nations Global Compact and the Forestry Stewardship council, both of which combine multiple stakeholders within a constructive tension, so that information is shared and each holds the other accountable for their public commitments in implementing sustainable development policies (Haas 2004b: 6).

The evolution of this polycentric system depends, however, on broader background beliefs, such as a certain conception of democracy. In particular, Vincent Ostrom's research on metropolitan systems points to the important role of civic education, which enables the intrinsic motivations of those motivated to solve problems on a conditional cooperative base. It thus seems that the contextual gain in cooperative behaviour through the multiplication of interactions between local experiments on self-regulation in a polycentric system depends in the long run on a broader theory of moral development. In particular, the experimental work on moral development by Kohlberg has shown, through numerous comparative studies on a longitudinal basis, that one cannot juxtapose the moral evolution of individuals and the evolution of a group as a practical space for experimentation on normativity (Kohlberg 1981). According to Lenoble and Maesschalck (2003: 155–68), an asymmetric relationship between two processes of moral development can be shown. The group constitutes a kind of intermediary culture, with its own references, its own codes. It enables experimentation with different types of behaviour without having to reassess them on the basis of already acquired attitudes or cultural codes in force. It is this incentive-reflexive role of the group that explains its enabling effect on the evolution of individual skills. Accordingly, evolution of the polycentric system will depend on the learning effects of these intermediary cultures on the different self-regulated sets of activity. These learning effects depend on collective experimentation with new norms of cooperation in the broader institutional environment.

The Contribution of Organizational Learning to Network Governance

The first model of network governance is based on the emergence of collective action through self-organization. However, it does not automatically imply the improved integration of a perspective of sustainable development into the network institutions in question. The network approach creates a self-adjustment process for the strategies used by the actors in different self-regulated sectors of activity; however, it does not develop initiatives geared towards a change in the larger background of legitimization that determines the overall normative orientation of the interaction between the different nodes in the network. In the specific case of sustainable development, this background is far from being stabilized. As Godard's analysis shows, the sustainable development criterion is open to several interpretations, and stabilization is, in turn, dependent on a series of legitimacy 'tests' that take a variety of forms according to the different orders of legitimization (Godard, Chapter 2 in this volume). Stabilization will therefore depend on a learning process enabling the different actors that make up this context to modify their background of normative beliefs in order to take into account the viewpoints of the largest possible community.

One example is the ambivalence of the environmental self-regulation policies of the European Commission's Fifth Environmental Action Programme (1993–2000). The aim was to organize environmental self-regulation through a set of incentive mechanisms such as eco-labels, voluntary agreements and environmental management systems. As it turned out, however, this incentive mechanism did not lead to the institutionalization of ecology in the social practices of production and consumption, but instead led to technocratic management by the main actors. In order to put forward an interpretation in the policy networks in terms of a democratic, ecological approach, there is a need for practical guarantees that environmental groups will be included in the evaluation and adaptation of the goals of self-regulatory arrangements (Neale 1997).

Another example, from the field of biodiversity governance, concerns the emerging regime of access and benefit-sharing in genetic resources. Indeed, in this field, in response to the lack of effectiveness of classical modes of regulation, the creation of collective norms of management by self-regulation can be seen (Ten Kate and Laird 2002: 300–89). For example, associations of biological resource users, such as botanical gardens or private corporations, have set up ethical codes of conduct or voluntary mechanisms of benefit sharing. This evolution has been especially important in sectors of greater homogeneity, as in the case of the international MOSAIC[8] code of conduct for the *ex situ* collections of microbial cultures, or the declaration of common principles on access and benefit sharing of the network of botanical gardens around Royal Kew Gardens in London.[9] In addition to these common initiatives, some companies have also created ethical codes on an individual basis, in the belief that this will improve their reputation as reliable suppliers of genetic material (ibid.: 302).

However, the level of compliance of the different initiatives of self-regulation with the requirements embodied in the different international regimes – Food and Agriculture Organization (FAO), United Nations Environment Programme (UNEP) and World Trade Organization (WTO) – actually depends only on reputation within a network of institutions or professionals in a certain sector. These strategies effectively increase the reliability of the member organizations, but it remains difficult to compare efficacy with regard to the goals of equitable access and fair benefit sharing as established in the Convention on Biological Diversity, or to evaluate the capacity of such institutional arrangements in order to guarantee a level of compliance in more heterogeneous sectors.

Thus, if one wishes to take into account the importance of the normative orientation of the governance networks from the point of view of the asymmetry of their contextual interpretation in the broader environment, a new question arises, which relates to experimentation in particular communities with normative background beliefs.

---

[8]   Microorganism Sustainable Use and Access Regulation.
[9]   Common Policy Guidelines for Participating Gardens on Access to Genetic Resources and Benefit-Sharing, available at <www.rbg.ca/cbcn/cpg_index.html>.

Social Learning in Epistemic Communities

This is why a second model of network governance focuses on the role of institutional framing in enabling learning processes on the background of normative beliefs. We can analyse this second model in greater depth on the basis of the research conducted by Ernst and Peter Haas on the conditions for organizational learning in international organizations. In their work, they reveal the important role that can be played by communities with a specific knowledge, known as epistemic communities, which are geared towards the development of organizational concepts and common intersubjective meanings with respect to a certain problem (Haas and Haas 2002*)*. In historical terms, these communities fulfilled an important role in the field of environmental governance. Well-discussed examples include the role of the scientists involved in the Villach Group in the field of climate change (Haas and McCabe 2001) and the ecological community monitoring pollution in the Mediterranean (Haas 1990). However, as their research clearly shows, the role of these communities with regard to the development of common intersubjective meanings can also be observed in other fields. For example, according to Peter and Ernst Haas, the United Nations Global Compact is also 'an effort to develop and apply within an institutional setting consensual knowledge about best corporate practices by trying to encourage participation from corporate actors, civil society and experts' (Haas and Haas 2002: 597).

With a view to clarifying the contribution of epistemic communities to international governance, Ernst Haas stresses the importance of two distinct learning processes. The first of these, learning as adaptation in its biological-cybernetic meaning, identifies learning as a form of 'error correction', whether through a process of 'trial and error', similar to natural selection, or a 'feedback' process from the environment. It is this form of learning that characterizes the self-regulated complex adaptive systems that we considered in the first section. The central idea of this first form is to enable an organization to maintain its principal functions within established limits, in order to guarantee survival under variable environmental conditions. In the context of learning theories, this first form comes up against the need to bring about a transformation process that makes it possible for an organization to meet the challenges posed by new demands, without having to reassess both the organization's programme in its entirety, and the justification that underlies its own legitimacy (Haas 1990: 34). However, organizations do not merely have a capacity for biological adaptation; they are also capable of reassessing their own fundamental principles. These self-programming abilities are the basis of a second learning process, allowing an organization to redefine its own organizational mission when confronted again and again with the unexpected or ineffective results of its own actions (Haas: 35–7). The important point about this second process is that it incorporates evaluation and monitoring processes that are not geared towards maintaining the stability of the organization, but rather towards changing the basic beliefs of institutions and encouraging the emergence of new possibilities of action that are necessary to promote an ethos of sustainable development.

According to Haas and Haas (1995), unlike the incremental adjustment process that is typical of the interactionist visions of organizational learning, the learning process that is possible thanks to epistemic communities leads to changes in the work programme of organizations by confronting them with a shared vision of cause-and-effect relationships between complex phenomena.[10] It is the change in the work programme of organizations as a result of a learning process that they designate as 'organizational learning'.

In a recent article, Peter Haas develops the different aspects of this concept of organizational learning in more detail. As such, organizational learning includes both a substantial aspect – on the level of the learning of common knowledge and common norms – and a procedural aspect – on the level of the process of transmission of the results of the learning process to the relevant organizations (Haas 2004a: 573). Current research on social learning in epistemic communities shows that one of the most important dimensions, on the procedural level, is the isolation of the learning process from the political process. As has actually been shown in several empirical studies, the independent character of the epistemic community enhances the influence of the ideas, and thus their transmission to the policy process. On the substantial level, the research shows the importance of a mechanism to include the widest possible community of interests in the production of the new ideas and to mobilise the widest possible knowledge base. Indeed, according to the concept developed by Peter Haas, the aim of social learning is to produce 'usable knowledge', which can eventually be integrated into the working programme of political institutions. Such knowledge should be accurate and of use to politicians and policy-makers (ibid.: 574), and can be characterized by the criteria of credibility, legitimacy and saliency (Siebenhüner 2002, 2003). In this light, organizational learning depends on precise, accessible knowledge that contributes to the achievement of collective aims.

On the basis of this research, empirical studies have tried to determine conditions for improving our governance institutions in such a way as to satisfy both the need for social learning and the development of appropriate procedures for linking the new ideas to the policy process. One of the most widely discussed examples in the literature on organizational learning is the role of the Intergovernmental Panel on Climate Change (IPCC) in the issue of global warming. According to Haas and McCabe, the key characteristics that made organizational learning possible in the field of climate science are, first, the existence of a learning process within the group of independent experts that

---

[10]   Indeed, as they state in their research on organizational learning, 'it is only a structured interpretation process, leading to the emergence of core beliefs around some operational models, that allows for knowledge production to be related to new policy programme proposals and to be integrated in the organisation's mission statement and activities' (Haas and Haas 1995: 266).

gathered for the Villach meetings between 1985 and 1988 (Haas and McCabe 2001) and, second, the establishment within UNEP, by its first Executive Director Maurice Strong, of an open policy process through which states were exposed to the consensual knowledge acquired by the Villach Group (Haas 2004a: 577). This group was able to propose new regulatory mechanisms in the field of climate change – introducing the concept of emission quotas – which were incorporated into the organizational activities of the United Nations Environment Programme. However, political control over climate science has increased in the years following the creation of the IPCC – which superseded the work of the Villach Group – and at present the IPCC reports suffer from a lack of legitimacy (ibid.: 582–3).

The learning process in the climate change community has served as a model for the organization of similar assessment processes in other fields. For example, in the field of biodiversity governance, in 1994 UNEP organized the Global Biodiversity Assessment, which aimed to gather relevant information on biodiversity and to structure it for policy makers. However, this assessment was not as successful as the climate change assessment, and the outcome was far less influential. In 2000, a second round of assessments in the biodiversity field got underway, via the Millennium Ecosystem Assessment. This second round presents major new initiatives, in that it aims to include contextual knowledge through local assessments, and starts from a broader conception of knowledge, making it possible to include traditional communities' perspectives on biodiversity.

Application to the Case of Sustainability Impact Assessment (SIA)

Impact assessment methods play an important role in improving European governance. They were originally conceived as a major step towards more transparent modes of governance, increasingly based on scientific evidence. Thus, according to Colin Kirkpatrick, who led the research into SIA methodology for the European Commission, impact assessment may be defined as 'a methodology for identifying the potential or actual impact of a development program' (Kirkpatrick 2003a: 32). As such, it may be regarded as an instrument for achieving 'better governance', making it possible to improve 'evidence-based decision-making and, by correlation, the quality of the decision-making process' (ibid.: 31).

In a Communication, the European Commission announced its intention to launch impact assessments as a tool to improve the policy development process (Commission of the European Communities 2002). In particular, all major policy initiatives would be subjected to the new sustainability impact assessment method ('phase III') elaborated by the Institute for Development Policy and Management (IDPM) of the University of Manchester. Below, we refer to this particular methodology as it has been applied and widely discussed in the sustainability impact assessment of trade liberalization policies by the DG Trade of the European Commission.

As stated in Chapter 13 of this volume (Knigge and Kranz), the specific aim of SIA of trade liberalization is to promptly identify and forestall potential negative effects, or, alternatively, to set up adequate measures to mitigate such effects. This particular use of impact assessments, in close connection with the negotiation process, poses new challenges in terms of research, causal-chain analysis, timing and legitimacy. We shall not explore these issues in any further depth here, but instead shall evaluate the possible contribution of SIA to improving current means of network governance by enabling a process of social learning on the issue of trade and sustainable development.

In the proposed IDPM methodology, the production of 'usable knowledge' for policy makers relies on a diverse set of methodologies, including modelling methods, methods based on data (statistical estimation) methods, descriptive (case study) methods, expert opinions and consultation. The principle used in the aggregation of this diverse set of data is to elaborate significant cause-effect links between trade liberalization and its eventual economic, social and environmental impact, and to provide for an empirical estimation of these impacts. As such, impact assessments can thus be considered as a further elaboration of the concept of integrated models that has been developed mainly in the field of environmental impact assessment (Janssen and de Vries 1998; Kirkpatrick 2003a: 40).

Representative examples of integrated models include not only the EU's trade liberalization SIA, but also the environmental impact assessment tools used within the North Atlantic Free Trade Organization (NAFTA), the impact assessment models for climate change used by the IPCC, or, previously, the models of limits to growth used by the Club of Rome. The belief underlying the construction of these integrated models is that, by integrating the human and natural dimensions of the change in systems into the same modelling procedure, these models will be able to help to create a hierarchy of priorities for public policies and research activities, and to reveal uncertainties and gaps in our knowledge.

Naturally, the principle of sustainable development, which serves as an optimization principle in these assessments, does not enable them to be stabilized unequivocally. In fact, the criterion of 'sustainable development', used in impact assessment, allows for a great many interpretations. Godard, for example, identifies at least three interpretations of sustainability (Godard, Chapter 2 of this volume):

1 a biocentric interpretation, which maintains that all living beings have an intrinsic value and must therefore be protected, whilst taking into consideration complex interdependences between all living beings in the biosphere;
2 an anthropocentric interpretation, which emphasizes the importance of preserving the earth's ecosystems in order to maintain human development potential;
3 an economic interpretation of sustainable development, which balances the long-term costs of the destruction of ecosystems in relation to the short-term benefits.

As a result, the social legitimacy of the models will depend on the practical acceptance of the principle of sustainable development from the viewpoint of these different interpretations. The legitimacy of the models will therefore depend not only on scientific data, but also on the collective preferences of the populations affected by the policies evaluated in the impact assessments. In the context of SIA, for instance, one example of conflict with regard to collective preferences centred on the priority to be given in the models to protecting the environment while promoting economic development in developing countries (Borregaard and Bradley 1999). Another major area of tension concerned the different concepts of trade liberalization to be considered in the assessments, ranging from liberalization without mitigation measures to the integration of scenarios of limits to growth (WWF 2002).

Such lack of consensus has severely limited the actual use of the SIA models. However, various signs of gradual change indicate an attempt to address these issues. From the outset, SIA was conceived as a multi-stakeholder process, and several inclusive stakeholder consultation processes have been implemented. These include the dialogue between contractors for the assessments and stakeholders with interests in individual sectors, or the meetings with civil society organized by the European Commission to discuss project reports (DG Trade 2002). Furthermore, the European Commission has already begun to address criticisms that have been voiced by stakeholders and civil society (Zerbe and Dedeurwaerdere 2003). For instance, it has committed itself to improving the timing of SIA by commencing the process at an earlier stage in trade negotiations so that SIA can have a more effective impact. It has promoted greater coordination between researchers and negotiators, and has trained negotiators regarding the potential value and use of assessment reports. In addition, it has increased opportunities for stakeholder input in the SIA process by hosting workshops within the EU, and by requiring stakeholder consultations in third countries when they are the focus of examination.[11]

Nevertheless, no methodology is complete, and several important gaps remain in the institutional implementation of the SIA tool. In particular, as mentioned above, the approach suffers from a lack of tools that specifically address the social learning process between the different stakeholders, making it possible to integrate information coming from different types of actors and to combine a heterogeneous set of social values.

First of all, with regard to information gathering, there is a major difficulty in the actual design to integrate contextual information into the assessment process. For example, in one major assessment concerning the ACP countries, several tools

---

[11]   The SIA of the ACP countries currently underway, for example, provides for four workshops to be held in Brussels, and two in West Africa and the Caribbean. Furthermore, it calls for the use of electronic communications and expert networks to provide additional opportunities for stakeholder and expert consultations during the whole assessment process (PriceWaterhouseCoopers 2003).

have been developed to address stakeholder participation, but in practice the major data used in the reports resulted from a compilation of existing World Bank data, because of the difficulty of obtaining direct information from the field in such a short time (Thirion 2003). Another example, also mentioned by one of the main contractors, concerns the restricted access of developing countries to electronic communication, which is one of the main tools used in current SIA for enhancing transparency and broad public involvement (Kirkpatrick 2003b).

Second, with regard to social values, there is real difficulty in developing contextual models in home countries that integrate local values more effectively, because of the lack of an institutional framework for producing local assessments. Therefore, there is no explicit construction of alternative ways of framing the problem of trade in sustainable development that is directly linked with *data* gathering and elaboration of models. Some NGOs have attempted to address this issue, such as in the long-term study of APRODEF on the impact of trade liberalization on the social status of women in Mozambique (Ulmer 2003). However, nothing is done to explicitly enable such local assessments to be carried out; nor are these initiatives connected with the overall assessment process.

It therefore seems that the institutional design of the social learning process on the trade and sustainable development *nexus* initiated by SIAs is still an important aspect to be addressed. SIA has been developed as a way of integrating sustainable development into the different policies of the European Commission, through improving the evidence base on which decisions are made, and hence the quality of decision-making. As such, the SIA experiment underway in the DG Trade has a broad-based ambition and can be considered as a potential extension of the Environmental Policy Integration (EPI) requirement mentioned in the EU founding treaties.[12] This requirement states that environmental considerations should be integrated into the design, adoption and implementation of policies in all policy sectors. With the methodology as it stands at the moment, this broad objective has been implemented through an institutional process that enables networking of independent experts, key negotiators and relevant stakeholders. As such, in a similar manner to the implementation of the EPI, it is a good example of the concept of network governance promoted by the European Commission. However, as we have argued throughout this chapter, long-term development of such networking can only be successful if it is simultaneously able to develop incentives for organizational learning in the broader institutional environment of the networks.

---

[12] Initially in the 1987 Single European Act; more recently in Article 6 of the 1997 Amsterdam Treaty.

Conclusion

The emerging networks of public-private partnerships and contracts aim to offer innovative answers, in the international context, to the present difficulties faced by the system of multilateral cooperation. Nevertheless, in most cases, these answers still remain confined to a functional adaptation to the new requirements for global regulation, and fail to take into account the reflexivity of the different actors in the construction of the networks. Indeed, the principle of these networks is to bring together, often by the use of contractual relationships, different areas of expertise and different types of actors around a common object, thereby attempting to bridge and articulate different levels of governance. However, there is no reflection on the mode of construction of a common perception or common norms in the networks, nor on the mode of organization of the rules for cooperation within the networks. It is this dimension that this chapter has developed, on the basis of case studies in the field of sustainable development, in order to enhance our understanding of the construction of such networks.

Our analysis has shown that it is possible to identify, through these network governance experiments, two phases in the improvement of our institutions for global governance. This improvement is particularly crucial in the case of sustainable development, where a plurality of principles of legitimation is put forward by different stakeholders. The first phase aims to mobilize the self-regulation capacity of the actors in order to improve the current governance arrangements. This first stage enables the construction of common perceptions or common norms among existing practitioners of sustainable development. The second phase tries to integrate the necessity for organizational learning into the institutional environment of the self-regulated sectors of network activity. This further phase considers the role of a polycentric set of institutions in enabling evolution of the background of normative beliefs, on which the successful implementation of sustainable development through self-regulation depends.

Following the critical analysis of Schout and Jordan of the concept of network governance in the European Commission's White Paper, this chapter has discussed the limits of a concept of network governance solely based on self-organization for implementing sustainable development policies. Indeed, as extensive research on self-organizing solutions to the management of common resources has shown, the sustainability of these initiatives depends on background beliefs in the broader institutional environment in which the networks are operating. That is why, relying on the work of Peter and Ernst Haas (1995, 2002), Godard (see Chapter 2) and Siebenhüner (2002), we have argued that the current network approach to sustainable development should be supplemented with initiatives that foster organizational learning in the institutional environment of the networks. In particular, the creation of appropriate institutions for social learning on the trade and sustainable development *nexus* should make it possible to enhance the credibility, legitimacy and saliency of the network institutions. As we have tried to show in our case study on Sustainability Impact Assessment, the further development of hybrid tools, such as contextual models that integrate social values more effectively, and the introduction of measures to enable local assessment capacity that broadens the information base from the field could enhance both the legitimacy and the credibility of the models.

References

Black, J. 2001. 'Decentring Regulation: Understanding the Role of Regulation and Self-regulation in a "Post-regulatory" World'. *Current Legal Problems* 54: 103–46.

Borregaard, N. and T. Bradley. 1999. 'Towards Understanding Costs and Benefits of Trade Liberalisation: A Developing Country Perspective'. Presentation at the OECD Workshop on 'Methodologies for Environmental Assessment of Trade Liberalisation Agreements', 26–27 October, OECD Headquarters, Paris.

Brousseau, E. 2001. 'Régulation de l'Internet, L'autorégulation nécessite-t-elle un cadre institutionnel?' *Revue Economique* 52 (hors série): 349–77.

Brousseau, E. and N. Curien. 2001. 'Economie d'Internet, économie du numérique'. *Revue Economique* 52: 7–36.

Commission of the European Communities. 2001. 'European Governance: A White Paper'. COM(2001) 428 final, Brussels.

Clark, A. 1993. *Associative Engines: Connectionism, Concepts and Representational Change.* Cambridge, MA: MIT Press.

Diani, M. and D. McAdam, eds. 2003. *Social Movements and Networks: Relational Approaches to Collective Action.* Oxford: Oxford University Press.

Dedeurwaerdere, T. 2001. *Action et Contexte, Du tournant cognitiviste à la phénoménologie transcendantale.* Hildesheim: Olms.

———. 2005. 'From Bioprospecting to Reflexive Governance'. *Ecological Economics,* forthcoming, April 2005.

DG Trade. 2002. *Trade Policy Dialogue with Civil Society: Sustainable Development and Trade.* Available online at <www.trade-info.cec.eu.int>.

Gadgil, M., F. Berkes and C. Folke. 1993. 'Indigenous Knowledge for Biodiversity Conservation'. *Ambio* 22.2–3: 151–56.

Godard, O. 2005. 'Is Sustainable Development an Alternative Principle of Justification?' This volume: ch. 2.

Gould, R.V. 1993. 'Collective Action and Network Structure'. *American Sociological Review* 58: 182–96.

Gunningham, N. and P. Grabosky. 1998. *Smart Regulation: Designing Environmental Policy.* Oxford: Clarendon Press.

Haas, E.B. 1990. *When Knowledge is Power: Three Models of Change in International Organisations.* Berkeley: University of California Press.

Haas P.M. 1990. *Saving the Mediterranean: The Politics of International Environmental Cooperation.* New York: Columbia University Press.

———. 2004a. 'When Does Power Listen To Truth? A Constructivist Approach to the Policy Process'. *Journal of European Public Policy*: 569–92.

———. 2004b. 'Addressing the Global Governance Deficit'. *Global Environmental Politics*: 1–15.

Haas, P.M. and E.B. Haas. 1995. 'Learning to Learn'. *Global Governance* 1: 255–85.

————. 2002. 'Pragmatic Constructivism and the Study of International Institution'. *Millennium: Journal of International Studies*: 573–601.

Haas, P.M. and D. McCabe. 2001. 'Amplifiers or Dampeners: International Institutions and Social Learning in the Management of Global Environmental Risks'. In *Learning to Manage Global Environmental Risks*, Vol. 1. Cambridge, MA: MIT Press: 323–48.

Hajer, M.A. and H. Wagenaar. 2003. *Deliberative Policy Analysis: Understanding Governance in the Network Society*. Cambridge: Cambridge University Press.

Hammer, M., A.M. Jansson and B.-O. Jansson. 1993. 'Diversity Change and Sustainability: Implications for Fisheries'. *Ambio* 22.2–3: 97–105.

Hodgson, G.M. 1999. *Evolution and Institutions: On Evolutionary Economics and the Evolution of Economics*. Northampton, MA: Edward Elgar.

Holland, J.H. 1995. *Hidden Order: How Adaptation Builds Complexity*. Reading, MA: Addison-Wesley.

Hutchins, E. 1995. *Cognition in the Wild*. Cambridge, MA: MIT Press.

Innes, J.E. and D.E. Booher. 2003. 'Collaborative Policy Making: Governance through Dialogue'. In M.A. Hajer and W. Wagenaar, eds. *Deliberative Policy Analysis: Understanding Governance in the Network Society*. Cambridge: Cambridge University Press: 33–59.

Janssen, M. and B. de Vries. 1998. 'Global Modeling: Managing Uncertainty, Complexity and Incomplete Information'. In C. van Dijkum, D. de Tombe and E. van Kuijk, eds. *Validation of Simulation Models*. Amsterdam: SISWO.

Joshi, N.V. and M. Gadgil. 1991. 'On the Role of *refugia* in Promoting Prudent Use of Biological Resources'. *Theoretical Population Biology* 40: 211–29.

Kahler, M. 1999. 'Evolution, Choice and International Change'. In D.A. Lake and R. Powell, eds. *Strategic Choice and International Relations*. Princeton: Princeton University Press.

Kirkpatrick, C. 2003a. 'Sustainability Impact Assessment Methodology: SIA Study of the Proposed WTO Negotiations'. Cepii Working Paper No. 2003–19: 27–52.

————. 2003b. 'Consultation and Participation in European Governance Reform: The Role of Sustainability Impact Assessment'. Presentation at the Sustra seminar on SIA, 28 March 2003, Université Catholique de Louvain, Louvain-la-Neuve.

Knigge, M. and N. Kranz. 2005. 'Public Participation in the EU's Sustainability Impact Assessments of Trade Agreements'. This volume: ch. 13.

Kohlberg, L. 1981. *Essays on Moral Development*, Vol. 1: *The Philosophy of Moral Development, Moral Stages and the Idea of Justice*. San Francisco: Harper and Row.

Lenoble, J. and M. Maesschalck. 2003. *The Action of Norms*. London: Kluwer International.

Lenschow, A. 1999. 'The Greening of the EU'. *Environment and Planning C* 17: 91–108.

Maesschalck, M. 2001. *Normes et contextes, Les fondements d'une pragmatique contextuelle*. Hildesheim: Olms.

Neale, A. 1997. 'Organising Environmental Self-regulation: Liberal Governmentality and the Pursuit of Ecological Modernisation in Europe'. *Environmental Politics* 6.4: 1–24.

Ogus, A. 2000. 'Self-regulation'. In B. Bouckaert and G. de Geest, eds. *Encyclopedia of Law and Economics*, Vol. V: *The Economics of Crime and Litigation*. Cheltenham: Edward Elgar: 587–602.

Ostrom, E. 1998. 'A Behavioral Approach to the Rational Choice Theory of Collective Action'. *American Political Science Review* 92.1: 1–22.

———. 1999. 'Coping with Tragedies of the Commons'. *Annual Review of Political Science* 2: 493–535.

———. 2000. 'The Danger of Self-evident Truths'. *Political Science and Politics* 33.1: 33–44.

———. 2001. 'Decentralisation and Development: The New Panacea'. In K. Dowding, J. Hughes and H. Margetts, eds. *Challenges to Democracy: Ideas, Involvement and Institution.* New York: Palgrave Publishers: 237–56.

Ostrom, E., J. Burger, C.B. Field, R.B. Norgaard and D. Policansky. 1999. 'Revisiting the Commons: Local Lessons, Global Challenges'. *Science* 284: 278–82.

Ostrom, V., C.H. Tiebout and R. Warren. 1961. 'The Organisation of Government in Metropolitan Areas: A Theoretical Inquiry'. *American Political Science Review* 55 (December): 831–42.

Posey, D.A. 1985. 'Indigenous Management of Tropical Forest Ecosystems: The Case of the Kayapo Indians of the Brazilian Amazon'. *Agroforestry Systems* 3: 139–58.

PriceWaterhouseCoopers. 2003. 'Sustainability Impact Assessment of the Trade Negotiations of the EU-ACP Economic Partnership Agreements: Final Revised Inception Report', 31 January 2003. Available online at <www.sia-acp.org>.

Reinicke, W.H. and F. Deng. 2000. *Critical Choices: The United Nations, Networks and the Future of Global Governance.* Ottawa: International Development Research Council.

Schout, A. and A. Jordan. 2003. 'Coordinated European Governance: Self-organising or Centrally Steered?' CSERGE Working Paper, EDM 03-14.

Siebenhüner, B. 2002. 'How do Scientific Assessments Learn?' *Environmental Science and Policy* 5: 411–27.

———. 2003. 'The Changing Role of Nation States in International Environmental Assessments'. *Global Environmental Change* 13: 113–23.

Singleton, S. 2000. 'Co-operation or Capture? The Paradox of Co-management and Community Participation in Natural Resource Management and Environmental Policy-making'. *Environmental Politics* 9.2: 1–21.

Steward, R.B. 2001. 'A New Generation of Environmental Regulation?' *Capital University Law Review* 29: 21–182.

Streck, C. 2002. 'Global Public Policy Networks as Coalitions for Change'. In D.C. Esty and M.H. Ivanova, eds. *Global Environmental Governance, Options and Opportunities.* New Haven: Yale School of Forestry and Environmental Studies: 121–40.

Suppe, F. 1989. *The Semantic Conception of Theories and Scientific Realism.* Chicago: University of Illinois Press.

Ten Kate, K. and S.A. Laird 2002. *The Commercial Use of Biodiversity.* London: Earthscan.

Thirion, M.-C. 2003. 'Sustainability Impact Assessment and Trade Liberalisation in the Developing World: The Case of the ACP Countries'. Presentation at the Sustra seminar on SIA, 27 March 2003, Université Catholique de Louvain, Louvain-la-Neuve.

Triantafyllou, M. and G. Triantafyllou. 1995. 'An Efficient Swimming Machine'. *Scientific American* 272: 64–71.

Ulmer, K. 2003. 'The Gender Dimension of Impact Assessment Studies'. Presentation at the Sustra seminar on SIA, 27 March 2003. Available online at <www.agro-montpellier.fr/sustra.

Weick, Karl E. and K.H. Roberts. 1993. 'Collective Mind in Organisations: Heedful Interrelating on Flight Decks'. *Administrative Science Quarterly* 9.38: 357–81.

WWF. 2002. 'Changing the Balance of Trade: WWF Briefing on Sustainability Assessment of EU Trade Policy'. Available online at <www.panda.org/epo>.

Zerbe, N. and T. Dedeurwaerdere. 2003. ,Sustainability Impact Assessment'. Sustra Policy Brief Paper. Available online at <www.agro-montpellier.fr/sustra>.

Chapter 13

Public Participation in the EU's Sustainability Impact Assessments of Trade Agreements

Markus Knigge and Nicole Kranz

Introduction

International trade is a policy area that frequently arouses suspicions of
illegitimacy. This is as a result of its traditional reliance on delegation, executive
authority and technicality. However, accompanying the shift in focus of
international trade policy from traditional trade barriers to new types of non-
tariff barriers that have major impacts on sensitive issues, such as food safety,
environmental protection and health, the participation of civil society becomes
even more important. However, this discussion has not only led to intensive
research activities in this area, but has also recently provided the impetus for
employing Sustainability Impact Assessments (SIAs) to allow for an *ex ante*
evaluation of potential negative impacts of trade agreements (see Elwell 2002 for
US and Canadian experiences). In the European Union (EU), an SIA programme
was launched in 1999 by DG Trade and Trade, committed to applying the SIA
process to all major policy initiatives. The prominent role given to SIAs by the
European Commission is underlined by the fact that a substantial share of DG
Trade's budget is dedicated to SIAs. The assessments are usually carried out
in several stages: in the planning stage, the SIA is launched and contents are
defined; the ensuing screening and scoping phase deals with the selection of
trade measures to be assessed, indicators, significance criteria and country case
studies, as well as evaluation methods. The actual assessment is then carried
out analytically and empirically, using models and case studies. This technical
analysis enables the assessment of possible flanking measures. In some cases the
SIA is supplemented by a follow-up study, including subsequent monitoring and
an *ex post* evaluation that allows for a direct comparison of projected outcomes
and the actual results.

Generally, impact assessments are nothing new, and indeed a broad base
of knowledge and expertise exists on how to assess the potential effects of
any planned activity of projects, in particular in the environmental arena.
The objectives of impact assessments are to promptly identify and forestall

the potential negative effects, or alternatively, to set up adequate measures for mitigating such effects. However, using SIAs in order to integrate sustainability concerns into trade policy poses new challenges in terms of research, causal-chain analysis, timing and legitimacy. A subsequent issue of major concern is how to integrate civil society better into these processes and procedures. This article addresses the question of how to improve the quality and legitimacy of SIAs by enhancing stakeholder participation. It starts with a short review of the benefits and costs of public participation in impact assessments. Based on this, major challenges and obstacles to participation are identified and analysed; in particular, the selection of stakeholders and the structure of participation in the different phases and stages are investigated in more detail. The article raises the question of whether, in the area of trade, a more decentralized approach to SIAs might be more appropriate. It concludes by making a number of proposals on how to improve SIA processes by increasing the participation of civil society. Special emphasis is given to the SIA process in the European Union context.

Benefits and Costs of Participation

Stakeholder participation entails significant costs and benefits. This is particularly true for trade agreements, given the complexity of impacts that trade measures could potentially have on a country's economy, environment and social development (Dalal-Clayton and Bass 2002: 193–5), as areas affected by international trade nowadays range from water services, agriculture and food security and environmental standards to intellectual property rights. Costs and benefits of stakeholder participation raise the question of what levels of participation are appropriate at different stages of SIAs. In terms of benefits, the additional knowledge and expertise that can be obtained through greater involvement of stakeholders is most important. Not only do stakeholders add further perspectives, but there are also thematic areas, such as biodiversity and indigenous knowledge, where it is widely acknowledged that local stakeholders alone are in the position to provide the knowledge and expertise necessary to integrate these issues into trade policy (OECD 2001).

However, stakeholder participation is not only fundamental to building a sufficiently broad knowledge base, but also to ensuring that SIAs are perceived as legitimate and independent (UNEP 2001: 17). Generally, transparent assessment processes and the involvement of interested parties contribute to building reciprocal trust between experts and stakeholders and improve the commitment to the process as well as the final strategy, thus facilitating its implementation. Again, this is especially important in the area of trade, where technical language and detailed knowledge tend to make involvement difficult for non-experts, and decision-making processes and negotiations are often accused of lacking transparency. In this respect, encouraging debate among experts and stakeholders is expected to lead to a better understanding of the different positions. In addition, it is hoped that participation processes in SIAs will raise awareness among civil society groups, and contribute to their understanding of the nexus between trade and sustainable development (WWF 2002).

Obviously, participation processes also impose costs on both those seeking input from participants and participating stakeholders themselves. These costs include the effort of identifying and inviting stakeholders, time needed for consultations, and direct costs such as travelling to meetings, renting meeting facilities, printing and disseminating information. All these costs may limit participation or cause a bias in the range of stakeholders who are able to participate. Consequently, costs and benefits need to be taken into account when thinking about the best way to organize efficient and effective participation processes.

To better gauge the benefits of their activities, it is essential for civil society groups to know about the relationship between SIAs and the trade negotiations whose potential impacts are being assessed. The criticism has been made that the effect of SIAs on negotiating positions and negotiation outcomes is unclear, and that it might actually be non-existent. Consequently, SIAs are frequently perceived as greenwash, or as a superfluous bureaucratic exercise (Joint NGO Statement 2000). If this was really the case, stakeholders should not devote their often-limited resources to participating in a process that has no impact on policy-making. In order to justify public participation in the SIA process, a stronger link needs to be established between the assessments and the negotiations. A starting point could be requiring negotiators to report on how their positions relate to the SIA, and on whether and how the progress of the negotiations was influenced by those positions. Another option might be the participation of stakeholders themselves in the negotiating process, which would allow them to contribute to the decision-making process more directly and exercise control over the way the SIA is used by policy-makers. Furthermore, the SIAs results could be disseminated before the end of the negotiation.

Selection of Stakeholders and Related Issues

It is obvious that the broad participation of a representative selection of stakeholders is the main goal of participative processes. The question, however, remains, who represents 'the public' and what selection of stakeholders would be representative of civil society. First, in terms of its political legitimacy, it is fundamental that the SIA addresses concerns of those affected by the trade measures under scrutiny, through the participation of relevant stakeholders. Here, a number of groups, including women, indigenous people and ethnic minorities, are frequently under-represented. Second, stakeholders representing societal interests and with a higher degree of organization are key to the inclusion of a broader knowledge base. Among these key groups, developmental, social and environmental NGOs and other public interest groups play a fundamental role. In addition, local authorities and agencies, trade associations and the private sector can add relevant views to the impact assessment process. Third, the participation of relevant experts and review by the respective scientific community, including research institutions and academia, is necessary in order to ensure the use of authoritative information and the scientific credibility of the assessment.

However, stakeholders may differ in their ability to actively participate and contribute to the process. SIAs are complex projects, and participation requires particular technical knowledge and expertise. This has to be considered against the background of traditionally opaque trade negotiations and a lack of expertise and experience on trade issues in a large number of environmental and developmental NGOs. Thus, capacity building among stakeholders might be a prerequisite for their successful participation in many cases.

Apart from the required knowledge and expertise, participation can also be costly in terms of time for preparation and participation in meetings, travel costs, the creation and dissemination of information material and so on. In order to level the playing field between all participants in SIAs, and to ensure effective and efficient participation, it might be necessary to financially support stakeholders participating in the SIA process.

As mentioned above, a broad range of stakeholders is a key factor for the success of SIA processes. However, there are two potential problems with regard to the selection of participants that need to be addressed. An excessively large number of stakeholders wanting to participate would pose time and resource constraints on the convenor, as it becomes difficult to actually consider all views and opinions and to deal with a large quantity of input. Written comments have to be read and integrated, and adequate feedback needs to be provided. Along the same lines, an excessive number of participants in open meetings or discussions might result in inertia and make it impossible to reach a consensus. A possible response to this kind of problem is to restrict the number of participants at certain events, and to encourage stakeholders to form constituencies and collectively submit statements or send representatives to discussion meetings. While stakeholders have already been associating and networking in order to negotiate common positions regarding SIAs in advance, and NGOs have submitted joint statements (WWF et al. 2002: 3), further resources might be required to strengthen this development without compromising overall representation.

Conversely, having too few interested stakeholders makes it more of a challenge to encourage participation and actively contact relevant stakeholder groups in order to ensure balanced and representative participation. Insufficient participation may occur for various reasons. One cause might simply be a lack of awareness and information. It has been suggested that too little is generally known about SIAs, both among policy-makers and stakeholders (WWF et al. 2002: 3). In order to raise awareness, the appropriate communication channels for disseminating useful information to the public need to be investigated. It might be necessary to identify and directly contact potentially affected groups. Reaching out to stakeholders by electronic means such as emails or newsletters has been proposed (PricewaterhouseCoopers 2003: 15), but in order to reach a larger group of people, other means should be taken into consideration, such as advertisements in local newspapers or the distribution of brochures or leaflets.

As mentioned above, the possibilities for participating in SIA consultations might also be hampered by a lack of resources. To ensure a more balanced presentation of stakeholders, civil society groups might need support to prepare and participate in the consultation processes (OECD 1999). To a limited degree, DG Trade already reimburses travel expenses of participants in dialogue with civil society in Brussels (European Commission 2002a). The rules and restrictions include the requirement that participants must not be based in Brussels, that only the main journey is being paid for, that no accommodation expenses are covered and so on. A similar system could be adopted, and maybe extended, to encourage and facilitate greater participation in the consultation process on SIAs.

The provision of financial support then raises the question of what is required from stakeholders to qualify for support, and how equal treatment of different actor groups can be ensured. Given the large number of potential requests, it might be reasonable to concentrate financial support on groups with the most limited resources and to define certain budget limits that determine eligibility for financial help. However, so far there are no clear rules and procedures in place for classifying NGOs according to their potential input and financial needs to participate effectively. Moreover, given the long-standing discussion on the lack of transparency and accountability of NGOs, there might be no easy answer to this question.

As international trade takes place between importing and exporting countries, the question arises as to which civil society groups from third countries should participate in the SIAs. For example, the European Commission's SIAs of trade negotiations usually include assessments of impacts on the countries of the trading partners. However, it is a much-debated issue to what extent and in what ways the trading partners or third countries and their respective civil society groups should be involved in the assessment process. Indeed, the lack of involvement of non-EU countries has been repeatedly pointed out and criticized by NGOs (WWF et al. 2002: 46). The potential hurdles to participation (lack of resources and information) that were mentioned above are likely to affect stakeholders from trading partners, and in particular from developing countries, even more seriously. While in some cases local groups in developing countries may not even be aware of SIAs taking place, in other instances, they will often lack financial and personnel resources to contribute actively and attend meetings.

For processes where participation by civil society representatives from developing countries is desired, some degree of decentralization will be essential. As seen in the SIA on the negotiations between ACP countries and the EU, meetings in the respective regions are imperative. Correspondingly, reports might have to be published in languages other than English to enable the participation of actors from the region. A Spanish version of the final report on the EU-Chile negotiations was requested by stakeholders to allow the Chilean fishing communities to participate in the SIA. The consortium conducting the study did not respond to this demand, claiming that the translation was not part of terms of the contract with the European Commission (Planistat 2002). In general, more of the communication would have to be conducted in local languages. As for the lack of resources of stakeholder groups in developing countries, the question again arises as to whether and how the European Commission should make financial support available for participation and capacity building.

There are several arguments in favour of more extensive participation in the SIA process by non-EU countries. Developing countries often perceive SIAs as biased towards environmental issues, and are concerned that they might be used as an excuse to maintain or create trade barriers. The involvement of developing countries in EU SIAs might help to build trust and ownership in the assessments outside the EU. Trading partners or third countries may have differing views and propose different indicators or assessment schemes, which could allow for an enriched design of the assessments and for more diverse feedback processes about the framework, which could lead to the evolution and elaboration of the SIA methodology and process.

On the other hand, this variety of views and goals might slow down the process and make it very difficult to reach a consensus on how to proceed. Since the number of participants could conceivably increase if the EU aimed for the integration of non-EU countries, it is necessary to ask whether it is feasible to do so, and whether the benefits gained would outweigh the costs.

Yet another issue is that there may be concerns within the European Commission that its own position in negotiations may be weakened by involving trading partners and third countries and spreading information about potential impacts. According to the confidentiality principle of the EU's negotiation strategy, its positions should not be revealed to its partners. This might be undermined by overly close cooperation with trading partners on SIAs (European Commission 2002c). One way to avoid these problems would be for every country taking part in the negotiations or likely to be affected by their outcomes to undertake its own impact assessment to inform its negotiating position (George, Nafti and Curran 2001). Since most mitigating measures will require national policy measures, national SIAs could have practical advantages for implementation.

NGOs have been requesting that the European Commission should provide support to developing countries to carry out their own SIAs (European Commission 2000). Splitting the SIAs up into national studies in the first place and then possibly sharing experiences and results afterwards might be an alternative to decentralizing a single comprehensive SIA integrating a range of countries.

Structuring Participation

At present, the consultation process with civil society on the European Commission's SIAs consists mainly of the publication of reports and other material on websites, the invitation for submitting written comments and inputs from stakeholders as well as open public meetings. Additionally, an international network of experts is maintained and is currently being extended (Kirkpatrick et al. 2002). In some cases, developing-country experts are called upon to provide specific input to country case studies, for example in the SIA of the EU-Chile negotiations (Planistat 2002). Generally however, the participation process does not seem to be subject to qualitative or quantitative change during the course of an assessment, although the stages of SIAs are different in character. Accordingly, different kinds of expertise may become relevant in the different stages, by dividing the consultation process into separate components that reflect the evolution of the assessment with time. Against this background, the organization of a larger number of smaller meetings during the course of an assessment would allow for more focussed discussion on the issues at stake during a certain phase. Central meetings could also be broken-up into working groups or round tables on individual issues. However, this approach would require the identification of the stakeholder groups eligible for participation in each phase of an assessment.

During the planning stage, in which the SIA is launched and contents are defined, the group of participants depends mainly on the convening institution, whose concerns are addressed by the SIA. However, the participation of stakeholders in the definition of the contents increases the probability that the assessment will address questions relevant to them (Eckley 2001: 8–9). In the current debate about how and by whom the contents of SIAs should be determined, the European Commission clearly states that it reserves the right to decide on the contents of the SIA study and possible scenarios (European Commission 2003). Its objective in conducting SIA studies is to inform negotiators of the possible range of impacts of a trade agreement within the framework of the negotiating mandate. However, if the concerns of civil society groups are to be integrated in the SIA process, it is essential for such groups to participate from the very beginning so that they will be able to influence the terms of reference for the SIA. In addition, the participation of experts might help with choosing the topics and methods to be used in the assessment.

Most of the decisions made in the scoping phase, such as the choice of indicators and significance criteria for the comparison, are not of a purely technical nature, but also have political implications (Cash and Clark 2001: 9–10). Thus, to ensure legitimacy and transparency of SIAs, NGOs and other interest groups need to be consulted during the scoping phase. When the final decision is made by the Commission and its contractors, adequate feedback should be provided, stating why indicators were eventually chosen or excluded. Similarly, the selection of individual countries for case studies may constitute politically sensitive judgements and should be conducted with the participation of stakeholders. It might also be useful to consult regional experts and research institutes, as well as trade associations or businesses involved with the respective countries on this issue.

In the actual detailed assessment, including the design and the handling of modelling, peer review by experts is crucial to enhancing the scientific quality of the study (Eckley 2001: 7). If possible, local research institutions and country experts should be involved in regional and sector studies. This principle was applied in the EU-Chile SIA study, which involved researchers at Chilean universities (European Commission 2003: 50). Apart from academic experts, NGOs and regional or local communities or groups should be consulted, as they might be able to provide valuable information about local conditions and potential impacts on the specific region.

The evaluation of results of the SIA and the decisions about which mitigation and enhancing measures should be taken are again essentially political questions. As a result, the outcomes of the evaluation will determine to a great extent whether the assessment as a whole is perceived as fair and legitimate. The criteria for adoption or exclusion of measures, such as their impact on sustainable development, their cost effectiveness and their feasibility (Kirkpatrick 2002), as well as their prioritization, should therefore be discussed with a broad range of interest groups and experts.

The major drawback associated with structuring the participation process in this way would probably be a significant increase in the workload for the Commission and its contractors. A substantially greater number of meetings would have to be organized, and increased coordination efforts would be required to integrate the results of the different working groups. Follow-up and feedback on every meeting would be necessary for the participants.

Another issue is that there might be too much of an overlap between the stakeholder groups participating in the different meetings, such that the division of efforts in the process would not be efficient and the resulting additional workload would not be justified. Moreover, whether there is sufficient interest and resources among stakeholders to guarantee that all meetings have a satisfactory attendance needs to be clarified in advance. Another question is whether participants or constituencies of stakeholders should actually be excluded from certain meetings, or if all meetings should be open to everyone in principle. If certain parties were to be excluded, it would be essential for this to be done in a transparent way.

Decentralization Approach – a New Way?

Currently, the implementation of SIAs is highly centralized. In the European Union, the main workload and responsibility lies with one consultant (or with a consortium of consultants) contracted by the European Commission.

An alternative to the current practice of impact assessments would be to decentralize the assessment process and change the institutional structures. This, for example, was proposed as part of the Global Environmental Assessment Project at Harvard University, which developed the idea of 'distributed assessment systems' (Cash 2000). The underlying idea is that national and international institutions have the resources and the capacity to undertake modelling studies, while research on a regional or local scale might be more appropriate for collecting local-specific data. Consequently, complementary advantages at each level should be integrated through an institutionalized system of multiple linkages. Scientific efforts on different levels and with different specializations and capacities would be coordinated, and links to decision-makers institutionalized across levels. This approach mirrors the complex multilevel nature of trade impacts on sustainable development, and the need to assess both large-scale dynamics and their local implications. Moreover, a network of semi-autonomous research nodes would allow the integration of differing assessment abilities and activities (Cash and Clark 2001).

A major practical obstacle to a decentralization of the European Commission's SIA efforts will certainly be time limits imposed by the negotiations themselves. To develop a well-functioning distribution system with reliable links and coordination between actors would take a long time. This is a serious shortcoming, given the need for SIAs for trade negotiations to start early enough and be completed in time to inform negotiators. Furthermore, a distributed assessment system would certainly require substantial deployment of financial resources and management efforts. Nevertheless, the European Commission might consider adopting elements of this approach in the near future and decentralizing its assessment system to some degree. For example, individual sectoral or regional studies could be delegated to research institutions based in the respective region, or projects could be assigned to consortia comprising a greater number of members.

The integration of multiple research centres into common projects may be hampered in the beginning by the fact that data come in differing formats and may be hard to compare. However, if cooperation is established and institutionalized, it might lead to a harmonization of data collection and methods in the long run. One step in this direction might be to include the trading partners, or even third countries, in the SIA processes. Thus, studies could be carried out only in cooperation with research institutions in the trading partners' countries. It might also be helpful to make the SIA tool available to interested parties who want to conduct preliminary assessments with a different focus. This would support the decentralization process, and at the same time give stakeholders more scope to influence the contents of SIAs. Moreover, such a procedure could leave more room for 'thinking outside the box' within SIA studies and for considering a broader range of scenarios, thus keeping more options open for innovative solutions.

With respect to public participation, it seems that decentralization of the SIA process could contribute to improving public participation in general. The division of the research tasks between multiple research institutes or agencies on different levels would increase the number of possible entry points for civil society contributions. Participation by local groups could be significantly fostered if local institutes were carrying out research on problems directly affecting the region. Meetings or discussions held at the local level would be more easily accessible for the public, and dealing with region-specific problems would lead to a heightened awareness of those affected. However, the costs of participation and the scarcity of resources available in civil society should not be overlooked. Thus, it should be kept in mind that with regards to participation efforts, a balance has to be found between the amount of time and resources invested in participation in SIAs and the actual impact such assessment have on the trade negotiations.

Conclusion

Given the financial and time resources needed for participation, and the existing doubts about the effectiveness of SIAs in civil society, it is fundamental to further clarify the role, opportunities and limits of SIAs in the trade negotiation process. As the impact assessments only indirectly feed into the negotiation process, civil society will only be willing to spend time and to provide knowledge to the process if the results and effects of their participation become more visible. A first step in this direction would be to provide detailed written feedback about how the input of civil societies was integrated into the final SIA, and how the SIA contributed to the negotiation process and its outcome.

Public participation in SIAs includes a number of traditional questions regarding effective participation that need to be addressed. It is crucial that experts, communities and NGOs affected by the trade agreements be adequately integrated into the impact assessment. Therefore, the issues of how criteria could be defined for the selection of participants in order to ensure a balanced representation of civil society and what means could be used to encourage participation by a wider range of stakeholders, should be analysed more closely. In this respect, capacity building and financial support is essential. In addition, participation should be structured according to the different stages of the SIA process. Given the distinct phases within SIAs, to better match participation in each phase with the respective needs and objectives, a scheme should be elaborated, eventually leading to more effective and efficient processes.

A possible way to enhance the quality of SIAs is to include trading partners, third countries and their respective civil societies. On one hand, involvement broadens the knowledge base of decision-makers and facilitates implementation. On the other hand, encouraging public participation in SIAs could contribute to raising awareness among civil society of trade impacts on other policy areas and thus support the creation of networks among different actor groups active in these areas.

Decentralization of the SIA process itself represents an opportunity to better integrate a larger number of voices and views into the impact assessment. A decentralized system would provide for more input from research as well as civil society. In addition, a system consisting of a larger number of actors would allow for more input of knowledge from all levels affected by the negotiations, and could prove more flexible in adapting participatory approaches to requirements emerging during the negotiation process.

In conclusion, it should be remembered that SIAs constitute a new and still-evolving tool. SIAs have the potential to play an important role in trade policy making and to render trade agreements and sustainable development mutually supportive. Public participation could increase the knowledge base, as well as increase the legitimacy of trade policy and thus facilitate its implementation. Moreover, based on a more decentralized system, SIAs would help in adapting trade agreements to local requirements. While the current practice is certainly a step forward, there is still room for improvement.

References

Cash, David and William Clark. 2001. 'From Science to Policy: Assessing the Assessment Process'. Faculty Research Working Papers Series. Cambridge, MA: John F. Kennedy School of Government, Harvard University.

Cash, David W. 2000. 'Distributed Assessment Systems: An Emerging Paradigm of Research, Assessment and Decision-making for Environmental Change'. Belfer Center for Science and International Affairs (BCSIA) Discussion Paper 2000–05. Cambridge, MA: Environment and Natural Resources Programme, Kennedy School of Government, Harvard University.

Dalal-Clayton, Barry and Stephen Bass. 2002. 'Participation in Strategies for Sustainable Development'. In IEED, UNDP and OECD, eds., *Sustainable Development Strategies*. London: Earthscan: 177–225.

Eckley, Noelle. 2001.' Designing Effective Assessments: The Role of Participation, Science and Governance, and Focus'. Report of a workshop co-organized by the European Environment Agency and the Global Environmental Assessment Project, 1–3 March, Copenhagen, Denmark. Research and Assessment Systems for Sustainability Program Discussion Paper 2001–16. Cambridge, MA: Environment and Natural Resources Programme, Belfer Center for Science and International Affairs, Kennedy School of Government, Harvard University.

Elwell, Christine. 2002. 'Sustainable Impact Assessment of the Earth Summit 10: A Canadian Perspective'. CIELAP. <www.cielap.org/sia.pdf> (16 February 2003).

European Commission. 2000. 'Key Issues Relating to the Development of the Methodology and Future Assessment: Summary Of Comments'. <europa.eu.int/comm/trade/miti/envir/siakey.htm> (12 February 2003).

———. 2002a. 'Communication from the Commission on Impact Assessment'. COM(2002) 267final. <europa.eu.int/eur-lex/en/> (7 February 2003).

———. 2002b. 'Communication from the Commission: Towards a Reinforced Culture of Consultation and Dialogue – General Principles and Minimum Standards for Consultation of Interested Parties by the Commission'. COM(2002) 704 final. <europa.eu.int/eur-lex/en> (12 February 2003).

———. 2002c. 'Presentation of the Sustainability Impact Assessment (S.I.A.) of the European Commission'. Available at <europa.eu.int/comm/trade/sia/index_en.htm> (28 February 2003).

———. 2002d. Webpage on DG Trade's dialogue with civil society. <trade-info.cec. eu.int/civil_soc/intro1.php> (6 March 2003).

———. 2003. 'Sustainability Impact Assessment of Trade Agreements – Making Trade Sustainable?' Background Paper: DG Trade Seminar, 6–7 February 2003. Brussels: DG Trade of the European Commission.

George, Clive, Rachid Nafti and Johanna Curran. 2001. 'Capacity Building for Trade Impact Assessment: Lessons from the Development of Environmental Impact Assessment'. *Impact Assessment and Project Appraisal* 19.4.

Joint NGO Statement. 2000. 'The EU Sustainability Impact Assessment of WTO Trade Liberalisation'. <www.fern.org/pubs/ngostats/wtosia.htm> (16 February 2003).

Kirkpatrick, Colin, Clive George, Jamie Franklin and others. 2002. 'Sustainability Impact Assessment of Proposed WTO Negotiations: Preliminary Overview of Potential Impacts of the Doha Agenda'. Project Inception Report to the European Commission. Manchester: IDPM.

NGOs. 2002. Joint NGO statement on Sustainability Impact Assessments of EU Trade Policy. <www.balancedtrade.panda.org/projectfiles/eur.html> (12 February 2003).

OECD. 1999. 'Timing and Public Participation Issues in Undertaking Environmental Assessments of Trade Liberalisation Agreements'. Issues paper for panel VII by the secretariat presented at the OECD Workshop on Methodologies for environmental assessment of trade liberalisation agreements, 26–27 October 1999.

———. 2001. *Citizens as Partners: Information, Consultation and Public Participation in Policy-making*. Paris: OECD.

Planistat. 2002. 'Sustainability Impact Assessment (SIA) of the Trade Aspects of Negotiations for an Association Agreement between the European Commission and Chile (Specific agreement No 1)'. Final Report. <trade-info.cec.eu.int/doclib/ html/112388.htm> (16 February 2003).

PricewaterhouseCoopers. 2003. 'Sustainability Impact Assessment (SIA) of Trade Negotiations of the EU-ACP Economic Partnership Agreements'. Revised Inception Report. Paris: PricewaterhouseCoopers.

Richardson, Sarah. 2000. 'A "Critique" of the EC's WTO Sustainability Impact Assessment Study and Recommendations for Phase III'. Oxfam. <www.oxfam.org.uk/what_we_do/ issues/trade/wto_sustainability.htm> (16 February 2003).

UNEP. 2001. *Reference Manual for the Integrated Assessment of Trade-Related Policies*. Geneva: UNEP.

WWF. 2002. 'An Effective Multistakeholder Process for Sustainability Assessment: Critical Elements'. WWF Position Statement. <www.balancedtrade.panda.org/pdf/en-effectiveSA.pdf> (16 February 2003).

WWF, Heinrich Böll Foundation and Caroline Lucas (MEP). 2002. Seminar Proceedings. 'Changing the Balance of Trade – A Seminar on Sustainability Assessments of EU Trade Policy', 9–10 July, Brussels. <www.balancedtrade.panda.org/pdf/en-effectiveSA. pdf> (16 February 2003).

Chapter 14

Transparency, Information Disclosure and Participation in Export Credit Agency Cover Decisions

Benjamin Görlach, Markus Knigge and Marcus Schaper[1]

Introduction

Export Credit Agencies (ECAs) play a substantial role in the international financing of infrastructure development in developing countries. As the activities of ECAs are backed-up by public resources, national governments have the power to set guidelines for ECA lending policies. Although the main function of ECAs is to promote exports by domestic firms, most governments also include social and environmental aspects in their ECA guidelines. As a result, the impact of investment projects on sustainable development is shaped by ECA policies. It is therefore important to understand their lending strategies: this article takes a closer look at the role of transparency, information disclosure and participation in the cover decisions of ECAs.

In the past, civil society actors have heavily criticized ECAs for their lack of transparency in decision-making, accusing them of excessive secrecy. Non-governmental organizations (NGOs) have repeatedly demanded that information about supported projects and the decision process be made publicly accessible. ECAs for their part, have argued that they and their clients operate in a highly competitive environment, and that openness, therefore, has to be restricted to a degree where confidentiality is guaranteed and competitiveness is not jeopardized.

NGOs gained considerable influence in ECA politics when they started to compile documentation of problematic projects and make it available internationally. This has particularly been the case for dams and large

---

[1]   This chapter is based on the results of a project commissioned by the German development agency (GTZ) as well as doctoral dissertation research conducted by Marcus Schaper at the University of Maryland. The aim of the GTZ project, carried out by Ecologic in 2003, was to give a survey of environmental and social standards in the lending practices of export credit agencies. The final report from the project is available at <www.ecologic.de/download/projekte/1800-1849/1809/1809wcd_ecas_en.pdf>.

infrastructure projects, such as the Chinese Three Gorges Dam, the Ilisu Dam in Turkey, the Maheshwar and Tehri Dams in India and the San Roque Hydro and Irrigation Project in the Philippines. By making projects that were previously concealed from public scrutiny more transparent, they raised the stakes for ECAs, who continued to insist on keeping project information secret.

In this way, increased transparency has also emerged as a way of circumventing discussions on appropriate and harmonized standards on which ECA cover decisions should be based. This assumes that stricter and internationally harmonized standards are less important as long as there is a high level of transparency and stakeholder involvement. If this assumption is accepted, transparency itself will provide for more rigorous project evaluation; even if relatively weak environmental standards are applied, civil society opposition to problematic projects will nonetheless be vocal. Following the same rationale, it can also be argued that increased transparency promotes better projects: project developers who know that Environmental Impact Assessments for their projects will be made public have an incentive to develop projects and assessments in such a way that NGO opposition is less likely.

This reliance on civil society, however, raises serious questions about the appropriate role and capacity of NGOs in monitoring ECA activity. This includes the issue of whether civil society has sufficient capacity to assume this monitoring function on a regular basis, and whether this may impact the autonomy of NGOs. It also raises the question whether the ubiquitousness of such vocal, well-organized and well-informed civil society actors can safely be assumed in all regions, at all times, and for all kinds of projects. Lastly, it is doubtful whether the burden of proof should indeed be with civil society, or whether it should be the responsibility of project developers and ECAs to monitor the impacts their projects will have.

Most ECAs tend to take a hands-off approach to the issue. In their view, monitoring of the implementation and enforcement of environmental standards is not their responsibility, as they only have limited influence over project sponsors and developers.[2] It is within the scope of this article to explain the fundamental role of transparency and public participation in ECA activities, and to discuss whether and how increased transparency by itself can have an impact on their cover decisions. The article also sets out the international negotiation process leading up to common, binding standards for ECAs at the OECD level, pointing out the difficulties in reaching a common position. With a view to the practical role and relevance of transparency, information disclosure and participation, it provides insights at the national level, draws comparison of different national approaches, and discusses their respective merits.

---

[2]   For a discussion of the role of ECAs, multilateral development banks, and private banks in greening infrastructure development, see Schaper (2005).

Export Credit Agencies

Nearly all OECD governments support their domestic economic interests through export credit agencies. In short, these agencies promote national exports by financing and insuring transactions in cases where support from the private market is not available at reasonable cost because of unacceptably high risks. Thus, government-supported export credit finance and insurance is commonly found in transactions or projects in developing regions and emerging-market economies, where political or other risks are considered to be high and unlikely to be insured by private means.

ECAs are an increasingly important source of financing for the private sector. From 1988 to 1996, export credits increased fourfold from US$ 26 billion to $105 billion per year (Rich 1998). In recent years, ECAs accounted for between US$50 billion and US$70 billion annually, exclusively for the support of large industrial and infrastructure projects in developing countries (Norlen et al. 2002).

ECAs are national institutions and differ widely not only in their institutional set-up, but also in their missions, mandates, and instruments at hand. First, the organizational forms of ECAs are diverse, and include forms such as sections of ministries, government departments, independent government agencies, semi-public joint stock companies, or private institutions operating partly under an agreement with the government (OECD 2001a). Furthermore, while the primary objective of most ECAs is to increase national exports, some also include other objectives, such as development goals. Some ECAs also handle export finance alongside export credit insurance and guarantees. All these differences have an impact on the capacity of the ECAs to influence environmental and social aspects of the projects they support. For example, providers of export finance and aid finance have more leverage over supported projects, because their stake in the projects is greater, and because they are involved earlier on in the project development process, than their counterparts which offer insurance (pure cover) only. As a result, there is a wide variety of standards and procedures in place, making it difficult to introduce common international standards and procedures into ECA activities.

ECAs and Civil Society

Given the massive environmental and social impacts of some ECA-supported projects (which include large dams, power plants, pipelines, mines, pulp and paper plants and other infrastructure projects), ECAs have been the targets of harsh criticism from civil society since the 1970s. In June 2000, the Jakarta Declaration was adopted by more than 350 NGOs from 45 countries, calling for common and binding social, environmental and human rights standards for ECAs that would correspond to internationally recognized standards, such as those of World Bank or the OECD Development Assistance Committee.[3]

Next to social and environmental standards themselves, transparency, information, and public participation procedures were also highlighted by several campaigns. It is widely acknowledged that public participation is crucially important to rendering lending policies and sustainable development mutually supportive. However, transparency and disclosure of information are both preconditions for the effective participation of affected stakeholders and civil society groups. Thus, not only have the rules and procedures for public participation been an integral part of demands from NGOs, but so have the standards both for information disclosure and transparency.

NGOs call for the adoption of binding environmental and social standards to which ECAs can be held accountable, and argue for transparency in ECA operations and their cover decisions. Such transparency provisions would allow the public to monitor ECA compliance with these standards, as well as observe their overall environmental, developmental and social performance.

NGOs have played a crucial role in putting environmental standards for ECAs on the political agenda. Environmental requirements for the American Export-Import Bank (Ex-Im) can be attributed in part to effective NGO work on the issue. A coalition of US NGOs succeeded in lobbying for the greening of the Ex-Im Bank, which led to the inclusion of a section on environmental requirements within the Export Enhancement Act of 1992. The law

> directs the Bank, for any transaction involving a project for which support of $10,000,000 or more is requested and certain environmental concerns exist, to establish procedures to take into account the potential benefits and adverse environmental effects of the goods and services which it may support under its lending and guarantee programs. Authorizes the Board to withhold financing for environmental reasons or to approve financing after considering the potential environmental effects of a project. Encourages the Bank to use its programs to support the export of goods and services that have beneficial effects on the environment or mitigate potential adverse environmental effects. (United States Congress 1992)

This provision for environmental requirements set a precedent for other export credit agencies. Up to this point, no ECA had explicit and codified environmental rules for its operations. Responding to a Green Party parliamentary inquiry, the German government asserted as early as 1985 that 'the consideration of ecological and developmental aspects occurs as part of the evaluation of an individual project's supportability based on available information and development policy objectives' (Deutscher Bundestag 1985), but no formal rules and basis existed

---

3   See <www.eca-watch.org/goals/jakartadec.html>. Note that NGOs advocate the application of World Bank Group standards despite their own criticism of the Bank's operations. This may serve as an indicator for the low level of ECA environmental performance.

for these considerations. Ex-Im responded to its Congressional mandate by developing environmental policies which were implemented in 1995 and have been refined and revised repeatedly ever since.

In the late 1990s, US NGOs took up the issue again and joined forces with the government in promoting international harmonization of environmental standards for export credit agencies. In Europe, the Berne Declaration first succeeded in the 1970s with its developmental critique of the Swiss ECA by broadening the scope of groups represented in ECA decision-making. The German ECA HERMES was also criticized, predominantly from a developmental perspective, throughout the 1980s. From 1983 onwards, the German Green Party gave the NGO campaign increased backing from within the Bundestag, but did not bring about major changes in HERMES activities until recently.

The international NGO campaign gained strength when groups in the ECA-Watch network compiled detailed documentation on controversial projects. Network meetings in 1998 and 2000 in Mesum, Germany, and in Jakarta, Indonesia, helped to bring campaign activists together and facilitate information exchange. The resulting compilation of problematic projects highlighted the need for environmental standards and transparency in ECA operations. By making the activities of ECAs and their impacts transparent, the NGOs placed transparency squarely on the ECA reform agenda.

Transparency and Information Disclosure

Transparency and information disclosure are both essential preconditions for increased openness in policymaking. Transparency entails greater access to information, as well as greater awareness of issues or policies. Operationally, this requires ensuring that the right to information (through a broad dissemination of activities to the general public and stakeholders, or through disclosure rules) is both practised and respected. In the context of ECAs, transparency, above all, implies not only a clear, open, and traceable decision-making process when approving applications for cover, but may also include the use of reporting and monitoring conditions to ensure compliance in the implementation of a supported project. In order to achieve such transparency, both decisions taken in the process and considerations of trade-offs with different countervailing objectives, should be communicated and documented to the public in a clear and understandable way. This includes information on the information sources used, as well as assessment of alternative options.

Not only NGOs, but also states which have a regulatory tradition of requiring environmental assessments and impact statements have been supportive of rules providing for the increased transparency in the approval process for export credits (Schaper 2006). It is often argued that transparency provision is required for both ensuring sincere implementation of binding environmental standards and for improving environmental project quality by increasing the risk to reputations stemming from environmentally problematic projects.

Transparency and information disclosure affect three different areas of ECAs' operations:

1 information about ECAs' environmental and social standards and guidelines;
2 information about the environmental and social impacts of particular projects (*ex ante* and *ex post*);
3 information about the role of environmental and social considerations in the decision-making process for a particular project.

In considering ECAs in several OECD countries,[4] it can be concluded that, by and large, the first aspect is generally covered very well. Information on environmental and social guidelines is available and easily accessible in most OECD countries via ECA websites, with the Norwegian Garanti-Instuttet for Eksportkreditt (GIEK) as the only exception.

With regard to the second aspect, relating to information on environmental and social impacts of supported projects, there is a remarkable overall trend towards better information disclosure – especially after the OECD Common Approaches, which were negotiated in the OECD's Export Credit Group from 1998 to 2003 and came into effect on 1 January 2004 (see below). Prior to this, only a small number of ECAs published Environmental Impact Assessments (EIAs) for projects that were expected to have a potentially significant impact on the environment (Category A projects in Impact Assessment terminology) prior to making a cover decision. Some ECAs either made the EIAs available on their website, or sent them out on request. This approach was practised, for example, by the US Ex-Im Bank, the Australian EFIC, and the Japanese Bank for International Cooperation (JBIC). Similarly, Export Development Canada (EDC) and the British Export Credits Guarantee Department (ECDG) did not publish EIAs for legal reasons, but encouraged their exporters to make EIAs available on request. Other ECAs published only selected pieces of information, e.g. the German EULER HERMES or the Swiss Export Risk Guarantee (ERG), which made a list of supported projects available online, identifying exporter, sponsor, duration and recipient country. The French COFACE presented a mix of both by publishing both general project information as well as a brief summary of the EIA. Most ECAs, including the Norwegian GIEK, the German EULER HERMES, and the Australian EFIC, addressed environmental and social impacts of supported projects in their annual reports. Most of this information, however, was only made available after an ECA had granted support for a particular project.

---

4   The following sections are based on a study conducted in 2003 that surveyed ECAs guidelines and lending practices in Australia, Canada, France, Japan, Norway, Switzerland, the UK and the USA.

The Common Approaches require ECAs to make environmental project information available to the public at least 30 days prior to making a cover decision. Certain ECAs moved forward in this respect before the establishment of this rule in the Common Approaches by providing information on applications before the final approval of an application. In this way, they are responding to demands by NGOs who see their participation rights curtailed if they are informed only about decisions that have already been taken. The Australian EFIC, the Japanese JBIC, the British ECGD, and the US Ex-Im Bank all took a lead role in this respect by making environmental information on pending projects available before final approval was granted. The Australian EFIC facilitates comments during a 45-day public consultation period, during which the EIA conducted by the project sponsor is available and open to comments through the EFIC website. The British ECGD maintains a website for high-potential impact cases on which EIAs can be found before decisions are to be made in regard to the project. In Japan, an *ex ante* evaluation is facilitated through the publication of Evaluation Reports after the loan contract has been signed for Official Development Assistance (ODA) loans conducted via JBIC (JBIC 2002). For these loans, there is also extensive and well-documented ex post evaluation. Similarly, the US Ex-Im Bank publishes a list of major projects, provides Environmental Assessments on request, and invites written comments on a list of other projects with potentially adverse effects.

It should be noted that the leeway for information disclosure is generally limited by legal provisions in the ECA's home country. Whereas some countries have a legal requirement for the disclosure of certain pieces of information,[5] other ECAs insist that publishing more information than is already currently the case would constitute a violation of national law, and that information disclosure generally has to take place voluntarily.[6] In other cases, more liberal information disclosure policies have been possible only in response to new legislation.[7]

The current Common Approaches provide for 30-day *ex ante* transparency, and thus represent a major NGO success. Responding to the new rules, a number of ECAs have changed their disclosure practices. The German HERMES, for example, now provides project information for pending cover decisions via the Internet. The client's consent, however, is required for publication. The Common Approaches provide for some flexibility, enabling ECAs not to make environmental project information available on any Category A projects that potentially have major impacts on environmental and social issues. Since these guidelines were agreed on only in December 2003, it remains to be seen what kind

---

[5] In the USA, information disclosure policies are based on the Freedom of Information Act 1966.

[6] See <www.exportkreditgarantien.de/publikat/einzelpr.html>.

[7] In Japan, JBIC's extensive disclosure policy has been influenced by the Public Information Act for the Japanese Governmental Agencies (unofficial translation), approved in November 2001.

of effect these provisions will have on the policies of those ECAs that previously did not make environmental project information publicly available before making a cover decision. In addition to the Common Approaches, the Aarhus Convention and the corresponding EU Directive require revision of transparency provisions in the policies of a number of ECAs.

Public Participation

The participation of civil society and other stakeholders in the reform of ECA practices and their implementation is closely connected to the concept of transparency, and has been subject to a similar dispute. Transparency is indeed a precondition for successful public participation, but transparency alone does not ensure a constructive dialogue which would allow the views of all major stakeholders to be accommodated. Public participation can range from relatively passive information exchange over substantive consultation through working groups or meetings, to active involvement in analysis and agenda-setting. By contrast, a lack of participation leads to allegations of illegitimacy.

In recent years, there has been a trend towards more proactive approaches in public participation in a number of ECAs. In some cases, stakeholder involvement is actively encouraged by ECAs, rather than fended-off by recourse to the confidentiality of business approaches. This trend is most pronounced in Japan and the USA, but there are also interesting examples in the UK, France and Australia.

One reason for the increased openness to public participation is that the damage to reputation resulting from badly managed and communicated projects is now recognized as a serious threat by ECAs and their clients alike.[8] Reputational risk is also increasingly seen as an economic risk with the potential to seriously affect the profitability of exporters. Somewhat less prominent is the risk that projects may fail altogether because of public resistance if environmental and social considerations are not given sufficient weight. This risk is generally less pronounced, as it poses a significant threat only for large-scale projects in very sensitive and controversial sectors that attract sufficient attention.[9]

---

[8]   Note also that many ECAs are connected to firms that are active on the private insurance market, where they face competition themselves. For example, in the case of the French COFACE and the German EULER HERMES, the officially supported export credit business is covered by subsidiaries of larger international insurance firms.

[9]   Cf. the debate concerning the Ilisu dam in Turkey: partly as a result of public resistance, the British construction company Balfour Beatty and the Swiss bank UBS withdrew their application for cover. Although extensive impact assessments were carried out for the Ilisu dam, these were seen as insufficient by NGOs and external reviewers alike <www.ecgd.gov.uk/finalermreport.pdf> or <www.evb.ch/cm_data/EIAR%20Ilisu%20Dam.pdf>.

Public participation is possible in different forms and at different stages of a project:

1   before or after approval, or during the implementation phase of a project;
2   during the designation of environmental guidelines;
3   during the evaluation and monitoring of the project.

Likewise, there are different stakeholders to be addressed:

1   local groups that will be affected by the supported projects;
2   NGOs in the ECA's home country;
3   firms that have to implement environmental standards (sponsors and exporters).

Participation by the affected local communities has to be regarded as the weakest spot of the three in the implementation of environmental and social guidelines in some ECAs. Although this point featured centrally, for example, in the final report of the World Commission on Dams, some room for improvement remains.

Most ECAs encourage or require the participation of the local affected population as part of an EIA for Category A projects. Consultation with local communities is strongly recommended by the Australian EFIC and the US Ex-Im Bank, and is obligatory as part of an EIA for the Canadian ECD or the Japanese JBIC. However, ECD also concedes that participation may be difficult to achieve because of differing cultural or legal backgrounds in recipient countries. JBIC further specifies the requirement for local participation, including the condition that information must be provided to local residents in a language they can understand, and that the outcomes of consultations must be documented. The German EULER HERMES encourages local participation in order to avoid opposition and complications at a later stage. In any case, participation of local affected groups is expected as part of the EIA for any large-scale project.

With regard to the participation of civil society actors in an ECA's home country, there have been interesting developments in some countries. One example is the cooperation between the Japanese JBIC and the NGO *Friends of the Earth Japan*, which has also been reflected in JBIC's revised environmental guidelines.[10] Likewise, a constructive dialogue has been conducted between the US Ex-Im Bank and the Washington-based NGO *Environmental Defense*.[11] The Australian EFIC publishes comments from NGOs concerning both EFIC's environmental policies and specific projects on its website, along with responses to the points raised. In a similar fashion, the British ECGD has included NGO comments on the ECGD Business Principles in its mission and status review (ECGD 2000).

---

[10]   Cooperation has taken place e.g. in the framework of the Study Group on Environmental Guidelines, see <www.sg-egl-jbic.org>.

[11]   See <www.environmentaldefense.org/washingtonwatch.cfm>.

However, NGO involvement does not necessarily result in 'greener' policies. JBIC's consultation process with Japanese groups has resulted in a set of standards that are considered weak in comparison to those of the OECD, and that proved to be a critical obstacle to agreement on OECD-wide standards.

In relation to the dialogue with other stakeholders, a number of ECAs have gathered comments on the guidelines from the main sponsors, or organized workshops to communicate and discuss the guidelines and their practical implications. The French agency, COFACE, staged such discussions during the development of its sectoral environmental guidelines. Similar consultations were held in Australia, Canada, Japan and Switzerland. In addition, the Japanese JBIC and the Australian EFIC have documented points of criticism brought forward by NGOs on their websites; in the case of EFIC along with the ECA responses.[12] Furthermore, a number of ECAs have hosted United Nations Environment Programme (UNEP) workshops on the environmental and social reform processes, which provided informal discussion fora for ECA representatives, practitioners and principal sponsors, as well as for NGO representatives.[13]

Somewhat less can be said about the role NGOs play in the selection and execution of projects. Some ECA officials have raised concerns that NGOs were not primarily interested in changing and improving projects, but rather wanted to stop them altogether. Other ECAs maintain that collection of comments from NGOs on projects for which cover is pending, and any respective changes to the project design are the responsibility of the project sponsor.

Trends and Developments at the International Level

In addition to domestic regulation, ECAs are subject to international regulation, such as the OECD Arrangement on Officially Supported Export Credits or the WTO Agreement on Subsidies and Countervailing Measures (Canas and Scharf 1996). Until the mid-1990s, almost all international negotiations with ECAs attempted to harmonize financial issues – such as lending periods and interest rates – at the international level. At the time, very few ECAs had formalized standards or guidelines that took account of environmental and social concerns in their operations.

Negotiations on common environmental and social guidelines for export credits began in the mid-1990s with the OECD Working Party on Export Credits and Credit Guarantees, and gained momentum following the 1997 Denver G8 Summit, which concluded that 'Governments should help promote sustainable practices by taking environmental factors into account when providing financing support for investment in infrastructure and equipment' (G8 1997), and urged progress on the issue in the framework of OECD negotiations. In late 1999, the

---

12   See <www.efic.gov.au/environment/eficresponse.asp>, <www.sg-egl-jbic.org>.
13   Personal communication with Ms Martina Otto, UNEP DTIE, 3 June 2003.

OECD Working Party on Export Credits and Credit Guarantees agreed to a voluntary environmental information exchange on larger projects. The six-point agreement includes exchanging environmental assessments on projects, sharing other information among ECAs and coordinating responses to exporters, lenders and other principle parties (Udall 2000). One objective of this agreement was to avoid negative downward competition among ECAs, so that projects which had been declined support on environmental grounds by one ECA would not receive support from another. Building on this, the next challenge was to agree on a set of Common Approaches in order to promote coherence among different ECA practices on the incorporation of environmental considerations, while taking account of institutional and other differences among ECAs.

In 2001, these negotiations resulted in the 'Draft Recommendation on Common Approaches on Environment and Officially Supported Export Credits (Revision 6)' (OECD 2001b) – commonly referred to as 'Common Approaches', or 'Rev. 6'. These recommendations were supported by all members of the Export Credit Group, with the exception of the United States and Turkey. All other members voluntarily implemented Rev. 6 from 2002 on. The United States denied Rev. 6 support because it fell short of US goals for binding standards and transparency. As a recipient country, Turkey opposed the agreement because it felt its interests were threatened by rules regarding ethnic minorities, cultural heritage and protected lands.

Revision 6 of the Common Approaches called for assessment and revision in 2003. In autumn 2003, the Export Credit Group set out to negotiate a text that would be acceptable to all its members. The current Common Approaches were negotiated from September to November 2003, and were passed by the OECD Council the following December. Since 1 January 2004, the current Common Approaches have provided the basis for national standard setting. Revisions to the OECD rules are being negotiated during the summer of 2006 to meet the group's mandate of completing review by the end of 2006.

At their core, negotiations about these environmental standards address two related issues: common and binding standards for project evaluation, and *ex ante* transparency of environmental assessments. The publication of information on projects and their environmental impacts prior to granting cover is of central concern here, because this provision enables civil society actors to monitor export credit agencies decisions and actions.

Regarding whether entire projects or individual components needed to be evaluated, which standards would be applied, and how this could best be done, Rev. 6 required international standards such as the World Bank Group's Safeguard Policies and Pollution Abatement Handbook to be used as benchmarks, but did not provide binding standards. The current Common Approaches have established international standards as minimum standards, and allow for other standards to be applied, provided they exceed the international ones.

Prior to the 2003 Common Approaches, some states allowed interested parties access to environmental assessments, and few consulted NGOs prior to granting cover (e.g. the US Ex-Im Bank), while other ECAs argued that this would not be possible, because it would infringe upon clients' business confidentiality. As mentioned before, the 2003 Common Approaches require that public access to environmental project information be granted 30 days prior to making a coverage decision. At the same time, however, they provide for deviation from this rule on a case-by-case basis. The deviation clause is a result of opposition to the *ex ante* transparency provision by some governments, which felt that such a provision conflicted with domestic regulations and national interests. It appears that states have made wide use of the deviation clause when implementing the Common Approaches nationally. The flexibility with regard to *ex ante* transparency is retained in paragraph 16 of the Common Approaches: 'In the case where environmental impact information cannot, for exceptional reasons, be made public Members shall explain the circumstances and report these in accordance with paragraph 19'. Paragraph 19, in turn, specifies the procedure for annual *ex post* reporting by ECAs to the OECD export credit group. The second sentence in paragraph 16 thus provides a major loophole for ECAs not to publicize environmental impact information for selected projects.

In summer 2004, ECAs reported on their implementation of the Common Approaches to the OECD Export Credit Group secretariat. Results of this survey are available as an OECD document comparing national implementation (OECD 2004). In this compilation of national responses, a number of countries cited national confidentiality rules limiting their ability to make environmental impact information available. Of the countries that had already implemented the current Common Approaches, Norway made no information available before a policy had been issued; and Belgium, the Czech Republic, Germany, Greece, Hungary and Luxembourg stated that confidentiality rules limited their ability to make environmental impact information available without their clients' consent. The Czech Republic, France and the UK required clients to make environmental impact information available to the public. Gerling NCM in the Netherlands and the US Export-Import Bank had the most far-reaching disclosure policy as they required the client's consent to publication as a basis for issuing a policy.

In spring 2005, the Export Credit Group conducted a follow-up survey and requested updated information from its Member States in autumn of the same year (OECD 2005) to gauge progress on the Common Approaches' implementation. Although there is still considerable variation among ECAs' transparency policies, more ECAs now require exporters' consent to disclosure of environmental impact information for category A projects. Australia's EFIC, Finland's Finnvera, Italy's SACE and Hungary have now joined the club of ECAs requiring their clients' consent to disclosure as a prerequisite for cover of such projects. However, Austria, Belgium, Greece, and Luxembourg still make no environmental information available, despite the Common Approaches' requirement to do so. Most of the remaining ECAs cite domestic legal rules limiting disclosure to those cases in which clients have consented to disclosure. Germany and Switzerland state that they are 'legally precluded from requiring the client to provide the disclosure as a condition of receiving ECA support' (OECD 2005, 55 and 60). More than a year after agreement on the Common Approaches, implementation of their disclosure requirements is still uneven and generally weak. NGOs also consider the partial and uneven implementation of transparency requirements a major shortcoming of the 2003 Common Approaches (OECD 2006).

The likely result of rules limiting *ex ante* transparency based on clients' consent to publication, without making such consent a prerequisite for cover, is a negative selection of environmental impact information available. Information for projects that are environmentally problematic is less likely to be publicized with the clients' consent than is information on non-problematic projects. Although the Swiss ERG, for example, claims in its response to the 2004 survey that 'very few exporters refuse to give approval' (OECD 2004), there is a distinct possibility that it is precisely these few problematic projects that are of greatest interest to civil society. The German HERMES followed a similar line of reasoning as the Swiss ERG until an inquiry by the German Bundestag revealed in 2003 that in 62 per cent of the applications for cover clients did not consent to the publication of environmental information (Deutscher Bundestag 2003). As long as ECA rules make it possible to withhold information on select projects, civil society's capacity to monitor ECA operations will be severely limited. The proliferating Dutch/US example of establishing consent as a prerequisite for coverage seems to be the most promising approach for reconciling national legal limitations with the public's right to know. Yet the German Euler-Hermes and the Swiss ERG are clear in their statements that national regulations do not allow them to establish such a prerequisite.

As the discussion above indicates, widespread use of the deviation clause appears to exist, rendering the Common Approaches less effective with regard to transparency. Overall, however, there is a trend towards increased transparency and more environmental information disclosure. Implementation of the Aarhus Convention on Environmental Information and the corresponding EU directive can be expected to provide for a more conducive regulatory environment for granting public access to environmental information as a number of ECAs cite national implementation of the directive (2003/4/EC) as a legal basis for reviewing their rules (OECD 2005).

The EU factor may also have a direct impact on national implementation of the Common Approaches. The confederate structure of the European Union becomes apparent in ECA politics. Depending on which aspect of ECA regulation is concerned, primary authority rests either with the EU or with the Member States. The EC treaty defines trade policy as an area in which the EU has exclusive competence. Environmental policy, on the other hand, is subject to shared competence. Here, the EU and the Member States regulate cooperatively. The principle of subsidiarity, however, requires regulation to take place at the lowest possible level. In regulating export credit agencies, both issue areas are affected. In addition to the individual Member States, the Commission is also represented in the OECD's Export Credit Group. In matters relating primarily to trade, such as the technical terms of the export credit agency regulation, the Commission negotiates and votes, leaving the role of observer to the Member States. In the case of the Common Approaches, however, the Member States negotiated and the Commission observed.

Apart from the purely legal question of how to classify EU and national authority on topics that cut across issue areas, the status of environmental standards in the EU is also politically relevant. If they do indeed fall within EU authority, then Brussels can issue a directive concerning their implementation. That way, ambiguity contained within the Common Approaches could be minimized within the EU, and lead to level implementation across all Member States. If the Common Approaches are considered to be within Member States' authority, implementation is most likely to be less equal; this, in turn, may lead to less than optimal effectiveness of the agreement. The transparency provision in particular is one of those ambiguously-regulated items within the Common Approaches. In terms of providing equal access to environmental information on ECA-supported projects, an EU directive could provide clarification.

Conclusions

In the past, the approaches of ECAs to the issue of information disclosure were markedly different. While there was much concern for business confidentiality in Europe, more proactive approaches prevailed in North America, Japan and Australia. Some arguments and experiences support the more proactive approach in the sense that NGOs find out about critical projects anyway, and that proactive information dissemination can therefore be in the ECAs' best interest. The 2003 agreement on the revision of the OECD Common Approaches has brought forward a move to more transparency. Still, the practical impact of this innovation remains to be seen. Increased transparency also facilitates compliance monitoring, as ECAs can and do rely on NGOs to identify instances in which rival ECAs violate the provisions of their domestic standards or those of the Common Approaches.

In many cases, participation is by now a well-established routine, with ongoing exchanges between ECAs' environmental practitioners and representatives of the NGO involved. However, despite laudable initiatives in some countries or for some projects, on the whole, participation tends to be less self-understood and institutionalized in European ECAs. Nevertheless, implementation of the Common Approaches and the EU directive on environmental information disclosure appear to provide for movement even among those ECAs previously considered most resilient to change.

The real test will be seeing the extent to which parties to the Common Approaches will make use of the deviation clause with regard to *ex ante* transparency in the future. Implementation of such rules means different things to different stakeholders. While activists may cherish them for improving accountability by governments, affected businesses may criticise them as being detrimental to their competitive position. After all, ECAs were created to facilitate exports, a task that conflicts with liberal disclosure policies. Businesses that could potentially profit from ECA support may decide to take assume risks that would normally be borne by ECAs, in order not to withhold project information that competitors could use against them.

Compliance monitoring by NGOs creates costs and extra work for them – efforts for which they are unlikely to be reimbursed. 'Outsourcing' of compliance monitoring and enforcement is inherent in the *ex ante* transparency provision of the Common Approaches, but at no point is it explicit. Can the existence and availability of critical and objective NGO review be taken for granted? Compensation is even more complicated by the fact that by monitoring their domestic ECAs, NGOs provide services that are particularly valued by public entities beyond their own borders.

This form of monitoring also raises the concern of accountability. NGOs monitoring state activity provide an important independent watchdog function, where legitimacy and accountability is only of minor concern. However, if states start relying on them to provide such functions as services, one has to ask where the NGOs' authority and legitimacy for such tasks rests.

The trend towards increasing transparency and environmental information disclosure may be interpreted by some as the application of an Anglo-Saxon straitjacket. Different institutional cultures prevail with regard to transparency policies, with the idea of transparency and cooperation with civil society actors being more common in the United States, Australia and Canada. To states with a divergent institutional culture, even the concept of making environmental impact statements publicly available constitutes a major challenge. Yet the convergence on such regulatory norms, as exemplified by the Aarhus Convention, turns this into a trend that appears not only inevitable but also irreversible. Resistance may be futile.

Even more challenging is the regulation of public participation in the target states. Environmental Assessments and Impact Statements build on the very concept of stakeholder consultation and involvement. This already provides challenges for some ECAs at home. But mandating public participation within the borders of another sovereign state, which may object to such practices, raises serious challenges to the legitimacy of such rules.

What can transparency provisions such as those discussed here provide for international agreements? From the empirical evidence and the discussion above it is clear that increased transparency exerts considerable pressure for the honest implementation of agreements. Members of the negotiating parties to the Common Approaches have gone as far as claiming that rigorous transparency provisions would make strict and binding standards almost obsolete by providing NGOs with a tool to confront ECAs over problematic standards. Nevertheless, only the combination of unmistakable standards and transparency promises to be an effective tool in the hands of NGOs. Arguing from a moral perspective that a project is problematic is one thing, yet being able to back up this claim with a rule violation and supporting evidence turns this ethical argument into potential political damage.

References

Berne Declaration, Bioforum, Center for International Environmental Law, Environmental Defense Fund, Eurodad, Friends of the Earth, Pacific Environment and Resources Center, and Urgewald. 1999. *A Race to the Bottom: Creating Risk, Generating Debt and Guaranteeing Environmental Destruction.* Available at <www.environmentaldefense. org>.

Canas, Rafael E. and Eric Scharf. 1996. Credit Insurance for Exports and the General Agreement on Tariffs and Trade. *ILSA Journal of International and Comparative Law.* 3: 173–175.

Deutscher Bundestag. 1985. Antwort der Bundesregierung auf die Große Anfrage der Abgeordneten Dr Müller (Bremen), Vogel (München), Tatge und der Fraktion DIE GRÜNEN: Haushaltspolitische, ökologische und entwicklungspolitische Risiken der Ausfuhrbürgschaften. Bonn: Deutscher Bundestag.

———. 2003. Antwort der Bundesregierung auf die Kleine Anfrage der Abgeordneten Rainer Brüderle, Dr. Rainer Stinner, Gudrun Kopp, weiterer Abgeordneter und der Fraktion der FDP: Transparenz bei Hermes Bürgschaften. Berlin: Deutscher Bundestag.

ECGD. 2000. ECGD's Mission and Status Review 1999–2000. Available at <www.ecgd. gov.uk/missionstatusreview.pdf>.

G8. 1997. Communiqué of the Denver G8 Summit, Denver, 22 June 1997.

JBIC. 2002. Environmental Report 2002. Available online at <www.jbic.go.jp/english/environ/report/2002/pdf/all.pdf>.

Knigge, Markus, Benjamin Görlach, Ana-Mari Hamada, Caroline Nuffort, Andreas R. Kraemer. 2003. *The Use of Environmental and Social Criteria in Export Credit Agencies' Practices.* Eschborn: Deutsche Gesellschaft für Technische Zusammenarbeit (GTZ).

Norlen, Doug, Rory Cox, Miho Kim and Catriona Glazebrook. 2002. *Unusual Suspects – Unearthing the Shadowy World of Export Credit Agencies.* ECA-Watch. Available at <www.pacificenvironment.org/PDF/UsualSuspects.pdf>.

OECD. 2001a. *Consultations between stakeholders and the OECD Working Party on Export Credits and Credit Guarantees.* 21 March 2001 TD/ECG(2001)3. Paris: Commissioned by OECD Working Party on Export Credits and Credit Guarantees.

———. 2001b. *Draft Recommendation on Common Approaches on Environment and Officially Supported Export Credits (Revision 6).* December 2001. TD/ECG(2000)11/ REV6, Paris. Available online at <www.oecd.org/dataoecd/2/32/2726700.pdf>.

———. 2004. 'Export Credits and the Environment: Review of Responses to the Survey on Members' Procedures and Practices Regarding Officially Supported Export Credits and the Environment – As of 18 June 2004'. Paris: OECD.

———. 2005. 'Export Credits and the Environment: Review of Responses to the Revised Questionnaire on Members' Procedures and Practices Regarding Officially Supported Export Credits and the Environment – As of 25 November 2005'. Paris: OECD.

———. 2006. 9th Informal Consultation between the OECD Working Party on Export Credits and Credit Guarantees and Civil Society Organisations – Initial Comments on the Review of the OECD Recommendation on Common Approaches on Environment and Officially Supported Export Credits: Letter Dated 6 January 2006 – ECA Watch – Room Document No. 2. Paris: OECD.

Rich, Bruce. 1998. 'Export Credit Agencies: The Need for More Rigorous, Common Policies, Procedures and Guidelines to Further Sustainable Development. Environmental Defense'. Available at <www.environmentaldefense.org/documents/ 470_ECA_NeedRigor.htm>.

Schaper, Marcus. 2005. 'Applying Financial Leverage to Green Infrastructure Development: Environmental Policies of the World Bank, Export Credit Agencies, and Private Banks'. Paper prepared for the Conference Global Governance and the Power of Business. Wittenberg.

———. forthcoming 2006. 'Export Promotion, Trade, and the Environment: Negotiating Environmental Standards for Export Credit Agencies across the Atlantic'. In M.A. Schreurs, S.D. VanDeveer and H. Selin, eds. *Enlarging TransAtlantic Relations: The Political Economy of Environment, Agriculture, and Energy Trade Politics across the Atlantic.*

Udall, Lori. 2000. 'Export Credit Agencies – Contributing Paper to the World Commission on Dams'. Available at: <www.damsreport.org/docs/kbase/contrib/ins207.pdf>.

United States Congress. 1992. *Export Enhancement Act of 1992 – Bill Summary.* 102nd Congress.

Appendix

Export Credit Agency	Acronym	Country	Website
Export Finance and Insurance Corporation	EFIC	Australia	\<www.efic.gov.au/\>
Export Development Canada	EDC	Canada	\<www.edc.ca/\>
Compagnie Française d' Assurance pour le Commerce Exterieur	Coface	France	\<www.coface.com/\>
Japan Bank for International Cooperation	JBIC	Japan	\<www.jbic.go.jp/ english/\>
Garanti-Instituttet for Eksportkreditt	GIEK	Norway	\<www.giek.no/\>
Export Risk Guarantee Agency	ERG	Switzerland	\<www.swiss-erg. com/e/\>
Euler-Hermes Kreditversicherungs-AG	Euler Hermes	Germany	\<www.exportkredit garantien.de/eng/ index.html\>
Export Credits Guarantee Department	ECGD	United Kingdom	\<www.ecgd.gov.uk/\>
Export-Import Bank of the United States	Ex-Im Bank	United States	\<www.exim.gov/\>

PART 4
Conclusion

Chapter 15

The Effectiveness of Participatory Procedures: Actors' Viewpoints

This roundtable was conducted by Isabelle Biagiotti at the beginning of year 2005 through telephone interviews. The objective was to give the opportunity to practitioners, policy-makers and scientists to comment together on the recent changes concerning participatory practices in decision-making processes, and to confront their viewpoints.

Sustra: Most international institutions working on sustainable development claim to be participative and have undertaken reforms to improve participatory procedures. From your point of view, what is the purpose of such a claim?

Daniel Esty[1]: I think that participation has emerged as a core principle for good governance at all levels, ranging from the local to the global level. In the world ahead, the principle of participation and the associated principle of transparency become critical elements of what is required for international decision-making to gain legitimacy.

Juan Mayr[2]: Participation is certainly a fundamental issue, and must be implemented at each level: people must be part of debates, of the definition of problems, of decision-making processes and of implementation of actions. One of the challenges of our time is to find organizations, and especially, international institutions, which genuinely use participation as a tool and have a sharp sense of participatory decision-making at a global level. Even at the local level, participation suffers from major problems.

Jorge Eduardo Durao[3]: The process of social participation is being subjected more and more to critical scrutiny and evaluation, even at the local level. For example, in Latin America, participation is increasingly separated from decision-making.

---

[1]   Daniel Esty is Director of the Yale Center for Environmental Law and Policy and Professor of Environmental Law and Policy at the Yale School of Forestry and Environmental Studies.

[2]   Juan Mayr is former Environment Minister of Colombia and a member of the United Nations Panel on UN – Civil Society Relations.

[3]   Jorge Eduardo Durao is Director General of ABONG, Brazilian Association of NGOs.

This is explained by the context, which severely limits democratic processes. Our governments have accepted a kind of voluntary servitude to economic policies, which reduces their capacity to develop their own social policies or development projects. What this gives us is a democracy with no substance, with very negative impacts on what is called participation. In Brazil, for example, in some cases, experiences of participatory budget management only involve a tiny share of municipal budgets, contrary to what is described in the media. We experience the same limitation at the national level, as a result of debt servicing, which drastically restricts our budgetary choices and therefore, our democratic choices as well.

Juan Mayr: I have been involved in the High-Level panel on Civil Society and United Nations Relations, launched by Kofi Annan.[4] We have held many discussions and consultations all over the world, and one of the main recommendations is the importance of civil society participation at the national level. It is at the national level that there is so often a lack of participation. You can have a great debate in New York and maybe you can bring people from NGOs and other civil society groups to participate, but even so, the consultation process remains limited. Enlarged participation of civil society at the national level and at the UN level would be good tools for improving this situation. This has been part of our final recommendations. We have 22 different UN agencies in Colombia – the highest concentration of UN agencies in one country, in the world – and I am currently working with the UN in the area of development and humanitarian assistance. It is clear that, through the UN, you can foster the participation of civil society in a country such as Colombia. Most of the time, national governments do not want to listen to civil society, and this is also the case in Colombia. But they are part of the international UN system, and this system is looking for ways to increase civil society participation, especially in discussion of important issues such as human rights. What has been achieved in Colombia, through the influence of the UN system, has been done step by step, and is extremely important. Through civil society participation in debates, you can verify whether policies are heading for the right direction, and increase their impact.

Bertrand Collomb[5]: I would go further and insist on the common interest for business and governments to make sustainable development happen. The UN is

---

[4]   The Panel of Eminent Persons on Civil Society and UN Relationships is part of the wider consultation process launched by Kofi Annan in 2002 on the reform of the UN. The panel was appointed in March 2003, under the chairmanship of the former Brazilian president, Fernando Henrique Cardoso. It has convened three times and has based its work on a wide survey of civil society actors around the world. Its final report was released on 21 June 2004, and can be found on the UN website: <ods-dds-ny.un.org/doc/UNDOC/GEN/N04/507/26/PDF>.

[5]   Bertrand Collomb is the Chairman of the Board of Directors of Lafarge and Chairman of the World Business Council for Sustainable Development (WBCSD).

now aware that global governance is no longer the sole domain of governments, that most of the successful initiatives to deal with emerging global threats are conducted by civil society. This is for me the reason for establishing a Panel of Eminent Persons on the United Nations and Civil Society Relationships.

Generally speaking, UN agencies and programs are more open to business than governments and other international bodies such as WTO or International Labour Organization (ILO). The United Nations Environmental Program, for example (UNEP), tries to set out guidelines on different subjects by organizing forums bringing together governments, business, NGOs and other representatives of civil society around global trends. These guidelines give the different actors a common visibility, and allow the whole of society to become involved: we could cite the major implication of UNEP in the Global Reporting Initiative (GRI)[6] in the field of transparency and accountability, or the work carried out by the sustainable construction forum. This forum has not as yet produced any concrete results, but the initiative would be worth repeating in order to mobilize all the actors concerned around the considerable environmental and social stakes involved in the construction industry, both in terms of climate protection and social progress.

Sustra: International organizations claim to have successfully brought new actors such NGOs and businesses onto the global arena. As representatives of these non-state actors, do you agree that the process is satisfactory?

Daniel Esty: I think it is important to distinguish between diverse kinds of participation. I think there has been some confusion about what an appropriate sort of participation might be in international environmental governance.

I would say that useful participation is anything bringing new ideas and new analysis to the decision-making process. In that respect, it would be important to give opportunities to NGOs to contribute to the governance process, and for that matter to businesses, to contribute to the decision-making process. It is important for those who are making the choices, those who are the decision-makers, to be pressed by competing ideas.

Bertrand Collomb: Although business is a major actor in the move towards balanced globalization, for a sustainable development, business is not alone. Construction of an efficient solid economy for the benefit of everyone cannot happen without the commitment of all the actors: governments, NGOs and business. That is the reason for having participative international institutions.

---

[6] The Global Reporting Initiative was launched in 1997 with UN support. It is a multi-stakeholder process, and has been an independent institution since 2002. Its mission is to develop and disseminate globally applicable Sustainability Reporting Guidelines. See <www.globalreporting.org>.

But even if awareness is now real, the place given to business remains insufficient, and business is still considered as separated from civil society: not one member of the already mentioned Panel of Eminent Persons on Civil Society and UN Relations came from the business sector, and the report acknowledged that 'the Panel gave little attention to this sector' (the private sector).

However, things are changing: we were pleased to see that the panel led by Mr Cardoso defined 'civil society' in its broadest sense, including the private sector, and in its report proposed to engage the private sector as a key constituency for partnership. In particular, it proposed to incorporate the Global Compact[7] into a proposed Office of Constituency Engagement and Partnerships, and to strengthen the Global Compact's capacity for engaging more businesses.

Let's take another example, the one of multilateral negotiations on trade. There is no doubt about the strong commitment of business to a successful Doha round: that is crucial for business. The private sector creates wealth, value, innovation and jobs, but needs good governance framework to be successful. The WTO trading system is a vital part of it. And despite the fact that the main, if not the sole, actors of international trade are companies, these are not really part of the process of the negotiations. Their voices are heard much less than those of NGOs, showing clearly that NGOs wish to be heard, while business prefer to be involved in solving problems. The fact that governments are often negotiating with their own agenda, challenged by their own NGOs on specific interests and disregarding the global agenda, hinders the process from moving forward and meeting business and development interests.

David Hartridge[8]: In the WTO, the governance processes today are wholly reserved to governments. Only they have obligations and rights under the WTO Agreements. But there has been a huge increase in interest and participation by non-governmental actors. Although they are not members of the organization, NGOs are much more involved than they used to be. The General Agreement on Tariffs and Trade (GATT) was almost an invisible organization. Hardly anybody knew it existed and what it did. But the WTO, though its purposes and working methods are essentially those of the GATT, is very well known, though still not well understood, and has even become notorious in a way because of events like the failure of the conference in Seattle and the anti-globalization campaign. So the WTO is much more publicly visible than the GATT ever was, and it makes far greater efforts to justify itself, and to provide access and information to civil

---

7   Launched in 2000, the Global Compact constitutes the main discussion forum between the UN and the corporate actors. Its nine principles define a basic social and environmental responsibility that will credit corporate actors' practice with UN approval. See <www.unglobalcompact.org/Portal/>.

8   David Hartridge has been working with the General Agreement on Tariffs and Trade (GATT), responsible for the coordination of the Uruguay Round Negotiations. He is former director of the Trade and Services Division at the World Trade Organization.

society. It seems to me that business has in general been less effective in taking advantage of this than other NGOs, with the result that the argument for open trade and governance through rules is being lost.

Daniel Esty: In my opinion, we need intellectual competition. It is important that those who are the decision-makers are those who have the power, and are forced to justify their decisions against alternatives that are advanced by external forces such as NGOs, businesses or various others. It is this process of being required to think about alternatives, to justify the decisions taken against those alternatives that make good decisions.

That's the logic of participation. But I did not suggest that NGOs should be entitled to vote in the international environmental processes. We should maintain the structure by which governments remain the ultimate decision-makers.

Jorge Eduardo Durao: I share the views of those in Brazil who have started to criticize the option of NGOs' participation. Brazilian NGOs have invested enormous efforts in the cycles of UN social conferences. I think that the participation of civil society, even if it has greatly influenced the results, compromises and decisions in these conferences, has failed to generate a sufficient level of influence on implementation. President Lula, himself, recognized during the last UNCTAD meeting (Sao Polo, June 2004) that some of the Millennium Development Goals will not be achieved in 140 years. Nowadays, we have a United Nations organization whose power is contested by the United States, and I think that we really need to ask ourselves whether all these development resolutions reflect genuine political will or not. I think that NGOs take a risk in participating in an illusory game. Is it the role of our organizations, of the civil society, to maintain illusions about the true nature of the processes going on? There are talks concerning social development or sustainable development, but all we see is the destruction of entire countries. I think that what we are experiencing now forces us to revise our premises, our *a priori*, and should induce us to rethink our strategies. In this sense, I think that the World Social Forum is the best forum in which to redesign the work of NGOs and other civil society organizations.

Juan Mayr: Before talking about the participation of non-state actors, we should mention the constitutive weakness of many governments. Because of this weakness, many international agreements that have been signed are being compromised. More and more countries realize they have done something wrong, detrimental to their future. You can see the domination, for example, in trade negotiations, by powerful countries over weaker countries. This power translates into a storm when people in the weaker countries realize that they are exploited by other countries – and that they do not even have their own voice when powerful countries have imposed some kind of trade rule that has a significant impact on their people, their culture, their traditions. Obviously such an agreement is detrimental to the weak countries, and international trade negotiations simply should not be implemented as being in their interests. In the coming years they will be recognized as unsatisfactory agreements. In this globalized world, where there are fast communication systems and where human rights are recognized as fundamentally important, it is clear that cultural diversity is going to be a driving force for development.

Sustra: How then, can one assess participatory procedures in the global arena?

Juan Mayr: Participation has just started to be an issue in global discussions and it is too early to assess its results. Participation in environmental issues can only be traced back to the early 1990s.

Sustra: In Rio?

Juan Mayr: In fact, it had started before that, but in practice, the Rio Summit was the first to gather people from all over the world to talk about environment and sustainable development. I was there as an NGO member at the time, and I remember that NGO participation was not really a concern. At all the preparatory meetings, it was possible to have some kind of consultation and debate, but the decisions were restricted to government representatives only. So it was possible to have some kind of impact, but it was not a democratic or participatory process in the way that we think decision-making processes must be conducted today.

Bertrand Collomb: Participation is clearly a by-product of sustainable development. Sustainable development gives a social role to non-State actors. I agree with Juan Mayr that until the 1990s, and it was still the case at the Earth Summit in 1992 in Rio, international institutions mainly focused on environment and development, not sustainable development. The economic and social dimensions of sustainable development were fully and genuinely integrated for the first time at the Johannesburg summit in 2002, and it appeared that the private sector had a major role to play, and had actually started several years before to contribute to satisfy the needs of local populations around their activities, in an economically efficient way.

David Esty: For me, the current participation predicament is related to an underlying serious issue of legitimacy that exists within all dimensions of global governance. The decision-makers are not elected at a global level – and this question applies to the WTO as well as to the UNEP, and many treaty secretariat or UN-sponsored negotiations. So we have the constant question of whether the policies, guidelines, dispute settlement decisions and regulation emerging, both formal and informal, have legitimacy. Traditional legitimacy, I would argue, comes from the decision-maker having been either elected directly by the people or appointed by people elected by the people. But in the international domain, legitimacy has more complicated foundations.

Traditional legitimacy comes from majority rule and the winning of elections. We might call this *Rousseauian*[9] legitimacy. There is a second kind of legitimacy, which is associated with delivering answers that are advancing social welfare and helping to promote cooperation. We might call this Kantian legitimacy, building on Kant's emphasis on reason as the foundation for decision. In this regard, the international trading system has been accepted as legitimate for a long time. The GATT delivered a trade liberalization process that governments were happy with. But as the GATT has evolved into the WTO and has increasingly affected domestic regulations and environmental issues, the confidence that it is delivering right and acceptable answers has been somewhat eroded. And so the WTO is now facing a challenge because it has emerged as an international environmental decision-maker without underlying legitimacy on these matters.

A third kind of legitimacy comes from being part of a system of checks and balances. What I call a 'systemic' legitimacy or, Madisonian legitimacy, after James Madison, one of the authors of the Federalist Papers that provide the logic for the US governmental structure. This legitimacy comes from a system of interlocked institutions which share power and, in doing so, discipline each other. We do not see this structure of checks and balances in global governance. Participation helps to overcome the legitimacy gap by giving some connection to the public – even if it is not through direct elections – and by giving a process through which the ideas that are emerging get tested to determine if they are actually good or right answers. Open processes that require decision-makers to justify their choices also create something of a 'check' on arbitrary and capricious official action.

The WTO has gained legitimacy in recent years by taking on board opinions from outside the trade commitments, and by opening its process – partially– to NGOs. We can also see that some aspects of the WTO process still lack legitimacy, particularly the dispute resolution process. It is still done behind closed doors, away from participation. Such secret tribunals are, almost by definition, not good governance.

David Hartridge: The legitimacy of the WTO rests on exactly the same basis as that of the GATT. It is an agreement among governments, and they hold all the power – to make, change, enforce and interpret the law. The organization, in the sense of the Secretariat, has none of these powers. I agree, though, that there is a danger of over-stretch, of asking the system to produce legal answers to what are essentially political questions involving environmental or welfare choices.

The question of the opening to the public of the WTO dispute settlement process has been raised increasingly in recent years – the United States in particular has been pressing for a dispute settlement function taking place in public and open to participation by interested parties, which would of course be in line with their own tradition of transparency. That has been resisted by many developing countries.

---

9   Inspired by the French philosopher Jean-Jacques Rousseau.

One factor underlying their opposition is that they know that in the developed world there are very powerful NGOs, trade unions and trade associations that can afford to send people to Geneva to attend meetings, to follow panel cases and perhaps to influence what goes on. It is true that civil society is much more highly developed in the rich world. These countries on the whole do not have such bodies at home, and they see a danger that opening the system to interested parties from civil society will stack the system further against them. So they want to keep it among governments. Many of the NGOs are pro-development, of course. But most of them are nevertheless bodies based in the North, in the rich world. Many of them also are strongly interested in things like environmental protection or labour rights – constraints on the employment of children and so on – which developing countries do not necessarily see as being in their own interest. For these reasons, a lot of developing countries do not want to open the dispute settlement process or the negotiating process to campaigners from the rich world.

Simply to sit and watch a panel hearing, as you can in a court, is well short of real participation, of course. But it is a lot more than is possible now. The reports and all the documentation in panel cases are published, but only post facto, when the case has been decided.

Sustra: What would be the main guidelines to give more room to participation today in global arena?

David Esty: Participation is both essential to good governance and insufficient for, good governance. Lacking participation, a process will have a hard time establishing legitimacy. But even with participation, it does not mean you have legitimacy. We also need global-scale administrative law – a commitment to a full set of procedures that promote transparency, public-minded decision-making, due process and robust debate. Even then, there is a limit to legitimacy at the global scale because of the distance between the decision-makers and the public, and because of the lack of political accountability.

Bertrand Collomb: There are many ways of being participative. For business, for example, the first step is to engage dialogue, to make its voice heard, considering the fact that in many cases, business is at the heart of the public-agenda issue. Further steps can take multiple forms from local public–private partnerships to tackle development issues, to technical or scientific input in governmental work and international negotiations.

Juan Mayr: Corporate actors today are fundamental. Many are more powerful than state governments. They are globalized corporations. And ethics is again the issue for all these corporations. There is a need for clear understanding of the impact of their actions, and how this impact can be a powerful tool for human and social development. This is the very discussion that we need. You may find good examples of corporations playing a positive role, and on the contrary there are many examples of negative impacts. Accountability is the key issue, covering information about the actions of corporations, the way they manage the world today and how they influence politics, for example. Politics and corporate actions are highly linked, and this is simply not fair, because politicians should look after the common good of all their constituency or people; but most of the time, the pressure of the corporations over governments results in what the corporations want and not what the people want or need.

We do not have clear ethical guidelines on how corporations or international institutions should act, and this is part of the problem. At the World Summit in Johannesburg (2002), the ethical dimension of sustainable development was put forward. You cannot talk about sustainable development without a clear definition of ethical behaviour. On the first page of the Plan of Implementation,[10] there is mention of the need for ethics, but my fear is that it will never happen. So many international agreements become just words on a paper, so what will happen to the issue of ethics? If you do not have a due respect for ethics, we cannot hope to resolve many of our global problems.

Sustra: What would be your recommendations in terms of institutional set-up at the global level to ensure enlarged participation and better governance?

Daniel Esty: Better-designed global governance institutions are quite critical. In this instance, I believe in focused institutions, such as a narrowly chartered but robust global environment organization. But all international bodies need to be connected into a web of institutions. That is why I think it is a huge mistake to talk about sustainable development governance. I think you need to have development-oriented processes, environmentally oriented processes – but distinct, not blended together. Of course, you want to test your development strategies against environment sensitivities. Likewise, environmental policies and programmes should be consistent with the necessities of development and economic growth. But it does not mean that you put it all decision-making in one big governance process. I think it is better to have multiple intertwined institutions that check and balance each other.

No country has successfully blended economic development and environment ministries into a single one. Several countries have tried – Mexico, Bolivia – but ended up abandoning this super-integrated approach. Sustainable development is an overarching goal. But development and environmental protection have distinct elements. Each requires a degree of expertise. You need to have environmental officials and development officials. They might all be charged with a common

---

[10] The Johannesburg Plan of Implementation is the main output of the 2003 UN summit on Sustainable Development. It aims to guide governments on the road to sustainable development. But to the utmost dismay of many, it does not set specific goals and means to achieve in a defined timeline. See: <www.johannesburgsummit.org/html/documents/summit_docs/2309_planfinal.htm>.

vision –sustainable development – and instructed to coordinate and collaborate. But cooperation does not mean that it is appropriate to bring them together for governance purposes.

I would draw the analogy that in a private company you would not set up a division for profitability. Everybody's job is profitability. Then you would set up separate divisions for production, marketing, research and so on, but you would never have a division for profitability. I think the same is true for sustainable development.

Index

Also published in the series

Agricultural Policy Reform
Wayne Moyer and Tim Josling
ISBN 978-0-7546-3050-0

Hard Choices, Soft Law
Edited by John J. Kirton and Michael J. Trebilcock
ISBN 978-0-7546-0966-7

Linking Trade, Environment, and Social Cohesion
Edited by John J. Kirton and Virginia W. Maclaren
ISBN 978-0-7546-1934-5

International Equity and Global Environmental Politics
Paul G. Harris
ISBN 978-0-7546-1735-8

Governing Global Biodiversity
Edited by Philippe G. Le Prestre
ISBN 978-0-7546-1744-0

Printed in the United States
by Baker & Taylor Publisher Services